Dirk Hansohm

Small Industry Development in Africa
– Lessons from Sudan –

Bremer Afrika Studien

herausgegeben vom

Informationszentrum Afrika (IZA)

Bremen

Herausgeber:

Barbro-I. Bruhns, Walter Folle, Jutta Franz,
Dirk Hansohm, Gabi Jaschok, Robert Kappel,
Peter Oesterdiekhoff, Rainer Wallentin

LIT

Dirk Hansohm

Small Industry Development in Africa
– Lessons from Sudan –

Bremer Afrika-Studien Bd. 2

Lit

Gedruckt auf säure- und chlorfreiem Recyclingwerkdruckpapier

Die Deutsche Bibliothek - CIP-Einheitsaufnahme

Hansohm, Dirk:
Small industry development in Africa : lessons from Sudan /
Dirk Hansohm. - Münster ; Hamburg : Lit, 1992
 (Bremer Afrika-Studien ; Bd. 2)
 Zugl.: Bremen, Univ., Diss., 1991
 ISBN 3-89473-223-7
NE: GT

© **Lit** Verlag   Dieckstr. 56   4400 Münster   0251/40022
                             Hallerplatz 5   2000 Hamburg 13   040/446446

for Jasmin and Aida

Acknowledgements

I am indebted to all the small industry producers in Nyala, especially to Mr Abbas Zakaria and Mr Faisal Abshanab of the Sudanese Craftsmen and Small Enterprises Union, who were always helpful and encouraged my work. The field work profited to a great extent by the assistance of the Ministry of Labour and Social Security which was rendered possible by Mr Mohamed El Murtada Mustafa. I am also indebted to Mr Gamal El-Din Abdulla Musa for giving institutional support. Special assistance was also given by Mr Hamza Zaroug, Mr Saad Al Din Ibrahim, Mr Yousif Bakhit Idris, Dr Abdin Ahmed Salama, and Mr El Fatih Abdel Sammed. Thanks are also due to all the other individuals and institutions in Sudan who provided information and commented results of my research.

During different phases of my research I benefitted by the personal assistance of Mr El-Khider Daloum Mahmoud, Mr Yacoub, and Mr Ahmed Abdelhameed Ali Dinar.

My special thanks go to my supervisor Prof. Dr. Karl Wohlmuth for his continuous encouragement and advice.

Previous drafts of my thesis benefitted also by valuable comments of Prof. Dr. Axel Sell, my second supervisor, Mrs Aida Abdel Rahim, Mrs Jutta Franz, Mrs Elke Grawert, and Dr. Robert Kappel. Last not least, I am indebted to Mrs Marlene Conrad for her patient proof-reading and Mrs Jutta Franz for her marvellous printing.

Contents

Preface

1 Introduction	1
1.1 The point of departure	1
1.2 A case for small industries	8
2 Methodology	11
3 Sudan: A case for economic reform	18
3.1 Is Sudan a typical case?	20
3.2 Development of a crisis	23
3.2.1 The colonial heritage	23
3.2.2 The "Breadbasket" strategy: an offensive attempt to restructure the economy	25
3.2.3 The "stabilization" period (since 1978)	29
3.3 Case study Nyala	32
4 Small industries: An introduction	35
4.1 The interest in small industries in developing countries	35
4.1.1 The interest in small industries in Sudan	38
4.2 Definitions and delimitations of small industries	40
4.2.1 Qualitative definitions	41
4.2.2 Quantitative definitions	44
4.2.3 Subdivisions	45
4.2.4 Definitions of small industries in Sudan	46
4.3 Industries in Nyala: An overview	48
5 Distinct advantages of small industries	61
5.1 Creation of employment	61
5.2 Income creation	75
5.3 Capital saving and capital mobilization	84
5.4 Efficiency	87
5.5 Strong linkages to other sectors	96
5.6 Utilization of local resources and low import intensity	102
5.7 Production for low-income markets	109
5.8 Wide geographical dispersion	116
5.9 Training ground for entrepreneurs	117
5.10 Ability to innovate and flexibility	124
5.11 Characteristics of small industries: a summary	129

6 Growth constraints of small industries	131
6.1 Lack of entrepreneurship	131
6.2 Managerial deficiencies	141
6.3 Lack of technical skills	147
6.4 Integration into family	149
6.5 Other internal constraints	152
6.6 Internal constraints: a summary	153
6.7 External constraints:	
Exploitation by large industry or the economy at large	154
6.8 Difficulties in access to raw materials and machinery	160
6.9 Difficulties in access to product markets	167
6.10 Difficulties in access to technology	172
6.11 Difficulties in access to credit	176
6.12 Government discrimination	180
7 Summary and conclusion	211
Abbreviations	219
References	221
Appendices	
1 Economic and social indicators of African countries	246
2 International Standard Industrial Classification (ISIC)	248
3 Price indices	250
4 Questionnaire	251
5 Employment in Sudanese industry: a micro-perspective	261
6 Light industries	263

Preface

Hardly any subject in the discussion on development policy in Africa has attracted so much attention during the last years as the role of small industry in the development process. This has several important reasons. The employment crisis has worsened; the informal sector has obviously reached the limits of its absorption capacity; the structural adjustment policy in Africa has had grave consequences for the existing import substituting industry.
New theoretical approaches with respect to industrialisation, notably strategies of agricultural-demand-led industrialisation, imply increased interest in small industries. But also concepts of export-led industrialisation rely on labour-intensive small industries. Last not least, the discussion about adequate structural adjustment policy for Africa is characterised by ideas of the utilisation of the specific advantages of small industry.
In that context this important study has to be seen. Although its empirical basis is limited to a region of Sudan, important lessons can be drawn for Africa: These lessons are indeed drawn systematically. In order to analyse the dynamics of the small industry sector, the study combines macro-, sector-, and micro-level analysis. This methodological approach, including different elements of quantitative and qualitative research, is explained in a separate chapter and can be taken as a guideline by anyone intending to do field research in Sudan or other African countries.
Starting point of the study are two hypotheses: firstly, because of its specific advantages, the small industry is suited to contribute to overcome the African crisis; secondly, there is a striking contradiction between this potential role of small industry and its real importance. The results with respect to the first hypothesis (ten alleged distinct advantages of small industry are analysed) show a differentiated picture. One has to discriminate clearly between traditional and modern small industries; some of the assumed distinct advantages are only true for the former group. However, this mixed picture reflects policy failures and past neglect - not immanent characterictics.
The second main part analyses growth constraints of small industry. It is shown that internal constraints as lack of entrepreneurship and management deficiencies are not immediate constraints. Traditional management training programmes as still recommended will fail, if they are not combined with an elimination of external constraints. In a discussion of the external constraints the hypothesis of an exploitation of the small industry sector by the large industry sector is disproved. However, the dependency of this sector on the activity level of the national economy is clearly shown. Access to raw materials and machinery as well as access to markets are identified as the main constraints. The final chapter analyses the

role of the government and its policies and identifies this as the central constraint of small industry development.

It is shown that a policy reform at several levels is necessary. Such a reform is possible and can fully mobilise the distinct advantages of small industries. However, reformed small industry promotion cannot replace a development policy in the sense of a new agricultural, industrial, trade, and export promotion policy.

This work is important for development policy for three reasons: firstly, the detailed inventory of the growth constraints for small industries in Africa; secondly, the evidence for the importance of policy reform on the basis of a consistent growth model; and thirdly, the substantiated warning against isolated programmes of small enterprise promotion. Theoretically important is not only the testing of the two starting hypotheses, but also the method to identify and to test the specific advantages of small industry and the constraints to their growth.

This outstanding study will set a standard for the research on Sudan and for the analysis of industrialisation processes in Africa. Industrial policy makers will have to examine this study carefully and development policy should take up this study to work out sustainable strategies for the promotion of small industry.

Prof. Dr. Karl Wohlmuth
Department of Economics
University of Bremen, Germany

1 Introduction

Promotion of small industry (SI) has been regarded by analysts and policy makers from different backgrounds as a way out or even *the* way out of Africa's crisis. This hypothesis is the starting point of the present study. The belief in a potential of SI is based on several *distinct advantages* ascribed to SI as compared with large industry (LI) with respect to economic development. The aim of this study is to verify these claims in the case of Sudan[1].

Despite those distinct advantages attributed to SI, its role in Africa did not come up to the hopes set in them in the past. The second issue the study addresses is the constraints for the development of SI.

The introducing chapter explains the frame of the study. Point of departure is the multi-dimensional crisis of African economies, with special regard to the industrial crisis (chapter 1.1). Since more than a decade attempts were made to redress this state - however, the crisis has deepened. During this period there were fierce debates about the course of reform policies. However, for some years now, some degree of consensus has been reached in important areas. The main points of both of these phases are summarized. This is the background to make a case for SI (chapter 1.2). Different methods have been employed to analyze the questions of research (chapter 2). The study was implemented on a country level: Sudan. Because of the dearth of data on SI in Sudan the macro-level analysis was combined with a micro-level analysis. For this the major urban centre of the most peripheral Northern region - Nyala - was selected (Sudan and Nyala are introduced in chapter 3). The next chapter gives an introduction to SI. In the following chapter the characteristics of SI which are considered as distinct advantages are discussed on a general level and their validity is examined in the cases of Sudan and Nyala (chapter 5). In the same manner the growth constraints of SI are analyzed (chapter 6). The concluding chapter summarizes the results and draws conclusions with respect to the role of SI in development (chapter 7).

1.1 The point of departure

The African continent is in a severe economic crisis, reflected in slow - for some countries even negative - growth, large unsustainable imbalances between exports and imports, investment and savings, and government revenues and expenditures. The extent and persistence of these gaps has resulted in indebtedness, paralyzed development efforts, and marginalization of Africa.

---

[1] Sudan was selected because of previous work and study experiences in the fields of SI promotion and analysis of structural adjustment policies (SAP) in this country (see the references).

More significant than the quantities of the crisis are qualitative aspects[2]:
- the lack of structural transformation of the colonial economies. Africa is still predominantly a supplier of agricultural and mineral raw materials. Its production base remains narrow, fragmented and disarticulated, with ill-adapted technology;
- lack of a functioning system of institutions;
- a degraded environment, due both to natural and human factors;
- declining food production;
- increasing regional inequalities, especially between cities and rural areas[3];
- widespread breakdown of the civil order and occurence of civil wars.

This had devastating consequences for the living conditions in Africa[4]:
- declining real incomes and the growth of absolute poverty
- increasing inequalities in income distribution
- increasing unemployment and underemployment
- increasing malnutrition and famines
- deteriorating quantity and quality of health and education services

Part of the economic crisis in Africa is a crisis of industrialization[5]. At the time of independence, in the early 1960s, in most of the African countries industrialization was regarded as the central way to move from the colonial pattern of heavy dependence on imported manufactures and primary exports and to achieve rapid modernization. For many policy makers and academics development was equated with industrialization[6]. The basic strategy pursued was one of import substitution, emphasizing greater self-reliance and direct public investment.

---

[2] For a comprehensive analysis of the crisis cf. Dumont (1988), Timberlake (1985), Harrison (1987); on the political-institutional aspects cf. Hyden (n.d.)

[3] On the pattern of rural-urban inequalities cf. the "urban bias" argument of Lipton (1977). The usefulness of this model for Africa has been doubted because of the interrelatedness of rural and urban income sources and because of decreasing urban incomes (Jamal and Weeks 1988). These authors argue that relations are much more complicated than to be analyzed in a dichotomy. This is actually one of the main arguments of that article - its title "the vanishing rural-urban gap" is thus a bit misleading. Although generally urban incomes in Africa declined more than rural incomes, for any visitor to Africa the contrast between city and countryside is so conspicuous that there can be no doubt about the existence of an urban bias. The different qualities of life cannot be measured by incomes alone. Furthermore, available information on rural areas is too scanty to allow for a comprehensive comparison (this lack of information is a part of the urban bias).

[4] On the social dimension of the crisis cf. Huang and Nicholas (1987), ECA (1988), Wohlmuth (1990a)

[5] The literature on industry in Africa is scarce, cf. Ewing (1968), Rweyemamu (1980a), Fransman (1982), Steel and Evans (1984), Meier and Steel (1989), Riddell et al. (1990)

[6] cf. Ewing (1968: XIII), who opened his book on "Industry in Africa" with the sentence "The main thesis of this book is that industry is the main lever of African development." This reflects a general understanding of development as a process of a shift of resources from agriculture to industry, prevalent in development economics (e.g. Kuznets 1966, Chenery et al. 1986).

Although industrial capacity and production grew rapidly and became more diversified in the post-independence period, since the late 1970s declining growth and capacity utilization indicated that this growth was neither sustainable nor did it represent a real transformation of the African economies. As main structural weaknesses have been described an overexpansion of industrial capacity to the debit of agricultural development, a neglect of the private sector, overinvestment in final-stage consumer goods relative to raw material processing and capital goods industries, lack of inter-industry and inter-sectoral linkages, and excessively high import and capital intensities[7].

Since the late 1970s most African countries have been forced to embark on *structural adjustment policies* (SAP)[8], mostly in cooperation with IMF and World Bank. These programmes were fashioned in a traditional way and concentrated on exchange rate reform, demand management, and aimed at export-oriented growth. Domestic policy inadequacies - inward-looking trade and exchange-rate policies, overextended public sectors and a bias against agriculture - were regarded as the chief factors behind[9]. They have been criticized by academics from the left[10] and by African governments[11] and a controversial debate continued[12]. Main issues of this controversy[13] were:
- a lack of integration of the structural adjustment programmes with - and even consideration of - the indigenous African development concepts[14];
- the self-assured, paternalistic character of the World Bank approach[15];

---

7   cf. Rweyemamu (1980b), Meier and Steel (1989)
8   This expression became excessively used. This is unfortunate because it springs from a narrow-minded and technocratic conception of economic crisis as resulting from "external or internal shocks". Since some years it has become clear that a much broader approach to economic crisis is necessary and that the issues of crisis policies are not separable from the issues of long-term development. Although the term "structural adjustment" is not appropriate to this, it has survived.
9   For the theoretical basis cf. Polak (1957). The central document expressing the World Bank approach towards Africa during the 1980s is World Bank (1981).
10 cf. Amin (1982), Harvey (1982), Daniel (1983), Godfrey (1983, 1985), Loxley (1984a, 1984b), Schultheis (1984), Girvan (1985), Malima (1986). For a general critique of the IMF approach to SAP cf. Killick et al. (1984)
11 cf. ECA (1982)
12 Further World Bank documents are World Bank (1983b, 1984c, 1986); others arguing on the same lines are Please and Amoako (1984), Berg (1984); other contributions to the discussion are Mkandawire (1982), Sau (1983), Shaw (1983), Allison and Green (1983, 1985), Gordon and Parker (1984), Madavo (1984), Paul (1984), Sender and Smith (1984), Shapiro (1984), Wheeler (1984), Wolde-Semait (1984), Green (1985a, 1985b), Helleiner (1985), Ouattara (1985), Lele (1986), Loxley (1986), Singh (1986). For a discussion cf. Hansohm (1987)
13 The literature cited serves to illustrate the dimensions of the crisis. The list does not claim to be exhaustive.
14 The central document of these concepts is the Lagos Plan (OAU 1981); defender of the World Bank approach in this respect are Please and Amoako (1984), Gordon and Parker (1984)
15 cf. Allison and Green (1983), Bienefeld (1983)

- the technical, economistic character, i.e. a lack of consideration of the underlying social and political factors, especially the role of the state[16];
- non-implementability[17];
- uniformity, i.e. lack of consideration of the specific country conditions[18];
- down playing of the external conditions, i.e. a critique of the export-led industrialization model, which relies on exports as the central motor of growth and development[19];
- the emphasis on cash crops to the debit of food crops[20];
- the fragility of the data base on which the recommendations are built[21];
- the underlying ideology of neo-liberalism, implying a reliance on market forces as the central mechanism of resource allocation[22]; central themes of this discussion are the appropriateness of price incentives[23] and devaluation[24], effects on income distribution, and on health and education services, and a failure to understand the peasant economy[25];

---

16 The government policies are simply described as "inappropriate policies" (e.g. Balassa 1981). For the critique cf. Hyden (1980, 1983), Bienefeld (1983, 1985), Griffith-Jones (1983), Loxley (1984b), Malima (1986)
17 cf. Leonard (1984), Shapiro (1984), White (1990)
18 Critics argue that the growth performance has been very diverse during the 1970s, both by country and period. Especially the categorization of states into etatist and market-oriented economies with less and more economic success resp. is challenged. Studies find little correlation between economic ideology and overall economic growth. Country studies show that countries that are presented as models (e.g.Malawi, Cote d'Ivoire) did in fact not follow closely the "World Bank path" (cf.Allison and Green 1983, Green 1983, Harvie 1983, Wheeler 1984).
19 On the strategy of export-oriented development cf. Krueger (1980), Balassa (1981, 1984), World Bank (1989: 78-94); critiques argue that the successes of East Asian NICs and others have to be understood as special cases due to favourable international demand conditions as well as socio-political and institutional structures and agricultural policies. Thus it is regarded as oversimplified and misleading to call exports the key to growth for all countries and all times, irrespectively of demand conditions. The danger is pointed out that increasing export volumes will result in reduced export earnings (the "fallacy of composition" argument). Furthermore, it is shown that the different arguments for trade liberalisation (economies of scale, competition, comparative advantage) are mutually inconsistent. For these reasons, the term "outward looking" is regarded as "too general and vague to present a good guide to policy" (cf. Diaz-Alejandro 1980, Cline 1982, Streeten 1982a: 169). The argument is supported with empirical data by Singer and Gray (1988). Cf. also the rejoinders of Balassa (1983) - who unfortunately fails to address the main issues raised by Streeten -, Henderson (1982), Streeten (1982b). On the African case cf. Bienefeld (1983), Daniel (1983), Griffith-Jones (1983), Schultheis (1984); on the "fallacy of composition" argument cf. Green (1983), Godfrey (1983, 1985), Loxley (1984a); against trade pessimism argue Berg (1984), Gordon and Parker (1984), Gusten (1984), Please and Amoako (1984), Sender and Smith (1984). On the risks of increased protectionism cf. also World Bank (1987d), Chapter 8 and 9. Recent evidence strikes a blow against the "trade liberalization" argument also from the import side: Because of weak market positions African countries appear not only to receive less for exports, but also to pay more for imports (cf. Yeats 1989).
20 cf. Dritte Welt Haus Bielefeld (1986)
21 On the quality of data on Africa's agriculture cf. Berry (1984)
22 Dell (1982) argues that stabilization programmes in their reliance on demand constraint have resulted in a process of "overkill", i.e. a process of economic retrenchment which went much further than would be strictly necessary in terms of reasonable objectives.
23 On low elasticities of African agricultural production cf. Bond (1983).
24 cf. Colclough (1983), Godfrey (1985), Singh (1986)
25 cf. Hyden (1980, 1983), Barker (1984), Berry (1984), Allison and Green (1985), Guyer (1984) on the neglect of the sphere of women's work; for a critique of Hyden cf. Kasfir (1986)

- the shift of emphasis from public to private sector;
- a neglect of industry[26].

The discussion had been very much based on ideological lines. For instance, the public sector has been regarded as a "bad thing" by the World Bank proponents, while devaluations, transnational corporations, the World Bank and the IMF, production and export of primary products were regarded as "bad things" by their critics - and vice versa[27].

After one decade of structural adjustment policies and further deterioration of economies and living conditions in Africa the discussion about appropriate policies has lost much of its antagonism and a convergence on many issues has been reached[28]. Elements of this consensus are:
- African low-income countries are a special case in the sense that they are characterized by a low level of development and structural deficiencies as fragmented markets, low literacy rate, poor health, poor infrastructure, i.e. the problems are deep-seated which means a "low capacity to transform"[29].
- The traditional, demand-oriented approach to stabilization is insufficient, it has to be complemented by supply-side policies, i.e. measures to increase the supply of real goods and services[30]; a structural approach, oriented at the real economy[31] is needed. Traditional measures as devaluation are necessary - but not sufficient.
- There is not *one* road to stabilization and economic reform (as often suggested by lending institutions). The combination of SAP measures has to be adapted to the specific country case and the respective development objectives[32].
- African solutions have to be found for African problems. The failure of the transfer of blueprints from other areas must not be continued[33].
- Any satisfactory set of policies must be jointly worked out by the lender and borrower - instead of being simply imposed by the lender[34].

---

26   cf. Brandt (1982), ECA (1982), Godfrey (1983), Bienefeld (1985), Riddell (1990)
27   On this argument cf. Sender and Smith (1984).
28   cf. ECA (1988, 1989), World Bank (1989a), Wohlmuth (1990a)
29   a notion of Kindleberger, cited by Killick et al. (1984: 286)
30   A forthcoming study reviewing the record of World Bank conditionality lending over the last decade (Mosley, Harrigan and Toye 1991, cited in: Munslow and Zack-Williams 1990: 5) found that the poorer countries could not benefit from World Bank programmes. For overviews of elements of SAP in developing countries cf. Crockett (1981), Khan and Knight (1982), Sharpley (1984), Khan (1987). On the case of commodity-based economies, i.e. economies where exports of minerals, raw materials and foodstuffs constitute more than 50% of total exports, cf. MacBean (n.d.).
31   On the "real economy approach" cf. Killick et al. (1984)
32   cf. Girvan (1985)
33   Belief in the "blueprint approach" is expressed e.g. in Lystad (1965b) and Kamarck (1965). For the critique cf. Hyden (n.d.), Korten (1980), Leonard (1987), White (1990).
34   cf. Stewart (1984)

- At the same time, conditionality is needed; the kind of conditionality is at issue, not conditionality itself[35].
- Donors have to take part of the responsibility for the failure of past development efforts as well as future successes by sufficient aid commitments[36].
- One has to think on a long term basis, going beyond the 1-3 year periods of traditional structural adjustment programmes[37].
- Stabilization policy has to be integrated with development policy.
- Growth of the economies is vital as the basis to raise living standards, and even to secure bare survival of the growing population ("adjustment with growth"). This means increasing volumes and values of exports and reducing net dependence on imports through efficient import-substitution[38].
- The human dimension must be at the centre of all efforts to conceptualize, achieve and measure development as well as impacts of SAP[39]. This implies, inter alia, an emphasis on basic needs provision, health and education services.
- Social equity and alleviation of poverty have to be objectives on their own. One cannot hope that they result automatically from growth[40]. While there are different opinions if adjustment policies have positive or negative impacts on poverty, a strong presumption can be made that macro-economic contraction will worsen poverty[41].
- Adjustment policies can no longer be confined to the macro-economic sphere but have to take account of the micro-level as well[42]. Measures on the supply side in developing countries generally tend to be micro-level measures.
- The dualistic structure of African economies has to be overcome, a structural integration, i.e. creation and intensification of domestic linkages, is important.

---

35 On the debate on conditionality cf. Killick et al. (1984: 287-288), Stewart (1984).
36 The inadequacy of unilateral adjustment from a moral as well as efficiency point of view is pointed out by Dell (1982), Bacha (1987) and Cornia et al. (1987). Gulhati and Nallari (1988) show that the foreign aid falls far short of requirements in Africa. Model simulations of Adelman et al. (1989) show that in Africa - in contrast to all other areas - even with appropriate policies domestic resources are not sufficient to create an adequate agricultural surplus - this has to be financed by foreign aid. On the lack of donor coordination cf. Morss (1984) and Whittington and Calhoun (1988). On reform of foreign aid to Africa cf. also White (1990).
37 "There are no 'quick fixes' in Africa" (Hyden n.d.: 40).
38 The growth of output can be attained by improved utilization of existing productive capacity and enlargement of this capacity. Concerning the second option, the important point is a relative increase in the output of tradeables - goods and services which enter significantly world trade, broadly speaking agricultural and industrial products, but also services which are directed to the productive sectors - vis-à-vis non-tradeables.
39 The central documents in this context are Cornia et al. (1987) and, with respect to Africa, the Khartoum Declaration (ECA 1988), cf. also Wohlmuth (1990a) on this.
40 On the traditional view, accepting growing inequality in the early stages of growth and believing in a later turn-around cf. Kuznets (1955), Lewis (1970), Chenery and Syrquin (1975). De Janvry (1983), de Janvry and Sadoulet (1983) and Adelman (1986) point out that equity does not necessarily result from growth. They argue for "redistribution before growth", while Chenery et al. (1974) propose "redistribution with growth". On policies to reduce poverty in developing countries cf. also Glewwe and van der Gaag (1987).
41 cf. Helleiner (1987)
42 cf. Cornia (1987)

- This means especially an emphasis on agriculture and a closer orientation of industrialization towards agriculture[43]. Historical evidence shows that to start industrialization a large overall agricultural surplus is needed. While in the long run a balance between agriculture and industry seems to be favourable, for the years to come some bias to agriculture appears to be necessary to correct for the past neglect[44].
- To raise the living standards of the broad population, a mass production of wage goods is necessary[45].
- Development efforts must be based more on domestic resources (labour, capital, food, manufactures), and the technologies employed must save capital and imports[46]. This strategy is also risk-reducing.
- Increased efforts must be made to mobilize domestic resources.
- Resources must be used efficiently.
- More labour-intensive technologies have to be utilized. In the course of development agriculture releases labour. Because of the anti-agricultural biases this process is already highly advanced in Africa. There is high pressure to create much productive employment.
- Price policies, i.e. alleviation of price distortions, are often necessary, but not sufficient - without complementing policies they may even be counter-productive[47].
- The industrialization strategy of import-substitution is widely discredited. The superiority of an open development strategy, i.e. non-discrimination of exports, is increasingly acknowledged. However, the feasibility of the pure export-led strategy for most African economies at the present time is also doubted by many[48].
- Regional integration and cooperation have to play a role.
- Although governments have to play a strong role in planning and setting favourable conditions for development, they cannot be regarded any longer as the main or even sole agent of change. The private sector, local communities and non-governmental agencies have to play a greater role[49]. At the same time, the "advantages" of the private sector have to be carefully assessed in the

---

43   On the emphasis on agriculture cf. Mellor (1986) and Bautista (1989), on industrialization based on agriculture cf. Adelman (1984) and Adelman et al. (1989).
44   cf. Adelman et al. (1989)
45   On agrarian wage goods strategies cf. Mellor (1976), Singer (1979), Hirschman (1981), de Janvry (1983).
46   This is all the more important in view of the democratization in the East, which attracts the resources of the industrial countries away from the developing countries.
47   Cf. Streeten (1987), who mentions "six ins" as necessary complementing policies: incentives, inputs, infrastructure, institutions, innovations, and information.
48   cf. Streeten (1982a) and Adelman (1984)
49   On participation cf. Goulet (1989); on the necessity of decentralization for progress in Africa cf. Davidson and Munslow (1990)

African context, free from ideological biases[50]. The "third sector" of local communities and NGOs, having been neglected by the dichotomous discussion of public vs. private sector, has to come to the forefront[51].
- A political renewal in Africa is necessary, i.e. increased participation by the people and national consensus building. Democratization can be regarded not only as an end (to be reached at a far point in future), but also as a necessity for the process of development in Africa itself[52].
- Environment conservation has to be given high priority[53].

1.2 A case for small industry

SI could play a positive role in a "new approach" to SAP as characterized in the preceding chapter. This idea is based on several characteristics, which are ascribed to small industries and which are in line with the criteria mentioned in the preceding chapter. Surprisingly the connection between the positive characteristics ascribed to SI and the necessities of SAP is hardly made - nor are the impacts of SAP on SI analyzed[54]. Prominent among those characteristics are[55]:
1. labour intensity
2. low capital and import intensity
3. mobilization of resources
4. production for the low income population
5. efficiency
6. strong linkages to other sectors, especially to agriculture
7. wide geographical distribution

These characteristics point to a positive role which small industries could play in structural adjustment and development policy. The characteristics of SI appear to

---
50 cf. Pickett (1989) on recent discussions on the role of the state vs. market forces. White (1990) remarks that the literature on privatization "often appears unduly vain".
51 cf. Hyden (n.d.), on African NGOs cf. Anheier (1987), Bratton (1987), Hansohm (1990b); the African Development Perspectives Yearbook 1989 devotes a chapter to this issue (RGADP 1990: 561-646).
52 This issue is coming more and more into the debate; cf. Munslow and Zack-Williams (1990) and other contributions in ROAPE (1990) as recent discussions. On the one hand there is increasing pressure inside African countries threatening one-party or other dictatorial regimes (e.g. Benin, Gabon, Cote d'Ivoire, Kenya); on the other hand there is pressure from outside: donors of development are beginning to introduce a political conditionality. Examples are the World Bank stressing the need for an "enabling political environment" (World Bank 1990) and the European Parliament tying aid to Namibia to the development of human rights (cf. Munslow and Zack-Williams 1990: 7).
53 On the ecological dimension of Africa's crisis cf. Harrison (1987)
54 Fuhr (1987) proposes a leading role for SI in the SAP in Latin America. Fitzgerald (1989) discusses the implications of SAP for SI.
55 For a detailed discussion cf. Chapter 5.

be congruent with the requirements of a "new approach" to the African crisis. This hypothesis is the starting point of the present study.
The second hypothesis is that the potential role contrasts with the actual role SI plays in Africa. This is due to different development constraints SI is facing. This hypothesis implies that there is a scope and a need for promotion of SI. This is, of course, not a new idea. For almost a decade now, SI promotion has its place in the programmes of governments and aid agencies, in Africa and elsewhere. The OAU's Lagos Plan of Action, for instance, urges to create a "network of small and medium-scale industries as well as actively promoting and encouraging the informal sector."[56]
As yet, although there is some history of SI promotion, there is a lack of comparative evaluation of programmes. However, there is a general suspicion that the effects of SI promotion have been rather disappointing. Critical points are[57]:
- fragmented approaches, i.e. lack of integration of different necessary measures;
- a neglect of the macroeconomic environment, reflecting the view that the problems at hand are internal to the SI enterprises;
- limited capacity to adapt to the socio-cultural environment; a transfer of blueprints;
- a wrong attitude towards the SI entrepreneur neglecting his inherent abilities with preconceived ideas what he should know and be able to do;
- a tendency to create an assistance mentality (to be "spoon-fed");
- a danger to destroy the strong points of SI by distortions of their economic environment, e.g. labour-intensity by cheap credits, flexibility by administrative regulations, and the use of local resources by incentives to import;
- a tendency to introduce new forms of enterprises, instead of building on that which is existing;
- biases towards the upper range of SI as well as urban industries, having negative repercussions on the lower range of SI and rural industries - although exactly those enterprises may have more desirable characteristics with regard to structural adjustment.

Furthermore, a strong argument can be offered that negative - wanted and unwanted - side-effects of government policies in other fields more than outweigh any positive measures of SI promotion. Actually, there is no consensus with respect to the "correct" measures of promotion[58], which is partly due to the great local differences. In general there is a lack of research on the role of SI in the macroeconomic context and specifically the effect of SAP on SI on the one hand and their role in SAP on the other hand.

---
56   OAU (1981), cited by: Page (1984: 1)
57   e.g. OECD (1974), Molenaar et al. (1983), especially Molenaar (1983)
58   cf. Wohlmuth (1990b: 11)

In order to determine the potential and the appropriate measures of promotion, the constraints have to be analyzed. This is what this study aims to achieve. It is not concerned with SI promotion itself, but with SI enterprises and the people working in them.

An analysis of the literature on SI shows that there is no consensus about these matters. There are several reasons for this:
1. people have very different conceptions of what is a SI;
2. there are very different approaches to SI: neo-liberal, marxist, anthropological, sociological, and others;
3. there is a lack of data; often the data are insufficient to justify the conclusions of the different approaches.

Thus, the most fruitful contribution to the debate about SI appears to be the collection of empirical data in order to evaluate existing theories. The scope for secondary analyses is limited because of a lack of comparability.

Those who occupy themselves with SI actually belong to two different worlds. On the one hand there are the "practical people", who assume certain constraints and concentrate on searching for appropriate measures to overcome them. On the other hand, there are the theorists, often with a socio-political outlook, who limit themselves to the analysis of constraints. These two worlds suffer from a lack of mutual fructification. Lack of communication, irrelevance of research, too narrow conceptions of those involved in the "development business" play a role. Parallel to this, there is a second gap between micro-level studies which neglect the macro-dimension and macro-level studies working with assumptions on the micro-level.

This study hopes to go some way towards filling these gaps. Thus, it is intended not only to contribute to the academic discussion, but also to produce relevant data for development efforts. This study is written with a belief in Sudan's small industrialists and craftsmen.

2 Methodology

The basis of this study is field work in Sudan in the period October 1987-October 1988 and again from January-April 1989. But also visits and academic exercises before this time as well as discussions with government officials during 1990 helped to form my picture.

Starting point of my work on SI in Sudan was an analysis of literature on SI in developing countries[1] in the context of a discussion of structural adjustment problems of Sudan[2]. The general conclusions relevant for research methodology were:

1. The far-reaching conclusions authors draw are often due to the ideological point of view of the analyst and not justified by the empirical basis. The ideological concept often turns out to be a straight-jacket, narrowing the field of vision. Examples are:
   - the "marginalization" approach, which starts with the presumption that SI are marginalized within the wider economic context; this denies prospects of accumulation and growth - instead of analyzing how they come about;
   - the pioneering ILO study on Kenya (1972), which takes government discrimination as the central constraint of SI; this gives the impression that if only governments support SI, every problem will be solved;
   - the comprehensive World Bank project on SI, regarding the question of comparative economic efficiency of SI vs. LI as the decisive matter - neglecting the question how these efficiencies come into being[3].

   All these approaches limit the scope of their analysis severely by certain assumptions. These are, however, not always made explicit. Any research, of course, has to start with assumptions. However, some of the assumptions made by the above approaches do not stand up to reality, as will be shown below.

2. The subject "small industry in developing countries" is, despite decades of research, still full of open questions and conflicting evidence. This points to the importance of approaching the research as open-mindedly as possible[4]. It implies for the economist the necessity to broaden his/her mind, and to listen

---

[1] Different terms are in use for this country group: less developed countries, underdeveloped countries, developing countries, Third World countries. All of them are unsatisfactory, because they imply a negative bias towards these countries, assigning an inferior position to them. This does certainly reflect reality, if we think in terms of economic and political power, but not otherwise. However, a more appropriate term seems not to be available. The term *developing countries* is used in this study - certainly these countries are developing, even though there is no agreement in which direction, and in spite of the fact that the *industrial countries* also develop.
[2] cf. Hansohm and Wohlmuth (1987)
[3] cf. also Andersson (1987) for such an approach
[4] Streck (1982b: 59) calls this "die Perspektive des Staunens".

to what other disciplines like sociology, anthropology, geography, political science, have to say about SI[5].
3. It is not useful to define "small industry" in qualitative or quantitative terms before starting research, because this would mean to replace research results by assumptions. If one defines, for example, SI as labour-intensive, one excludes capital-intensive SI from one's analysis, and one confirms, of course, one's belief that SI are labour-intensive. Or if one deliminates SI from LI by a certain number of employees or amount of invested capital, this will necessarily be arbitrary. Thus, the field research for this study tried to record all non-agricultural productive activities, without any upper limit, and left it to a later stage to decide what is "small" and what is "large".
4. SI is a very heterogenous sector. Thus it is not useful to take it as a unity. Instead one has to disaggregate the sector. The failure to do this is one main handicap of several concepts, for example the "informal sector" concept, which lumps together activities at the lower margin of existence and highly profitable businesses. Cross-sectional surveys, working with pre-set questions and coded answers in order to secure comparability, only allow for very general conclusions. This limits the possibility to identify the complex specific realities. It is more useful to discuss SI in the context of branch-specific studies[6].
5. To understand the dynamics of SI the macro-economic context has to be considered[7]. As mentioned above, many studies fail to do this.

This study does not claim to present a new theory on SI. This would need comparative field studies, direct studies of external determining factors (especially demand factors and linkages to agriculture) and intertemporal comparisons. This was beyond the scope of this study. Rather, the approach is eclectic: different assumptions and theories are evaluated in the light of Sudanese reality.
A review of the state of research on SI in Sudan and own experiences[8] led to the following methodological considerations:
1. Starting point of the study was the belief that SI producers play an economic role which is important for the national economy, but which should be promoted to contribute more. It is believed that the task of research is to highlight this sector in order to make that promotion possible. It is not believed that research can be "objective" in the sense of value-free. On the contrary, the

---

5   Arguments for an integration of different approaches, namely economy and anthropology, are also given by Geertz (1963), Peattie (1980), Hugon (1982), and Moser (1984).
6   This point is made by Schmitz (1982a).
7   This point is also made by Elwert (1985: 73) and Lewin (1985: 131) - who also argue to include the socio-cultural dimension.
8   These consist of a consultancy on SI in Darfur and Kordofan and an unpublished survey of SI in Omdurman (cf. Hansohm 1986a, Hansohm and Wohlmuth 1989)

failure of much research to expose the underlying value-orientations leads to much confusion[9].

2. The literature and data basis on SI in Sudan is very weak. On the one hand, there are programmes which are derived from standard theory or based on political statements rather than empirical fact. On the other hand, there are several micro-level studies, most of them very limited in scope and formulation of questions. Virtually all are based on single visit interviews. Some broad conclusions about some of the major characteristics can be drawn from their analysis, but no comprehensive comparative study is possible. Furthermore, the macro-economic context of SI is not, if at all, considered adequately. Thus, it is necessary to combine an analysis of the macro-level environment of SI with a micro-level case study. Because the "urban bias" towards the capital area - the "Three Towns" - is believed to be one of the major structural deficiencies in Sudan, and that thus one major objective should be the promotion of rural areas (defined as all of the country except of the province of Khartoum), the Three Towns (Khartoum Province) were not included in the micro-level analysis, although this was suggested by many because of the major economic importance of the Three Towns. Because regional inequality is one of Sudan's root problems, the most peripheral region was selected for the micro-level study: Darfur Region[10]. The study was implemented in the regions major urban centre, the capital of South Darfur province, Nyala.

3. SI in Sudan is for the major part not registered statistically. For example, in the city of Nyala, according to the industrial statistics there are 7 "factories" with 25 and more employees, and 18 SI enterprises. The own comprehensive survey, however, came to 1263 industrial units. This shows that the available surveys are of no use as a sampling frame. This is a contrast to countries like Colombia, India, Philippines, South Korea and other ASEAN countries where comprehensive studies of SI have been done[11], but typical for African countries. No available material can serve as a frame for a comprehensive micro-level study on SI - one has to start from scratch.

In short, from the scientific point of view, SI in Sudan is still new ground - no accepted wisdom is available. Qualitative methods of empirical research[12] must be applied in the centre of analysis. Traditional measures of empirical research - standard questionnaires with pre-coded questions and a one-shot visit - are not

---
9   For a discussion of these issues cf. Myrdal (1969)
10 The Southern Regions are more marginalized on almost all terms, but security reasons did not allow to select this region for the study.
11 cf. Schwarz (1980) and Cortes et al. (1987) on Colombia, Bruch (1983) on the ASEAN countries, Schneider (1986) on the Philippines and Little et al. (1987) on India.
12 On qualitative methods cf. Warwick and Osherson (1973) and Berg (1989).

suitable to generate new knowledge, to go beyond the surface[13]. They rather tend to accumulate a mass of meaningless data and to pretend objectivity[14]. This is due to several factors:
1. Research is a (social) process. Before beginning and during the course of research, some degree of confidence from the side of the interviewees has to be gained. In this process several cultural barriers have to be overcome. The two most prominent are given if the researcher is, first, a foreigner[15] and second, perhaps even more importantly, a non-small industrialist. In Sudan, as in other countries, the world of industry is socially discriminated against. The "educated" people are looking down on manual work and are to some degree despising the surrounding sphere. This can be stated generally, despite the considerable differences in evaluation of different industrial branches. As a *pendant* to this the small industrialists view outsiders with a degree of suspicion. Despite of many connections - even within families - to the outside world, SI production is very much a world of its own.

Generally speaking, the notion of "scientific research" is not well known[16]. Furthermore, for those who had been interviewed, it had often been a negative experience. They did not see their benefit and felt exploited by people who did not care for their interest. My position (affiliation with the Ministry of Labour) was an advantage with regard to the research process, but of course it also implied problems which had to be overcome - in any case, this position had to be explained[17].

Thus it is an important first step which one must really be sure to have taken in order to establish a degree of confidentiality. It is not as easy as it might look at first sight, to find out if this first step is done, because due to the great politeness which is inherent to the Sudanese personality, rarely will you not get an answer to your question. However, to establish reality may be a different story. Nevertheless, the "courtesy bias"[18] cannot be characterized as an unequivocal "constraint" for research, but this attitude also makes field research easier in some respects - and in any case pleasurable.

---

[13] This point is also made by Bienefeld (1975b), Bienefeld and Godfrey (1975), Schwarz (1980). On the problems of application of social research methods in developing countries cf. Mitchell (1965), Schönherr and Gupta (1975), Hippel (1980), Bulmer and Warwick (1983) and Rafipoor (1988). Especially on the African context cf. different contributions in O'Barr et al. (1973), especially Cohen, Drake and Ijomah.
[14] On the discussion of objectivity cf. Myrdal (1969). Unfortunately much research still pretends to be "objective" and neglects its underlying value orientations.
[15] For a discussion of the role of foreigners as researchers in developing countries cf. Myrdal (1968), Streeten (1974).
[16] This is true not only for the industrialists, but also for the government service.
[17] There was a previous acqaintance with the craftsmen and small industrial entrepreneurs of Nyala organized in the Sudanese Craftsmen and Small Enterprises Union (SCSEU) in the context of a consultancy. This made it clear that my interest was something more than a pure desire to obtain an academic degree and proved to be very helpful to establish a good relation.
[18] cf. Jones (1963)

2. Besides this, there is a linguistic problem. Language is not only a means of communication about reality - it constructs reality. Even for some of the quantitative data questions, which appear at first sight to be quite simple and unequivocal, different meanings co-exist, which may become obvious only at a later stage. Of course, for qualitative, non-standardized questions, this problem is all the more pronounced.
3. Inevitably, the answers of small industrialists are influenced by certain perceptions and expectations toward the researcher. The scope for these perceptions is very large because it is so unfamiliar that an outsider is interested in SI.
4. Large differences in the level of the interviewees' education result in different perceptions of questions. Thus, simply to ask the same standardized questions to SI entrepreneurs and workers may distort the results.
5. These problems are further complicated if translators are employed. Inevitably, they bring in their own conceptions about the research subject and the people interviewed. This is a problem facing every field researcher working with translators. But it is even more severe when studying a group so distinct as small industrialists. Interviewers tend very much to have biased views. This is exacerbated by the, sometimes subtle, differences in the languages spoken by interviewers and interviewees. My own knowledge of the local *lingua franca*, a dialect of Sudanese Arabic, allowed to dispense with translators. Instead the interviews were carried out in team work with a Sudanese assistant.
6. One visit is not sufficient to get reliable and correct information on all of the relevant questions. It is often impossible to get at once reliable information about sensitive subjects as income, profit etc. For understandable reasons people hesitate to give information which might be turned against them. Furthermore, the production in most branches is highly variable due to supply and demand constraints. Also there are high seasonal variations. Reliable information about a number of factors can only be obtained in a process of repeated visits during different seasons.

In this context the traditional methods of empirical work fail. The division between formulating a questionnaire, testing, re-formulating, and main interrogation, breaks down. Instead, during the process of research new perceptions and new questions are coming up continuously, questions are dropped, and questions are re-formulated. In such a situation to stick to standard methods of statistics would mean not only to forego information, but also to arrive at wrong conclusions[19]. Thus, producers were selected as case studies, being visited several times in a process of supplementing, changing and updating

---

[19] An analysis of previous studies gives evidence for this. See below

information. To get a clear picture in general is a continuous process. Furthermore, it needs a continuous awareness.
7. The appropriate methods for the study of SI in Sudan have something in common with "ethnological" methods[20]. Some degree of understanding of the interviewee's point of view is necessary, his meaning construction, which is in effect understanding of a culture. This requires some extent of an active interaction with the people. However, I do not believe that the degree of understanding is a function of the level of participation (the researcher will never be a part of the interviewees' culture). It is rather a question of subtle intuition, sensitivity, the competence of introspection and the ability to reflect on experience[21]. To obtain objectivity in field research is not a question of formal procedures. The ambiguity of the researcher's position cannot be overcome.

Qualitative methods alone are not sufficient because they fail to establish representativeness. Thus, a combination of qualitative and quantitative methods is necessary[22]: quantitative methods have to establish the frame in which qualitative interviews are carried out.
In general, for the research on SI, different methods have to be combined. To do research on SI is like working on a puzzle[23]. The methods employed were:
- literature review;
- questioning and discussion with craftsmen/small industrialists and their workers, observation of their activities (case studies and short interviews);
- questioning and discussion with citizens, consumers, SI unions, chamber of commerce, city council, ministries on different levels, institutions of SI promotion and research institutions. To facilitate the discussion of the research results interim reports in English and Arabic languages were distributed[24].

In Nyala a total survey of industries in the two industrial areas and on the markets was carried out (on 8 markets industrial activities were identified). From all working enterprises basic characteristics were collected (sex of entrepreneur, kind of activities, kind of workplace, nature of accomodation, number of workers (skilled/unskilled, male/female), number of family-related workers, possession of license, type of ownership/management, age of enterprise, possession of electric machines).

---

20 On ethnological methods cf. Spradley (1979) and Ellen (1984).
21 The graphical description of the irrationalities, mistakes and embarassments of fieldwork described in Bohannan's "anthropological novel" (Bowen 1964) gives a feeling for the difficulties of fieldwork in developing countries - much better than any textbook.
22 For a discussion of the relation of quantitative and qualitative methods cf. Schönherr and Gupta (1975), on the African context cf. Cohen (1973), Ijomah (1973)
23 Schwarz (1980: 8) makes the same point.
24 cf. Hansohm (1988a, b)

This survey did not, however, cover 100% of the industries. First, some of the activities are carried out partly or completely out of the markets, in the open or at home. These activities had to be estimated. Second, many activities are not carried out continuously, mostly either for lack of raw materials or because people work exclusively on order. For this reason, at any point in time, a survey will miss some producers. However, with a combination of different methods, reasonable estimates of the total number of producers can be made.

The basic information collected on all of the SI enterprises and individuals provided a sampling frame for a selection of enterprises and individuals representing different industries and, within the industries, representing different sub-groups according to the characteristics mentioned above. The case studies concentrated on four industrial branches representing a wide spectrum: Two of them are traditional, i.e. of indigenous character and with a primitive technology (blacksmiths and tinsmiths), the other two are modern, i.e. of recent origin and with sophisticated technology (metal and carpentry workshops). Within these branches, case studies were selected to represent different types with respect to size and equipment.

For the analysis of the case studies, a manual of questions was drafted in English, translated and re-translated[25]. This manual contained the questions believed to be relevant. It was not used as a questionnaire, but rather in a loose, open way, subject to any interruption, discussion, suggestion coming up. Additionally, a short questionnaire was developed to be applied for complementary short interviews.

---

25 see Appendix 4

3 Sudan: A case for economic reform

Sudan is the largest state in Africa, covering more than 2,500,000 square kilometers. With an estimated population of 26.2 million (1989)[1] the population density is very low (10.5 per square kilometer) - however, the rate of population growth is obviously high (2.7% p.a. between 1983 and 1989[2]). Sudan has access to the Red Sea and borders on eight states: Ethiopia, Kenya, Uganda, Zaire, Central African Republic, Chad, Libya, and Egypt (see map).

SUDAN

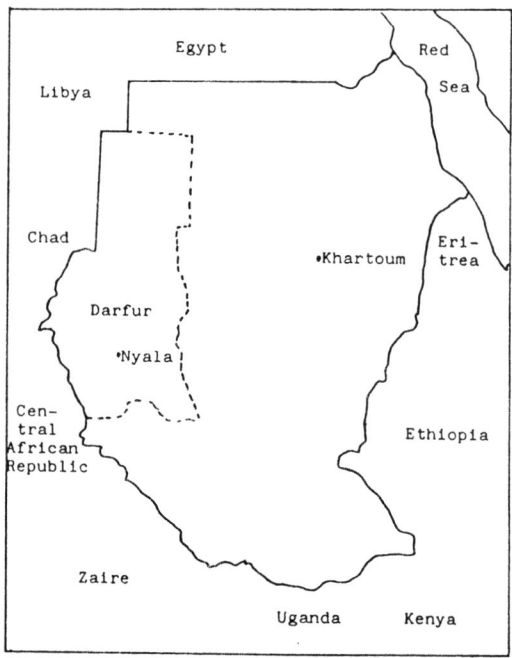

---

[1] cf. GoS (1990: 1). Estimations of population in Sudan are characterized by a high degree of uncertainty. Most of the people live in rural areas, outside of any close supervision of the government. Additional factors complicating population estimations are the devastating effects of the civil war on the one hand and the high number of refugees from neighbouring countries (mainly Ethiopia and Eritrea) on the other hand. This number is estimated to be as high as 1.2 mill.; this makes Sudan, after Pakistan, the second largest host country for refugees. On the other hand, the numbers of Sudanese refugees in Ethiopia and Uganda are estimated to be 250,000-350,000 and 43,000 resp. (cf. SBA 1990: 23).

[2] cf. SBA (1990: 18)

As most African states, Sudan is a product of colonial rule. Before colonial rule, part of the area was organized in two states (Funj and Darfur), but most of the people lived in state-less societies. During the 19th century a large part of present Sudan became a Turkish-Egyptian colony, and since 1898 (since 1916 in its present borders) Sudan was a British-Egyptian colony. Sudan became independent as one of the first African countries in 1956.

Sudan is in a state of deep crisis since the late 1970s. All attempts to steer clear of this crisis have been in vain - the crisis has on all accounts (economically, politically, socially) become deeper:
- The GDP growth is slightly negative in absolute terms and clearly negative in per capita terms: -1.4% and -4% between 1980 and 1987 resp.[3] (between 1965 and 1988 GDP growth per capita was 0.0[4]).
- The country is highly indebted (the debt was estimated to be US$ 12-13 billion in 1988[5] - within Africa second only to Nigeria). Debt service amounted to 756% of exports in 1988[6]. Sudan is the largest debtor of the IMF (end of 1990).
- Since the mid 1970s there is a persistent high trade balance deficit: the value of imports has been constantly more than double of export value (1988: 223%, 1989: 199%[7]). The terms of trade have been moving against Sudan; the prices for most of its export products have declined and the perspectives are no less gloomy.
- There is a parallel gap between domestic savings and investment - savings are negative (savings and investment were -2.7% and 7.7% of GDP in 1984/85-85/86[8]).
- The gap between government revenues and expenditures is in a process of persistent expansion: the central budget deficit increased from 4.8% of GDP (1977/78) to 8.1% in 1988/89[9].
- Increasing financing through bank loans (47% of the budget in 1987/88[10]) is heating the inflation (officially around 80% in 1989 but estimated to be more than 100%[11]); the money circulation increased by 475% between 1985 and 1989[12].
- Reform efforts of the government have become increasingly paralyzed and the flow of foreign development aid declined. Sudan has been declared "non-cooperative" by the IMF on September 14, 1990 - this is the most extreme

---

3   cf. BfA (1989: 6)
4   see Table 3.1.
5   cf. GoS (1990: 18) and BfA (1989: 19)
6   cf. GoS (1990: 18)
7   cf. MFEP-E (1990: IV)
8   cf. GoS (1990: 28)
9   cf. GoS (1990: 1)
10   cf. BfA (1989: 16)
11   cf. BfA (1989: 17)
12   cf. MFEP-E (1990: IV)

measure the IMF can take vis-à-vis his members. This should have severe repercussions with regard to foreign finance.
- One important dimension of the crisis is the breakdown of institutions and the increasingly bizarre and unworldly role of economic planning.
- Interwoven with the economic crisis is a political crisis. This has an ethnic and religious character, but main reasons are regional inequality and structural heterogeneity. This crisis today questions the very existence of Sudan itself. It is mainly a North-South conflict, but during the 1980s the conflict also spread to the West and the East. Most of its existence Sudan has spent in a state of civil war - only 11 years she enjoyed peace (1972-1983)[13].
- A second dimension of the political crisis is the repressive character and fragility of the political system. Sudan spent most of her life until now under military rule: 1958-1964, 1969-1986 and 1989 until the present (end 1990). Worse than this is the fact that the civil regimes have betrayed most of the hopes of the citizens, so that Sudan was an easy prey to the military. The performance of the civil regimes with respect to socio-economic development and even human rights records was hardly better - this is not to deny that military rule has had much more devastating impacts on the population[14].
- This *human dimension* of Sudan's crisis is the result of all the factors mentioned above and its most severe aspect: low and declining incomes, lack of basic goods, wide-spread malnutrition, lack of essential services (education, health).
- Last not least Sudan's crisis is an ecological crisis[15].

3.1 Is Sudan a typical case?

Can Sudan be considered as a typical African low-income country? The great diversity of country experiences in Africa[16] makes any generalization hazardous. Furthermore, at first sight, Sudan might be considered as a special case because of its Afro-Arab identity and the problems connected with this fact. However, a closer look shows that other African countries are plagued by similar conflicts and the

---

13 On the origins and history of the "Southern problem" cf. Omer Beshir (1968, 1975), on the general neglect of the Southern region in government attention cf. Yongo-Bure (1989), on the background of the second civil war and its terrible impact on the population cf. Mawut (1986) and Twose and Progrund (1988) resp. The basic problem of nation-building is excellently portrayed in Deng (1986). Many discussions about possible solutions of the political crisis have taken place (cf. Deng and Gifford 1987 and Ahmed and Sorbo 1989)

14 The last civil government came hardly under international pressure for its blatant human rights violations shortly before its fall; cf. Amnesty International (1989), Deutscher Bundestag (1989); for the terrible human rights record of the present military regime cf. Africa Watch Committee (1990a) and Committee for Peace and Reconstruction in Sudan (1989-1990).

15 cf. Ibrahim (1984), Osman (1990)

16 For an illustration of this see the African Development Perspectives Yearbook 1989 (RGADP 1990).

economic, social and political structures are similar. An analysis of the industrial structure, in particular, indicates similar problems.

Sudan is often characterized as an "Arab", rather than as an African country. A comparative analysis of economic and social data with the other member countries of the Arab League shows, however, that Sudan cannot be taken as representative of this country group, while the country fits into the picture of an African low-income country[17].

Table 3.1. compares some indicators of social and economic development in Sudan with sub-Saharan Africa (SSA) and the OECD countries[18]. While the health services are better developed in Sudan, primary school attendance is lower there than on the average in SSA (on the secondary school level the picture is opposite). Anyhow, these differences are dwarfed by the gap to the industrial countries. The GDP per capita in 1988 is almost 50% higher in Sudan than in average SSA, which is, however, exceptional. One year before Sudan's GDP per capita was exactly the SSA average (330 US $). The growth rate is a bit lower (0.0% and 0.2% resp.). The industrial sector is much smaller (in terms of GDP share, manufacturing value added per capita, manufactured exports), while the size of the services sector is far more extraordinary (in terms of labour force, however, these differences are far less significant). Sudan received higher development aid, but was worsely affected by terms of trade deterioration.

Table 3.2., depicting the industrial structure, shows that with a concentration on consumer goods industries, and especially food industries, Sudanese industry is at a lower level of structural evolution than other low-income SSA countries. However, the share of capital goods production is not significantly different.

In terms of SI policy, there are similarities between Sudan and most SSA countries. While programmes give a priority to SI promotion, reality looks different: SI promotion is negligible and does not outweigh negative biases of industrial and other policies. However, the data basis on SI is much weaker in Sudan than in many other SSA countries.

In conclusion, it seems reasonable to regard Sudan as a typical African LLDC[19].

---

17 Appendix 1 provides comparative indicators of social and economic development on African countries.
18 These data have to be interpreted with care. Their comparability is limited by a high degree of irreliability.
19 For a discussion of this cf. also Wohlmuth (1989: 357-362)

Table 3.1. Comparative data on Sudan, sub-Saharan Africa (SSA) and OECD countries (1988)

	Sudan	SSA	OECD
life expectancy at birth (years)	49	50	76
inhabitants per doctor (1984)	10100	23850	450
population growth in % (1980-88)	3.1	3.2	0.6
percentage in primary school (1987)	49	68	103
percentage in secondary school	20	17	94
daily caloric supply per capita (1986)	2208	2096	3390
urbanization rate	21	28	77
GDP per capita (US $)	480	330	17470
average annual growth rate 1965-88	0.0	0.2	2.3
percentages of GDP			
agriculture	33	34	
industry	15	27	
manufacturing	8	10	
services	52	39	
1985 MVA per capita (US $)	21	53	
annual growth of ind.prod.			
1965-80	3.1	9.4	3.1
1980-88	3.6	-0.8	2.2
manufactures as % of exports	7	16	81
terms of trade (1980=100)	86	92	103
ODA receipts per capita (US $)	38.6	28.9	

Sources: Meier and Steel (1989), World Bank (1989b), World Bank (1990)

Table 3.2. Composition of manufacturing value added in Sudan, Sub-Saharan Africa (low-income, middle-income), and World in % (1984)

	Sudan	low-income SSA	middle-income SSA	World
food, beverages, tobacco	53.8	35.0	27.5	11.2
textile, apparel, leather	11.7	15.9	9.9	8.4
wood and wood products	2.1	3.4	6.1	3.2
paper and paper products	2.2	5.0	6.5	0.1
chemicals, petrol., plastic	14.3	28.5	14.2	17.7
non-metallic mineral products	6.7	2.8	5.3	4.7
basic metals	1.8	1.5	5.2	8.1
metal prod., machinery	7.1	7.5	21.7	38.9
other manufactures	0.3	0.3	3.5	1.8
consumer goods	65.8	51.2	40.9	21.4
intermediate goods	27.1	41.2	37.3	33.8
capital goods	7.1	7.5	21.7	38.9

Sources: DoS (1987), Meier and Steel (1989); consumer goods: ISIC 31, 32, 39; intermediate goods: ISIC 33-37; capital goods: ISIC 38

3.2 Development of a crisis

As shown above, the record of development in Sudan has been more than disappointing so far. To explain this phenomenon one has to start with the impact of colonial domination. This will provide a basis for an evaluation of the following different phases of development policy.

3.2.1 The colonial heritage

Basically speaking, colonialism imposed a new, foreign dominated economic structure on the existing indigenous economy - or rather, economies. Whatever economic development took place during this period can be attributed to the dynamic export enclaves which were surrounded by a stagnant traditional sector. The main economic linkages did not connect sectors of the Sudanese economy but connected its modern sectors with Great Britain, the colonial power, via:
1. export of agricultural raw materials
2. import of consumer goods and capital goods.

In this way the Sudanese economy became highly dependent on external factors for its own reproduction[20]. This economic structure, described as "unbalanced" and "dualistic", has been in existence to this day: two economic spheres are co-existing, greatly differing in regard of income, mode of production, forms of property, technological standard etc: the "modern" sectors of irrigated and mechanized agriculture, cattle ranches, modern industry, trade and transportation on the one hand, and the "traditional" sectors of subsistence-oriented agriculture and informal non-agricultural activities in which the overwhelming majority of the population earns its living (still more than 3/4) on the other hand. This structure is usually described as "dualistic". However, the dual economy approach is based partly on false assumptions, neglecting the interdependence, the very close interrelations of the two sectors. A more appropriate characterization would be "structural heterogeneity"[21].

Colonialism had a clearly negative impact on the existing industries (handicrafts). A combination of sanctions and competition by imports hindered their development[22]. Hardly any modern industries were established (the only exception being agricultural processing as cotton ginning and edible oil)[23]. Only supply shortages

---
[20] This typical structure has been analyzed in a model by Amin (1977); on the African context cf. Rodney (1972); for the case of Sudan cf. Mustafa Salih (1977).
[21] cf. Cordova (1973)
[22] cf. Nimeiri (1976b: 77), Mahmoud (1984: 53), Oesterdiekhoff (1984), Abu Affan (1985: 10-12), Wohlmuth (1989: 363)
[23] According to Mahmoud (1984: 53) there were only 10 modern industrial establishments in 1944.

during the Second World War resulted in the establishment of some import substituting industries. However, when the war-induced import blockage was over, most of these industries turned out to be uncompetitive and collapsed[24].

After independence, the national government, being more development-oriented, began to recognize the importance of state activity and to institutionalize development planning. In 1962 the first comprehensive plan for economic development was presented: the *Ten Year Plan 1961/62-1970/71*. For the first time this document formulated broad national objectives. However, neither did the plan aim at public sector leadership, nor did it present a strategy for the private sector investment - its behaviour was simply assumed. The plan did not aim at any substantial transformation of the economy. Furthermore, development policies remained confined to the modern sectors. A sectorally and regionally concentrated "spearhead" strategy was pursued[25]. The successor, the *Five-Year-Plan 1970/71-1974/75*, was more elaborate, more detailed in its objectives and more ambitious. However, although inspired by Soviet planners, it represented no major turnaround[26].

None of the development plans achieved a basic restructuring of the economy. Neither a developed internal sector of mass consumption goods production nor an adequate domestic capital goods sector had come into being. Thus, the agricultural sector had to overtake the function of a "quasi-capital goods sector".

In the face of low productivity the export income was critically dependent on the competitiveness of exports and thus on the low remuneration of agricultural labour. Labour incomes were significant as a cost factor only. This limited the development of a broad domestic market.

A large part of the population remained living in the "subsistence economy", characterized by:
- a low share of market goods for reproduction;
- production targets which do not give the highest priority to maximal exploitation of labour and natural resources. Instead the security of material existence and an optimal relation of work effort and material result have first priorities.
- no monetary value for work and land. Work extending the scope of a family is organized on a reciprocal basis. Land is owned by communities. In rainfed agriculture land is allocated to cultivators through usufruct rights. Only on irrigated land there are permanent land rights.
- low intensity of land use;
- low standards of technology and productivity.

---

24   cf. Homoudi (1976: 46), Abu Affan (1985: 12)
25   cf. Bishop (1962), Wynn (1971), Ahmed Suliman (1975), Abdel Wahab (1976)
26   cf. Awad (1973), Ahmed Suliman (1975), Abdel Wahab (1976), Nimeiri (1976a)

However, this does not mean that the subsistence economy was self-sufficient. The main linkages to the "modern" economy are:
1. seasonal working migration
2. cash cropping

Neither of these two allowed for a "trickle down" of resources making a parallel growth of both the modern and the traditional sectors possible[27].
Independence was the start of modern manufacturing. The investments in industry came mainly from the private sector, while the government invested in the field of agro-industries[28].

3.2.2 The "Breadbasket" strategy: an offensive attempt to restructure the economy

In the 1970s the Sudanese government initiated an ambitious development programme called the "Breadbasket Strategy" - Sudan was to become the Arab world's food supplier[29]. This strategy involved a massive restructuring of production and foreign trade in order to take advantage of a regional Arabic division of labour. Arab capital, Sudanese manpower, land and animals, and western technology were to be combined[30]. The strategy has to be seen in the context of the surplus of capital as a result of the two "oil shocks" in the beginning of the 1970s and of the counter-threat of the USA to impose a food embargo over the Arab oil exporters.
The *Breadbasket Strategy* was a very ambitious programme of a gigantic size (more than 100 projects), aiming at high production increases[31] and a rapid economic transformation. At first sight, the objectives reflect a fundamental change in economic policy, an attempt to overcome the economic and social deficiencies resulting from the deformed economic structure (see above):
- Balanced and accelerated growth is aimed at.
- Regional and sectoral distribution of development efforts is to become more equitable.

---

27 cf. Wohlmuth and Hansohm (1984: 14-17)
28 cf. Affan (1985: 12-20), Wohlmuth (1989: 364-365)
29 cf. Awad (1983), Oesterdiekhoff and Wohlmuth (1983a, b), Wohlmuth and Hansohm (1984: 26-43, 1987: 209-211)
30 The objectives and the corresponding strategies are set out in the documents of the *Six-Year Plan of Economic and Social Development 1977/78-1982/83* (MNP 1977), the *Food Investment Strategy* (MAFNR 1977), and the Arab Fund's *Basic Programme for Agricultural Development in the Democratic Republic of the Sudan 1976-1985* (Arab Fund for Economic and Social Development 1976).
31 cf. the planned production increases of the *Basic Programme* ranging between 115% (pulses) and 640% (sugar) for the period 1972/73-1985 (Arab Fund 1976: 20) and the export targets of major agricultural commodities for 1985 as a percentage of the average exports of the years 1970-73 ranging between 10% for cotton (lint) and 1070% for meat & fish; cf. also the planned revenue surplus and additional fiscal effort covering 61% of the domestic resources (MNP 1977a: 56).

- Development is to be combined with social equity.
- The traditional agricultural sector is to be developed and modernized.
- Self-sufficiency in selected food and other agricultural commodities is to be reached.
- The country's natural resources are to be conserved.

However, the plan objectives are not integrated in any way, and some of them remain abstract declarations of intention - they are not reflected in the allocation of resources. The actual catalogue of measures in some instances even has contradictory effects. This assessment is exemplified in the following points:
- The regional inequalities were not overcome. While private investments expanded to some degree to the West, public investments were still concentrated on Eastern and Central Sudan. Investments to the South amounted to an insignificant 1.4% of total private investments in the *Six-Year-Plan*[32]. Not more than 4.8% of total public sector investment were allocated to regional development[33].
- Neither were the sectoral biases overcome. The emphasis is on agriculture, based on the "comparative advantage"-argument. However, leaving aside the question if these advantages really exist, this policy committed Sudan to continue the concentration on export of a few primary goods, and thus prevented it from overcoming its extreme dependence on the world market. While the manufacturing sector had the highest growth rate (9.5% in the *Six-Year-Plan*), its intra-sectoral structure of investments followed the inherited structure (see below). The limits of export- and import-substitution prevented the development of a dynamic structure of specialization.
- The concentration on the modern sectors was upheld as well. Only 3.0% of total investment in agriculture went to "traditional agriculture" - despite the evidence of the high potential of traditional agriculture as a net foreign exchange earner[34]. But even the small amount devoted to traditional agriculture is of doubtful value, because the strategy of "modernizing the traditional sector" aimed at an expansion of modern cultivation practices - like mechanization of rainfed crop production, establishment of modern ranches in the savannah region - instead of modernizing the existing farming systems. This kind of modernization was inaccessible for the small peasants. Thus it helped to strengthen social inequalities rather than to reduce them[35].

---

[32] On the economic neglect of the South cf. Yongo-Bure (1989).
[33] cf. MNP (1977a: 153)
[34] cf. D'Silva (1983)
[35] An alternative was formulated by the ILO (1976), emphasizing the development of the traditional sector. However, this document suffered from naive and unrealistic conceptions (vast land resources, co-existence of traditional and modern sectors, elastic supply response of traditional agriculture, efficient labour markets) and neglected institutional constraints (cf. Wohlmuth and Hansohm 1984: 41-43)

- The huge production increases envisaged were planned to be arrived at by horizontal rather than vertical expansion, i.e. by area expansion more than by higher yields[36]. This strategy was based on the widely spread belief that the Sudan has a surplus of "vast untapped land resources". This assumption has to be questioned. In fact, all parts of the country, even the desert, are used by its people. In most parts this use is extensive rather than intensive - however, this low intensity has its roots in and is adapted to the prevailing natural conditions (weather, soils, etc.) and the available technologies. The low population density can in fact be interpreted as a result of those conditions. As Lebon stated already in 1965, "statistical underpopulation has little correspondence with reality"[37]. Indeed, presently a lot of evidence points to a condition of acute and increasing shortage of land[38].
- A case in point of the kind of development intended by the Breadbasket Strategy is the expansion of mechanized farming schemes to the western savannahs and to other areas. In spite of its profitability the feasibility in technical, economical, ecological, and social terms has to be doubted[39].
- In the irrigated sub-sector (where most of the public funds were concentrated) modern capital- and import-intensive projects were implemented, which not only marginalized traditional land users, but also turned out to be unfeasible from the national economic point of view[40].
- The distribution problem was neglected. Even assumed that the high production rates would in fact turn out to be realistic, the problems of transportation and - more importantly - effective demand would remain. As the *Breadbasket Strategy* enforced the displacement of traditional agricultural producers (nomads and farmers), the result was that the people in need were not able to benefit from the increase of mechanized grain production.
- The unproportionate growth of the tertiary sector - which makes up one half of GDP since the mid 1970s (see Table 3.3.) reflects the distorted incentive structure.

The expansion of the tertiary sector is due to the high growth of the public sector (accompanied by declining efficiency)[41] and of unproductive activities in the trade sphere. For this reason Sudan has been described as a case of "pseudo-

---

36   cf. MNP (1977b: 7)
37   cf. Lebon (1965: 158)
38   cf. F. Ibrahim (1984), Wohlmuth and Hansohm (1984: 36), Osman (1990)
39   see below chapter 6.12.
40   see below chapter 6.12.
41   On the unproductive growth of the public sector see Hassan Ahmed (1986)

development"[42]: instead of industry, unproductive activities in the services sector have been expanding.

The agro-industries, established at that time, were of a gigantic, capital- and import-intensive character, often misplanned and had no relation to the existing industrial structure[43].

The three programmes are characterized by over-optimism, high dependence on foreign resources (52% of the *Six-Year-Plan*)[44], high dependence on imports[45], high dependence on deficit financing[46], and plan inconsistencies and methodological shortcomings which contributed to a serious underestimate of required foreign resources[47]. Last not least the envisaged projects went beyond the government's planning and implementation capacity. A top-down, state-centred approach was implemented, instead of relying on the existing structures and capabilities of the society[48].

By the measurement of development in structural terms, but also the measurement in terms of its own targets, the *Breadbasket Strategy* has to be considered a failure. The discussion whether the reasons of this are internal or external are of a pure academic nature, in fact they all worked together in an inseparable way:
- in the face of a tightening credit market and declining levels of international assistance the government embarked on a high level of short term borrowing in order to maintain its investment levels;
- declining terms of trade;
- declining export quantities[49];
- the cost explosion of the import dependent development projects[50];
- the infeasibility of the idea of *Pan-Arabism* which had inspired the concept of the Breadbasket Strategy. This concept had implied a transfer of capital resources primarily for political reasons. In reality, the Arab states (Saudi-Arabia and Kuwait in the first instance) were willing to invest in projects, but not to give balance of payment aid on other than IMF terms.

---

42 cf. UNIDO (1985: 5)
43 cf. Wohlmuth (1989: 365-366)
44 The analyses of Yongo-Bure (1984) and Farzin (1988) show that the scale and terms of Sudan's loans were not appropriate to Sudan's economic situation. Instead of contributing to growth, they were a heavy burden for the economy.
45 Yongo-Bure (1984) shows the negative impact of high fluctuations in export earnings on the supply of intermediate and capital goods.
46 38% of the domestic share of the public investment of the *Six Year Plan* (MNP 1977a: 56)
47 cf. Ezzat (1980), El-Shibly and Thirlwall (1981) and El Sheikh and Fadlalla (1985).
48 For Tignor (1987) this is the central reason of the *Breadbasket Strategy*'s failure. On the deficiencies in planning and plan implementation see also Abdel Wahab (1976), Kuku (1980), Yongo-Bure (1984), Moharir and Kagwe (1987)
49 As Umbadda and Shaaeldin (1983: 10) show, the falling quantities of export quantities in the 1970s were more important as an explaining factor of the decline of the export incomes than the terms of trade decline.
50 As the most prominent example take the Kenana sugar scheme, the largest integrated sugar scheme in Africa, which was calculated to cost $ 150 m. in 1973, but whose actual cost was estimated to be as high than $ 1 bn. (ACR 1977-78: B 134).

Table 3.3.: Sectoral structure of the economy (percentage shares in GDP)

	1955/56	1965	1976/77	1981/82	1986/87
primary sector	60.7	47.7	35.2	37.2	34.4
secondary sector	10.5	14.8	14.1	13.5	14.6
o/w manufacturing	4.4	6.0*	8.3*	6.1*	7.1*
tertiary sector	28.7	37.5	50.6	49.3	51.0
o/w government	6.0	10.4	9.3	11.8	11.9
o/w commerce	n.a.	14.7**	19.0	18.5	14.6

Sources: 1955/56: Harvie and Kleve (1959: 14); 1965: El-Hassan (1976b: 8); 1976/77-1986/87: Bank of Sudan (1976, 1982, 1987)
* incl.mining ** incl.hotels

By 1978 the balance of payments situation of the country had become precarious. Total foreign indebtedness had increased by 387% in the period from 1973-78 and was estimated to be more than $ 2 bn. and the Bank of Sudan's foreign reserves were exhausted - debt services amounted to more than one third of total export earnings. Huge gaps between exports and imports, government revenues and expenditures, and domestic savings and investment had opened[51]. SAP became necessary. It is important to keep aware of this - some of the critique of SAP loses credibility by holding SAP responsible not only for its results, but also for the emergence of the crisis itself[52].

3.2.3 The "stabilization" period (since 1978)

Since mid 1978 the Sudanese government pursued a stabilization policy in consultation with World Bank and IMF[53]. The government programmes[54] fell more and more in line with the advice of IMF and World Bank. The cooperation between government, IMF/ World Bank, and aid donors was coordinated in a "consultative group". In spite of the disastrous results and virtual end of cooperation with regard to SAP, the programmes continued to have the hand-writing of IMF and World Bank. Even the *Four-Year Programme 1988/89-1991/92*, which

---

51 cf. Wohlmuth and Hansohm (1984: 44-55)
52 e.g. Ali 1985, 1988; for a critique cf. Hansohm (1989a)
53 cf. Hansohm (1986b, 1989a), Wohlmuth and Hansohm (1984: 62-77, 1987: 213-216)
54 The relevant documents are: *Second Three Year Public Investment Plan 1980/81-82/83* (MNP 1981), *Prospects, Programmes and Policies for Economic Development 1982/83-84/85* (MFEP-P 1982), *Prospects, Programmes and Policies for Economic Development II 1983/84-85/86* (MFEP-P 1983), *Prospects, Programmes and Policies for Economic Development III 1984/85-86/87* (MFEP-P 1984), *Four Year Salvation, Recovery and Development Programme 1988/89-1991/92* (MFEP-P 1988a, b), and *Three Year Economic Salvation Programme 1990-93* (Republic of Sudan 1990)

clearly breathes their spirit, was not shelved by the military regime, which seized power in mid 1989 - its own programme[55] offers no significant change.

Central points of the programmes are:
- devaluation;
- overall ceiling of domestic credit;
- reduction of government budget;
- rehabilitation of existing agricultural and industrial projects;
- removal of state regulations (price controls, subsidies);
- encouragement of the private sector;
- concentration on economic fields which offer a comparative advantage;
- concentration on quick-yielding projects.

These programmes went astray (see the results listed in the introduction) because they did not really touch the structural deficiencies inherited from the colonial past (see above), many objectives were simply not implemented (as in other programmes before), and some turned out to be not implementable:
- Devaluation did not work to promote exports and to reduce imports because of the structural rigidities in the economy and the nature of the markets for Sudan's exports. Thus devaluation tended to heat up inflation, instead of changing economic price relations[56].
- More important to prevent a correction of the biases has been the political power of interest groups like the urban population and the merchants.
- The impact of the marketing structure, which prevents producers to reap the benefits of incentives, was neglected.
- The frequent separation of ownership and actual operation of irrigated tenancies also helped to divert incentives[57].
- In the run for quick-yielding projects the neglect of infrastructure was continued, so that its state is even worse now than at the beginning of the SAP.
- In the same manner, the neglect of the traditional sector was continued[58].
- Instead the concentration on the irrigated sub-sector was enforced in a technocratic manner (the "colonial bias"[59]), neglecting its negative performance as a foreign exchange earner, neglecting the policy failures at the bottom of the

---

[55] cf. Republic of Sudan (1990)
[56] cf. Diab (1984); also the discussion on the effectiveness of devaluation in Sudan between Nashashibi (1980), Nureldin Hussain and Thirlwall (1984), Nashashibi and Clawson (1986), and Nureldin and Thirlwall (1986); see also the argument of Ali (1985) on the non-appropriateness of devaluation and the comment of Hansohm (1989a: 271-273)
[57] cf. Shaaeldin (1983)
[58] This was in contradiction to the government's "Strategy for Development of Rainfed Agriculture" issued in 1985 (MFEP 1986). This very comprehensive policy document was obviously never implemented. For an evaluation cf. Wohlmuth (1987).
[59] cf. Wohlmuth (1987: 13)

problems of the rainfed sector, and completely disregarding the fact that the vast majority of people live on rainfed agriculture.
- The preponderance of the tertiary sector was not changed.
- Nor were the regional inequalities overcome.
- The notion of "vast land resources" is still held in most quarters, although it is co-existing uneasyly with a growing consciousness of the ecological destruction.
- There is an unreserved praise for the "private sector". However, evidence does not support the view that the private sector always is more efficient than the public sector. Some of the foreign investment on the contrary had an exploitative character[60].
- Also the concept of the "private sector" itself[61] behind the drive for privatization is not adequate to Sudanese conditions. This sector consists of elements which are very differently affected by policy measures. On the one hand, the traditional sector and the informal sector are part of the private sector, on the other hand there are investors from the modern sector, mainly the tertiary sector, as well as foreign investors. The trend in the past had been to marginalize the former and to give advantages to the latter. The stabilization policies have enforced this pattern rather than overcome it: Almost all of the planned measures aimed at the second sub-sector at the expense of the former sector. Social inequalities have been widened.

In short, the chance for a fundamental restructuring of the economy in the course of crisis and SAP has been missed. Instead, the country fell back into the traditional pattern in terms of concentration on traditional agricultural exports as well as trade partners[62], although in the face of the terms of trade development the perspectives for Sudan on the road of export-oriented development are gloomy. Short-term crisis management, characterized by overoptimism and wishful thinking[63], has been the order of the day. The result have been:
- decreasing incomes;
- even faster decreasing living standards[64];
- increasing inequality;
- collapsing public services (education, health);

---

60 see for instance the literature on the Kenana Project: Oesterdiekhoff (1982), Wohlmuth (1983), Grawert (1984), Wohlmuth and Hansohm (1985)
61 as formulated e.g. by Waterbury (1985) and Tignor (1987)
62 On the limited success of efforts to diversify trade to developing countries and East Bloc countries see Hansohm and Wohlmuth (1988)
63 Informative are the meeting protocols of the Consultative Group (World Bank 1983a, 1984a), or programmes which state a negative growth, prescribe the same tablets and expect a growth of 5%.
64 due to the development of terms of trade and the high cost for the civil war

- malnutrition and famines[65];
- internal and external refugees.

Foreign aid has contributed to many of Sudan's present problems. It is often characterized by by-passing of the government institutions, non-integration into its plans and priorities, and lack of coordination[66]. Because of the large size of foreign aid compared to the government resources, this impact is very serious[67]. A special case is food aid, which saves human lifes in the short term, but creates the "dependency syndrome", i.e. it undermines attempts of rural development planning, regional self-reliance and has negative impacts on agricultural production[68]. Despite its lack of coordination with government policies, foreign aid helped to prevent change by subsidizing governments, which were unwilling to implement changes[69].

3.3 Case study Nyala

Many of the crisis symptoms described in the preceding chapter are present in a multiplied form in Darfur Region. Except for the South, this region is the most marginalized region of the country, in terms of economic development, incomes, and provision of government services (education, health)[70]. This region belongs also to the regions least integrated into the national economy[71]. Further, the region has been hardly hit by desertification and famine[72]. Thus Darfur is an ideal candidate for an examination of Sudan's crisis.

---

65 It is now widely recognized that the famines in Sudan were not primarily a result of drought, but of policies; see Ahmed Abdel Ali (1988) on the 1984/85 famine, Africa Watch Committee (1990b) on the 1989/90 famines in the South, the Western (Darfur, Kordofan) and Eastern (Red Sea Province) peripheries and in the Central Region and the *Three Towns*, Osman (1990) on the general context.
66 cf. Whittington and Calhoun (1988)
67 Yassin (1982) evaluates Sudan's foreign exchange gains through aid vs. trade by comparing the grant element in foreign aid with the excess cost of tying. His results - 31.1% and 92.6% resp. - throw a negative light on foreign aid.
68 On the ambivalent impact of food aid in Sudan see Abdel Gadir Mohamed (1989) and Bickersteth (1990); on the case of Darfur Region see de Waal (n.d.: 129-147) and Buchanan-Smith (1990).
69 Even the humanitarian aid, to which Western aid is now more or less reduced, helps to finance the government policy, because foreign funds are changed at the official rate, which is only a fraction of the real value (LS 4.5/US-$ vs. approximately LS 40/US-$ at the end of 1990); this gain is a significant proportion of the government's budget.
70 For indicators cf. ILO (1987: 46) and El Sammani (1987)
71 Rural Darfur is still to a large extent a separate economic entity (see above chapter 3.2.1.) with its own rationality. This has been described as *subsistence ideology* by de Waal (n.d.: 5-25); on this rationality see also Barth (1967) and Hansohm and Woltersdorff (1983: 57-134).
72 On the effects of desertification on Darfur cf. F. Ibrahim (1984) and Dar Fur Region and UNDP (1985), on the famine Bush (1988).

Nyala is the major urban centre of Darfur region[73] (see map on page 18). The city belongs to the most rapidly growing urban centres in Sudan. In comparison with eight other Sudanese towns which had a population between 10,000 and 20,000 inhabitants in 1955/56 (year of the first census), its growth between 1955/56 and 1973 was only second to Juba; its population increased by 320% from 13,986 to 59,583 during this period[74]. In this period it outstripped the regional capital of El Fasher and the other towns of Darfur, its growth rate being more than twice as high as that of all the Darfur towns taken together. The 1983 population census counted 111,779 inhabitants[75]. Presently the city has certainly more than 200,000 inhabitants. Population projections for 15 principal cities of Northern Sudan - including Greater Khartoum - for the period 1980-2000 estimate the highest growth rate for Nyala in each of the four quinquennial periods[76]. According to these figures in 2000 Nyala would be the third largest city in Sudan, after Greater Khartoum and Port Sudan. This growth rate is all the more remarkable since in the early 1920s Nyala was only a nomadic camp with a small weekly market and four shops[77].

However, the growth dynamics of Nyala have been described as "a relatively extreme case of a general phenomenon rather than as atypical or totally different"[78]. Urban development in Southern Darfur started only when road and motor transport supplanted caravans as the principal mode of transport. Other contributing factors were the progressive deterioration in the physical environment of towns in Northern Darfur, the increasing scale of eastward migration in the context of *hajj* (pilgrimage to Mecca), and the emergence of demand for labour in East Sudan by the Gezira Scheme, which opened in 1925[79]. Nyala became the headquarters of the British Assistant District Commissioner for South Darfur in 1931. This contributed to an increase in commercial activities. Further pushes were given by the end of the "closed district" policy[80] after the Second World War and by the extension of the railway to Nyala as the terminal station in the West in 1960. With the administrative reorganization of the provinces in 1974 Nyala became provincial capital of South Darfur. Two migration flows are held responsible for Nyala's "urban explosion": east-west migration of traders, investors, and government officials, and west-east migration (from within Darfur and

---

73 As a part of Darfur's marginalization, also the information basis on its urban development is very small. On Nyala cf. Hale (1977), Abu Sin (1980) and A. Ibrahim (1984); on urbanization in Western Sudan see Ali el Dawi (1975).
74 cf. Abu Sin (1980: 375)
75 cf. DoS (1988)
76 cf. Farag (n.d.: 40)
77 cf. Khogali (1964: 220-221), cited by Abu Sin (1980: 352)
78 cf. Abu Sin (1980: 365)
79 cf. Abu Sin (1980: 355)
80 This policy banned traders from most regions of the Sudan.

neighbouring West African countries)[81]. The result is a high proportion of "transient" migrants and the preservation of a "somewhat 'rural' demographic profile" and a high dependence on agriculture[82].

---

[81] Classical works on the dynamics of migration in Sudan are Mather (1956) and Ali el Dawi (1975).
[82] cf. Abu Sin (1980: 363-371)

4 Small industries: An introduction

4.1 The interest in small industries in developing countries

In the development theories of the 1950s and 1960s SI did not figure prominently. Development was equated with economic growth. It was believed that economic growth would lead automatically to overall development of the society. The prevailing modernization theories conceived development as a repeatable and cumulative process of modernization, based on the example of the industrialized countries. Thus, development was regarded as a transfer of technologies, organization structures, and behaviour of industrial societies from outside and from above.

In this process industrialization plays a central role[1]. Industrialization was equated with the development of modern large industry. The advantages of modern technology were considered as overwhelming, since this usually entails a larger scale of production and greater capital intensity. For this reason it was believed that total factor productivity would be very high, offsetting the high cost of the use of scarce capital[2].

The view of the development theories of the 1950s and 1960s on development and industrialization was shared by policy makers in developing countries - in many countries, among them Sudan, it is still prevalent. As Little et al. note, the neglect of small industries at the time is readily understandable: The policy makers of the developing countries wanted to create a lot of industry very fast from a very small base. Furthermore, it was believed that the social base for industrialization was very small[3]. This led to the prevalence of large units, capital-intensive investments, public sector investment and foreign management. Other reasons for the preference of capital intensive methods were the prestige and promotion of advanced country technologies, ignorance of alternatives or a belief in the inferiority of alternatives (the belief in "fixed proportions" of labour and capital), a belief in higher profits, savings and reinvestment rates related to capital-intensive production[4], preference by the rich for import-equivalent goods, difficulties of dealing with large numbers of inexperienced workers, and government policies that tend to favour the use of capital[5]. Industrialization was promoted in 3 main ways: trade regulation, investment incentives as interest rate manipulation and credit control, and public sector investments - all of the three discriminating against SI.

---

1 Kuznets (1959: 110) summarized his fundamental research on economic development by describing "modern economic growth as the adoption of the industrial system".
2 cf. Gerschenkron (1952), Cortes et al. (1987: 1)
3 - the "lack of entrepreneurship" (see below Chapter 6.1.)
4 For this argument cf. Galenson and Leibenstein (1955).
5 cf. World Bank (1978: 16-17)

SI was simply omitted in the dualistic models of economic development and migration of Lewis and others, which treated activities outside the "modern sector" as a form of temporary unemployment or "waiting room" for this sector[6]. The existence of traditional SI, if considered at all, was regarded as inferior[7]. It was believed that SI would simply be displaced by LI in the course of development. At the most, SI was introduced in development theory as the starting point of, or as a contrast to, LI[8]. Many believed that persistence of SI was due to market imperfections and implied sub-optimal use of resources[9].

The judgment of SI as inferior was shared by the marxists as well. Marx believed that SI necessarily will be destroyed by LI, "petty industry" will create the material forces for its own destruction[10]. Lenin believed that LI will completely "squeeze out" SI and considered promotion of SI as reactionary, because it helped to preserve pre-capitalist social relations and retarded the development of industry and fully fledged capitalism[11]. This belief is shared by modern Marxists analysing developing countries[12]. With regard to Africa, this ideology implies a belief that the indigenous industries would be destroyed by mass-produced imports in the course of colonialism. The most that could survive the colonial impact would be an industry directed to tourists[13].

The "inferiority view" of SI resulted in an almost total lack of study on SI in developing countries. The marginality of SI in economic research on developing countries persists until today, as exemplified by the discussion on SAP - neither the neo-liberal theorists nor their critics take account of SI in designing and evaluating structural adjustment policies[14].

However, since the 1970s there is a gradual change in mind among development economists. SI has started to gain interest[15]. There are different reasons for this change. One is the recognition that despite the predictions to the contrary, SI continue to exist or even flourish in developing countries. For example, a 1987 review of evidence on SI indicates that in 14 developing countries industrial firms with less than 10 employees account for 40-90 % of industrial employment, the 6 African countries being in the upper range[16]. The most detailed study on SI in Africa, on Sierra Leone, apportions 99.9% of enterprises, 95.6% of industrial

---

6   cf. Lewis (1970), Todaro (1969), Harris and Todaro (1970)
7   e.g. Bottomley (1965). An exception is Hirschman (1958: 130-131), who emphasized the importance to preserve small industries besides large industries.
8   cf. Hoselitz (1959)
9   cf. Cortes et al (1987: 1)
10 cf. Marx (1963)
11 Lenin, cited by Schmitz (1989: 1); also Lenin (1936: 331), cited by Bromley (1985b: 323);
12 cf. Warren (1980) and Abu Affan (1985)
13 cf. Rodney (1972: 253)
14 cf. Fitzgerald (1989), Haggblade et al. (1986), Schmitz (1989)
15 For Africa cf. Page and Steel (1984: 1-5)
16 cf. Liedholm and Mead (1987: 15)

employment, and 43% of industrial value added to SI[17]. In Africa, during the process of industrialization, SI production has not only been preserved, but actually expanded - there is no process of ousting the SI comparable to the industrial countries[18], which is partly due to the failure of large scale industrialization. However, the role of SI is still more important in other developing countries, notably in India and other South Asian countries, but also Latin America[19]. Besides this, it has been recognized also that the idea that SI had vanished in the industrial countries during the process of industrialization was mistaken. Industrialization and the emergence of factory industry transformed rather than displaced non-factory SI. While some product lines were pushed out, other activities were created (repair, installing, servicing of factory goods, subcontracting to LI). While new products and new technologies made some traditional crafts obsolete, new ones were created. And changes in social structure and rising income levels resulted in declining markets for some goods, but expanding markets for many more[20]. It has been observed that in many countries the trend towards concentration has slowed down or even reversed[21]. SI has continued to play a vital role in development, it especially explains part of the success of countries like Italy, Japan and West Germany. Furthermore, SI is re-discovered as a solution to the West's industrial crisis[22].

The reason most often mentioned for the increasing interest for SI in developing countries is the increasing "employment problem". Agriculture has proved to be unable to absorb the increasing population. Though absorbing huge investments, LI created a small amount of productive employment, concentrated in urban areas. But even there, it has been totally unable to cope with the "labour force explosion"[23]. The result is a flourishing urban informal sector, consisting of SI and tertiary activities, but also of poverty. It is recognized that the category "unemployment" is not suitable to developing countries, especially to the African context. It has been replaced by the concepts of "underemployment" or "disguised unemployment"[24].

In general, it is emphasized that patterns of development using more (unskilled) labour were preferable, independently of evidence of either unemployment or underemployment, from the point of view of availability of assets - capital, not labour, is the scarce factor.

---

17 cf. Chuta and Liedholm (1985: 14ff.)
18 cf. Bragina (1974: 128). On the growth of the informal sector in Africa cf. ILO and JASPA (1989), Wohlmuth (1990b); for two notable country studies cf. van Dijk (1986a, b)
19 cf. Thomas (1988)
20 cf. Staley and Morse 1965: 45; for the structural changes SI undergo cf. also Anderson (1982)
21 cf.Harper and Soon (1979: IX), Little et al (1987: 16)
22 cf. Schmitz (1989) for literature on this topic
23 cf. Frank (1968), Friedmann and Sullivan (1974), Morawetz (1974)
24 A wide academic discussion about measurement of the size of the "unutilized labour pool" set in, which did not arrive at any productive conclusion (cf. Bienefeld and Godfrey 1975).

A related point is the realization that up-to-date technologies are not the panacea as believed, because new technologies can significantly increase output only with a much higher capital investment than available in most developing countries[25], especially in Africa. Some even doubt that LI is likely to be efficient at all under the production factor (labour/ capital) availabilities in developing countries[26]. LI production may be inefficient under conditions of small, scattered, seasonal or fragmented markets, maintenance and management difficulties and workers being not used to factory discipline[27]. A related view takes an evolutionary perspective and regards SI as a stage of development on the way to the development of LI, which can hardly be bypassed[28].

For many authors SI plays a role in the wider context of a re-definition of development[29] or a radical critique of traditional development concepts. The re-definition of development includes other economic objectives as alleviation of poverty, unemployment, and inequality, participation and self-reliance - besides growth[30] - or sees development as a part of a wider process of social change[31].

Others go much further, regarding SI as the central element of a complete re-orientation of development policy. An example is Schneider-Barthold (1984b), who questions not only growth as an objective (rather than as a result), the imitation of Western models in Africa, but also the industrial system itself. Biguma Napoleon (1990) sees the SI as a germ of an alternative social organisation.

4.1.1 The interest in small industries in Sudan

Sudan is a classical example of a total neglect of and bias against SI in developing countries. Policies of the independent government have in this respect been a continuation of colonial policy, which tended to drive out the traditional industries (all of them SI), mostly by import of manufactured goods, but also by direct measures, i.e. through bans[32]. The national government continued in this line by promoting exclusively LI and capital-intensive technologies. Its policy has been based on ignorance and prejudices - an attitude generally shared by the elite: government officials and academicians.

---

25 cf. Cortes et al. (1987: 2): The argument of *appropriate technology* was forcefully developed and made popular by Schumacher (1974)
26 cf. Little, Scitovsky and Scott (1970: 91), cited by: Cortes et al. (1987: 2)
27 cf. Marsden (1970: 478)
28 cf. Spiro (1972)
29 cf. Seers (1974)
30 cf. Amedon (1982), Schwarz (1980), Vorlaufer (1988)
31 cf. McCormick (1988)
32 see above chapter 3.2.1.

This point of view is, for instance, expressed in the comprehensive standard work on Sudan's industry[33]. Here it is argued that SI units "are generally known to be less economical and efficient than large scale industries where the law of increasing returns prevails". While it is acknowledged that SI may be appropriate to the scattered character of population and demand, it is argued that if SI compete in larger cities instead of one LI, this would be a waste, because "the inevitable result of such a state of affairs is a high level of excess capacity and uneconomical inefficient use of capital assets and higher costs". Furthermore it is argued that larger units are more efficient, even if their production capacity is larger than the existing demand, because it is to be expected that "the pattern of increase in demand may, over time, be such as to make it economical to install plants which have excess capacity over shorter periods in preference to smaller uneconomical ones". Further, SI tend to produce "lower quality products". Lastly, it is argued that the recommendation of SI on the grounds of employment creation is to be rejected because "Sudan is not as overpopulated as other underdeveloped countries". These citations are representative for the arguments (or unexpressed beliefs) heard again and again when speaking with government officials and other concerned people in spite of the fact that virtually all of these arguments are disproved or irrelevant (see below). Another typical attitude of academics towards SI is complete neglect[34]. The results of this general ignorance are not only a lack of promotion for SI and a biased policy, but also a severe lack of knowledge about SI activities[35].

Sudan's imposed capital-intensive and dependent LI is in a severe crisis and on a declining trend since 1978. Manufacturing value added per capita has decreased from $71 in 1970 to $36 in 1985[36], and production figures are at best stagnant (see Table 4.1.).

The industrial decline is a result of the LI's inappropriate character and the impact of SAP, which undermines its artificial distinct advantages vs. SI.

As a result of the crisis the need for new industrial policies is long since overdue. In this context Sudan's donors have emphasized the positive performance of SI and the need to redress the neglect and discrimination of this sector[37]. Promotion of SI was also advised by Sudanese intellectuals and development agencies[38]. SI is also regarded as a possible channel for migrants' remittances. Lastly, the promotion of

---

33 Abu Affan (1985: 133-134)
34 e.g. Kaballo (1979), for whom SI are units with 25-50 workers.
35 See the literature overviews on traditional industries by Madani (1981) and Oesterdiekhoff (1984), on SI by Hansohm and Wohlmuth (1987) and Ibrahim (1989).
36 cf. UNIDO (1989: 15)
37 The ILO made this emphasis as early as 1976 (ILO 1976: 56), while other organisations followed later; see also ILO (1987b: 82-83), UNIDO (1989: 57); the World Bank (1987a: 67) included in her comprehensive industrial report the promotion of SI as one of 14 proposed fields of action.
38 e.g. Bakhit (1979), Amara (1987), MDC (1987, 1988)

SI has also been advised as a part of programmes in an effort to diversify income sources to combat desertification[39].

Table 4.1. Production changes of selected commodities 1986/87-1988/89

commodity	unit	1986/87	1987/88	1988/89
cigarettes	'000 kg	1.5	1.2	1.2
flour	'000 ton	859.7	796.7	268.3
soft drink	mill. dozen	0.2	0.09	10.5
sweets	LS mill.	67	44	34.7
kitchen utensils	LS mill.	12.8	9.9	6.1
ready-made cloth	LS mill.	15.9	10.7	7.9
cosmetics&perfume	LS mill.	31.3	25.1	16.5
tiles	'000 m2	965	2131.1	249
paint	LS mill.	40.7	38.7	58.6
electric goods	LS mill.	13.3	6.1	13.7
batteries	LS mill.	28.4	6.1	20.4
soap	LS mill.	54	55	43

Source: MFEP-E (1990: 62)

However, these proposals were hardly translated into action - neither by the donors nor by the government. Almost the only result were a lot of consultancy studies[40]. The few attempts of SI promotion had mixed success[41]. In the context of SAP the emphasis on industrial policies (of donors as well as the government) was laid on rehabilitation of the existing LI. But more important was the general tendency of declining interest in industry as a whole.

Although SI is also mentioned in several of the government programmes[42], in the face of the actual lack of action this appears to be a mere gesture. The above described anti-SI ideology turned out to be extremely persistent and stubborn and determines government policy until today. The 1979 assessment of one of the few intellectuals consistently making an argument for SI that "a strong movement for development of SSE emerged in 1975" because of increasing dissatisfaction with the record of LI[43], is unfortunately not borne out by the facts.

4.2 Definitions and delimitations of small industries

In this study "industry" is defined in a narrow way as manufacturing (ISIC codes 31-39) plus repair of manufactured goods (ISIC code 95), i.e. mining, construction,

---
39 cf. Tubiana and Tubiana (1977: 91-92), F. Ibrahim (1984), Hansohm (1986a)
40 e.g. Ahmad (1978), Sen (1985), Hansohm (1986a), Bakhit et al. (1987), Niazi (1987)
41 cf. Hansohm and Wohlmuth (1987: 183-186), Oehler (1989)
42 see below chapter 6.12.
43 cf. Bakhit (1979: 1.1.1.)

electricity, water and gas are excluded. This definition is in line with most approaches[44].
Definitions of SI vary a great deal[45]. They depend on the context and purpose of the definition. The meaning of "small" depends on the location - a small factory in Germany may be regarded unequivocally as large in an African developing country. It is a question of time: what is considered as a LI today may be considered as a SI tomorrow - or vice versa - depending, for instance, on the development of technology. It depends on the industry: What is small in one industry may be large in another. Principally there are two ways of defining a SI: firstly, qualitative, functional, and secondly, in quantitative terms. The first way is the more satisfactory, because the justification of the use of the term "SI" bases on the assumption that it is functionally different, which makes SI's problems and opportunities different. However, because of measurement difficulties, quantitative definitions are predominating. A problem arises because both ways are often combined, i.e. it is assumed that enterprises of a certain size do have certain characteristics - an assumption not always standing up to evidence[46].

4.2.1 Qualitative definitions

The classical work on SI mentions four functional differences of SI: relative little specialization in management, close personal contacts, handicaps in obtaining capital and credit, and the sheer number of SI units[47]. Berg characterizes SI as an industry equipped with simple, often non-electrified tools and machines with little division of labour, and the proprietor is both entrepreneur and artisan[48].
Schneider-Barthold[49] characterizes African SI (including crafts) by:
- production on demand and/or small series for direct sale to consumers;
- lack of division of labour and specialization;
- lack of book-keeping, calculation and formal education;
- predominant employment of family workers.

---

[44] cf. Liedholm and Mead (1986)
[45] A survey of 75 countries conducted in 1975 found over 50 different definitions being used (cf. Auciello et al. 1975, cited in: Liedholm and Mead 1987: 2)
[46] An example is the apparently first attempt to define SI with respect to Africa, made by the ILO in 1962: "SI units comprising small-scale and handicraft undertakings are understood to mean establishments for manufacturing, processing and service activities which differ from larger establishments inter alia, by a significant lack of specialization in management. Such undertakings vary from craft shops in which the self-employed owner works together with his family, to the small mechanical factory which may employ up to some 50 workers." (cited in: ECA 1969: 25)
[47] cf. Staley and Morse (1965: 10)
[48] cf. Berg (1978: 20)
[49] cf. Schneider-Barthold (1984b: 128)

Page and Steel, from the point of view of project design, define small scale enterprises as "enterprises engaged in activities involving barriers to entry in the form of human or physical capital that do not have ready access to institutionalized credit and incentives without special assistance"[50].

The qualitative definitions stand in the tradition of dual theories. To dichotomize the economy of developing countries is a classical analytic approach in development economics[51]. The most prominent and widely discussed dual theory is the "informal sector" (informal sector) - "formal sector" division. An analysis of the extensive literature is beyond the scope of this study[52]. Although the majority (in Africa 70-80 % in terms of employment[53]) of informal sector activities are tertiary activities (especially petty trade) rather than industry, the literature on the informal sector is all the more relevant, because a great proportion of SI activities are too small even for the interest of economic studies on SI.

The term "informal sector" was apparently made known by Hart (1973), who equated informal sector activities with self-employment. The concept was made popular by the ILO study on Kenya (1972), which characterized informal sector activities by:
- ease of entry
- reliance on indigenous resources
- family ownership of enterprises
- small scale of operation
- labour-intensive and adapted technology
- skills acquired outside the formal school system
- unregulated and competitive markets[54]

The informal sector concept can be regarded as a progress compared with earlier dualist models which often implied a bias against the "traditional" sector by assigning attributes like passivity, "un-economic behaviour" (limited wants, backward-sloping supply curves of effort and risk-taking), inability to develop, to the sector. In contrast, the ILO report emphasized its modernity and dynamics. Weeks (1975) defines the informal sector by its limited access to resources and the freely competitive nature of its product and factor markets, whereas Mazumdar

---

50 cf. Page and Steel (1984: 13)
51 It goes back to Boeke (1953), who dichotomized the economy in capitalist and pre-capitalist sectors. Other examples are Lewis (1970) with a capitalist and subsistence sector, Higgins (1955) with a modern and a traditional sector, Geertz (1963) with firm centred and bazaar economies, McGee (1973) with capitalist and peasant forms of production, and Santos (1975) with upper and lower circuits.
52 For a review of literature see Moser (1978), Dick and Rimmer (1980), Hugon (1982), Moser (1984), Richardson (1984), Märke (1986), and Turnham et al. (1990).
53 an estimate of ILO/JASPA (1985: 41)
54 ILO (1972: 6)

(1976) defines the informal sector as the not-protected sector in contrast to the protected sector (protected by government, trade unions). However, there are several shortcomings of the informal sector concept. Firstly, because of the combination of different criteria/variables, it is logically inconsistent. It often leads to an assumption of an identity of different criteria for the dichotomy. Secondly, it includes very different activities and gives the wrong impression that a single policy prescription can be applied to all. Thirdly, there is a tendency to confuse neighbourhoods, households, people, activities, and enterprises. One common feature is to equate the informal sector with the urban poor[55]. It is not useful to speak of neighbourhoods, households, and people, because these may be active in both the informal and the formal sector. The term "enterprise" does not seem broad enough, because there are many activities below this size. Fourthly, there is a danger that the dichotomization directs attention away from the diversity of informal sector activities and the linkages between them and the formal sector, their incorporation in a larger economy[56]. Fifth, another danger is that the informal model, being static, fails to capture the dynamics of informal development[57]. Sixth, one can argue that it has a function to divert attention from the underlying political structures and thus helps those who oppose social transformation[58]. Seventh, there is no satisfactory method of defining the informal sector empirically. It is not clear, for example, why all the enterprises with less than 11 workers in manufacturing, construction, transport, trade, and service should meet the characteristics of the informal sector enterprises as defined by Sethuraman (1981a). He tries to solve half of the problem by including also enterprises with more than 10 workers if they meet one of the informality measures, but also this is arbitrary. The basic problem of the informal sector concept seems to be that it is essentially a descriptive category which is used as an explanatory variable[59].

Some of these critical arguments can be incorporated in the informal sector model. For instance, the existence of two separate sectors does not necessarily imply a neglect of their linkages. Also the "continuum view" does not necessarily preclude the informal sector concept[60].

A group of critics of the informal sector model developed the "petty commodity production" approach, based on Marxist theory[61]. While Marx viewed the petty

---

55 cf. Bromley (1978), ILO and JASPA (1985: 16)
56 cf. Leys (1973), Breman (1976), Bromley (1978), Dick and Rimmer (1980), Moser (1984)
57 cf. Coing et al. (1982)
58 cf. Connolly (1985)
59 cf. Moser (1984: 153).
60 cf. Sethuraman (1981a: 19). For the continuing discussion on the usefulness and appropriateness of the informal sector concept cf. van Dijk (1986a, 1986b), Peattie (1987), Chandavarkar (1988), Coing et al. (1982), Khundker (1988), Mezzera (1988), Sethuraman (1988), Boehm/Kappel (1990), in this volume especially Kappel (1990) and Wohlmuth (1990b), Hugon (1990), King (1990), Lachaud (1990).
61 cf. Deblé and Hugon (1982), Moser (1984), Vorlaufer (1988)

commodity production as a transitional mode[62], its application to developing countries sees it as a more permanent feature/ mode. It emphasizes the determination of the petty commodity production activities by their linkages to the wider economy, more exactly, its subordination. Vorlaufer lists the following characteristics of petty commodity production:
- the entrepreneur is taking part in production;
- wage labour is of little, family labour of much significance;
- producers have control over their products;
- beside or even before the principle of profit maximisation pre-capitalist aspects and systems of social security have significance;
- subsistence-production is significant[63].

The main point is that not capital realization but reproduction security is the objective. A close look shows that the difference to the informal sector concept does not go very much beyond a linguistic difference[64]. Similar criticisms have thus been brought forward against the petty commodity production approach[65].

Lipton (1980) proposed to re-define the informal sector as the family mode of production, which in his view, as the core of the informal sector, possesses all the decisive characteristics: a substantial overlap between providers of capital and providers of labour, prevalence of perfect, or rather near-perfect, competition, and prevalence of unorganized, unincorporated enterprises[66]. For Lipton, it is individuals, households, enterprises, economic activities, neighbourhoods - all of these units are relevant[67].

The actual weakness of the qualitative definition is the measurement difficulty. An often occurring result of this are unwarranted assumptions.

4.2.2 Quantitative definitions

There are many possibilities to define SI in quantitative terms: by number of employees, capital investment, turn over, profit, value added, etc. or a combination of several of these. Because of simplicity, the use of the first measure of these is predominant. The International Labour Conference in 1986 defined small and medium enterprises as those having up to 50 employees[68]. Many studies follow this

---

62 cf. Marx (1962: 591-802)
63 cf. Vorlaufer (1988: 76); own translation
64 cf. Lipton (1980)
65 cf. Lewin (1985), Portes (1983)
66 Lipton (1980: 199-201)
67 Lipton (1980: 203)
68 cf. Vorlaufer (1988)

definition (some, however, take "less than 50" as the limit)[69]. Others define SI much narrower, by up to 10 employees (or less than 10)[70]. Few give it a broader definition, by up to 100 employees[71]. Shortcomings of quantitative definitions are:
1. They are arbitrary: The size of establishments being small in the sense of having distinct characteristics, differs by industry branch, by location, by level of development. An industry with few employees can nevertheless be highly capital intensive.
2. At the lower end of SI there is an ensemble of part-time activities, not well described by this concept.

4.2.3 Subdivisions

To cope with the great diversity many analysts have subdivided the sector. There are many different concepts of sub-sectors. Staley and Morse (1965) arrange different dimensions of subdivision. A basic division is made between factory and non-factory SI. Another way is to distinguish between traditional, partly modern, and modern SI, differing in four main respects: outlook, products and product design, physical technology of production, and social technology of organization and management[72]. Schneider-Barthold (1984b) divides SI[73] in four subsectors along the lines modern/traditional, rural/urban. Mars (1977) discriminates between three types: artisan-simple unit, workshop, and factory, along the dimensions technology, expansion pattern, product pattern, production pattern, division of labour, skill levels, authority structure, spatial networks, and outlet type. Most authors divide in only two subsectors: Bruch (1983) distinguishes craft and home industry (small enterprises with less than 10 employees) and larger SI with 10-49 employees. LeBrun and Gerry (1975) distinguish between those who have the accumulation of wealth as the principal end-result of their activities and those whose activities only result in reproduction of subsistence[74]. Mwene-Milao[75] distinguishes crafts from SI, which is a "relatively modern SI establishment characterized by greater division of labour, using relatively sophisticated technology, power or manual labour."

---

69 cf. Hoselitz (1959), Bruch (1983), Haggblade et al. (1986), Liedholm and Mead (1986), Cortes et al (1987), Little et al. (1987), Seibel and Holloh (1988)
70 cf. Steel (1977), Schmitz (1982b), McCormick (1988)
71 cf. Staley and Morse (1965), Vepa (1971), Schwarz (1980), Anderson (1982), Nanjundan (1986), Schneider (1986)
72 Staley and Morse (1965: 4)
73 in German "Handwerk und Kleinindustrie"; the English *pendant* "handicraft" is not employed in this study because it connotes traditionality and/or artistic crafts
74 LeBrun and Gerry (1975: 22-23)
75 Mwene-Milao (1985: 4)

House (1984), Steel (1977) and Steel and Takagi (1983) introduce an intermediate sector, which is regarded as dynamic, competing with the modern sector, labour intensive and efficient, and contrasting with the lower end of the SI activities. These are defined by Steel as economic activities without fixed assets or a permanent place of business, which are assumed to have a marginal productivity of zero[76]. House calls them the "community of the poor" and characterizes them by a "lack of motivation and perhaps means to seek informal activities with growth potential or to invest in their current activity because they view their situation as temporary"; they are stagnant, residual and under-employed. In contrast, the intermediate sector is characterized by higher incomes and is more likely to aspire to formality[77]. Child[78] defines the third sector as combining the relatively simple technology and small-scale characteristics of the traditional sector with the improved market orientation of the modern sector.

These classificatory approaches have as well been criticized to be static and being unable to analyze the dynamics; a disaggregation by occupation or by product would be preferable[79].

4.2.4 Definitions of small industries in Sudan

Many different definitions of SI are in use in Sudan (see Table 4.2.), which renders the comparison of data difficult. Most definitions take the number of workers (25, 30 or 50), others combine this with the sum of investment, or take only the sum of investment. Also qualitative definitions are in use.

The matter is complicated by the fact that most of the institutions dealing with SI have changed their definition. The Department of Statistics, for instance, defined SI as having less than 30 workers when starting its activities[80], but later shifted to "less than 25 workers", which became the most widely used definition[81]. Despite of the wide use, this division between SI and LI has never been explained and appears arbitrary. Others, like the Ministry of Industry, the Industrial Bank of Sudan, and the investment encouragement acts have no formal definition of SI.

---

[76] Steel (1977: 169)
[77] House (1984: 280, 291)
[78] cf. Child (1977: 9)
[79] cf. Sinclair (1976)
[80] cf. Harvie and Kleve (1959)
[81] The last industrial survey (1981/82) claims to represent all licensed establishments. This limitation rests on the belief that the organized sector represents "the major if not the total activity" in the industrial sector (UNIDO 1986: 25). The survey attempted to cover 100% of LI, but took a 20% sample of establishments with 10-24 workers, a 5% sample of establishments with less than 10 workers, and a 1% sample of traditional bakeries and flour mills employing less than 10 workers. The validity of the results of this survey is limited by several methodological shortcomings: limited and undefined coverage, poor extent of response, suspect randomness and ad hoc stratification, lacking indication of representativeness (UNIDO 1986: 28-31).

Table 4.2. Some definitions of small industry in Sudan

DoS, AIDO, Industrial Survey 81/82	<25 employees
Harvie and Kleve (1959), Bakhit Idris (1979)	<30 employees
Gumaa et al. (1987)	<50 workers
Management Development Centre	<25 employees and <LS 500,000 investment
Shadeed Mohamed Zein (1988)	<50 workers and < $500,000 investment
Institute for Ind. Research & Consultancy	LS 40,000-200,000 investment and 10-50 workers
Sudan Rural Development Corporation	<LS 25,000 investment
Dept. of Cooperation	10-15 workers
Sen (1985)	<50 workers, <LS 350,000 investment
Ahmed (1989b)	<50 workers, owner or part-owner management and control, independence in ownership, management & control and decision making
Bakhit Idris (1979)	own finance, personal management, small geographical operating area
Faisal Islamic Bank (Sudan)	possession of license, employing workers, location in industrial areas

The definitions including sums of investment face the problem of comparability because of the high inflation rate in Sudan, which lead to continuing changes in definition. Shadeed Mohamed Zein (1988) solves this problem by denominating the investment sum in US$. However, all the definitions based on this criteria suffer from arbitrariness - no explanation is given why it makes a difference to invest less than LS 25,000, LS 40,000, LS 350,000, LS 500,000, or $ 500,000. The same is true for the definition based on the number of workers, but these have at least the advantage of being unambiguously comparable.

Qualitative definitions are prevalent to subdivide the SI sector - or the industrial sector - in modern and traditional industries. Generally a modern, large scale, organized sector and a traditional, small-scale, informal sector are contrasted[82]. For Harvie and Kleve (1959) in their first industrial survey of Sudan the difference between modern and traditional industries (manufacturing and crafts) seemed to be so obvious that they dispensed with a definition altogether. This tradition of division between modern and traditional industries is continued in the national income accounts[83]. However, they record only part of the traditional industries by definition: only in the sub-sectors of food, textile, wood, and other non-metal minerals industry (ISIC 31, 32, 33, 36) are traditional industries identified. This means that important traditional industries are neglected, e.g. the blacksmiths.

More complicated definitions are proposed by Bakhit (1979) and Ahmed (1989b; see Table 4.2.). The Sudanese Craftsmen and Small Enterprises Union (SCSEU) defines crafts as those industrial activities that produce without the use of modern equipment and with the use of local raw materials. Miro et al. (1986) define

---
82 e.g. Naseem (1977)
83 cf. DoS (1977), DoS (1979), DoS (1987)

handicrafts as industrial activities which produce without using progressive machines. The UNIDO[84] defines them as the traditional activity, mostly very small with an average of 5 workers, utilizing few machines and simple tools and generally processing local raw materials. The Industrial Sector Workshop (1987) defined them as depending basically on labour and its skilfulness and utilizing uncomplicated tools and equipment. Curtis (1979, 1980) classifies industries on the basis of the technologies they use: he distinguishes between units operating with hand, power, and machine technologies.

This study works - for the time being - with the two prevalent definitions: 1. units with less than 25 employees, 2. traditional industries (understood as those industries having a long history and dispensing with electric machinery).

4.3 Industries in Nyala: an overview

Different surveys came to different numbers of industrial establishments in Nyala. Not all of them differentiated between SI and LI. According to the most recent country-wide industrial survey (1981/82) there are 7 LI establishments, i.e. establishments with more than 25 employees, in Nyala: three oil mills, two chemical factories, one textile factory, and one grain mill. SI was represented by 18 enterprises[85]. An industrial survey carried out by the Labour Office Nyala counted 62 establishments[86]. A 1989 publication arrived at the following figures with respect to "factories and handicraft workshops": 8 oil crushers, 4 soap factories, 23 decorticators, 200 multi-purpose workshops, an unknown number of carpentry workshops, 1 modern tannery, 6 cottage tanneries, 1 soft drink factory, and 4 others, i.e. a total number of 247[87]. The Sudanese Industry Association (SIA) counts five soap factories, one oil mill, and one macaroni factory as its members in Nyala.

The wide differences in scope and number of these figures are conspicuous in themselves. They point to the arbitrary character of definitions. However, how limited all these figures and estimates are, is made evident by the own survey of industries in Nyala: Working with a broad definition of industry[88] 1263 industrial units and 33 branches were identified[89]. Compared with this the figures of the other surveys appear negligible. This finding implies that the knowledge about SI

---

84 cf. UNIDO (1989: 34)
85 Ministry of Industry; this figure excludes traditional bakeries and flour mills.
86 The only information included in this survey was "name of the establishment", "branch", and "number of employees" - for 51 of the establishments.
87 cf. Seisi Mohamed and Fadlalla (1989: 7); this report provides no information about what is a *factory* or a *handicraft workshop*.
88 see chapter 2
89 Even this does not represent the totality of industries (see chapter 2)

as included in the statistics does only cover a fraction of the actually existing SI and consequently the prevalent evaluations of SI are extremely biased.
Industrial activities in Nyala range in scale from part-time activities done at home to a large textile factory. They can be classified by several dimensions: branch, location, size, sex and ethnic origin of entrepreneurs and workers, permanence of activity, part time vs. full time activities, type of machinery, kind of work place, nature of accomodation, legal status, type of ownership and management.
33 industries were identified in Nyala city[90] in December 1987/ January 1988 (see Table 4.3.). The survey was confined to the two industrial areas and the market areas. Industries located in the residential areas or carried out at home had to be estimated. In the case of four industries - traditional sweets, pottery, bricks, and palm leaves products - estimations were found to be too hazardous and thus abandoned.
Industrial activities are distributed over the town area (see map on next page), but not evenly: some are confined to one or more areas. There are two industrial areas: The *Heavy Industrial Area* consists of all decortication plants and oil mills, one sweets factory, one snuff factory, one soap factory, and one oil container factory. In the *Light Industrial Area* the only soft drink factory, some carpentry and most of the metal workshops, a few blacksmiths, car electricity workshops, some painting workshops, one grain mill and two bakeries are located. The textile factory is located at the outskirts of the city. Industrial activities are carried out in the central market area and on seven markets. Of these the main markets with most activities are *Suq Um Dafaso* (the central traditional market), *Suq ash Shabi* (the Peoples market) at the outskirts of the city and *Suq al Mawashi* (the former cattle market). With respect to numbers tailors are the most important activity, followed by leather work and different kinds of metal work.
The smaller markets - *Suq Congo, Suq Texas, Suq al Geneina* - are of no big importance in terms of industrial activities. These are mostly confined to tailors. There is a number of additional small markets all over the town, but apparently without any industrial activities.
Grain mills and bakeries are scattered all over the city. Also the larger part of carpentries are located in the residential areas. Tailors, leather workers (shoe makers), blacksmiths, tinsmiths and different repair activities are concentrated in the markets, but a few are also scattered across the city.
Traditional tanneries are situated besides the railway in the mountain quarter (*Haj al Jebel*)[91]. Also the foundries are located in this area, the reason being that these two activities are almost completely confined to one ethnic group: the *Fellata*

---

90 Only those people and enterprises were counted, which were actually operating. Quite some enterprises are idle for long periods (or even never worked), especially a lot of capacity is unutilized in the Heavy Industry Area.
91 There is one modern tannery - a public sector project which, however, never worked due to lack of energy supply.

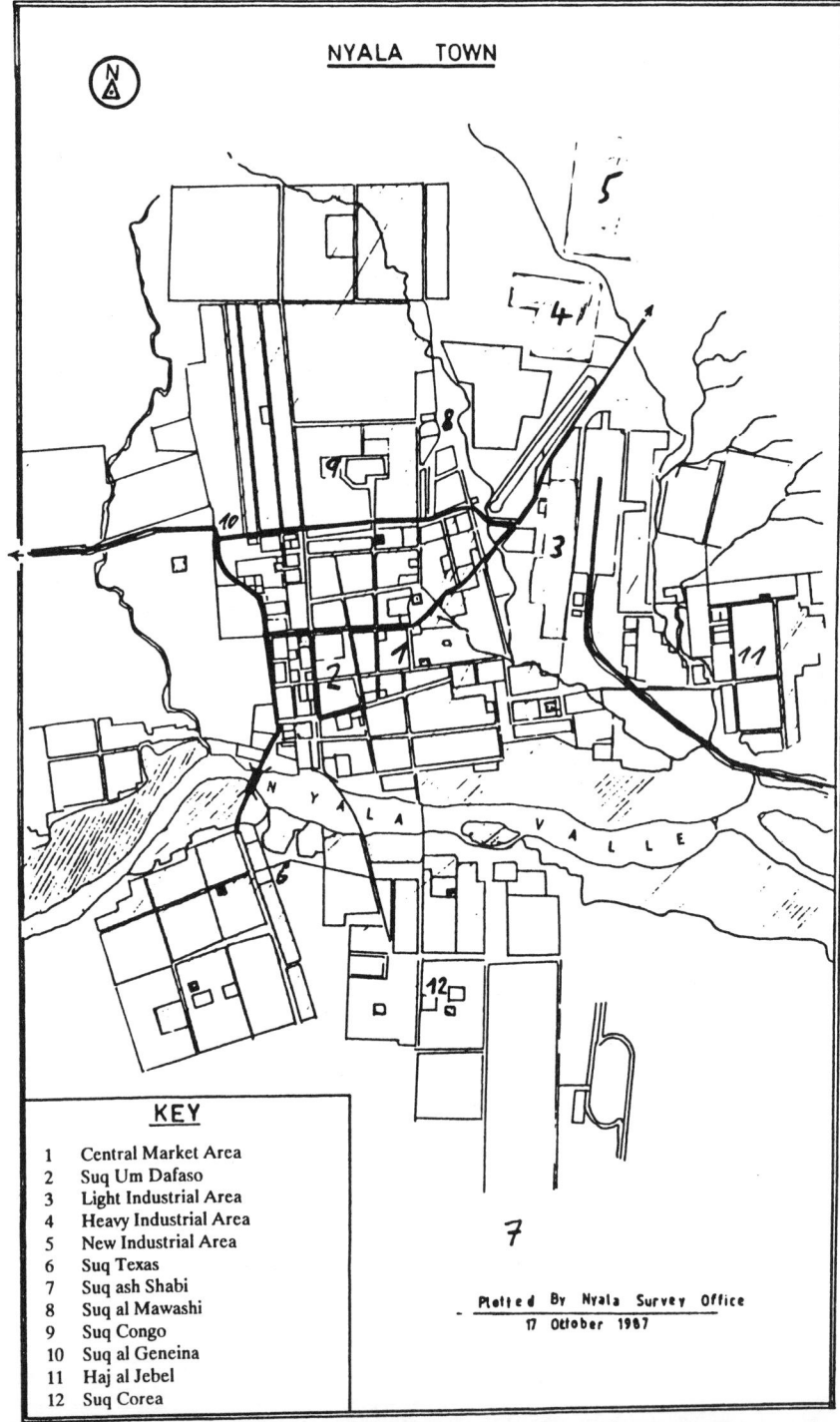

(West Africans). The activity of pottery is carried out at home, palm leaves products are made at home or at markets. The brickworks are located at the raw material sites near the river bed.

Table 4.3. Industrial Survey Nyala 1987/88 (numbers of establishments and workers, average no. of workers per unit)

Industries	December 1987/January 1988			August 1988		
	establ.	workers	workers/establ.	establ.	workers	workers/establ.
decortication	8	302	37.8	-	-	-
oil mill: traditional	3	3	1	-	-	-
oil mill: modern	8	372	46.5	6	269	44.8
grain mill	86	258*	3	86	258*	3
bakery	97	403*	4.2	97	403*	4.2
sweets factory	1	48	48	-	-	-
traditional sweets						
soft drinks and ice	1	31	31	1	33	33
snuff factory	1	11	11	-	-	-
textile	1	195	195	1	195	195
tailors	329*	353*	1.1	239*	242*	1.0
tannery	5	114	22.8	4	24	6.0
leather work	147	249	1.7	72	115	1.6
carpentry	168*	458*	2.7	131*	342	3.4
printing	2	20	10	2	25	2.5
soap	1	31	31	-	-	-
gum & plastic: informal	40	61	1.5	23	25	1.1
gum & plastic: modern:	1	20	20.0	1	20	20.0
tyre repair	5	16	3.2	4	14	3.5
pottery						
bricks						
metal work						
modern workshops	156	822	5.3	140	671	4.8
blacksmiths	69*	183*	2.7	58*	131*	2.3
tinsmiths	27	57	2.1	21	39	1.9
goldsmiths	9	43	4.8	9	43	4.8
foundries	9	39	3	6	18	3
bicycle repair	11	21	1.9	15	27	1.8
watch repair	20	23	1.2	24	24	1
radio, tv etc. repair	33	71	2.2	24	34	1.4
car electricity	11	52	4.7	3	14	4.7
painting and dyeing	4	4	1.0	3	6	2.0
palm leaves products						
mattress	10	30	3.0	2	5	2.5
total	1263	4290	3.4	972	2977	3.1
modern industries	312	2325	7.5	282	1677	5.9
traditional industries	951	1965	2.1	690	1300	1.9

Source: own survey; * = estimate

According to the most common definition of SI (less than 25 employees), five industrial branches emerge clearly as LI: the textile factory with 195 employees, the soap factory with 31 employees, the sweets factory with 48 employees, the soft drinks and ice factory with 31 employees and the modern oil mills with an average of 47 employees (see Tables 4.4. and 4.5.). The decortication factories include both factories with less and with more than 25 employees, the average being 38. As a whole, SI constitutes 98.6% of industrial units and 78.1% of workers. Among the SI units, the very small units (less than 11 workers) make up the bulk: 96.4% and 68.0% of the total units and workers resp. On this definition, there is no clear-cut, unequivocal difference between SI and LI. While all those branches included in the LI category, clearly appear to have the characteristics associated with LI, among the SI there are similar highly modern establishments as well, e.g. a semi-automatic factory for plastic containers.

At first appearance there is a dichotomy between traditional industries working with simple, indigenous tools on the one hand and modern industries operating with sophisticated, imported tools on the other hand. To this second category belong decortication factories, modern oil mills, grain mills, electric bakeries, the sweet factory, the soft drinks and ice, snuff, and textile factories, electric carpentry workshops, printing shops, soap and plastic container factories, and electric modern metal workshops. It constitutes 24.7% of industrial units and 54.2% of employment. However, a closer look shows a more differentiated picture (see below).

Most economic activities and virtually all industrial activities are strictly segregated by sex, i.e. there are few economic and no industrial activities which are done both by women and men. Womens' traditional crafts are pottery and palm leaves products. Furthermore, women work as unskilled labour in modern factories (oil mills, sweets factory, soft drinks, textile). It was not possible to arrive at reasonable estimates of the extent of traditional female crafts (pottery, palm leaves products). Furthermore, these are part-time activities. However, it was found that pottery is a main or sole income source for female drought refugees. Among the industrial labour force 391 women, equal to 8.8% of the industrial labour force, were counted. Most important branches in this respect are modern oil mills, decortication, and textile with 123, 121 and 62 female workers resp.

Some of the traditional industrial activities are carried out exclusively or predominantly by certain ethnic groups (tannery, pottery, brick making).

It is generally known that small industries are subject to seasonal variations. It is believed that the level of industrial activities is low in the rainy season (June to September). However, this has not been taken into consideration in the industrial surveys. In order to quantify the variation the own Nyala industrial survey in December 1987/January 1988 was repeated in August 1988.

Table 4.4. Size distribution of industries in Nyala (number of enterprises)

number of employees	1	2	3-5	6-10	11-24	25-50	51+
decortication	-	-	-	-	2	3	3
oil mill: traditional	3	-	-	-	-	-	-
oil mill: modern	-	-	-	-	-	6	2
grain mill	-	-	86	-	-	-	-
bakery	-	-	97	-	-	-	-
sweets factory	-	-	-	-	-	1	-
soft drinks and ice	-	-	-	-	-	1	-
snuff factory	-	-	-	-	1	-	-
textile	-	-	-	-	-	-	1
tailors*	308	20	1	-	-	-	-
tannery	-	-	-	-	5	-	-
leather work	90	30	26	1	-	-	-
carpentry	3	139	17	7	2	-	-
printing	-	-	-	1	1	-	-
soap	-	-	-	-	-	1	-
gum and plastic: informal	26	9	5	-	-	-	-
gum and plastic: modern	-	-	-	-	1	-	-
tyre repair	1	1	3	-	-	-	-
metal workshops	7	16	70	50	13	-	-
blacksmiths*	6	48	11	2	2	-	-
tinsmiths	14	5	7	1	-	-	-
goldsmiths	1	1	4	2	1	-	-
foundries*	-	-	6	3	-	-	-
bicycle repair	2	8	1	-	-	-	-
watch repair	17	3	-	-	-	-	-
electric repair	10	14	8	1	-	-	-
car electricity	1	1	5	4	-	-	-
painting and dyeing	4	-	-	-	-	-	-
mattress	-	1	9	-	-	-	-
total	493	296	356	72	28	12	6

Source: own survey (December 1987/January 1988); * = estimate

The dry season census (December 1987/January 1988) gives the following picture: In terms of enterprises/units the tailors are most important (mostly one person-establishments), followed by carpentry, leather work, tannery, bakery, and car repair workshops. In terms of employment the order changes: car repair, carpentry, bakery, modern oil mills, tailors, metal workshops, decortication. In total 1263 enterprises with 4290 employees/workers were counted/estimated. The average number of workers per establishment was 3.4.

The rainy season census shows that the numbers of industrial establishments and workers declined by 23% and 31% resp. The order of importance of industries changed: In terms of number of enterprises tailors are followed by carpentry, bakery, grain mill, leather work and car repair. In terms of employment bakery is followed by car repair, carpentry, metal workshops, modern oil mills and grain mills (see Table 4.3.). The differences between dry and rainy season by industry are expressed in Table 4.6.

Table 4.5. Size distribution of industries in Nyala (no. of employees/workers)

number of employees	1	2	3-5	6-10	11-24	25-50	51+
decortication	-	-	-	-	40	96	166
oil mill: traditional	3	-	-	-	-	-	-
oil mill: modern	-	-	-	-	-	253	119
grain mill*	-	-	258	-	-	-	-
bakery*	-	-	403	-	-	-	-
sweets factory	-	-	-	-	-	48	-
soft drinks and ice	-	-	-	-	-	31	-
snuff factory	-	-	-	-	11	-	-
textile	-	-	-	-	-	-	195
tailors*	308	40	5	-	-	-	-
tannery	-	-	-	-	114	-	-
leather work	90	60	92	7	-	-	-
carpentry*	3	278	85	64	28	-	-
printing	-	-	-	7	13	-	-
soap	-	-	-	-	-	31	-
gum and plastic: informal	26	18	17	-	-	-	-
gum and plastic: modern	-	-	-	-	20	-	-
tyre repair	1	2	13	-	-	-	-
metal workshops	7	32	257	356	170	-	-
blacksmiths*	6	96	39	14	28	-	-
tinsmiths	14	10	23	10	-	-	-
goldsmiths	1	2	16	13	11	-	-
foundries*	-	-	21	18	-	-	-
bicycle repair	2	16	3	-	-	-	-
watch repair	17	6	-	-	-	-	-
electric repair	10	28	26	7	-	-	-
car electricity	1	2	18	31	-	-	-
painting and dyeing	4	-	-	-	-	-	-
mattress	-	2	28	-	-	-	-
total	493	592	1304	527	435	459	480

Source: own survey (December 1987/January 1988); *=estimate

The table shows that, on the one hand, the seasonal differences are surprisingly small, compared to the general opinion that industrial activities would be very much a function of the agricultural cycle and would virtually stop during the rainy season: On the whole, 77.0% of establishments are working during the rainy season with 69.4% of their work force. The ratio of worker per establishment declined by 9.8%. The results point to a low dependence of Nyala city on its agricultural environment; formulated differently, to a high independence of the urban economy. On the other hand, there are wide inter-industry differences: The seasonal differences range between 0 and 150%. Thirdly, there are different reasons behind the seasonal differences which are not all directly connected to the seasons:

1. seasonality due to the agricultural cycle (decortication, oil mills);
2. lack of raw materials due to transport difficulties, which is higher during, but not specific to the rainy season (e.g. sweets and soap factories);
3. lack of demand due to low incomes at the end of the agricultural year;
4. agricultural activity of the industrial workers (a major factor e.g. in tannery, leather work, mattress).

Table 4.6. Seasonal differences in the levels of industrial activities (numbers of establishments and workers in rainy season as % of dry season)

industry	establ.	workers
decortication	0	0
oil mill: traditional	0	0
oil mill: modern	66.7	72.3
bakery	100.0	100.0
sweets factory	0	0
soft drinks and ice	100	106.5
textile	100.0	100.0
tailors	72.6	68.6
tannery	80.0	21.1
leather work	49.0	46.2
carpentry	78.0	74.7
printing	100.0	125.0
soap	0	0
gum & plastic: informal	57.5	41.0
gum & plastic: modern	100.0	100.0
tyre repair	80.0	87.5
metal work		
modern workshops	89.7	81.6
blacksmiths	84.1	71.6
tinsmiths	77.8	68.4
goldsmiths	100.0	100.0
foundries	66.7	46.2
bicycle repair	136.4	128.6
watch repair	120.0	104.3
radio, tv etc. repair	72.7	47.9
car electricity	27.3	26.9
painting and dyeing	75.0	150.0
mattress	20.0	16.7
total	77.0	69.4

Source: Table 4.3.

The last reason is generally presumed to cause a major decline of industrial activities, especially in the traditional industries which are characterized as slack season activities. The Nyala results defeat these assumptions. The difference between employment in traditional and modern industries is not very significant: While 72.1% of the workers in modern SI are active during the rainy season, the corresponding figure for traditional industries is 66.2% (see Table 4.3.).

One of the characteristics ascribed to SI is its *informality*. As a proxy for informality the possession of a licence is often taken. SI branches can be ranked according to the percentage of enterprises which have a licence (see Chart 4.1.).

Chart 4.1. Formality of industrial enterprises in Nyala (percentage possessing a licence)

industry	0	10	20	30	40	50	60	70	80	90	100
decortication											100
modern oil mill											100
grain mill											100
bakery											100
sweets factory											100
soft drinks and ice											100
snuff factory											100
textile											100
printing											100
soap factory											100
goldsmiths											100
mattress											100
modern gum and plastics											100
tyre repair								60			
car electricity							55				
metal workshops							53				
tinsmiths						41					
radio, tv etc.repair					30						
leather work				25							
painting				25							
carpentry			20								
blacksmiths			20								
watch repair			20								
tailors		<10									
gum and plastics	2.4										
traditional oil mill	0										
traditional sweets	0										
tannery	0										
pottery	0										
bricks	0										
foundries	0										
bicycle repair	0										
palm leaves products	0										

Source: own survey

13 industrial branches are formalized by licences completely (100%), while 8 are completely unformalized. 12 branches range between 2.4 and 60% of formalized units. There is a correlation between modernity and formality of industrial enterprises: All of the industries operating with modern machinery possess licenses. However, the correlation is not as clear-cut and unequivocal as often assumed: Also some traditional industries include a high percentage of licensed enterprises (e.g. goldsmiths, mattress producers, traditional bakeries, tinsmiths). Most

importantly, in those industries including both formal and informal establishments there is no unequivocal difference between those industrial units operating with and without licenses, i.e. formality as defined by possession of license is not a meaningful criterion to classify industries.

Chart 4.2. Industries in Nyala: Kind of working place

	at home	in the open air	raquba	terrace	wood/corrugated iron workshop	brick house
decortication		x				x
oil mill: traditional		x				
oil mill: modern						x
grain mill						x
bakery						x
sweets factory						x
traditional sweets	x					
soft drink and ice						x
snuff factory						x
textile factory						x
tailors	x	x	x	x	x	x
tannery		x				
leather work		x	x		x	
carpentry	x		x	x	x	x
printing						x
soap						x
gum and plastic: informal			x			
gum and plastic: modern						x
tyre repair			x		x	x
pottery	x					
bricks		x				
metal work						
modern workshops		x	x	x	x	x
blacksmiths		x	x			
tinsmiths			x		x	
goldsmiths					x	x
foundries	x					
bicycle repair		x	x	x	x	
watch repair				x	x	
radio, tv etc.repair				x	x	x
car electricity			x		x	x
painting and dyeing		x	x		x	
palm leaves products	x	x	x			
mattress		x		x		x

Source: own survey

The industries can be classified according to a kind of working place: at home, in the open air, under a straw roof or in a straw hut (raquba), on a terrace in front of a shop, in a workshop of wood and corrugated iron, in a brick house. Except for the first, these categories correspond to increasing size, i.e. the smallest activities (in terms of employment and capital investment) are carried out in the open air, while LI units are accomodated in brick houses. There is a similar correspondence to the continuum of traditional to modern industries, i.e. traditional activities tend to be located at home, in the open air or in raqubas, while modern activities tend to be situated in brick house and wood/corrugated iron workshops. However, these correspondences are not rigid. There are many exceptions: Decortication machines are located invariably in the open air, tailors practice their trade in all kinds of working places, etc. (see Chart 4.2.).

A classification by type of machinery shows that industries operate at very different levels of technology. Three types of machinery can be distinguished: hand tools, animal-driven machines and power-driven machines. These can be further divided according to the place of manufacture: self-made, locally made, domestic or imported. In this way six types of machinery are identified: self-made hand tools, locally-made hand tools, imported hand tools, locally-made animal-driven machines, locally-made or assembled power-driven machines, and imported power-driven machines (see Chart 4.3.).

It is significant that:
- Intermediate technologies using animal-driven machines are almost absent (the only instance is the traditional oil mill driven by camels).
- A significant number of industries - especially traditional industries - use locally made hand tools, but few manage to dispense with imported hand tools. This contradicts the image of traditional industries based on local machinery.
- Very few power-driven machines are made or assembled locally. The local capital goods industry is concentrated on the production of few types of hand tools.
- A dichotomy is perceptible between industries using self-made or locally-made hand tools and industries using imported power-driven machines. Six branches use only instruments of the first category: traditional bakery, traditional sweets production, tanneries, potteries, brick works, blacksmiths. Eight branches use only machinery of the second category: modern oil mills, grain mills, modern bakeries, the sweets, the soft drinks and ice, textile, and soap factories, and the printing shop. However, these clear cases make up only 41% of the industrial branches. The majority of industrial branches does not fit into the dichotomous picture.

Chart 4.3. Industries in Nyala: Types of machinery

	self-made hand tools	locally-made hand tools	imported hand tools	locally-made animal-driven machines	locally-made or assembled power-driven machines	imported power-driven machines
decortication					x	x
oil mill: traditional				x		
oil mill: modern						x
grain mill						x
bakery: traditional	x					
bakery: modern						x
sweets factory						x
traditional sweets	x					
soft drink and ice						x
snuff factory					x	
textile factory						x
tailors			x			
tannery		x				
leather work		x	x			
carpentry		x	x			x
printing						x
soap						x
gum and plastic: informal		x	x			
gum and plastic: modern						x
tyre repair		x	x			
pottery	x					
bricks	x					
metal work						
modern workshops		x	x		x	x
blacksmiths	x					
tinsmiths	x	x	x			
goldsmiths		x	x			x
foundries	x	x	x			
bicycle repair			x			
watch repair			x			
radio, tv etc.repair			x			
car electricity			x			
painting and dyeing			x			
palm leaves products	x					
mattress			x			

Source: own survey

The overview of industries in Nyala shows a very differentiated picture which does not allow an easy categorization of industries, nor does it allow clear-cut conclusions about the character of industries. The questions posed in this study with respect to the characteristics of SI and their development constraints need a specific analysis of industrial branches, which will be carried out in the following chapters.

5 Distinct advantages of small industries

Several characteristics are ascribed to SI in developing countries which are at the bottom of their positive assessment. In these characteristics SI differs from LI, for this reason they are termed *distinct advantages*. The objective of this chapter is to examine these arguments, to formulate them in operational terms, to look at available evidence from developing countries, especially from Africa, and to confront this with the evidence from Sudan and Nyala. The propositions are often not as straightforward as one might think at first sight. Some are contradicting others, some are not seen as an advantage by all (instead as a constraint)[1], many are overlapping with the discussion of constraints[2], often the evidence is inconclusive or lacking, and there are difficulties to operationalize the arguments[3].

5.1 Creation of employment

It is widely agreed that there is an "employment problem" in African countries, especially in the urban areas, but also in the rural areas[4]. Development can be visualized as the structural change from an agrarian to an industrial economy, i.e. a shift from agriculture to industry as the major sector of employment. In developing countries, and especially in Africa, industrialization has not fulfilled its function of employment creation sufficiently. First, industry grew at a low rate. Second, the increase in employment did not even keep pace with the meagre rate of output increase[5]; Africa's industrialization is biased towards capital[6]. This bias cannot be explained by a lack of alternatives - as the argument of "fixed proportions" claims[7] - but rather by the deviation of the market prices of labour and capital from their

---

[1] Hirschman (1965) discusses the ambiguous and ambivalent character of "obstacles to development".
[2] see below chapter 6
[3] The theoretical discussion does not claim to be exhaustive. The purpose is to identify relevant research questions for the study of SI in Sudan.
[4] There is a strong argument that the problem is not one of people having no work, but rather having no income, a "poverty problem". Also the concept of unemployment makes only sense in an economic system in which people can afford to be unemployed, i.e. where they receive unemployment benefits. On the notion of employment in the African context cf. Weeks (1973a, b). But if the employment problem is redefined as an income problem, this does not change the matter much, because there is evidence that the most efficient way to generate income is employment; it appears to be superior to other options as income transfers (cf. Demery and Addison 1987; Huang and Nicholas 1987).
[5] The employment needed to produce a given increase in output is only one sixth of that in agriculture (ILO 1983: 76).
[6] It can be expected that industrialization implies a faster growth rate of output than of employment - due to capital deepening and technical change. However, the very high differences between the two rates in developing countries are far beyond what can be explained by those factors (for evidence cf. Morawetz 1974 and White 1978: 29).
[7] For evidence on manufacturing elasticities of substitution cf. Morawetz (1974), White (1978), Haggblade et al. (1986).

true social value. This is mostly due to government policies, reflecting an ideology regarding the technology of industrial countries as superior, regardless of factor prices, which is widely spread among engineers, economists, and policy makers[8]. This tendency is also partly explaining another constraint - the lack of information about labour-intensive techniques. Other factors behind the employment problem are the rapid population growth rate, release of labour from agriculture, and urbanization. At the same time, in the specific critical economic situation in SSA stabilization policy implies costs in terms of employment[9].

The absorption of labour is the most often cited argument in favour of SI[10]. In this context there are two hypotheses relevant. The first focuses on the absolute extent of employment in existing SI, in comparison with the total number of employed in industry and in the total economy. The proposition is that SI employs a significant part of the labour force.

The evidence from developing countries shows that SI often represents a large share of industrial employment. Out of 14 countries analyzed in a recent comprehensive literature analysis on SI, only in one country (South Korea) LI employed more than 50% of the industrial labour force. A mean of 71% of total industrial employment was generated by SI in the 14 countries. The African countries range from 59% (Kenya) to 95% (Sierra Leone)[11]. It can be assumed that the figure on Sierra Leone is the most accurate of all studies on African countries, because in no other African country has SI been studied so extensively[12]. Most of this employment is concentrated at the lower end of the size spectrum (less than 10 employees), while there are few establishments in the larger size of 10-49 employees[13]. The total importance of SI employment is determined by two opposing effects: First, in higher-income countries the share of industrial employment is usually higher; second, in the lower-income countries the share of SI employment in industrial employment is generally higher. If it is assumed that policy-induced constraints impede the development of SI (which is reasonable to do), the actual number of employed people will perhaps not say much about its potential.

---

8   cf. White (1978), who also presents evidence that there are feasible and efficient labour intensive alternatives in industry of developing countries. Besides this, economic history shows that industrialization generally started with labour-intensive techniques (cf. Mendels 1972).
9   According to optimists this is a transitory problem which will be alleviated after a time lag (Demery and Addison 1987, Huang and Nicholas 1987). The evidence in many developing countries, especially in Africa, however, seems not to support this optimism: the "employment problem" is deeply seated and unlikely to disappear in the near future.
10   cf. Oshima (1971), World Bank (1978: 62-70)
11   Liedholm and Mead (1987: 15)
12   Estimates of employment in SI regularly underestimate this employment, because of the large number of part-time and "invisible" home activities. On can argue that by definition it is only possible to measure and enumerate employment in the formal sector (Breman 1976: 1872).
13   Liedholm and Mead (1987: 14)

The second hypothesis is that SI produces more labour intensively than LI, i.e. it uses less capital per worker than LI. This can be regarded as positive because if it is true, SI creates relatively more employment and generally its production function is more suited to the availability of the production factors labour and capital in developing countries.
The evidence on this issue in developing countries is mixed, but affirmative for Africa. Most come to the conclusion that, in developing countries, SI produces more labour intensive[14]. For Africa the data show consistently that SI creates more employment per unit of capital[15]. Chuta and Liedholm (1985) find that in Sierra Leone SI produces approximately 17 times more labour intensive. Schneider-Barthold (1984b) argues that additionally the indirect employment effects would be greater because of stronger domestic linkages[16]. However, a detailed study on SI in India found that, while the proposition holds at a sectoral level, it frequently fails, when the sector is disaggregated. The differences in labour intensity were found to be great between industrial branches, but small within branches. Furthermore, there are great variations in labour intensity within size groups, and many SI enterprises are not the most labour-intensive enterprises. The authors conclude that to find labour intensity one has to look to technology, not to size[17]. In Africa also intra-industrial differences are generally much smaller than those between industries and between countries[18].

Employment creation of small industry in Sudan

Sudan's population and accordingly its labour force are growing rapidly (see Table 5.1.1.). This points to the need for an active policy of employment generation.
In the 27 years between the first population survey at independence and the most recent survey in 1983 the population doubled, with an average annual increase rate of 2.6%. For the period 1983-1989 the rate is estimated to be 2.7%. The UN forecasts the annual population increase in the 1990s at 2.8%. This estimate has, however, to be regarded as conservative in the face of the prevalent pro-natalist policy of the government and attitude of the population. Thus, a higher population growth can be expected[19].

---

14 cf. Hoselitz (1959), Morawetz (1974), Cortes et al. (1987)
15 cf. Page and Steel (1984: 19), ILO and JASPA (1985: 19-21), Liedholm and Mead (1986: 315)
16 see below Ch.5.5.
17 cf. Little et al. (1987)
18 cf. Page and Steel (1984: 19)
19 There are contrasting opinions how a high population growth should be evaluated. In the industrial countries people regard the high population growth in the developing countries as negative and threatening - both for the developing countries and the industrial countries. In Sudan, however, another opinion is prevalent: Sudan is regarded as underpopulated and a high population growth thus as not only tolerable, but beneficial or even necessary. In the face of present living conditions and how these are developing, this opinion expressed by government

Table 5.1.1. Estimates of population and labour force 1955/56-1983

year	total population ('000)	population (15-65 years) ('000)	economically active popul. ('000)	crude activity rate (%)	refined activity rate (%)	annual rate of labour force growth (%)
1955/56	10,263	5,560	3,497	33.3	61.5	
1983	21,593	11,517	6,653	30.8	57.8	2.4

Source: MFEP-E (1990: 94); the second column shows the population supposed to be at working age (in the age of 15-65 years). The "economically active population" refers to the labour force, i.e. all persons who represent the supply of labour, including the employed and unemployed; the crude activity rate measures the labour force as a proportion of the total population, while the refined activity rate measures the economically active population as a proportion of the population in working age.

Consequently the labour force has been growing fast, according to the official statistics by 2.4% between 1955/56 and 1983 (see Table 5.1.1.). This estimate is, however, an underestimate. Especially the activity of women is severely underestimated: the refined activity rate of women in 1983, for instance, is estimated to be 26.1% - in contrast to the male rate of 89.5%[20]. Another example of underestimation is the "informal sector", whose activities are largely (if not completely) ignored by the statistics. It can be assumed that the growth rate of labour force is higher than the population growth rate because of rising activity rates[21].

The statistics on unemployment (13.1% in 1986) are a doubtful indicator of the situation on the labour market, because of the lack of an official social security system - a situation which allows few people to be unemployed: the majority of the people classified as unemployed are in fact working temporary and/or in the "informal sector"[22].

Table 5.1.2. Structural changes of the economy (% shares in GDP and employment)

sector	1955/56 GDP	1955/56 EMP	1970/71 GDP	1970/71 EMP	1979/80 GDP	1979/80 EMP	1988/89 GDP	1988/89 EMP
agriculture	60.7		41	69.5	35.4	65.7	35.2	60
industry	10.5		17	6.0	13.8	6.7	13.8	
o/w manufacture	1.0	0.5	9.4	3.3	7.6	3.5	6.8	4
services	28.7		42	24.5	50.8	27.6	51.0	

Sources: 1955/56: Harvie and Kleve (1959); 1970/71: DoS (1976), Nimeiri (1976b); 1979/80 GDP: UNIDO (1986); 1979/80 employment and 1988/89 GDP: SBA (1990); 1988/89 employment: GoS (1990)

---

officials appears to border on cynicism. However, a discussion of this subject involves many non-economic issues and a discussion beyond ideology seems overdue in Sudan (cf. the illuminating discussion of the different arguments by Killick 1981: 72-105).

20   cf. MFEP-E (1990: 94). The degree of underestimation is illuminated by an ILO study which estimates that 38% of economically active women in Khartoum were not covered by the 1983 census (cf. SBA 1990: 38).
21   cf. also Murtada Mustafa (1988) on the discussion and projection of activity rates.
22   cf. SBA 1990: 41

Table 5.1.2. shows the development of the demand for labour in the economic sectors. The table shows that agriculture remained the most important sector in terms of employment generation. Its share in employment declined only slightly, although the share in GDP declined considerably. Already in 1970/71 the services sector produced a higher share of GDP, but remained second in employment generation. The share of manufacturing remained comparatively insignificant. The first economic survey (1955/56) did not provide employment figures, but the share of manufacturing was estimated to be less than 0.5%, i.e. less than half of its share in GDP. Compared with the other sectors, manufacturing (and industry in general) showed an impressive growth from 1955/56-1970/71. However, later the share of industry declined. The main structural shift of Sudan's economy in terms of GDP, less in terms of employment, was from agriculture to services. Furthermore, one can see that the growth of employment in manufacturing has been consistently less than one half of its GDP growth. This finding is in line with the development in other developing countries (see above). The most recent estimate of employment (4%; see Table 5.1.2) seems incredible and, in any case, cannot be taken as evidence for a shift to more labour-intensive industrial growth, but indicates the low capacity utilization of LI. One can summarize that industry - as far as recorded in the statistics - did not generate employment to any meaningful extent.

How do LI and SI compare in employment generation? The first economic survey did not give separate data for SI and LI, but discriminated between *manufacturing* and *craft industries*. A definition of both categories was not given, probably the difference was regarded as being self-evident[23]. As Table 5.1.3. shows, a qualitative definition was used to discriminate between both categories. Although most of the manufacturing firms were probably quite small in terms of employment, in comparison with craft industries they were the LI.

This table shows that the contribution of craft industries was far more important than that of manufacturing, despite the fact that only those crafts producing consumer goods were considered[24]. Unfortunately employment figures are not given for the craft industries. However, the kinds of industries leave no doubt that craft industries were more labour-intensive than manufacturing. This implies that in terms of employment creation craft industries were even more important.

The statistics on national income accounts continued the tradition of the 1955/56 survey to discriminate between "traditional" and "modern" industries (see Table

---

[23] Because of a lack of data this survey had to work with a lot of assumptions, which makes its figures especially shaky. Paradoxically, at the same time this survey gives richer and more comprehensive information than the more recent surveys. It includes, for instance, information on linkages between the sectors (input-output table) and takes informal and illegal activities (e.g. merissa making, prostitution) into account. Both of these categories are simply neglected in all later surveys.

[24] Other crafts were ignored because of difficulties to estimate (Harvie and Kleve 1959: 33). In general, an underestimation of crafts is implicit because manufacturing industries are more visible.

5.1.4.). However, they also tend to underestimate the former category[25]. These statistics do not pertain to employment and thus can only be indicative.

Table 5.1.3. Structure of industrial employment and production in 1955/56

sector	manufacturing				craft industries	
	net output (LS '000)	%	no.of employees	%	net output (LS '000)	%
oil mill	1009	36.5	2698	22.0	-	-
flour mills	340	12.3	3353	27.4	-	-
sweet factories	84	3.0	596	4.9	-	-
ice factories	106	3.8	260	2.1	-	-
merissa-making	-	-	-	-	2816	28.8
brewing	137	5.0	134	1.1	-	-
mineral water fact.	347	12.6	1696	13.8	-	-
snuff-making	-	-	-	-	384	3.9
spinning & weaving	-	-	-	-	230	2.4
mat-making	-	-	-	-	443	4.5
rope-making	-	-	-	-	404	4.1
tailoring & cap-making	-	-	-	-	2802	28.7
tannery	-	-	-	-	127	1.3
shoe-making & repairs	-	-	-	-	390	4.0
carpentry	-	-	-	-	685	7.0
carpentry workshops	67	2.4	256	2.1	-	-
printing	77	2.8	245	2.0	-	-
soap factories	131	4.7	589	4.8	-	-
pot making	-	-	-	-	1466	15.0
cement factory	228	8.3	236	1.9	-	-
tin factories	38	1.4	97	0.8	-	-
goldsmiths	-	-	-	-	15	0.2
engineering workshops	152	5.5	844	6.9	-	-
ivory-making	-	-	-	-	4	0.0
other	46	1.7	1253	10.2	-	-
total	2762	100.0	12257	100.0	9766	100.0
all industries	12528					

Source: Harvie and Kleve (1959: 31, 33, 83)

Table 5.1.4. Comparative development of traditional and modern industries 1955/56-1983/84 (% of value added at factor cost)

	1955/56	1966	1970/71	1975/76	1980/81	1983/84
HC	78.0	36.3	31.5	27.4	34.8	39.8
MF	22.0	63.7	68.5	72.6	65.2	60.2

Sources: 1955/56: Harvie and Kleve (1959), 1966-1970/71: Elnur Ahmed (1977), 1975/76: DoS (1979), 1980/81-1983/84: DoS (1987); HC=traditional industries (handicraft), MF=modern manufacturing

---

[25] Only in the food, textile, wood and other non-metal minerals sub-sectors (ISIC 31, 32, 33, 36) a division between traditional and modern industries was made. The other sub-sectors were simply counted as modern. This points to a neglect of important branches of traditional industries, for instance blacksmiths and other traditional metal work.

According to this statistics, the clear predominance of traditional industries in 1955/56 had already been reversed ten years later. The importance of crafts declined further to almost one third of modern industry in 1975/76. However, since then its share increased again. In 1983/84 (the most recent available data) traditional industries constituted again 2/3 of modern industries.

For the years 1975/76-1983/84 details by two-digit ISIC class are available (see Table 5.1.5.).

Table 5.1.5. Comparative development of traditional and modern industries 1975/76-1983/84 (% of value added at factor cost)

ISIC	sector	1975/76	1980/81	1983/84
31	food, beverages and tobacco	21.9	48.9	61.3
	MF	10.1	24.8	30.3
	HC	11.8	24.1	31.1
32	textile, weaving & apparel and leather products	29.1	12.4	7.3
	MF	19.2	7.0	3.6
	HC	9.9	5.4	3.7
33	wood and wood products incl. furniture	4.5	6.2	2.7
	MF	1.0	3.2	1.4
	HC	3.6	3.0	1.3
34	paper and paper products	3.2	4.7	2.5
35	chemicals & chem. products incl. prod. of petrol. & coal	32.0	16.5	7.9
36	other non-metal minerals	5.8	5.1	8.4
	MF	3.6	2.7	4.8
	HC	2.2	2.3	3.6
37	basic metal industries	1.2	0.9	1.6
38	fabricated metal products and machinery	2.2	4.4	7.9
39	other manufacturing industries	0.0	0.9	0.2

Sources: DoS (1979), DoS (1987); HC = traditional industries (handicraft), MF = modern manufacturing

The predominant sector is food production (ISIC 31), for both modern and traditional industries. The textile sector (ISIC 32) lost in importance, but the share of traditional industries in this sub-sector increased from one third to half of textile production. On the other hand, in the wood processing sub-sector their share deteriorated from 80% to half. In the non-metal sector their share increased slightly from 37.5% to 43.2%.

The national income accounts give no information on employment, but the division of modern/traditional bases on the distinction made in the 1955/56 survey. Thus it is obvious that traditional industries are more labour-intensive.

The other statistical sources on comparative employment in SI and LI are the industrial surveys 1970/71 and 1981/82 as well as the handicraft surveys 1970/71 and 1987. The next table shows that the employment in LI is far more important than employment in SI (as far as they are considered).

Table 5.1.6. Employment in SI and LI 1970/71-1981/82

ISIC	1970/71				1981/82				%change		
	all	SI	LI	% SI	all	SI	LI	% SI	all	SI	LI
31	18194	2999	15195	16.5	87739	26302	61437	30.0	382.2	777.0	304.3
32	15972	185	15787	1.2	28409	984	27425	3.5	77.9	431.9	73.7
33	1361	757	604	55.6	2091	1467	624	70.2	53.6	93.8	3.3
34	2498	207	2291	8.3	4225	796	3429	18.8	69.1	284.5	49.7
35	4017	250	3767	6.2	5336	1232	4104	23.1	32.8	392.8	8.9
36	2007	244	1763	12.2	4741	2059	2682	43.4	136.2	743.9	52.1
37	78	-	78	-	777	64	713	8.2	896.2	-	814.1
38	5022	1719	3303	34.2	10803	6431	4372	59.5	115.1	274.1	132.4
39	67	32	35	47.8	382	-	382	-	470.1	-	991.4
total	49216	6393	42823	13.0	144503	39335	105168	27.2	193.6	515.3	145.6

Sources: DoS (1976), Nimeiri (1976b), UNIDO (1986)

In 1970/71 only in the small sector of wood industry SI employed more workers than LI. The only other sector with a major share of SI employment was *fabricated metal products and machinery* (ISIC 38), a minor industrial sector in Sudan. In textile industry, the second most important branch in terms of employment, SI employed only 1.2%, while in food industry, the most important branch, they came to 16.5%. Of total industry, 13.0% were employed in SI.

However, the survey of 1981/82 indicates a major shift. The share of SI employment more than doubled to 27.2%. In every sub-sector the growth rates of SI employment were faster than the average, the share of SI employment increased, with the only exception of the minor sector ISIC 39 (*other industries*), which recorded no SI enterprises in 1981/82. Remarkable is the increase in the food sub-sector, which consolidated its position as the most important industrial branch by its high growth (including 60.7% of all employees in 1981/82).

A detailed look at the size structure of Sudanese industry shows a familiar pattern: the "missing middle", i.e. a bimodal structure with very small enterprises on the one hand and very large enterprises on the other hand with a small number of enterprises of intermediate size (25-100 workers). As Table 5.1.7. shows, this tendency became stronger in the 1970s - on all counts (number of enterprises, number of employees, and gross output) the enterprises of medium size lost importance.

Another statistical source of information on SI are the handicraft surveys of 1970/71 and 1987 (see Table 5.1.8.). They throw light on another part of SI which is neglected by the industrial surveys[26].

---

[26] Although both kinds of surveys have been done by the same institution (the Department of Statistics), no mention about the relation of the two is made in either report. However, an analysis of the data shows that the activities analysed in the handicraft surveys are additional to the activities covered in the industrial surveys.

Table 5.1.7. Sudanese industries by size class 1970/71-1981/82 (numbers of establishments <EST> and employees <EMP>, gross output <GO>)

	1970/71						1981/82					
	EST		EMP.		GO		EST		EMP		GO	
size	No.	%	No.	%	LS mn	%	No.	%	No.	%	LS mn	%
>25	1067	83.6	6393	13.0	6360	7.2	6412	94.9	39335	27.2	525.1	34.2
25-50	79	6.2	3974	8.1	6837	7.7	131	1.9	4679	3.2	66.1	4.3
51-100	56	4.4	3974	8.0	10396	11.8	79	1.2	5432	3.8	82.7	5.4
100>	74	5.8	36110	73.4	64659	73.3	137	2.0	95057	65.8	862.2	56.1

Source: UNIDO (1986)

Table 5.1.8. Employment in handicrafts in 1970/71 and 1987 (numbers of establishments <EST> and employees <EMP>)

	1970/71				1987			
	all		Khartoum		Khartoum		all	
branch	units	EMP	units	EMP	units	EMP	units	EMP
food products, drinks & tobacco	4521	10696	668		1191	8280		
clothes	9308	13096	1532		2219	8885		
furniture	941	11946	88		849	4245		
leather, plastic & tannery prod.	1232	2220	56		1010	4000		
goldsmith & blacksmith products	1733	3466	168		2049	9773		
palm leaves products	670	716	8		30	90		
pottery	465	3669	180		110	550		
unclassified	172	632	36		943	6187		
total	19022	36441	2736	9084	8401	42010	39516	200000

Sources: 1970/71: DoS (1974), 1987: BCHLI (1987), Industrial sector Workshop (1987); the second survey refers to the first survey and compares the results of both; however, the empirical base is restricted to Khartoum, the figures for the other regions are extrapolated. The comparison of data between the two surveys, as attempted in the 1987 document, is quite hazardous with such a small and unrepresentative data basis of the second survey. Even the 1970/71 survey does not give a complete view of handicraft activities - village, part-time and home activities are neglected.

This information qualifies the view concerning the relative weight of SI and LI offered by the industrial statistics. Adding the SI recorded in the industrial statistics and in the handicraft surveys, it appears that employment in SI and LI were of the same size in 1970/71. Bearing in mind that the SI is likely to be underestimated, especially with regard to its rural[27], informal, and part-time segments while there is no such underestimate with regard to LI, it is clear that SI were far more important than LI in terms of employment generation in 1970/71.

The employment in handicrafts increased by 449% between 1970/71 and 1987, while in industry the rate for the period 1970/72-1981/82 was only 194% (515% and 145% for SI and LI resp.).

---

[27] The finding of El Sammani et al. (1977), that there is a dearth of information about non-agricultural employment in rural areas, does not have to be qualified 13 years later.

There is no recent detailed estimate of employment in industry. However, there is information on the number of industrial enterprises in 1988. Comparing this with the 1970/71 and 1981/82 figures gives the following picture:

Table 5.1.9. Industrial enterprises in 1970/71-1988

ISIC	1970/71	1981/82	1988	% increase 1970/71-88
31	670	5275	896	33.7
32	42	138	136	223.8
33	135	182	270	100.0
34	34	97	93	173.5
35	51	118	139	170.6
36	42	81	72	71.4
37	1	12	8	700.0
38	298	854	934	213.4
39	3	2	1	-66.7
total	1276	6759	2549	99.7

Sources: 1970/71: DoS (1976), Nimeiri (1976b); 1981/82: UNIDO (1986); 1988: MFEP-E (1990: 61)

Similar as the number of handicraft units, the number of industrial establishments almost doubled between 1970/71 and 1988. However, the latter was accompanied by a significant internal growth of handicraft enterprises (see Table 5.1.8.). On the other hand, one cannot assume a similar internal growth of industrial enterprises. On the contrary, the share of small industrial enterprises increased, i.e. the growth of employment was lower than that of enterprises.

What is more, the doubling of industrial enterprises masks the dramatic decline by almost 2/3 since 1981/82, which is due to a tremendous decline in the number of enterprises in the food industry.

There are only assumptions on the size and composition of the "informal sector". The few studies are concentrated on the urban areas, mostly on Khartoum. The general picture is that the informal sector has been growing rapidly (about 7% p.a.), represents a considerable part of the urban labour force (the estimations vary between 25 and 50%), and it is assumed that this growth will continue in the future[28]. However, concerning the composition of the informal sector the studies point to a prevalent orientation at trade activities - industrial activities are only of minor importance in the informal sector. Nevertheless, it is clear that SI activities are heavily underestimated in the statistics. In reality, SI is much more important than LI. If the distortions against SI would be alleviated (see chapter 6.12.), its role would be even more important.

The second criterion to evaluate the employment generation by SI is its employment intensity compared with LI. This can be measured in terms of capital per employee (see Table 5.1.10.).

---
28 cf. El Bagir and Gibreal (1984), ILO (1987: 39-41)

Table 5.1.10. Capital intensity in SI and LI in 1970/71 and 1981/82 (capital per employee <K/EMP> in LS '000, capital intensity in SI as % of LI)

ISIC	1970/71				1981/82			
	all	SI	LI	SI/LI	all	SI	LI	SI/LI
31	2.52	1.65	2.69	61	7.54	4.25	8.95	47
32	2.19	3.42	2.18	157	6.64	7.44	5.61	133
33	0.89	0.65	1.19	55	7.15	9.22	2.28	404
34	1.96	2.02	1.95	104	3.46	6.07	2.86	212
35	2.82	3.78	2.76	137	21.39	7.11	25.67	28
36	4.21	1.16	4.63	25	6.51	3.31	8.97	37
37	5.03	-	5.03	-	3.54	5.42	3.37	161
38	1.05	1.17	0.99	118	4.24	2.57	6.71	38
39	1.01	1.06	0.97	109	5.67	-	5.67	-
total	2.29	1.53	2.40	64	7.44	4.32	8.61	50

Sources: 1970/71: DoS (1976), Nimeiri (1976b); 1981(82: UNIDO (1986). The figures of both years cannot be compared because of different calculation methods.

The difference in labour intensity between SI and LI is striking. While in 1970/71 in the majority of branches more capital per worker was invested in SI, the overall picture shows a clearly lower capital intensity of SI: 64% of LI. Among the branches with a higher capital intensity of SI only ISIC 38 (*metal products, machines & equipments*) is an important field of SI (with 26.9% of SI employment), altogether these branches represent 37.4% of SI employment. In the main industrial branch, *food* industry (ISIC 31), the capital intensity of SI is only 61% the capital intensity of LI.

Perhaps more interesting is a comparison with the 1981/82 data. Again a very patchy picture emerges, but on the whole the relative capital intensity of SI declined to 50% of LI's values. In the main sector, *food* industry (employing 2/3 of the SI labour force), the distinct advantage of SI has been increased (now it needs less than half of the capital required in LI to employ one worker) and the surprisingly disadvantageous performance of SI in the *metal products, machinery & equipments* sub-sector has been turned into an advantageous position. Surprising is the high capital intensity of SI in the *wood and wood products* sector (ISIC 33).

A detailed look at the industrial structure[29] reveals the great variations by branch and size. Industries are assigned to 49 ISIC four digit classes. It is conspicuous that SI and LI are mostly active in different branches, rather than competing with each other. In 17 branches only LI is active, while in 2 branches only SI is working. Thus in 30 classes SI and LI compete (of these 8 classes unite different industries not elsewhere classified, so that only 22 "proper classes" are left). These branches tend to be dominated by either LI or SI. There are only two branches - *cement*,

---

29   see Appendix 5

quicklime & plaste (ISIC 3692) and *structural metal products* (ISIC 3813) - in which the shares of SI and LI are comparable.

Are the SI activities concentrated in those branches in which they produce less capital-intensive and vice-versa? A first look seems to confirm this. In 9 branches (plus 3 uniting not elsewhere classified industries) where there are less SI units, these produce more capital-intensive than their LI competitors, while in 7 branches, where they predominate, they also produce less capital-intensive. On the other hand, there are only 3 branches (plus one) in which there are more SI establishments, although they produce more capital-intensive and 4 branches (plus two) in which there are less SI establishments, although they are less capital-intensive.

But looking at the importance of these classes employment-wise, the picture becomes even less clear-cut. The first two branches unite 18.6% and 25.1% of the workers employed in the branches in which SI and LI compete resp., while the second two branches unite 18.3% and 38.0% resp. This seems to imply that a considerable part of the industrial workforce is not employed under capital-saving conditions, which points to distortions of the economic environment of industrial producers[30].

In summary, the available data confirm the hypothesis that, firstly, SI plays a substantial and increasing role in employment generation and secondly, on the whole SI is less capital-intensive than LI. However, the second finding is qualified by the fact that SI and LI tend to operate in different sub-sectors which are characterized by different capital-intensities and there is no clear-cut division between SI and LI on the count of capital-intensity.

Creation of employment: Nyala

Out of the 1263 industrial establishments surveyed in Nyala, 1245 or 98.6% belong to SI according to the official definition (see Table 4.4.). In terms of employment, SI accounts for 3351 or 78.1% of industrial employment in Nyala (see Table 4.5.). During the rainy season, the picture shifts even more towards SI: Some of the large industries close down, bringing the shares of small industries in units and employment to 99.2% and 88.4% resp. (see Tables 4.4. and 4.5.). With respect to traditional vs. modern industries, the former category constitutes 46% of employment. Still these figures imply a downward bias, because while large industries could be totally included in the survey, an unknown part of small industries could not be covered.

---

[30] This assessment is underlined by the evidence on factor substitutability: see Ali (1977a), Mohamed Ahmed (1980) and the case of sugar industry analysed by Seisi Mohamed (1976).

The figures correct the prevalent picture of the importance of SI and LI (see above). The true relative importance of SI on the national level is even higher because of the rural industries, which are 100% SI.
To quantify the importance of employment in SI in the whole economy of Nyala is more difficult. Data on the extent of employment in the formal sector are not available. Clearly the employment in trade and services activities are far more important than industrial activities. An indication of this importance is given by a comparison of the number of secondary and tertiary activities in the industrial areas and on the major markets (Table 5.1.11.).

Table 5.1.11.   Secondary and tertiary activities in the industrial areas and on the major markets of Nyala (number of units)

market	secondary units	tertiary units
Light Industrial Area	201	164
Heavy Industrial Area	23	35
Suq Um Dafaso	499	1372
Suq Al Kabir	80	566
other markets	141	963

Source: own survey; "other markets" are: Suq Al Gencina, Suq Mawashi, Suq Congo, Suq Texas, Suq Corea; if not indicated otherwise, all tables concerning Nyala refer to the year 1988.

The tertiary sector comprises as diverse activities as cigarette sellers, boys roaming about with a few pieces of soap for sale, tea ladies, fruit sellers, restaurants, food shops, petty traders, hair dressers, laundries etc. - the quick census summarized in Table 5.1.11. is likely to be an underestimate. The figures do not show the true importance of the secondary vs. tertiary activities because they do not pertain to numbers of employees but units. They are likely to imply an underestimate of tertiary activities, because many of them employ more than one person, while the majority of industrial activities in the markets are one-person establishments. For instance, more than half of the secondary units in the largest market (Suq Um Dafaso) are tailors. Furthermore, all those many small markets which have no industrial activity are not included in the survey. On the whole, it is clear that in comparison the industrial activities are much less important than trade and other services. Although it is found that industrial activities are much more extensive than indicated by the industrial statistics, they are small in comparison with the total population.
The second dimension of employment creation is the relative *labour intensity* of SI. In order to evaluate not only the present importance of SI in Nyala, but also to assess its potential role in future development, it is important to know if they produce particularly labour intensive.

In order to make the data on SI in Nyala comparable to the data of the official industrial surveys, capital intensity is expressed in annual capital expenditure per worker. The results are presented in Table 5.1.12. The next table shows the capital intensities of SI and LI in Darfur region.

Table 5.1.12. Capital intensity of small industries in Nyala (annual capital expenditures per worker)

industry	no.of units	no.of workers	average K/EMP	current prices min. K/EMP	max. K/EMP	average K/EMP	1981 prices min. K/EMP	max. K/EMP
blacksmiths	13	30.33	251	150	500	34	20	68
tinsmiths	11	20	60	21	150	8	3	20
metal workshops	33	176	424	13	941	57	2	127
electric	22	132.67	521	150	941	70	20	127
non-elec.	11	43.33	127	13	740	17	2	100
carpentry	26	110.67	575	25	2860	78	3	386
electric	7	51.33	1139	134	2860	154	18	386
non-elec.	19	59.33	87	25	235	12	3	32
total	83	337	436	13	2860	59	2	386

Source: own survey; for units with differing numbers of workers the average number of workers is given (if the number differs in the dry and rainy seasons, they are weighted with 8 and 4 months resp.).

Table 5.1.13. Capital intensity of SI and LI in Darfur in 1981/82

ISIC	sector	SI	LI
31	food, beverages and tobacco	1692	6815
32	textile, weaving, leather	-	16825
34	paper & paper products	1786	-
35	chemicals and chem. products	3163	1787
38	fabricated metal products	1902	-
	total	1769	9441

Source: UNIDO (1986); no data for Nyala city were available; of the 10 LI enterprises registered in Darfur 7 are in Nyala - four food industry firms (out of seven), one textile factory (100%), and two chemical plants (100%).

A comparison of the data on Darfur's industry (Table 5.1.13.) with the national data (Table 5.1.10.) shows that the difference between SI and LI are more pronounced in Darfur region: The value for Darfur's SI is 59% lower, while the value for Darfur's LI is 10% higher than the national average. More striking, however, is the difference between the own field survey and the official survey data (Tables 5.1.12. and 5.1.13. resp.). All of the SI branches surveyed need only a fraction of the capital used by the SI establishments included in the official survey - not to speak of the LI. Even the maximum invested in the surveyed industrial establishments is less than the statistical averages.

5.2. Income creation

Results of the economic crisis in Africa have been increasing poverty and a deteriorating income distribution. SAP aim at improving this situation. However, at least in the short run stabilization effects are likely to lead to contractions. Because of this, SAP have to be designed in a way so as to minimize these costs.

From an economic point of view, the importance of employment for the employed lies in the income it creates. The proposition advanced by those who propagate SI promotion is that the wages and profits[31] in SI are significant, comparable to those in other sectors[32]. However, this hypothesis is not undisputed. Firstly, it contradicts traditional perceptions of SI as a backward, low-income sector. Secondly, "marginalists" also emphasize low, and declining, incomes in SI. A third related argument regards incomes as low but explains this as a positive factor, because it reflects better the factor availabilities (labour/capital) - in contrast to the LI with its artificial high wages (the *labour aristocracy*[33] and *labour market segmentation*[34] arguments).

The evidence from developing countries is not conclusive. Studies do not only indicate wide variations in SI wages and profits[35] as well as urban labour markets[36], but also differences in definition of SI. This reflects great difficulties to measure incomes and profits in SI[37]. Furthermore, to be comparable, incomes in SI and LI have to be analyzed in their different contexts. For example, it has to be analyzed if family labour is involved (which might not have the opportunity to work elsewhere), how hard the work is, how long the working day is, how regular the income is, which other benefits (social) are connected to the income. Most of these factors are, however, not considered[38].

Keeping these qualifications in mind, the evidence can be summarized as follows[39]. Many studies conclude that incomes in SI are low - often this is a defining

---

[31] In SI wages and profits often coincide because of self-employment. At least it is often not possible to discriminate perfectly.
[32] e.g. Cornia (1987), who sees in SI a survival strategy with strong potential for protecting the poor and the children during periods of economic decline.
[33] cf. Arrighi (1973)
[34] cf. Steel and Takagi (1983) on literature supporting the "labour market segmentation" argument; cf. also chapter 6.12.
[35] cf. Anderson (1982), Hugon (1990)
[36] Kannappan (1989) summarizes evidence on urban labour markets and rejects the argument of segmentation.
[37] cf. Schmitz (1982b: 36-43) on the difficulties to come by reliable information on incomes in SI (calculation of returns on capital, division of wages/ profits, assessment of family labour, payment in kind, high percentages of non- or biased responses)
[38] Other reservations one has to keep in mind are: If incomes are low, one has to find out if this reflects lower productivity or if it is due to policy-induced distortions. Only in the first case low incomes are contradicting the hypothesis.
[39] Most income comparisons are, unfortunately, restricted to comparisons with LI, in few cases with agriculture, although an economy-wide comparison would be necessary to get a comprehensive picture.

characteristic of the informal SI and other informal sector activities[40]. However, a generalization seems to be misleading, because there are wide variations. The comprehensive study of Little et al. (1983) finds large wage differentials between SI and LI, but an erratic relation of profitability and size. Many mention an extensive use of apprentices being paid very low wages[41].

Other studies, however, give a different picture, describing incomes as comparable to those in LI, or at least overlapping with the wages in LI and the formal sector[42]. There is also evidence showing that people left jobs in the formal sector to join SI - because of low wages in the formal sector[43]. The few studies on SI profits show a sustainability. Also, the high percentage of self-financed growth points to profitability[44]. A disaggregation of SI shows a wide variation of wages and profits[45] - the main reason to introduce a third sector in its analysis[46]. A secondary analysis concludes that no clear picture of the earnings in the small scale sector arises and therefore states that "the image of the small scale sector as that of the poor, and the large-scale sector as that of the privileged, is questionable"[47]. Mazumdar (1976) points out that a disaggregation of wages in LI shows a wide variety: According to this analysis, there seems to be a two-tier urban labour market, but it does not correspond to the LI-SI distinction. It is also argued that to describe the traditional apprenticeship as exploitative because of low wages is mistaken because of the efficient role the system would play in transmitting skills and as a springboard to formal employment[48]. Compared with incomes in agriculture, although some say that for many SI incomes are not higher[49], others found them to be high above incomes in agriculture[50].

Income creation: Sudan

Data on incomes other than government are scarce. Up to the 1970s the government was a wage leader, i.e. government wages were higher than other wages. According to the *Minimum Wages Order* (1974) the minimum wages paid in the private sector had to be equal to the minimum wages paid in the public sector

---
40 cf. Hoselitz (1959), ILO (1972), Leys (1973), Page (1979), Bromley (1985), who speaks of "hyper-exploitation", ILO and JASPA (1985: 17), Stearns (1985)
41 cf. LeBrun and Gerry (1975), Steel (1977), Nihan and Jourdain (1978), Nihan, Demol and Jondoh (1979), Kennedy (1980), Hugon (1990)
42 cf. Nihan and Jourdain (1978), Sethuraman (1981c), Richardson (1984)
43 cf. Schmitz (1982b, 156
44 cf. Aryee (1981), Sethuraman (1981a)
45 cf. Page (1979), House (1984)
46 see above chapter 4.2.3.
47 cf. Schmitz (1982b: 41)
48 cf. Nihan, Demol and Jondoh (1979), Lipton (1980)
49 cf. House (1984: 285-8)
50 cf. ILO (1972), Sethuraman (1977)

(within a transitional period of two years; see Table 5.2.1.). Seasonal agricultural labourers, workers outside the urban areas (i.e. Khartoum and the provincial capitals), workers in establishments employing fewer than 10 employees, and workers under the age of 18 were excepted from this regulation, i.e. one may say roughly that they are applied for the modern sector enterprises.

Table 5.2.1. Minimum wages (LS)

	monthly	yearly
1968 (public sector)	13.50	162
1973 (public sector)	15.00	180
July 1974 (public sector)	16.50	198
Oct.1974 (private sector)	11.50	138
Oct.1975 (private sector)	14.00	168
Oct.1976 (private sector	16.50	198
1978	28.00	336
January 1983	31.00	372
1985	60.00	720
December 1988	300.00	3600

Sources: MFNE (n.d.), SBA (1990: 94)

The modern sector in Sudan up to the 1970s fits into the picture of a protected high-wage sector, contrasting with a low-wage marginalized informal sector[51]. However, since the second half of the 1970s the picture changed dramatically. Incomes of government employees deteriorated drastically, especially in the higher echelons: a deputy undersecretary's salary in 1986 was only 8% of his 1975 salary[52]. For the development of government wages and salaries see Table 5.2.2.

Table 5.2.2. Government wages and salaries 1980 and 1988 (ground salary + allowance, LS, per annum, current and 1980 prices)

group	1980	1988 (current prices)	1988 (1980 prices)
first	5025	24000	2603
nineth	1060	7980	866
tenth	1646	7440	807
eighteenth	352	3240	351

Source: MFEP-E (1990: 119)

This development gave the private sector the lead in labour incomes[53]. Furthermore, incomes abroad are estimated to be 6-15 times higher for skilled labour than in Sudan[54].

---
51 cf. Kannappan (1977), Oesterdiekhoff (1979b)
52 cf. Fallon (1987: 29)
53 cf. Fallon (1987)
54 cf. Fallon (1987: 37)

The information on agricultural incomes is scarce. A 1985/86 survey on traditional agriculture arrives at an average family income from crop production of LS 784.58 per annum for an input of 183.14 mandays of family labour, i.e. an income of LS 4.24. per manday (including the labour income as well as the return to land)[55]. Another calculation comes to a per capita income of LS 152.20-LS 159.56 per annum (derived from a household income of LS 1064.70-LS 1116.95.[56] Compared to this, incomes from mechanized farming are very high: Total annual household income is calculated at LS 271,925 on a farm of 5,000 fd. For a typical farm of the size of 1,000 fd this makes LS 54385[57].

Wages for agricultural labourers in traditional agriculture are calculated at LS 0.52-0.91 per day (1979/80)[58], and at LS 3.49-4.56 per day (1985/86)[59].

An evaluation of industrial incomes has to distinguish between wages and profit incomes. The industrial surveys give only limited information on industrial wages, because their information is confined to the wage sum, i.e. it is possible to calculate the average wage, but the wage differentiation cannot be considered. Table 5.2.3. shows average industrial wages in 1970/71 and 1981/82; the following table shows the wages in handicrafts in 1970/71.

Table 5.2.3. Comparative wages in SI and LI 1970/71 and 1981/82 (LS per annum)

ISIC	branch	1970/71				1981/82			
		all	SI	LI	SI/LI	all	SI	LI	SI/LI
31	food, beverages, tobacco	267	141	291	48	857	860	859	100
32	textile, wear. app.& leather	307	232	308	75	1266	798	1282	62
33	wood & wood products	184	172	200	86	1301	1484	870	171
34	paper & paper products	263	213	268	79	1508	1141	1593	72
35	chemicals & chem. products	320	256	324	79	2197	942	2574	37
36	other non-metal minerals	306	180	323	56	908	372	1320	28
37	basic metal industries	782	-	782	-	1893	766	1994	38
38	fabr. metal prod. & mach.	285	217	320	68	1485	1275	1794	71
39	other industries	210	188	229	82	1442	-	1442	-
	total	286	176	302	58	1068	926	1129	83

Sources: 1970/71: DoS (1976), Nimeiri (1976b); 1981/82: UNIDO (1986)

The data for 1970/71 appear to confirm the hypothesis of low wages in industry and in SI particularly. The average industrial income was LS 286, compared to a minimum wage of LS 162. Because of the wage differentiation it is clear that the minimum industrial wage is lower than this, although the difference cannot be quantified.

---
55 cf. El Hanan et al. (1987: 33)
56 cf. El Bashir Mohamed (1986: 106-107)
57 cf. El Bashir Mohamed (1986: 106-107)
58 cf. Bashir Mohamed (1986: 132)
59 cf. El Hanan et al. (1987: 10)

Table 5.2.4. Wages in handicrafts 1970/71 (LS per annum)

food products	147
drinks	83
clothes	102
furniture	116
leather, plastic & tannery products	95
goldsmith& blacksmith products	98
palm leaves products	87
pottery	49
tobacco	105
unclassified	90
total	102

Source: DoS (1974: 33)

On the average, wages in SI were only 58% of those in LI, while the wages in handicrafts were only 34%. In no branch did SI wages exceed those in LI. Similarly there was a wage gap between the modern SI recorded in the industrial statistics and the traditional SI registered in the handicraft survey. The only exception is *food, beverages and tobacco* production (ISIC 31), where in the subsector of food the incomes of both coincide.

This picture changed in the 1970s, as the 1981/82 data show. The gap between the minimum wage in the formal sector (LS 336) and the average industrial income (LS 1068) widened considerably. In 1980 this income was equal to the salary of the nineth grade (LS 1060), which is the starting income of graduates and comparable to the income of a senior unskilled worker. This means that a wage gap between industrial and public sector incomes no longer existed.

Concerning comparative wages in SI and LI, the gap narrowed considerably. On an average the incomes in SI come to 83% of those in LI. Most remarkably is the development in the main sector, food production, where incomes equaled. However, the direction of comparative wage developments was not unequivocal. While in 3 two-digit ISIC classes SI wages improved relatively, in 4 others they deteriorated. Furthermore, on the four-digit level, only in 3 branches were SI wages surpassing LI wages: *bakery, macaroni & noodle production* (ISIC 3117), *preparing wood and saw mills* (ISIC 3311) and *wood products incl. furniture* (ISIC 3320). Thus the picture is one of a diminished, but still existing wage gap between SI and LI.

The evidence on profits of industrial establishments give a different view. The industrial surveys provide information on the operating surplus of enterprises as a percentage of fixed capital. The data allow to compare the profitability of SI and LI (see Table 5.2.5.).

Table 5.2.5. The return on equity in SI and LI 1970/71 and 1981/82 (in %)

	1970/71			1981/82		
ISIC	all	SI	LI	all	SI	LI
31	12	16	11	53	194	25
32	13	9	17	-6	61	-8
33	6	25	-6	18	18	16
34	18	16	18	17	-2	27
35	18	44	16	20	27	19
36	7	14	7	22	55	12
37	44	-	44	209	6	238
38	25	19	29	46	61	37
39	16	32	0	-10	-	-10
total	15	19	14	37	141	18

Sources: DoS (1976), Nimciri (1976b), UNIDO (1986). The data for both years are not comparable because of different methods employed. The 1986 attempt of UNIDO to evaluate the 1981/82 industrial survey measures the rate of return on equity indirectly by subtracting wages and depreciation from value added to arrive at an estimate of the "operating surplus", which is divided by fixed capital. The 1970/71 data do not provide information on depreciation, so that an own calculation tries to approximate operating surplus by subtracting wages from value added; the result is divided by gross invested capital.

The data of the two surveys are not comparable (see note to the table), but allow to compare the relative profitability of SI and LI in the two years. In 1970/71 SI was on an average 36% more profitable, but this masks large differences between sub-sectors - in five sub-sectors SI is more profitable, while in three sub-sectors the picture is reversed. The differences by size are in both cases mostly quite significant. In 1981/82 the difference between SI and LI became even more significant - on an average SI was almost 8 times as profitable as LI. This is mostly a result of the increasing gap between the two industries in *food* production, the main industrial sector. But the relative improvement of SI in two other sub-sectors, in which SI had been less profitable than LI ten years before, also contributed to this: *textile* and *metal products* (ISIC 32, 38).

Table 5.2.6. Comparative profitability of modern and traditional industries (profitability of traditional industry <handicrafts> as a percentage of profitability of modern industry <manufacturing>)

ISIC	1975/76	1980/81	1983/84
31	5717.8	751.8	1707.8
32	734.6	(14532.0)	(151.0)
33	667.6	401.1	702.7
36	359.6	3333.3	5683
total	898.7	1064.0	1358.8

Sources: 1975/76: DoS (1979), 1980/81-1983/84: DoS (1987)
The profitability is measured by division of the "operating surplus" by "consumption of fixed capital". The differences in profitability are measured by dividing the profitability of traditional industry by that in modern industry. Values in brackets indicate a negative profitability of modern industry.

The income accounts provide information allowing for a comparison of profitabilities of modern and traditional industries (see Table 5.2.6.).
This table indicates clearly that the profitability of traditional industries, understood as the surplus in relation to invested capital, is clearly higher than in modern manufacturing. One main factor accounting for this is the low capital investment in traditional industry, compared with modern industry. The large changes between the years are due to high variations in profitability of modern manufacturing - the rate in traditional industries is, in contrast, rather stable. The data must, however, be interpreted with care and the increasing overall gap does not indicate a secular trend, but results from different sources. While in the first period the gap is mostly due to increasing profitability of traditional industry, in the second period it is a result of a profitability of handicrafts cut in half but being overcompensated by the dramatic loss of profitability in modern manufacturing.

Most of the micro level studies confirm a high profitability of modern SI, informal sector and craft activities, but do not bear out the impression of low wages given in the macroeconomic statistics. While there are high variations in labour incomes of different activities, relatively high incomes in small manufacturing activities are reported in most reports[60]. These incomes are comparable with those in LI. They compare also well with those in other sectors. Some studies, however, uncovered that while profits were high in SI, these were contrasting with - and based on - low wages[61].

Income creation: Nyala

Wages in SI show a high variety. They are characterized by a lack in stability and vary according to the enterprises' profits. The figures in Table 5.2.7. indicate this. High wages as in the tannery trade are relativized by the seasonal character of the work. In many branches monetary wages are supplemented by payments in kind (e.g. tea, food) - these are not included in the calculations on which Table 5.2.7. is based. Incomes are high in most activities, both in traditional and modern branches, in comparison with incomes in LI (the textile factory) and other incomes obtainable in Nyala (see Table 5.2.8.). Higher incomes are possible in electric metal workshops and electric carpentry as compared to their non-electric counterparts, but there is no clear wage gap. The incomes for unskilled labour in LI and the modern SI branches (decortication, oil mill, sweets, soft drinks and ice, and soap factories) tend to be lower than comparable incomes in the more

---
[60] cf. ILO (1976: 383), Bilal (1980), Jenkins (1981), Miro et al.(1986: 33), Fallon (1987: 28), House (1987)
[61] cf. Anand and Nur (1984, 1985), Howard (1988), Mohamed Osman et al.(1985)

traditional SI branches. Even apprentices can earn much more in comparison. It is conspicuous that with the exception of the textile factory (a public sector project) the modern industries rely to a high degree on unskilled labour - this is not the case in SI. A comparison with national data (see Table 5.2.3.) does not show a wage gap between SI and LI.

Table 5.2.7. Wages in small industries in Nyala (apprentices, unskilled, semi-skilled, skilled labour)

industry	apprentice	monthly (current prices)			appr.	annual (1981/82 prices)		
		unsk.	semi-sk.	skilled		unsk.	semi-sk.	skilled
blacksmiths	10-1000	-	-	625-1250	18-1829	-	-	1143-2287
tinsmiths	125	-	-	83-1667	229	-	-	152-3049
metal workshop	21-208	-	-	146-1042	38-380	-	-	267-1906
electric	21-208	-	-	146-1042	38-380	-	-	267-1906
non-elec.	21-146	-	-	167-250	38-267	-	-	305-457
carpentry	21-313	-	104-729	208-1875	38-573	-	190-1334	380-3430
electric	21-313	-	104-729	333-1875	38-573	-	190-1334	609-3430
non-elec.	21-167	-	-	208-1042	38-305	-	-	380-1906
snuff factory	-	500	-	-	-	915	-	-
bricks: porter	-	250	-	-	-	457	-	-
brickmaker	-	-	250-500	-	-	-	457-915	-
kiln builder	-	-	313	-	-	-	573	-
pottery	-	-	-	125-150	-	-	-	229-274
palm leaves prod.	-	-	-	200	-	-	-	366
grain mill	-	125	-	-	-	229	-	-
trad. bakery	-	100	100-300	-	-	183	183-549	-
electric bakery	-	450	-2000	-	--	823	-3659	-
tannery	-	-	-	1250-6750	-	-	-	2287-12348
pounding	-	200-300	-	-	-	366-549	-	-
gum sandal prod.	-	-	-	600-1250	-	-	-	1098-2287
leather products	-	-	-	375-750	-	-	-	686-1372
goldsmith	75-400	-	-	750-2500	137-732	-	-	1372-4573
foundry	250-375	-	-	375-750	457-686	-	-	686-1372

Source: own survey; a month is calculated with 25 working days.

Table 5.2.8. Monthly wages and other incomes in Nyala (LS)

industry	unskilled	skilled	% of skilled labour
decortication	200-250	250-1050	10.1
oil mill	175-450	250-800	20.7
sweets factory	150	200-400	4.1
soft drinks and ice	120-	1100-1600	16.1
textile	115-	-1015	74.4
soap	250-375	300-550	9.7
building: worker	125-750	625-1250	
cart transport	300		

Source: own survey

The following table shows profits of Nyala SI. For comparison with the nation-wide industrial surveys the return on equity is calculated (see Table 5.2.9.).

Table 5.2.9. Profits and return on equity in small industries in Nyala

industry	profit		return on equity	
	range	average	range	average
blacksmiths	598-2461	1352	1079.2-7116.71	2678.4
tinsmiths	217-1118	733	416.1-6150.0	1367.6
metal workshops	-208-13693	2400	-135.2-16628.6	798.9
electric	397-13693	2870	69.8-4327.6	705.2
non-electric	-208-10088	1461	-135.2-16628.6	1713.5
carpentry	199-3506	1572	114.0-19166.7	524.8
electric	1040-3506	2334	114.0-1745.6	314.2
non-electric	199-2973	1291	242.1-19166.7	1170.7

Source: own survey; profit per enterprise owner. The profits are calculated on an annual basis. They are not comparable to the wages which are calculated on a weekly basis. The return on equity is the profit divided by fixed cost.

Compared with the national figures (see Table 5.2.5.), the return on equity of Nyala industries is much higher, due to the small amounts of capital used by them. For the same reasons, there is a similar gap between more traditional and more modern industries within Nyala industries.

There is an argument that SI exploits cheap labour, especially apprentices. In fact, the incomes of apprentices differ significantly from those of skilled workers. However, the picture differs by industry.

In the *carpentry* trade, apprentices are generally paid per day, in most cases 5-10 LS/day. Skilled workers are often paid piece-wise, which, over a time and between individuals, results in high variations. The average incomes of carpentry workers range between 208 and 1875 LS/month. Apprentices contribute a significant part of the labour force: on an average apprentices make up 32% of the labour force. 2 of the 26 case studies employed only apprentices, i.e. their only skilled worker is the owner. On the other hand, 8 establishments employed no apprentices. Those workshops employing only apprentices are at the lower profit margin, while those dispensing with apprentices include high-profit as well as low-profit establishments. However, the average profit of the latter group is LS 411/month, i.e. 11% higher than the overall average of carpentry workshop profits. This evidence does not support the proposition that the exploitation of low-paid apprentices is a vital factor for the profitability.

In *metal workshops* apprentices are also paid per day. Their incomes are between 21 and 208 LS/month and are thus considerably below those of skilled workers (LS 146-1042/month), although the incomes of apprentices in one workshop may be higher than the incomes of skilled workers in another workshop. Apprentices play a much more important role in metal workshops than in carpentry, contributing

49% of the labour force. Only 2 (6%) of the metal workshops (at the low end of profits) employ no apprentices. 10 workshops (38%) employ only apprentices, all of them at the lower end of profits.

In the *blacksmith* trade apprentices earn the comparatively highest incomes of all SI branches in Nyala, ranging from 10-150 LS/week, equal to 42-625 LS/month. Nevertheless, apprentices' incomes are clearly lower than those of skilled workers which range between LS 625 and 1250/month. In this trade, however, there is no clear demarcation line between apprentices and skilled workers. It is open to judgment who is to be regarded as an apprentice and who as a skilled worker. With this qualification the information has to be taken that 29% of blacksmith workers are regarded as apprentices. While this rate is lower than in the other trades, the role apprentices play in production is generally more significant. This is reflected in higher wages and in the fact that 5 (38%) of the case studies consist of the owner and one apprentice. Those units are in the medium range of profit incomes, as well as those 4 units which employ no apprentices, i.e. no correlation does appear between employment of apprentices and profits.

Of the 11 analyzed *tinsmith* units 7 are one person establishments, i.e. only 4 use additional workers. Of these only one has (exclusively) apprentices. These earn the "minimum wage" found for apprentices in SI in Nyala, LS 5/week.

In all trades apprentices are generally provided with food during their working hours, irrespective of the amount of work. While their income is much lower than that of skilled workers, it is also more stable, less subject to fluctuations according to the amount of work. The low wages of apprentices reflects their marginal role in production and a lower productivity compared with that of skilled workers rather than an exploitative relationship. The hypothesis of exploitation of family labour is also not supported by the Nyala experience. In the blacksmith trade, for instance, where the use of family labour is most important, family as well as non-family apprentices earn comparatively high wages.

Nyala data do not show either wage gaps between SI and LI nor do they show an unequivocal separation between modern and traditional industries.

5.3 Capital saving and capital mobilization

Capital is a scarce factor in Africa. In spite of this, industrialization has been characterized by increasing capital intensity. Factors contributing to this bias are[62]:
- the relative cheapness of capital, encouraging the transfer of labour-saving technologies;

---

62   cf. ILO (1983: 76)

- a bias in effective demand in favour of products based on less labour intensive production processes (because of international competition and a skewed income distribution);
- the shortage of domestic skilled labour.

In addition to these factors, the flow of foreign resources has declined in the time of crisis. For these reasons it is important to produce in a way that saves capital as well as to mobilize domestic capital.

It is hypothesized that SI plays a positive role in this respect. Two propositions are relevant in this context:

1. SI produces with low capital intensity (see above chapter 5.2.) and thus needs less capital than LI. Means to save capital are the use of second-hand machinery and production inputs (recycling)[63], and on-the-job training[64]. These factors substitute for imports and other production inputs and for vocational training. Many studies give evidence for this.
2. SI mobilizes capital. Most evidence shows that SI main, if not only source of investment is self-finance[65]. It is assumed that the capital initially invested is largely additional capital, which would otherwise not be spent as investments or not come into being at all[66]. There is a lot of evidence on the ability of the poor to save, accumulate capital and reinvest it[67].

Capital saving and capital mobilization: Sudan

The available data on Sudan bear out that SI needs far less capital per worker. However, the statistics give no information and data are scarce on the way SI manages to save capital. Several micro studies tend, however, to confirm the hypotheses that SI contributes to capital saving by using second-hand inputs[68] and on-the-job training[69]. With respect to capital mobilization, SI enterprises undoubtedly are largely self-financed[70].

---

63 cf. Streck (1983), Werobèl-La Rochelle and Bliss (1989)
64 cf. Page and Steel (1984: 24)
65 cf. Sethuraman (1981a), Page and Steel (1984: 24-25)
66 cf. Staley and Morse (1965: 236), Sethuraman (1981a), Nanjundan (1986: 11)
67 cf. Allal and Chuta (1982: 17-18), Anderson and Khambata (1982: 20), Stearns (1985: 31-32). However, the ability of the very small enterprises to reinvest may be limited. Traditionally it was believed that unequal income distribution would be favourable because of higher savings. However, this arguments neglects possible dissavings of the poor under highly unequal income distribution; for that reason it does not follow that more equal income distribution will reduce total net savings (Oshima 1971: 174-176)
68 cf. Streck (1983), Bliss (1989)
69 cf. chapter 6.3.
70 cf. chapter 6.11.

Capital saving and capital mobilization: Nyala

The analysed SI units in Nyala use very little capital. Do they save capital by using inexpensive equipment, e.g. domestically produced, self-produced and second-hand tools and machinery? There is a dichotomy between traditional and modern SI branches. Blacksmiths work almost exclusively with self-produced tools, as a rule made out of second-hand material. More than half of the interviewed tinsmiths, on the other hand, worked exclusively with new tools - the rest exclusively with second-hand tools.

Among the non-electric metal workshops almost two thirds possess exclusively machinery bought new; only one had only second-hand tools. Among the electric metal workshops, half had only new tools, while none had only second-hand tools; only two worked with some self-produced tools.

Among the electric and non-electric carpentry workshops 71% and 58% resp. use only newly bought machinery, while the rest uses partly second-hand machinery. No self-produced machinery is used by either branch.

Another kind of capital saving is on-the-job training. This is the predominant form of training, of entrepreneurs as well as workers. Concerning the entrepreneurs, all of the blacksmiths are trained on the job exclusively. Of the tinsmiths one was enjoying a part-time institutional training at the time of the survey (at the Youth Training Centre). Of the metal workshop owners 6 (18%) completed an institutional training. For carpentry the corresponding figure is 3 (12%).

Institutional training for workers plays only a marginal role. All the workers in the blacksmith and tinsmith trades are trained on the job. Ten workers of the metal workshops and one worker of carpentry enjoyed some kind of institutional training (in a Youth Training Centre, Vocational Training Centre, Technical School, or Technical Institute)[71].

One may conclude that with respect to training, all SI branches save capital by high reliance on self-training. However, with respect to tools and machinery, only the traditional SI branches conform to the expected picture; the modern branches show an astonishing high dependence on imports.

With respect to capital mobilization, SI in Nyala fulfills the promise of SI, as Table 5.3.1. shows.

As Table 5.3.1. indicates, the analysed SI branches in Nyala are almost exclusively self-financed, i.e. financed by own or family savings. Only one **carpentry workshop** relied on a merchant credit to finance part of his initial investment. Astonishingly, even family savings play a marginal role.

---

71 On-the-job training can only be considered as capital saving if this training is efficient, i.e. if it enables to work productively. For a discussion of this see below, chapter 6.3.

Table 5.3.1. Sources of initial capital of small industries in Nyala

industry	own savings	family savings	merchant credit
blacksmiths	9 (69%)	5 (38%)	-
tinsmiths	9 (82%)	2 (18%)	-
metal workshops	32 (97%)	7 (21%)	-
electric	22 (100%)	5 (23%)	-
non-elec.	10 (91%)	2 (18%)	-
carpentry	26 (100%)	-	1 (4%)
electric	7 (100%)	-	1 (14%)
non-elec.	19 (100%)	-	-
total	76 (82%)	14 (17%)	1 (1%)

Source: own survey

5.4 Efficiency

The scarcities in Africa and the inability of the supply systems to satisfy even the basic needs, point to the importance of an efficient use of available resources. From this point of view, the central criterion for the assessment of SI enterprises is their relative efficiency in comparison to LI[72]. If labour intensity of SI is higher than in LI, reflecting more closely the social opportunity costs of labour and capital in developing countries, this points to a better, in the sense of more appropriate, use of labour and capital.

However, it is possible that SI enterprises need not only more labour, but also more capital per output unit. In this case they are "technically inefficient"[73]. To be economically efficient, a firm (and an economy) has not only to be technically efficient, but also price efficient, i.e. to combine the production factors in the combination appropriate to the relative factor prices.

Principally, there are two sources of technical inefficiencies: First, failures to reach the optimum possible with the applied production technique; this may be due to managerial shortcomings or lack of information. Second, use of technologies which are not at the "technological frontier", i.e. which need both more capital and more labour than the most modern techniques. In this second case, there may be an employment-output trade-off, i.e. a conflict between the development objectives of employment maximization and output maximization. While in the neo-classical world such a conflict cannot exist because every type of machine can be associated with any amount of employment, other economists assume that it must necessarily

---

[72] This is the central theme of the extensive studies of Little et al. (1987) and Cortes et al. (1987); cf. also Andersson (1987) for this approach.
[73] cf Farrell (1957); in his terminology a firm is technically inefficient if it does not obtain a maximum output from its inputs

arise[74]. This idea is based on the belief that new techniques are always superior in the sense that they need less labour *and* less capital. Concerning SI, there is a lot of evidence that many SI branches use different technologies[75]. A pessimistic view of their efficiency is wide-spread[76].

Efficiency can be measured by the economic rate of return, reflecting profit when all inputs are valued at their opportunity cost (total factor productivity). However, there is a lack of data on total factor productivity in developing countries. The few studies on economic rates of return indicate higher rates in SI[77]. There are virtually no data on this in the African context[78]. The productivities of labour and capital have to be taken as proxies. In the African context there is some evidence that SI uses capital more productively than LI (because of constraints in access to capital). On the other hand, labour productivity is generally lower in African SI. Although this appears to be offset by higher capital productivity, it is not clear if the total factor productivity (in terms of the true economic cost) is higher or lower than in LI[79]. However, most of the evidence points to a higher efficiency of SI[80]. These findings are in line with evidence from other developing countries, which also point to higher capital productivities and lower labour productivities of SI. Some evidence from other countries also points to higher efficiency of SI, so that there appears to be no output-employment conflict[81].

The usefulness of measures of efficiency in developing countries is restricted in several ways:

1. The concept of *technical efficiency* is "somewhat elusive"[82]. While it is obvious that the assumption of traditional static micro-economic theory that all enterprises adopt technically efficient production processes is not realistic, it is not clear how they combine different sources of inefficiencies (and which). The elusiveness and ambiguity of the concept is partly due to different definitions in use[83] and partly to the fact that non-economic factors (psychological, cultural

---

74 e.g. N.Kaldor, S.Amin, cited in: Stewart and Streeten (1971: 148); cf. the comment of Schumacher (1974: 183): "There is no conflict between growth and employment. Not even a conflict between the present and the future. You will have to construct a very absurd example to demonstrate that by letting people work you create a conflict between the present and the future. No country that has developed has been able to develop without letting the people work. On the one hand, it is quite true to say that these things are difficult; on the other hand, let us never lose sight of the fact that we are talking about man's most elementary needs and that we must not be prevented by all these high-faluting and very difficult considerations from doing the most elementary and direct things."
75 cf. Banerji (1978)
76 cf. Hoselitz (1959: 609), Cortes et al. (1987: 31)
77 cf. Liedholm and Mead (1986: 316)
78 cf. Page and Steel (1984: 20)
79 cf. Page and Steel (1984: 21)
80 cf. Chuta and Liedholm (1979), Byerlee et al. (1983); ILO and JASPA (1985: 26) state that "there is overwhelming evidence that the informal sector masters run their enterprises efficiently".
81 cf. Steel (1977: 167), World Bank (1978: 19), Sethuraman (1981c: 199), Schneider (1986: 433)
82 cf. Page (1979: 15)
83 cf. Page (1979: 41)

factors) are involved. The concept of efficiency bases on the belief in the exclusive objective of production maximization, which is unrealistic - not only in developing countries. It neglects differences between objectives of workers and firm owners, other economic objectives and necessities - e.g. security, continuance of production and input supply) - as well as non-economic objectives, e.g. leisure[84].

2. The measurability of technological efficiency is limited by the fact that it always reflects the quality of the enterprise's inputs[85], i.e. a comparison of enterprises operating with different inputs also has to reflect this.

3. The objective of output maximization is ambiguous because output consists of heterogeneous products. Thus as a part of definition of the objective they have to be weighted[86].

4. The objective of employment maximization is not unambiguous, either. Types of employment differ, in duration, in effort, by regions, by payment, as well as being skilled or unskilled[87].

5. Capital is also a heterogeneous factor in developing countries - not all forms of capital are equally scarce in developing countries.

6. Choice of technique is neither unlimited as assumed by neo-classical theory nor completely determined (a technological process as labour- and capital-saving), but rather a historical process, i.e. "the range of techniques available to produce a particular good arises from the historical development of the industry in question." Early labour intensive techniques do not necessarily become inefficient; especially at a small scale they may remain efficient. The scale is important in determining the efficient range of production possibilities[89]. This implies also that efficient techniques of production are different in different locations[90]. In the process of technical progress new techniques become available, but also, others get lost, because they become inefficient. The bulk of research & development is carried out in the industrial countries, which are driving towards capital intensity. Labour intensive techniques may be unaffected by technical progress and therefore become eventually inferior. Developing countries are transfering those techniques to their economies. Conflicts arise because those techniques are appropriate to a different level of economic development (in terms of factor prices, incomes)[91]. Techniques which would be appropriate to developing countries are not available or only available at higher prices - and thus appear to be inefficient - than they would

---

84 cf. Leibenstein (1966), Shapiro and Müller (1977), Oesterreich (1980)
85 cf. Farrell (1957: 260)
86 cf. Marsden (1970), Stewart and Streeten (1971: 145), Stewart (1972: 114)
87 cf. Stewart and Streeten (1971: 145)
88 cf. Stewart (1972: 103)
89 cf. Stewart (1972: 107); Stewart and Streeten (1971: 146-147)
90 cf. Anderson (1982: 921-922)
91 This is the core of the *appropriate technology* argument.

be if appropriate research would be carried out because of the different levels of economic development and the different research & development interests of industrial countries .
7. Different techniques produce different products, which are substitutes (e.g. plastic and leather shoes, bricks and cement, cotton and synthetic fibres). It is assumed that in order to produce an identical product the choice of technique is very limited[92]. A meaningful measurement of efficiency comparing industries producing different goods has to give weight to their contribution to the society's needs. These needs have to be ranked in an order of importance. Products, like techniques, are transferred from industrial countries. The same problem of appropriateness occurs. Goods may overkill in relation to given needs, i.e. they may satisfy more than the given need[93]. Besides, there may be external diseconomies of consumption[94].
8. Value-added estimates are generally biased downwards because of the exclusion of human capital formation[95].
9. The concept of efficiency implies a strict separation between work and leisure, as well as between economic and non-economic activities. In practical life, for those involved in SI in developing countries, it may not be possible to draw this separation.

The use-value of the concept of efficiency thus becomes very limited. If SI and LI produce different goods, use different techniques, face different factor prices, and their factors are qualitatively different, efficiency comparisons become difficult to interpret. Available studies do not appear to sufficiently take into account the points made above.

Even if SI is found to be at an efficiency disadvantage, this does not have to lead to a pessimistic conclusion[96]:
1. Among SI there is an especially high proportion of failures of new enterprises.
2. Other factors than size appear to be more important.
3. Many will grow big, thus a longer-run efficiency assessment would be preferable.
4. Firms can raise their productivity without growing in terms of employment.

Furthermore, it can be suggested that even when there is an output-employment conflict, it might be considered sacrificing output for employment. Stewart and

---

92   cf. Stewart (1972: 109-114)
93   cf. Stewart (1972: 110)
94   i.e. buying as a result of created wants or habits. If capital-intensive products are wanted because others buy it, it was bought in the past or wants are created through advertising, the welfare loss will be smaller than indicated by nominal values - or it may be regarded as a welfare gain (cf. Stewart and Streeten 1971: 167)
95   cf. Sethuraman (1981c)
96   cf. Cortes et al. (1987: 205)

Streeten give four reasons to do so: wage payments may be the only mechanism to redistribute income to those who would otherwise be unemployed, unemployment is demoralizing, work might be regarded as intrinsically good[97], unemployment has political destabilizing effects[98].

Efficiency: Sudan

It is believed by many that SI in Sudan suffers under low productivity[99]. However, it is difficult to assess the comparative efficiency of SI because the macro-economic statistics[100] as well as micro-level studies show that SI and LI operate largely with different activities. They appear to produce different products and to use different technologies. Accordingly, most micro-level studies do not provide information on comparative efficiency of SI and LI. An exception is Bakhit Idris, who reports on a study by the MDC in 1976 comparing 5 SI and 5 LI in 5 activities, showing consistently higher labour productivity of the SI[101]. In general, the evidence on LI points to wide-spread inefficiencies and low capacity utilization rates[102].

The industrial surveys provide information on labour productivity as well as capital productivity expressed as a percentage of gross output to number of employees and invested capital resp. (see Tables 5.4.1., 5.4.2.).

Table 5.4.1. Comparative labour productivity of SI and LI 1970/71-1981/82 (gross annual output per worker, LS)

ISIC	1970/71			1981/82			% change*	
	all	SI	LI	all	SI	LI	SI	LI
31	2355	938	2634	12605	16309	11019	157.2	-38.1
32	1210	1843	1203	3726	12057	3428	-3.2	-57.8
33	584	624	533	4890	5700	3960	35.1	9.9
34	1225	865	1257	7590	4080	8400	-30.2	-1.1
35	2596	3716	2521	26052	24656	26471	-1.8	55.3
36	1335	652	1429	6087	4199	7540	-4.7	-21.9
37	9359	-	9359	22360	2480	24140	-	-61.8
38	1638	795	2076	8387	5320	12901	-1.0	-8.1
39	2433	3094	1829	17924	-	17924	-	45.0
total	1793	995	1912	10630	13349	9613	98.5	-25.6

Sources: DoS (1976), Nimeiri (1976b), UNIDO (1986)
*: In real terms deflated according to price indices (see Appendix 3).

---

[97] a perhaps doubtful part of Puritanism, which is, however, conducive for development - thus work morale "may have to be accepted along with the rest"
[98] Stewart and Streeten (1971: 151-152)
[99] e.g. Güsten and Künkel (1963: 232), Elnur Ahmed (1977: 60), Abu Affan (1985: 133-135)
[100] see Appendix 5
[101] The activities are textile, oil mill, soap, garment, shoe (1979: 4.4.7., App. N)
[102] cf. Umbadda (1985), World Bank (1987a: 13, 41-43), UNIDO (1989: 38)

Table 5.4.2. Comparative capital productivity of SI and LI 1970/71-1981/82 (gross output per capital, LS)

ISIC	1970/71			1981/82			% change	
	all	SI	LI	all	SI	LI	SI	LI
31	1.01	1.88	0.98	1.67	3.84	1.23	104.3	25.5
32	0.56	2.05	0.55	0.56	1.62	0.52	-21.0	-5.5
33	0.89	2.70	0.45	0.68	0.62	1.30	-77.0	'88.9
34	0.66	1.27	0.64	2.19	0.67	2.94	-47.2	359.4
35	0.97	2.39	0.91	1.22	3.47	1.03	45.2	13.2
36	0.32	1.87	0.31	0.94	1.27	0.84	-32.1	171.0
37	1.86	-	1.86	6.32	0.46	7.17	-	285.5
38	1.81	1.34	2.09	1.98	2.07	1.92	54.5	-8.1
39	4.18	19.80	1.88	3.16	-	3.16	-	68.1
total	0.83	1.83	0.80	1.43	3.09	1.17	68.9	46.3

Sources: DoS (1976), Nimeiri (1976b), UNIDO (1986)

In 1970/71, as expected, labour productivity in SI tended to be lower as compared with LI (amounting to 52% of LI productivity), while capital productivity was on the whole higher (229% of LI productivity). However, the picture was not uniform. With respect to labour productivity, in four sub-sectors (*textile, wood processing, chemicals,* and *other industries* - ISIC 32, 33, 35, 39) SI had higher rates - in general, the rates were very different in the sub-sectors. With respect to capital productivity, only in the sub-sector *metal products* (ISIC 38) SI did not have higher rates.

In 1981/82 the picture was quite different. On the whole, labour productivity decreased by 12% during the decade (adjusted prices), but there are significant differences between SI and LI: while the former category almost doubled its labour productivity, the performance of LI declined by 1/4. The preponderance of LI explains the overall negative development. Labour productivity in SI was on the whole 139% of LI, which contradicts expections. However, the picture is not uniform. The good performance of SI is mainly due to the performance in the main sector of *food industry* (ISIC 31), but also to an improvement in the *wood processing* sector (ISIC 33). At the same time, in the five other sectors with SI activity the relative performance deteriorated. In only one sector - *chemical industry* (ISIC 35) LI performed better than SI in terms of labour productivity.

With respect to capital productivity, there was an overall increase by 72%. The gap between SI and LI widened - the rate of SI increased to 264% of LI. This reflects highly diverse sub-sectoral performances. While SI improved its distinct advantage in *food industry*, this is qualified by deteriorations in other sectors. In two sub-sectors (ISIC 33 and 34) SI lost its distinct advantage, while in *metal products* (ISIC 38) it became slightly better than LI.

An analysis on the 4 digit level further qualifies the pictures of strict distinct advantages of either SI and LI in terms of labour and capital productivity. Out of the 30 classes in which SI and LI compete, in 13 classes SI is better on both terms, while in 5 classes SI is more capital productive and in 4 classes more labour productive; in 8 classes it is neither.

The income accounts, which divide industries into modern and traditional industry, provide only information on capital productivity (see Table 5.4.3.).

Table 5.4.3. Capital productivity in traditional and modern industry (productivity of traditional industry as a percentage of modern manufacture's productivity)

ISIC	1975/76	1980/81	1983/84
31	450.1	245.1	533.9
32	404.5	408.3	40.6
33	117.1	215.4	305.1
36	160.2	264.9	320.1
total	284.5	237.1	174.2

Sources: DoS (1979, 1987). Capital productivity is calculated by dividing gross output by consumption of fixed capital.

As expected, here the picture is more uniform, because both kinds of industries clearly present different technologies. Except for one exception (*textile industry* in 1983/84), the small amounts of capital employed by traditional industries is consistently used more productively. The rates represent highly different developments of traditional and modern industries.

The handicraft survey (1970/71), in contrast to the income accounts, provides only information on labour productivity (see Table 5.4.4.).

Table 5.4.4. Labour productivity of handicraft units (1970/71) (gross output per employee)

branch	GO/EMP
food products	1436
drinks	240
clothes	309
furniture	112
leather, plastic & tannery products	412
goldsmith & blacksmith products	709
palm leaves products	74
pottery	171
tobacco	602
unclassified	3125
total	596

Source: DoS (1974)

As expected, the labour productivity of handicrafts is considerably lower, as compared with SI and LI - it comes to 59.9% and 31.2% of their values resp. (see

Tables 5.4.1., 5.4.4.). However, there are remarkable differences between sub-sectors. The rate of the combined *food, drinks and tobacco* sub-sector, for instance, is with LS 962 higher than the rate of SI (LS 938). This questions the characterization of traditional SI as low productive.

With respect to capital productivity, the data on Sudanese industry confirm the hypothesis on a better performance of SI; the gap between SI and LI has been increasing, while between traditional and modern industries it has been decreasing. With respect to labour productivity, according to expectations, SI had a worse performance in 1970/71. But one decade later the situation was reversed.

Efficiency: Nyala

Nyala's industries are characterized by a high variety of production performances, which is due to the high instability of demand as well as supply. This is indicated by the high variation of output. It qualifies the significance of the average output figures (see Table 5.4.5.).

Table 5.4.5. Labour productivity of small industry in Nyala, 1988 (gross annual output per worker)

industry	average output			range
	current prices	1981/82 prices	1970/71 prices	current prices
blacksmiths	22398	3414	505	13005-34892
tinsmiths	26720	4073	595	3276-92040
metal workshops	31334	4777	707	666-159011
electric	34788	5303	785	5543-115123
non-electric	20759	3164	468	666-159011
carpentry	32142	4900	725	10400-60007
electric	38126	5812	860	21876-65994
non-electric	26969	4111	608	10400-98800
total	30521	4653	688	666-159011

Source: own survey

Compared with the industrial survey of 1981/82, the average output of Nyala's industries is only 35% of the national average; compared with the 1970/71 survey 69%.

The figures on capital productivity, on the other hand, show that because of the small amounts of capital used by Nyala's industries they use capital much more productively not only than LI, but also than the SI recorded in the statistics (see Tables 5.4.6., 5.4.2.).

Table 5.4.6. Capital productivity of small industry in Nyala, 1988 (gross output/capital expenditure per year, LS)

industry	annual capital expend.[103]	range of capital expend.	output/ capital	range of output/ capital
blacksmiths	584.6	300-1000	89.4	26.9-157.4
tinsmiths	109.1	50-250	445.3	65.5-745.7
metal workshops	2259.2	100-15000	74.0	9.7-2114.8
electric	3138.9	415-15000	66.8	9.7-414.2
non-electric	500.0	100-3700	163.5	24.4-2114.8
carpentry	2447.8	50-28600	55.9	8.3-1267.8
electric	8353.6	1075-28600	33.5	8.3-213.5
non-electric	271.9	50-1250	309.7	93.4-1267.8
total	1771.0	50-28600	70.0	8.3-2114.8

Source: own survey

Comparing the industries of Nyala, as expected, the capital productivity is the highest in those industries which use least capital. When the industries are ranked by capital expenditure (see Table 5.4.7.), it can be seen that this relation is unequivocal.

Table 5.4.7. Capital productivity of small industries in Nyala (ranked by annual capital expenditure)

industry	annual capital expend.	output/ capital
tinsmiths	109.1	445.3
carpentry (non-elec.)	271.9	309.7
metal workshop (non-elec.)	500.0	163.5
blacksmiths	584.6	89.4
metal workshop (elec.)	3138.9	66.8
carpentry (elec.)	8353.6	33.5

Source: own survey

The results of a comparison of the Nyala survey with the national statistics has to be interpreted with much care, however: a comparison has to be qualified in many respects. In chapter 5.1. it was shown that SI and LI are largely active in different fields: this is indicated by the statistics, but becomes more evident by a comparison with the industries in Nyala, which are mostly not included in the statistics. These industries produce different goods, use different technologies, use mostly different inputs (which they obtain often from different sources and in any case through different channels than LI and formalized SI), and to some degree, they use different kinds of capital (second-hand equipment, self-produced equipment).

---

84 For hand tools, the entrepreneurs estimated the annual expenditure. For power-driven machines, a life-span of 5 years is estimated, i.e. a depreciation of 20% p.a.

Furthermore, they face to a high degree production interruptions due to supply and/or demand factors and a high mobility of workers. Lastly, the economic rationality of SI producers in Nyala cannot properly be interpreted by the output maximisation theorem on which the concept of efficiency is based. These factors render a strict comparative evaluation of SI in terms of efficiency impossible. Nevertheless, the data provide evidence to refute claims of a principal inferior position of SI with respect to efficiency.

5.5 Strong linkages to other sectors

The importance of linkages for economic development has become widely recognized. In the broadest sense, linkages perceive development as "the record how one thing leads to another"[104]. Linkages focus on how productive activities lead to new activities. More specifically, linkage effects are defined as investment-generating forces of a given product line "that are set in motion, through input-output relations, when productive facilities that supply inputs to that line or utilize its outputs are inadequate or nonexistent"[105]. Basically, one has to discriminate between:
- backward production linkages (leading to new investment in input-supplying facilities);
- forward production linkages (leading to new investment in output-using facilities);
- consumption linkages (leading to new investment in industries producing consumption goods as a result of that activity).

Originally the focus of this discussion was on industry, based on the belief that agriculture is weak in terms of linkages to other sectors[106]. More recent research, however, emphasizes the importance of agriculture as a stimulator of industrial development[107]. The former negative assessment of the linkage potential of agriculture was partly based on the neglect of the consumption linkages, which in fact appear to be not only as important, but even more important than the production linkages[108]. Another reason for the negative assessment of the linkage potential of agriculture was the underestimate of the rural non-farm activities. It is

---

104 cf. Hirschman (1981: 75; see also idem, 1958: 98-119)
105 cf. Hirschman (1981: 65)
106 cf. Hirschman (1958)
107 cf. Johnston and Mellor (1961), Mellor (1976, 1986, 1989), Bautista (1989)
108 cf. Hazell and Röell (1983), Hazell (1984)

now well established that non-farm activities play an important role in terms of employment as well as income[109].
Economic development in Africa and industrialization in particular have been processes of imposition of foreign techniques rather than a development of the indigenous forms of production. This has led to a coexistence of two separate economic spheres with weak linkages between them[110]. LI is not linked to the remaining sectors of the domestic economy, but instead strongly linked to foreign economies. The absence of domestic linkages is also a central argument of the Latin American dependency and development of underdevelopment approaches[111].
There is a consensus that the degree of linkages, especially in Africa, depends very much on the government policy regarding agriculture. Many studies emphasize that the fate of rural industries is closely connected to that of the agricultural sector. In a study on 6 eastern African countries (Kenya, Malawi, Sudan, Tanzania, Uganda, Zambia) Johnston (1984) for example contrasts the present capital-intensive labour-saving, urban-biased agricultural strategy which makes a participation of the majority in productivity and income gains impossible with a more broadly based strategy which maximizes the positive interactions between agricultural and industrial development.
It is widely believed that SI has stronger linkages to other domestic sectors, especially to agriculture[112], as well as inter-industrial linkages. The scarce and uncompatible evidence shows significant differences between Africa and other continents, especially Asia: This continent is characterized by much more integrated economies. Inter-industrial linkages of SI[113] as well as linkages to agriculture[114] are strong. In Africa, industrial linkages are strong to the agricultural sector, as far as backward linkages (crop processing) are concerned, but weak in terms of forward linkages (production of agricultural inputs). However, detailed studies in Sierra Leone indicate that the SI-agriculture linkages are stronger than those between LI and agriculture, which is especially due to stronger consumption linkages[115]. Linkages appear to be especially weak between SI and LI[116]. The informal sector enterprises appear to have strong backward linkages, but weak forward linkages to the formal sector[117].

---

109 cf. Anderson and Leiserson (1980), Binswanger (1983), Haggblade et al. (1987), Liedholm and Kilby (1989)
110 cf. World Bank (1978: 68), Liedholm and Mead (1986)
111 cf. Cordova (1973), Girvan (1973), Amin (1977)
112 e.g. Spiro (1972)
113 cf. Chaudhuri (1989)
114 e.g. Oshima (1971), Child and Kaneda (1975)
115 cf. King and Byerlee (1978)
116 cf. Haggblade et al. (1987), Liedholm and Mead (1986: 314-315)
117 cf. Hugon (1982: 36), ILO and JASPA (1985: 29-31); an exception to this assessment are, however, the studies of van Dijk (1986a, b), who find also important forward linkages of the

Linkages: Sudan

There is a lack of data on the extent of linkages. There are virtually no data on consumption linkages. Only indirect conclusions on the state of affairs can be taken.
The rising import dependence of industry was accompanied by domestic linkages between economic sectors as well as within the industrial sector becoming weaker. According to the economic survey already in 1955/56 the overall degree of interdependence between sectors was low: Only 11% of total sales by all sectors was directed to other sectors, the rest was for final consumption[118]. This estimate, however, underestimates the actual interlinkages, because non-monetary subsistence and other informal activities are not sufficiently considered. For instance, those craft industries which produce capital and intermediate goods were not included.
The intensity of backward linkages from industry to other sectors in 1955/56 can be seen in Table 5.6.1. (next chapter). From the industry's point of view, these were quite strong: 69.4% and 95.3% of total inputs for manufacturing and craft industry resp. came from agriculture. However, from the agriculture's point of view (forward linkage of agriculture), this was only a small amount: 2.0% and 1.9% of total agricultural production resp. (63.7% of agricultural output was for final consumption and 33.4% for export). The forward linkages of the manufacturing sector[119] were directed to agriculture (5.9% of its output to the livestock subsector), to transport & distribution (3.0%), to building & civil engineering (7.6%) - a total of 16.7% of output as intermediate goods for other sectors - , 17.8% to export, and 62.5% to final consumption[120]. Inter-industrial linkages are not considered in this calculation.
The only other input-output table available seems to be for the year 1962/63. It considers four economic sectors: agriculture, food processing & agro-allied industries, constructing & mining and transport, utilities & services (see Table 5.5.1.).

---

informal sector to the formal sector and emphasize the integrating function of the informal sector.
118 cf. Harvie and Kleve (1959: 74)
119 No data are available on the craft industry, as only those producing for final consumption were considered.
120 cf. Harvie and Kleve (1959: 74)

Table 5.5.1. Abridged input-output table 1962/63 (LS '000)

Producing sector	Agriculture	Intermediate demand				Total intermediate demand	Total final demand	Total demand
Purchasing sector		Food processing and Agro-allied industries	Construction and mining	Transport utilities and services				
Agriculture	1,900	10,248	2,637 a/		40	14,825	242,482	257,307
Food processing and agro-allied industries	1,200	0	2,050 a/		840	4,090	41,729	45,819
Construction and mining	0	19	75 a/		2,147	2,241	54,928	57,169
Transport, utilities and services	20,089	6,833	6,171		3,299	36,392	85,372	121,764
Total intermediary inputs	23,189	17,100	100,933		6,326	57,548	424,511	482,059
Value added	222,861	19,676	27,632		100,317	370,486		
Total production at factor costs	246,050	36,776	38,565		106,643	428,034		
Imports	10,046	6,180	15,452 a/		7,020	38,698		
Taxes on imports	1,211	2,863	3,152 a/		8,101	15,327		
Total input	257,307	45,819	57,169		121,764	482,059		

Source: Computed from ECA Statistical Bulletion for Africa, No. 2, Part 2, March 1967.
a/ Construction only.

Source: Sheira (1968: 32)

This table gives an impression of the overall weak domestic intersectoral linkages. However, this picture is incomplete as only those industries allied to agriculture are included - not to mention informal SI. According to this table, agro-allied industry received 44.0% of its inputs from agriculture and 26.5% from imports, thus being the most intensively backward-linked sector. Its outputs go mainly to final consumption (91.1%). Only 8.9% are intermediate goods - 2.6% go to agriculture, 4.5% to construction & mining and 1.8% to transport utilities & services.

Available input-output tables are deficient in 3 respects. First, they are out of date; second, they give a partial view; third, they do not allow to evaluate the comparative performance of SI and LI with regard to intensiveness of backward or forward linkages. A division of industries by output provides information to go some way towards a temporal evaluation of industrialization (see Table 5.5.2.).

Table 5.5.2. Classification of industries by output (shares in gross value added)

	1955/56 LI(MF)	1970/71 all	1970/71 SI	1970/71 LI	1981/82 all	1981/82 SI	1981/82 LI
consumption goods	74.9	69.0	44.4	71.8	81.5	88.7	74.5
intermediate goods	19.6	21.8	30.5	20.9	11.8	4.6	18.9
capital goods	5.5	9.0	25.1	7.3	6.6	6.6	6.6

Sources: Harvie and Kleve (1959), Nimeiri (1976b), DoS (1976), UNIDO (1986); consumption goods: ISIC 31, 32, 39; intermediate goods: ISIC 33-37; capital goods: ISIC 38

The table confirms the information that industries are predominantly consumer goods-oriented. It appears that a structural shift towards the production of intermediate and capital goods, implying an intensification of linkages - an attribute of industrialization - had gone some way during the 1960s, but was radically reversed during the 1970s. In terms of structural change the industry was back on square one - if not worse (see the shares of intermediate goods).

The 1970/71 survey gives the impression that SI is more engaged in the production of intermediate and capital goods and thus stronger linked intra- as well as intersectorally. However, this picture was reversed ten years later: While the share of total intermediate production almost halfed, SI produced only 15% of its former share, while the LI share declined only slightly. With respect to capital goods, the total share declined by 27%, also mainly due to the decline of SI production, now being on the same percentage level.

The micro studies on SI hardly elaborate on the linkages - neither forward, backward nor consumption.

The strength of external linkages are indicated by the foreign trade statistics. Exports of industrial goods are insignificant: they are consistently much less than 10% of total exports and consist of agricultural processed goods (mainly edible oil, oil cakes, yarn). The statistics on imports is especially unreliable, because of the high extent of unofficial and illegal imports (estimated as high as 50%). However, it is safe to assume that the vast majority of those illegal imports are consumer goods. The statistics give the following picture:

Table 5.5.3. Import structure (% of total imports)

	1981	1987/88
food, drinks, tobacco	22.1	14.0
crude materials	20.3	20.8
chemicals	8.2	17.1
manufactured goods	21.3	20.1
machinery & equipment	13.9	14.4
transport equipment	10.8	11.7
textiles	3.5	2.0

Sources: 1981: BoS (1984), 1987/88: IMF staff estimates

Together with the domestic production structure, this table gives an indication of the strength of domestic vs. external linkages.

The import of machinery & equipment in 1981 amounted to LS 120.5' mill., while the domestic production of the comparable sector (ISIC 38) in 1981/82 amounted to LS 36.9 mill. (gross value added)[121]. Although the industrial statistics do not allow to discriminate perfectly between intermediate and consumer goods, it is

---
[121] cf. UNIDO (1986), BoS (1984: 117-119)

clear that the production of intermediate goods falls far short of the demand. This confirms the data on import dependence in the preceding chapter and indicates a weak capability of the industry to supply its own production basis.
But more significant than this is the situation with respect to agricultural production goods - agriculture being the main productive sector. The agricultural sector has a bimodal structure. On the one hand, there is the traditional sub-sector, which gives a living to the majority of the population and relies almost completely on agricultural hand tools, which are locally produced by SI (blacksmiths - not included in the industrial statistics). On the other hand, the mechanized rainfed sector relies totally on imported machinery[122]. However, this constitutes a problem, as the imports (about 1200 tractors, 100 combine harvesters annually, and some small implements) are irregular, due to foreign exchange shortages and cover only a fraction of demand - not to mention potential demand[123]. The production of fertilizers and pesticides, other important agricultural inputs, ceased apparently. These have to be totally imported (LS 19.8 mill. in 1981). Only minor agricultural inputs for modern agriculture (mechanized farming, irrigated farming) are produced (e.g. jute sacks, assembly of trailers).
Although the backward linkage of food industry to agriculture is comparatively strong, it falls short of the potential (as seen by the great majority of unprocessed agricultural exports). At the same time, the development of infrastructure and marketed agricultural surplus did not keep pace with the rapid expansion of food processing and textile industries in the early 1970s. Many sub-sectors do not refer to the domestic raw material base or are not in a position to do so under present circumstances. Examples are the grain mills, relying mainly on imported wheat, sugar mills relying for a long time mainly on imports, textile mills requiring short staple cotton (while Sudan is a major producer of long staple cotton) and relying mainly on imported yarns, and the leather factories working with low capacity due to superior competition by exporters of raw hides & skins[124].
The high share of food imports points to a limitation of consumer linkages as well, because the large majority of imported food items belong to the category of basic rather than luxury goods.

---

[122] cf. ILO (1987a); attempts to assembly tractors in Sudan were apparently not successful (Bedri 1979; Osman Abdel Nour 1987), limited manufacture for irrigation appears to be done (Bedri 1979).
[123] According to Osman Zein El Abdin (1987: 77) the actual tractor park of 9500 contrasts with a "potential park" of 100,000.
[124] cf. Oesterdiekhoff (1979b), UNIDO (1989)

Linkages to other sectors: Nyala

The origin of industrial inputs will be discussed in Chapter 5.6.2. The information for both machinery and raw materials is summarized in Table 5.5.4.

Table 5.5.4. Backward linkages of small industries in Nyala (annual raw materials and capital consumption)

industry	input consumption as % of gross output	local inputs (%)	domestic inputs (%)	imported inputs (%)
blacksmiths	46.6	100.0	-	0.02
tinsmiths	75.9	66.4	-	33.6
metal workshops	72.7	0.03	17.4	82.6
electric	73.5	0.03	19.6	80.3
non-electric	68.4	0.02	5.0	95.0
carpentry	66.4	26.7	4.9	68.4
electric	68.2	19.7	4.8	75.6
non-electric	64.0	36.3	5.0	58.7
total	68.9	17.2	11.4	71.4

Source: own survey

Blacksmiths are almost totally backwardly linked to the local economy; imports are negligible. The second best locally linked industry are the tinsmiths. The other industries are more linked to the external economy than to the local economy. On the third rank are the non-electric carpentry workshops which receive a bit more than one third from the local economy, followed by the electric carpentry workshops. The metal workshops are insignificantly linked to the local economy.
The linkages to other parts of the country, for all industries, are much weaker than the links to the external economy. They are strongest for the metal workshops, due to the consumption of metal raw materials.
The forward linkages of SI are also stronger for the more traditional industries of blacksmiths and tinsmiths, than for carpentry and metal workshops (see Chapter 5.7.2.). Nyala SI produces mostly consumption goods, but these do not constitute a large share in the consumption basket of the population.

5.6 Utilization of local resources and low import intensity

Past development efforts in Africa have relied highly on foreign resources and foreign technologies. It is by now widely accepted that Africa to a far higher degree has to rely on her own resources. First, this will reduce the high dependence on outside help which has in the past impaired the capacities of economic decision making as well as implying other economic costs. Second, perhaps more importantly, it will reduce the disastrous psychological side-effects of a high dependence on foreign aid, stifling any spirit of development. Third, in the present economic and political situation it is quite obvious that despite well-intentioned appeals of international organisations for more aid to Africa, this is not forthcoming.

SI can play a role to achieve the aim of more reliance on own resources. It is hypothesized that SI:
1. uses more local resources than LI (labour, machinery, raw materials);
2. imports less of these resources than LI;
3. is able to exploit discarded materials and second-hand materials.

Here a distinction is made between *domestic* and *local* resources. Compared to domestic resources, the use of local resources has some additional advantages as promotion of regional development and saving of transport costs, which is of special importance in the African context in view of the low level of infrastructural development.

Various studies provide evidence for the use of local resources, less imports[125] and discarded materials[126]. However, the evidence is sketchy and some studies contradict the first hypothesis by claiming a high dependence of SI for inputs on the formal sector[127].

Utilization of local resources and low import intensity: Sudan

Data on the origin of industrial inputs are scarce. The industrial surveys neglect the source of industrial inputs; only the 1955/56 survey provides information on the composition of inputs (see Table 5.6.1.):

Table 5.6.1. Input structure of industries in 1955/56 (percentages of gross output; MF = manufacturing, HC = craft industries)

	MF	HC	total
agricultural inputs	33.2	26.6	29.6
transport & distribution	20.5	0.1	9.3
total domestic inputs	57.9	27.6	41.3
imported inputs	15.3	0.4	7.1
gross value added	24.7	71.9	50.6

Source: Harvie and Kleve (1959)

---

125 cf. Cortes et al. (1987)
126 cf. Oshima (1971: 167), Sethuraman (1977), Bromley and Gerry (1979), Sethuraman (1981d: 181-183)
127 cf. Hugon (1982: 36)

On the whole, industries show a high reliance on domestic inputs - imports were only 7.1% of gross output, while total domestic inputs amounted to 41.3%. However, the difference between modern and traditional industries was considerable. For the latter imports were insignificant (0.4% of gross output), while modern industries relied to some degree (15.3% of gross output) on imports. The difference in costs for transport and distribution (20.5% and 0.1% for modern and traditional industries resp.) implies that craft industries relied totally on local raw materials, while modern industries depended more on materials from other regions or from abroad.

Oesterdiekhoff's comprehensive analysis of the industrial structure reveals that Sudan's LI became highly - and increasingly - dependent on imports (see Table 5.6.2.).

Table 5.6.2. Input structure of industrial branches 1968/69 (local and imported intermediate inputs in % of production costs)

sub-sector	local	imported
agricultural food processing	45.34	23.13
agricultural non-food processing	24.78	27.20
non-agricultural manufacturing	17.14	33.22
services	0.03	39.20

Source: Oesterdiekhoff (1979b: 44); agricultural food processing: ISIC 31, agricultural non-food processing: ISIC 32, 33, 3411, 3412, non-agricultural manufacturing: ISIC 35, 36, 37, 38 (excl. 3813); services: ISIC 3420, 3813

This table shows a cascading structure of increasing import dependence: While *agricultural food processing* industry needs almost double as much local than imported inputs, *services* depend almost totally on imported inputs; but even the import dependence of the first category is surprising. A comparison with data from 1977/78 appears to confirm the tendency of increasing import dependence. As far as the data on the 4 digit level can be compared, they show consistently higher rates. Most branches appear to import the majority of their inputs and some in fact 100%. Even the agro-processing industries import a high percentage of their inputs (e.g. flour milling 76.4%, macaroni 57.8%, ice and mineral water 56.8%, cigarettes 86.4%)[128].

In contrast to this, most studies on SI in Sudan argue that they - and especially their lower end of traditional, informal and rural industries - largely use local resources[129]. However, other studies are contradicting this argument - they found that also SI may be highly import dependent[130].

---
128 cf. Abu Affan (1985: 163), Oesterdiekhoff (1979b: 46); cf. also UNIDO (1989: 22)
129 cf. Babiker (1982: 52), Jenkins (1981), UNIDO (1989: 34)
130 cf. Anand and Nur (1985), Bakhit Idris (1979), Mohamed Osman et al. (1985), Shadeed Mohamed Zein (1988)

Unfortunately these studies did not analyse the industrial input structure by size. More recent industry surveys give only indirect information on the input structure, namely the degree of processing (the share of gross value added in gross output). A low degree of processing indicates high costs for inputs which points to a large share of imported inputs (see Table 5.6.3.).

Table 5.6.3. Comparative degree of processing in SI and LI (gross value added as a percentage of gross output)

ISIC	1970/71			1981/82		
	all	SI	LI	all	SI	LI
31	23.8	43.7	22.4	38.7	55.8	27.9
32	56.2	29.0	56.7	24.4	44.4	21.8
33	41.3	53.1	23.9	53.0	55.4	41.8
34	50.4	60.9	49.8	27.8	25.1	28.1
35	31.9	51.6	29.9	24.6	11.5	28.3
36	46.5	52.8	46.1	36.3	46.7	32.2
37	31.8	-	31.8	41.6	44.0	41.6
38	33.5	55.6	29.1	40.8	53.5	33.0
39	15.3	17.2	12.5	4.9	-	4.9
total	34.6	47.6	33.5	36.3	52.5	27.8

Sources: DoS (1976), Nimeiri (1976b), UNIDO (1986)

Table 5.6.4. Comparative degree of processing in traditional and modern industries 1975/76-1983/84 (gross value added as a percentage of gross output)

ISIC	1975/76	1980/81	1983/84
31	24.9	30.6	35.6
MF	18,7	21.8	28.2
HC	53.5	52.0	53.6
32	55.0	25.7	13.4
MF	54.2	18.3	9.9
HC	56.7	54.8	56.6
33	62.9	58.8	58.9
MF	43.0	46.7	51.4
HC	72.5	70.5	71.3
36	54.7	40.0	42.9
MF	52.3	32.1	36.2
HC	59.3	59.3	59.1
total	33.6	26.4	25.2
total MF	29.7	24.7	19.9
total HC	57.1	55.6	54.8

Sources: DoS (1979), DoS (1987)

In 1970/71 the gross value added in gross output was 42% higher for SI, which is consistent with the assumption of higher dependence on local raw materials. Only in one sub-sector (*textile*, ISIC 32) it was lower than for LI. During the 1970s the degree of processing in SI increased, while it decreased in LI (on an average it was 89% higher in SI in 1981/82). This is also consistent with the evidence on increasing import dependence of LI. However, the picture became less uniform than in 1970/71: Now in two sectors SI had a lower processing rate (*paper* and *chemical products* - ISIC 34, 35).

As expected, the income accounts, dividing industries in traditional and modern industry, show a uniform picture (see Table 5.6.4.).

The processing rate is consistently very much higher in traditional industries, and often the difference tended to increase. This reflects an almost stable processing rate of traditional industries. As for modern industries, it is rising in the *food* and *wood processing* sub-sectors and declining in the *textile* and *non-metallic products* sub-sectors - declining on the whole by 1/3 over the period. While the processing rates of traditional industries are consistently higher, the differences between industrial branches are considerable.

Utilization of local resources: Nyala

The resources used by SI are machinery, raw materials and labour. The results of the examination of the origin of machinery is summarized in Table 5.6.5. It is significant that SI branches differ significantly in this respect.

Table 5.6.5. **Origin of machinery of small industries in Nyala, 1988 (LS)**

industry	value of machinery	self-produced (%)	local (%)	domestic (%)	imports (%)
blacksmiths	12565	50.6	48.2[131]	-	1.1
tinsmiths	5482	2.7	61.5[132]	-	35.8
metal workshops	331995	0.4	1.5	2.0	96.1
electric	299460	0.4	1.4	2.0	96.3
non-electric	32535	0.4	2.3	2.5	94.8
carpentry	339808	-	2.8	-	97.2
electric	294445	-	3.0	-	97.0
non-electric	45363	-	1.9	-	98.1
total	689850	1.1	3.5	1.0	94.4

Source: own survey

Most *blacksmiths* produce all their tools (anvils, bellows, hammers, tongs, wedges, etc.) themselves - 10 (77%) of the sample. If blacksmiths use any purchased tools, these are in addition to their stock of self-made tools and play only a marginal role. The raw material for the production of tools is generally scrap of lorries, other automobiles and the railway. The scrap originates from Nyala or, in most cases,

---
[131] second-hand material for own production of machinery
[132] including 7% second-hand material for own production of machinery

from Greater Khartoum. It was not possible to determine the shares of local and other domestic places of origin. In any case, the scrap utilized by the blacksmiths is not imported for this purpose, but comes from vehicles no longer in use.
Blacksmiths are the only trade which produces tools for own use in any significant scale. More than half (55%) of the analyzed *tinsmiths* use some self-produced tools, but these constitute only a tiny share of their machinery (see Table 5.6.5.). However, most of their tools are locally produced, only about one third is imported. Concerning the use of second-hand tools, tinsmiths are split into two groups: 6 units use only new tools, while 5 units use only second-hand tools. It could be expected that the utilization of second-hand tools is concentrated on the low-income units, but in the case studies there is no clear relation to profitability.
In contrast to the trades of blacksmithing and tinsmithing, the modern metal workshops and carpentry are extremely import dependent. For *carpentry*, ten (38%) do not have any local tools, and 85% have more than 90% of their machinery imported. Interestingly, even the non-electric workshops are not less import dependent, in the case of carpentry, their import share is even slightly higher. This reflects the fact that in the field of hand tools only very simple and inexpensive wedges are locally made, while for electric machines there are several instances of locally produced frames implying a higher value added. An extreme contrast to modern carpentry is represented by the only traditional bed-maker included in the survey. His tools are completely locally made, but with a value of only LS 50 they constitute a marginal part of total machinery. Of the carpentry workshops 16 (62%) work exclusively with new tools and machines. Also in this trade there is no clear association of high profit and use of new tools.
For *metal workshops* the picture is less extreme, only 5 (15%) have exclusively imported tools. The same number needs less than 90% imported machinery. Most (73%) use locally produced tools, only 6 (18%) use machinery from Khartoum. However, in terms of value the last category is higher, because the local tools most have are only wedges. Of the metal workshops a majority (18 or 54%) use only new tools. 12 units (36%) use partly second hand tools, only one works exclusively with second hand tools. Very few (3) units work with self-produced tools. However, these are confined to one type of tools (wedges) and make up only a marginal part of even their tools. Those, working partly with second hand tools, are evenly distributed among high-profit as well as low-profit workshops.
In the origin of the processed *raw materials* there are also wide differences between various trades or rather, products. The differences in respect to raw material origin are more suitably analyzed product-wise than industry-wise, because most of the analyzed trades produce different products which are distinguished especially by different raw materials.

The only exception are the blacksmiths, who process almost exclusively local (charcoal) and second-hand (scrap) raw materials. These are included in the category "local", because they are purchased in Nyala, mostly from merchants, but also from lorry drivers and owners. However, the greater part of the scrap is brought from Khartoum by merchants for sale in Nyala. The percentage cannot be quantified. In any case, they are of domestic origin. No scrap seems to be imported to Sudan.

Tinsmiths, on the one hand, use second-hand sheet metal of motor oil containers, of milk-powder tins (imported) and of *tahnia* (indigenous sweets, factory-made) tins, sheet metal strips of packing material of tea and cotton. On the other hand they use imported sheet-metal, corrugated iron, solder, colour and nails.

Some products are available both in a low-cost type based on second-hand material and in a "luxury" type based on new raw materials. Examples are metal suitcases, stoves, shovels. Five of the analyzed units use mainly second-hand material (90% or more), while on an average it is calculated that 33.6% of the consumed raw materials of tinsmiths are imported (see Table 5.6.6.).

Table 5.6.6. Origin of raw materials of small Industries In Nyala, 1988 (LS)

industry	consumed raw mat.(LS)	local[133] (%)	domestic (%)	imported (%)
blacksmiths	308932	100	-	-
tinsmiths	404508	66.4	-	33.6
metal workshops	3933852	4.5	13.1	82.3
electric	3324412	5.0	15.0	80.0
non-electric	609440	2.0	3.0	95.0
carpentry	2330796	27.4	5.0	67.6
electric	1317368	20.4	5.0	74.6
non-electric	1013428	36.5	5.0	58.5
total	6978088	20.0	9.1	70.9

Source: own survey; for the metal workshops estimated; for elec.carpentry projected from analysis of 3 units; for non-elec.carpentry projected from analysis of 4 units.

The metal workshops, by contrast, are almost totally dependent on imported inputs for their raw materials (metal rods, metal sheets, metal discs, etc.). Few of these raw materials are made in Sudan (Greater Khartoum). There are examples of substituting second-hand material for new material, for instance doors made out of motor oil barrels, but these play only a marginal role. The share of second-hand materials is not more than 5% of total raw material consumption. The analyzed units import 82.3% of their raw materials. The percentage is even higher for the non-electric units, because 9 (82%) of them practice only car repair, which is totally import dependent.

According to raw material source, there are four kinds of carpentry products:

---

[133] Darfur region

1. Traditionally there were only two kinds of furniture used: beds (angareb) and stools (banbar) made of local tree branches and rope of local plants. This kind of furniture is produced in the villages, although the traditional beds are widely used in Nyala. Only one producer of angareb and banbar was identified in Nyala.
2. The first products of modern carpentry were based completely on the wood locally available, only the non-wood ingredients (nails, screws, wire mesh, paint, glue etc.) had to be imported. These products have an import content of less than 30%. However, due to the declining availability of local wood and to the sophistication of tastes implying a rising import content, this kind of products is no longer of much importance.
3. Most furniture is made mostly - if not totally - of imported wood, coming either from neighbouring Central Africa (white wood) or from overseas via Port Sudan and Greater Khartoum. These products have an import content of 60-100%.
4. A few workshops utilize mainly second-hand material (mostly packing material like tea boxes) to build very simple, but low-cost products (one in the sample). These products have an import content of less than 30%.

The third product group is predominant, so that the total import intensity of carpentry is higher than 60%. A detailed study of 7 workshops arrived at an average import intensity of 67.6%. The import intensity is significantly higher for the electric units, because the first and fourth product group are only produced by non-electric workshops, and the second product group is concentrated on non-electric workshops.

These results defeat the belief in a locally-based SI. Instead, a dichotomy appears between traditional locally-based SI on the one hand and heavily import-dependent SI on the other hand.

5.7 Production for low-income markets

One main deficiency of African industrialization is its direction towards luxury goods, bypassing the needs of the broad population. In this way it strengthens structures of inequality. One of the objectives of SAP reform is to direct industrial activities to a mass production of wage goods.

It is widely believed that SI produce predominantly inexpensive consumption goods (tending to be of lower quality) for the low-income population groups[134].

---
[134] c.f. Oshima (1971: 178), Weeks (1975: 8), Steel (1977: 18), Nihan and Jourdain (1978), Sethuraman (1981d), Amedon (1982: 204), Richardson (1984: 21), Schneider (1986: 111), Chuta

Furthermore, it is suggested that production for low-income markets goes together with employment intensity, reliance on local resources, and low import intensity[135]. For this reason, however, high inequalities have also to be regarded as demand constraints for SI[136].
The propositon implies that:
1. A large share of SI production is directed to the demand of low-income groups (larger than that of LI).
2. A large share of the expenditure of low-income groups is directed to SI products. In contrast LI produces predominantly for high-income groups.

The evidence on Africa is very sketchy. An ILO/JASPA study estimates that 75% of value added in the informal SI is concentrated on the basic needs (food, clothing, housing)[137]. Foreign demand for SI products is relatively small[138].

Production for low-income markets: Sudan

Several micro-level studies claim that SI is directed towards the needs of the lower-income groups[139]. However, most studies do neither address the markets SI operates on and competes with other products[140] nor the expenditure structure of lower-income households by product origin. Thus, the extent of SI production for lower-income markets is a question of estimation.
The statistics on consumption structure differentiates merely between very broad product groups, which do not allow to distinguish between goods produced by SI and LI. Nevertheless, the figures allow some conclusions. A comparison between the years 1955/56-1983/84 shows that the predominance of *food & beverages* in the consumption budget has not declined. On the contrary, the share of expenditures on this product group increased over time from 59.4% to 64.5% resp.[141]. Other expenditures are dwarfed by this. The expenditures on *fuel, light & water* and on *clothing & footwear* declined from 11.3% to 6.1% and from 8.9% to 4.3% resp. On the other hand, expenditures on housing increased from 7.6% to 10.8%. Other expenditure groups characteristic of a rising standard of living actually decreased

---

and Liedholm (1984: 306) with respect to rural SI. For Schneider-Barthold (1984a: 15) this is the most important argument for promotion of all.
135 First claimed by the ILO (1970); cf. Weeks (1975: 8), Steel (1977: 18), Schneider-Barthold (1984a: 27), King and Byerlee (1978: 197); King and Byerlee report, that in Sierra Leone rural low-income households have a strong inclination to consume goods and services of rural SI - but not of urban industries.
136 cf. Chapter 6.8.
137 cf. ILO and JASPA (1985: 16)
138 cf. Liedholm and Mead (1986: 315), Liedholm and Mead (1987: 59-60)
139 e.g. Jenkins (1981), Oesterdiekhoff (1984)
140 cf. chapter 6.8. on this
141 cf. Harvie and Kleve (1959: 40), DoS (1977, 1979, 1987)

slightly: expenditures on *furniture, furnishing, household equipment & operations* and on *recreation, entertainment & education* from 4.5% to 3.4% and from 1.1% to 0.8% resp.
This suggests that the argument about inferior goods produced by SI loosing markets because of rising incomes is not relevant for Sudan at the present time and points to the importance of production directed at the basic needs. Formulated differently, it points to the severe limitations of industries not directed at these needs.
The most recent household expenditure survey differentiating by income group gives the following picture (see Table 5.7.1.):

Table 5.7.1. Detailed consumption structure (by income group, urban/rural, selected groups, in %) 1978-80

items	urban <500	urban 1000-1999	urban >3000	rural <500	rural 1000-1999	rural >3000
food, beverages, tobacco	64.6	58.8	44.4	71.5	65.2	60.1
clothing & footwear	4.7	4.2	4.4	6.1	7.2	7.0
housing	8.7	11.3	24.8	7.4	6.8	5.3
fuel, power, water	8.8	6.8	4.7	4.6	5.1	5.6
furnit.,household equipm.,etc.	4.6	5.6	7.1	6.7	8.9	9.3
medical care & health	5.8	7.8	6.9	2.4	3.6	5.0
transport & comm.	2.1	3.5	5.4	0.8	1.9	6.1
recr.,entert.,educ.	0.7	2.0	2.3	0.6	1.2	1.6
total C (per capita, LS)	113.36	207.83	363.37	84.42	129.15	203.52

Source: MFEP (1984)

One point is conspicuous: the similarity of urban consumption structures on the one hand and rural consumption structures on the other hand, despite large income differences.
The relative high urban expenditures on housing point to some potential of industrial activity - which is lacking in rural areas. But the expenditures on other goods with a potential for domestic production - *clothing & footwear, furniture, furnishings, household equipment & operations, recreation, entertainment & education* - remain minor categories even for high income groups.
How do the products of the Sudanese industry correspond to its population's needs? Based on a detailed analysis of consumption structure, Oesterdiekhoff classified industrial products according to their "basic needs" or "luxury" character[142].
On the basis of the data presented above and many discussions with representatives of different income groups a reformulation of Oesterdiekhoff's catego-

---

142 cf. Oesterdiekhoff (1979: 99)

rization is attempted here. In the light of the development of the last decade, some of the products classified as "luxury goods" are now so widely used that they have to be regarded as wage goods. Furthermore, a dichotomous model is no longer adequate to describe the different consumption structures in rural and urban areas. To account for this, a three-tier classification of consumption goods is applied here. A third category is introduced including those products which are now wage goods in urban areas, but hardly consumed in rural areas. Luxury goods (see Table 5.7.2.) here are understood as those goods which play no role for the reproduction of the population majority, because they are either only consumed by a small minority of the population or because they are non-essentials. The limits of these categories are, however, fluid.

Table 5.7.2. Luxury goods, urban wage goods, and mass consumption goods

luxury goods:	slaughtering and preparation of meat
	dairy products incl. ice cream
	canning & preserv. of fruits & vegetables
	canning & preserv. of fish & fish products
	sugar confectionary, cocoa & choc. products
	food industry not elsewhere classified
	prepared animal food
	distilled alcoholic drinks
	soft & carbon drinks
	tobacco, cigar & cigarette
	blankets, bed sheets & towels
	knitting, needle works, socks & stockings
	ready made apparel excl. footwear
	leather & substitute products excl. footwear
	footwear excl. plastic & rubber
	wood products incl. furniture
	other industries not elsewhere classified
urban wage goods:	grain & mill products
	bakery, macaroni & noodle products
	printing & publishing
mass consumption goods:	vegetable & animal oils & fats
	sugar industry & refinery
	drugs & medicines
	soap, cleaners & toilet products incl. perfume

According to this classification, the domestic production of consumer goods can be classified as follows:

Table 5.7.3. Classification of consumer goods 1981/82 (% shares in gross value added)

	all	SI	LI
luxury consumption goods	13.6	9.2	18.7
urban wage goods	59.3	88.9	25.0
mass consumption goods	27.1	1.9	56.3

computed from: UNIDO (1986)

While a majority of branches producing consumer goods fabricates luxury goods (17 out of 24), only a minority of production is taking place in these fields (13.6% of value added). However, this does not mean that the other industries produce for all lower-income population groups. Almost 3/5 of production are destined to the urban people. Wheat bread has replaced the traditional food (sorghum and millet) and is now consumed widely by urban people - but not by the people living in the rural areas.

As far as the activity of SI vs. LI is concerned, the following picture emerges: SI appears to be much less active in luxury goods production - only half of the resp. category of LI. But SI production is highly concentrated on the production of urban wage goods, and less than 2% produce mass consumption goods. The LI, on the other hand, concentrate over half of their production on this field.

Thus, according to the industrial statistics, a different picture of SI appears: As expected, they are less active in luxury production, but do not concentrate on products consumed by lower income groups, but rather on urban people.

This characterization of SI, however, is not perfect, because many categories of SI are not included in the statistics. Micro-level studies tend to conclude that the informal and traditional SI branches not included in the statistics are more directed towards the needs of the lower income people[143].

Production for low-income markets: Nyala

Blacksmiths produce predominantly agricultural hand tools. Besides that they make other production hand tools (trowel, wedge, hammer, plier, pincer, etc.), knifes, scissors, pestles and other goods. They are generally inexpensive goods. The only exception is the plough (see Table 5.7.4.).

Table 5.7.4. Blacksmith products in Nyala, 1988 (LS)

product	price
hoe	5-15
sickle	3-30
pestle	15
knife	5-50
ax	10-25
wedge	5-20
trowel	10
plough	150-250

own survey; this list serves to illustrate products and prices of blacksmiths with examples of most important products. It is not comprehensive.

---

143 e.g. Jenkins (1981), Oesterdiekhoff (1984)

The non-agricultural tools are competing with imported goods which are generally much more expensive but also more durable. They are directed at low-income population groups who prefer them because of their low price. The agricultural hand tools, on the other hand, do not face any competition from imports. The hand tools are directed at the low-income small peasants, while the ploughs aim at higher income peasants who own draught animals and are rich enough to afford ploughs. Thus they have a limited market. More than half of the interviewed blacksmiths (54%) produce ploughs, but the share of ploughs in total blacksmith production is less than 35%.

The *tinsmith* products are generally directed at low-income population groups. The charcoal stove, however, their most important product, is found in virtually every household. Even those enjoying the privilege of being connected to the electric mains need them as a substitute in case of electric stoppages, which occur frequently.

Table 5.7.5. Tinsmith products in Nyala, 1988 (LS)

product	raw materials[144]	prices
stove	second-hand	15-75
	new/second-hand	25-120
metal suitcase	second-hand	20-75
	new	60-150
lamp	second-hand	2-5
coffee-pot	second-hand	5-7
small table	second-hand	20
wash basin	second-hand	40
jug	second-hand	20
window	second-hand	50-125
door	second-hand	350

Source: own survey; this list illustrates products and prices of tinsmiths - it is not comprehensive.

Other products are low-cost low-quality substitutes for imports (suitcase, shovel, lamp), but more importantly for products of local carpentry and metal workshops (table, door, window). None of the tinsmith products is directed at higher-income markets.

Metal workshops have a different clientele. They concentrate on modern furniture, windows and doors. They satisfy new, urban and - in relation to the prevailing income levels - "luxury" wants (see Table 5.7.6.).

Rural society did not know any furniture except traditional beds and stools. For the poor majority, in rural areas as well as in Nyala the situation did not change much until now. From the modern furniture, only chairs are spread to some degree. Most metal workshops confine themselves to the production of consumption goods. Very

---

[144] This refers to the basic material, metal. Also products categorized as "second-hand" here have an import content (nails, paint etc.)

few metal workshops also produce capital goods. Examples are tobacco mills and decortication machines. A major activity of metal workshops is car repair. 90 workshops (58%) even restrict their activity to this. As far as they maintain lorries - being the main life-line to the outer world - they have a vital function for the whole population, but as far as they serve other private cars, this can be clearly categorized as a "luxury" want.

Table 5.7.6. Metal workshop products Nyala

product	prices
chair	75-250
bed	300-1000
table	150-270
cupboard	1000-2000
window	400-500
door	650-2500

Source: own survey; an illustrative selection

As argued above, modern furniture has to be categorized as "luxury" goods. This is all the more true for carpentry products, which are more expensive than their metal counterparts (see Table 5.7.7.). There is, however, a number of carpentry workshops which serve the low-income market with products made out of second-hand material.

Table 5.7.7. Carpentry products

product	raw material	prices
traditional bed	local	25-70
traditional stool	local	7-10
bed	local/imported	350-750
arm chair	local/imported	250-350
side-board	local/imported	750-1000
cupboard	local/imported	350-3000
table	local/imported	450-3500
	second-hand	50
cigarette box	second-hand	50

Source: own survey; an illustrative selection

The conclusion is that the more traditional SI branches (blacksmiths, tinsmiths) tend to serve low-income groups, while the more modern SI branches (metal workshops, carpentry) serve the high-income groups. In terms of production and employment, the latter are by far more important. Thus, the presumption that SI as a whole serves low-income groups has to be denied in the case of Nyala city.

5.8 Wide geographical dispersion

One of the results of the economic distortions of development in Africa are grave regional inequalities - inequalities between regions and between urban and rural areas (the "urban bias"[145]). The industrialization process has its share in this development: LI is concentrated in a few urban centres. Rural areas - including medium- and small towns - and industries are neglected, accompanied by high and increasing income inequalities. Decentralization of industry can help to redress this bias[146].

It is hypothesized that SI is more geographically dispersed and can thus help to redress the geographical inequalities - in terms of supply with industrial goods, employment and income generation. Furthermore, rural industries can make use of labour during the agricultural slack season - thus the classical problem of competition between agriculture and industry for labour does not occur[147].

In most developing countries the vast majority of SI is located in rural areas, the employment in rural SI even seems to exceed that of all urban industries[148].

Wide geographical dispersion: Sudan

Sudan's industry is heavily concentrated on the "Three Towns" (Khartoum, Omdurman, Khartoum-North). This is due to several inter-related factors:
- a large market (in terms of population and income);
- the centralization of the government machinery and of political power in general;
- better infrastructure;
- industries attract new industries[149].

Although virtually all development plans emphasize the need for regional development, not much progress was made in this respect.
How did SI and LI compare in terms of regional distribution? Table 5.8.1. shows the regional distribution of SI, LI and handicrafts.

---

145 cf. Lipton (1977)
146 cf. Marsden (1970), Braun (1981)
147 The first phase of industrialization generally consisted of rapid growth of rural industries - only in the second phase a major shift to urban areas took place (cf. Mendels 1972).
148 Liedholm and Mead (1987); Oshima (1971: 167) on Asia
149 cf. El Bushra (1966); for an elaborate analysis of the regional development of Sudan's industry see Mohamed Ali (1980)

Table 5.8.1. Regional distribution of SI, LI and handicrafts (HC) (% of gross output)

	1955/56	1970/71				1981/82		
	all	all	SI	LI	HC	all	SI	LI
Khartoum	57.6	65.3	39.1	66.1	41.5	39.2	30.4	43.8
Central Region	11.6	16.4	28.7	16.1	24.4	36.3	37.8	35.6
Northern Region	-	2.8	9.0	2.6	7.8	2.7	4.3	1.8
Eastern Region	-	12.4	10.8	12.7	10.2	15.7	15.8	15.7
Kordofan	29.o	2.4	8.6	1.7	11.6	3.8	7.0	2.2
Darfur	-	0.3	3.8	0.2	4.6	1.8	4.5	0.4
Southern Region	1.8	0.4	-	0.4	-	0.4	0.2	0.5

Sources: 1955/56: Harvie and Kleve (1959); 1970/71: Nimeiri (1976b) and DoS (1976); 1981/82: UNIDO (1986). "All" stands for SI and LI. Handicrafts are only represented in 1970/71 - and only for the Northern regions. For 1955/56 Khartoum, Northern and Eastern Regions are counted together, as well as Kordofan and Darfur. In 1970/71 in the South SI is not covered, and only LI in Bahr al Ghazal is represented. In 1981/82 in the South only Equatoria is covered.

The table shows an increasing concentration of industries on the *Three Towns* (Khartoum) between 1955/56 and 1970/71. During the 1970s some deconcentration took place, but this was almost exclusively to the benefit of the Central Region. Only the Eastern Region increased its share in industries, all the other regions had relatively more industry at the time of independence. According to the table SI is not concentrated to the degree of LI. The best performance with respect to regional distribution has handicrafts (only data for 1970/71 are available). These informations, however, underestimate the differences between LI and SI. Clearly SI and especially handicrafts are underestimated in rural areas. It is, for example, not credible that in the Southern Region only 0.5% of output is produced, and LI is more important than SI. This means that the significantly higher concentration on Khartoum of LI as compared with SI and handicrafts in all years as shown in Table 5.8.1. is in fact more pronounced.

5.9 Training ground for entrepreneurs

It is widely believed that a class of entrepreneurs is vital to promote development. It is debatable if there is a "lack of entrepreneurship" in developing countries[150] as presumed by socio-psychological modernization theorists. However, the non-existence of a class of industrial entrepreneurs in developing countries is less debatable. It is hypothesized by many that in view of their great number and the use of appropriate technologies SI units can be a seed-bed, training ground and outlet for entrepreneurs[151]. This assumption rests on two hypotheses:

---
150 see below Ch. 6.1.
151 cf. World Bank (1978), Page and Steel (1984: 22)

1. There are low entry barriers for SI. The discussion centres on capital, but other barriers are important as well: knowledge, training. Thus the hypothesis can be operationalized as: Little capital, little previous knowledge, little education and training are necessary to enter SI[152]. As a proxy for low entry barriers the age of entrepreneurs has been taken as well[153].
   The evidence is, however, mixed and the hypothesis of low entry barriers has been challenged by many[154].
2. A related hypothesis behind the concept of SI as a training ground for entrepreneurs is the view of SI as a transitory stage in an upward mobility of agriculturalists to modern sector entrepreneurs or wage earners[155]. According to this proposition, a large part of SI entrepreneurs must come from agriculture and must be on the way to the modern formal sector.

The first issue can be analyzed by information on the job history of the entrepreneurs. The second issue can only be analyzed indirectly, by a discussion on future plans of entrepreneurs. Indirect inferences can also be drawn from enterprise histories (growth, change in technology, change in product range).
The evidence, however, challenges this view. First, studies show that some SI entrepreneurs are former modern sector employees. Actually, a related hypothesis can be formulated that SI can be an outlet for former government officials being dismissed in the course of structural adjustment[156]. Second, studies show that many have come to stay in the SI sector, i.e. it is not as transitory as believed[157].

Training ground for entrepreneurs: Sudan

No nation-wide evaluations of entry barriers and of job histories exist but the following picture emerges from the various micro-level studies: In terms of initial capital, wide variations exist by branch and size of SI. A recent study (1987) in Khartoum finds, for instance, initial investments ranging from LS 10 (palm leaves production) to LS 30,000 (bakery)[158]. However, the opinion prevails to regard this

---

152 cf. ILO (1972), Sethuraman (1976)
153 cf. Bienefeld (1975b), House (1984), Hugon (1990)
154 cf. Bienefeld (1975b), King (1975), Breman (1976), Schmitz (1982b), House (1984), Richardson (1984), Wohlmuth (1990b). The argument is supported e.g. by Sethuraman (1981c: 191), Hugon (1982: 35), idem (1990).
155 The "urban traditional sector" in the models of Todaro (1969) and Harris and Todaro (1970)
156 Wohlmuth (1989a: 11) claims that the absorption capacity of the informal sector in this respect is limited.
157 cf. Bienefeld (1975b), Richardson (1984)
158 BCHLI (1987); cf. also Miro et al. (1986) and Seisi Mohamed and Fadlalla (1989) on the high variations.

entry barrier as low and does not consider it as a barrier preventing the growth of the majority of SI activities[159].
Also education appears not to be regarded as a barrier[160]. It is found that other skills are more important to start a business[161]. Higher education is regarded by some as a result of business success, rather than its cause[162]. Furthermore, a great percentage of highly educated people in some activities is interpreted by a lack of appropriate employment rather than by any requirement for or advantage of higher education concerning the SI business[163]. Young age of entrepreneurs is also cited as a sign for low barriers of entry[164].
In conclusion, one can say that first, there are high variations with respect to necessary initial capital, but in most activities this is not a major obstacle for the growth of the sector as such. Second, formal education seems not to be a requirement for success nor to be related to success.

Training ground for entrepreneurs: Nyala

The evidence on entry barriers for SI in Nyala shows significant differences between the branches (see Table 5.9.1.).

Table 5.9.1. Initial investments on tools and machinery in SI in Nyala (LS)

industry	average	range
blacksmiths	469	327-969
tinsmiths	125	30-360
metal workshops	1765	70-6500
electric	2456	100-6500
non-electric	382	70-1220
carpentry	1428	20-13300
electric	3818	150-13300
non-electric	548	20-1900
total	1233	20-13300

Source: own survey

In the *blacksmith* trade the necessary initial investments are quite uniform. The average is LS 469 (investment on tools). This sum can be covered by own or family savings. It is small in itself, but besides this, it does not have to be invested all at

---
159 cf. Bakhit Idris (1979), Babiker (1982), Mohamed Osman et al.(1985), Howard (1988: 81), Mohamed Nur (1988)
160 cf. Jenkins (1981), Miro et al.(1986), Gumaa et al. (1987: 93), Isehaq and Adam Mohamed (n.d.)
161 cf. Mohamed Nur (1988: 36), Mohamed Osman et al. (1985)
162 cf. Ali El-Dawi (1972) in a study on businessmen in El Obeid
163 cf. Anand and Nur (1984: 25)
164 cf. Jenkins (1981), Bilal (1985: 18), Miro et al. (1986: 30), Howard (1988: 81)

the same time, but as a rule is acquired one by one during the apprenticeship. Thus capital cannot be considered an entry barrier.

For *tinsmithing* the initial investment is even smaller. Ranging between LS 30 and LS 360, the average is only LS 125. This sum can easily be covered by own or family savings.

The picture is different for the modern industries. The *metal workshops* need an initial investment of LS 1765 on an average. This is due to the electric metal workshops which need LS 2456 on an average. But also this comparatively high sum is qualified by the fact that the tools are normally acquired one by one over several years of work as apprentice and later as worker in other workshops. The non-electric metal workshops need on an average only LS 382, a sum even lower than blacksmiths. However, capital is less an entry barrier for blacksmiths because their capital is self-produced. As discussed above (see Chapter 5.3.2.), metal workshops were also exclusively financed by own and/or family savings.

The capital entry barrier is high also for *carpentry*: LS 1428 on an average. For electric and non-electric carpentry workshops the figures are LS 3818 and LS 548 resp. But even the comparatively high capital requirements of carpentry (as far as electric workshops are concerned) could be financed by own and family savings, with only one exception (out of seven).

Initial capital could be a barrier, if at all, for the two industry branches working with electric machines, being more than eight times as high than their non-electric counterparts (see Table 5.9.1.). In all the trades the figures imply an upward bias because most of the entrepreneurs accumulate their tools and machines over the time they are learning their trade in other workshops, i.e. they do not have to have the amount of initial capital available at one time. Besides this, the two electric industries practice a strategy of "starting small and growing big" if capital is a constraint. 86% of the electric metal workshops had more machines at the time of the survey than when they started their business. Almost one third started as non-electric units. In contrast less than half of the non-electric workshops acquired more tools over a period of time.

Like in the metal workshops, most electric carpentry workshops - with the exception of only one - started small and increased machinery over a period of time financed out of profits. Almost half started as non-electric workshops. From the non-electric carpentry workshops only a little more than half increased the stock of tools over time.

In summary, one can say that capital does not constitute an entry barrier for the analysed SI branches in Nyala. For most activities the capital requirements are small, and the industries working with electric machines start with a small investment making the larger investments later, financed by profits. A strategy to

start on a big scale in electric industries is to work abroad. Five (12%) of the entrepreneurs followed this strategy.
Other possible entry barriers are education and training. *Blacksmiths* are all trained on the job and have a low formal educational profile. Almost half (46%) of the analyzed entrepreneurs have no formal education at all, 31% passed the traditional Koran school (khalwa), and 15% joined the government school for 3 years (see Table 5.9.2.).

Table 5.9.2. Educational profile of SI entrepreneurs in Nyala (type of formal education)

industry	no education	khalwa	primary school	secondary school	university
blacksmiths	6	5	2	-	-
tinsmiths	2	3	4	1	1
metal workshops	3	4	18	8	-
electric	-	1	14	7	-
non-electric	3	3	4	1	-
carpentry	-	7	13	5	1
electric	-	1	1	4	1
non-electric	-	6	12	1	-
total	11	19	37	14	2

Source: own survey

The analyzed *tinsmiths* are also all trained on the job. Two had no formal education, two passed *khalwa*, and 6 joined the government school, for 3-11 years, one of them is a university graduate. For these two traditional trades neither education nor training can be considered as an entry constraint.
In the modern SI branches, formal education and training play a greater role. From the *metal workshop* entrepreneurs only three have no formal education, three passed *khalwa*, and the rest passed government schools between 2 and 12 years, with an average of 6 years. Six entrepreneurs (18%) passed some form of formal training, mostly short-term courses. At the other extreme, three entrepreneurs had not any training before starting their enterprise, and the rest was trained on the job before.
From the *carpentry workshop* owners, there is not one without any formal education, seven (27%) passed *khalwa*, the rest government school, between 4 and 12 years, with an average of 6.3 years. One is a university graduate. Three (11.5%) enjoyed some formal training, only one of them a real long-term training (3 years). For modern SI, a higher level of schooling indicates an entry barrier to some degree, but training plays such a minor role, that it cannot be considered as such.
A proxy for low entry barriers is the age of entrepreneurs at the time of starting their enterprise (see Table 5.9.3.).
For the traditional industries of blacksmithing and tinsmithing the age figures are not very meaningful, because these trades are carried out at a very young age,

either by helping the father (or other relatives) or by working on their own account. But there can be no clear distinction between these two, thus it is a question open to interpretation when a blacksmith or a tinsmith considers himself as an "own unit" or when as part of a larger unit. In any case, it is clear that there is not a significant entry barrier in terms of capital, formal education, training or otherwise in these crafts. The age figures are more meaningful for the other two industries, to whom it is more clearly recognizable what is the establishment of an industrial unit. On an average, for these the ages are 2-3 years higher. But this cannot be taken as a significant difference. First, the figures have some upward bias because some of the entrepreneurs had workshops before in other towns or at home - the ages refer to the present workshops. Second, higher age of some reflects the fact that they come from other professions. The age figures conform with the concept of low entry barriers.

Table 5.9.3. Age of entrepreneurs at the time of starting their enterprise (years)

industry	average	range
blacksmiths	24.8	8-48
tinsmiths	21.3	11-41
metal workshops	26.2	17-54
electric	25.8	23-36
non-electric	26.9	17-54
carpentry	27.2	14-44
electric	27.3	14-44
non-electric	27.2	15-37
total	25.6	8-54

Source: own survey

The view of SI as a training ground for entrepreneurs views them as a transitory stage in an upward mobility of agriculturalists to modern sector entrepreneurs or wage earners. The origin of entrepreneurs can be illuminated by a look at their *job history* as well as their *father's profession* (see Table 5.9.4.). Their future way can be illuminated by a view on their enterprises' development and on their future plans.
Of the blacksmiths and tinsmiths very few had any other profession, while of metal and carpentry workshops about one fourth did. But only one out of all (1.2%) has been a farmer. Those previous professions include very different kinds, but they do not support the hypothesis of a social upward movement: More than half have been skilled employees in the formal sector, one in another SI, two have been merchants, and only four were unskilled workers (fitting in the picture of upward movement). These figures indicate changing perceptions of the benefit to work in the formal and informal sectors - the SI sector already plays a role in the process of privatisation, which is a part of SAP.

Table 5.9.4. Professional career and social origin of SI entrepreneurs (previous occupation, father's occupation)

industry	previous occupation			father's occupation		
	same	farmer	other	same	farmer	other
blacksmiths	11	-	2	10	1	2
tinsmiths	10	-	1	-	6	5
metal workshops	25	-	8	1	15	17
electric	16	-	6	1	9	12
non-electric	9	-	2	-	6	5
carpentry	18	1	7	2	12	12
electric	6	-	1	1	3	3
non-electric	12	1	6	1	9	9
total	64	1	18	13	34	36

Source: own survey

The picture changes with regard to the *father's occupations*. 41% were farmers or nomads, but even more (43%) had other occupations. These include very different kinds: unskilled worker (36%), police/army (22%), SI (17%), merchant (14%), skilled worker (8%), and others. The fact that only 16% had the same profession reflects the young age of SI in general. The only exception is blacksmithing. Thus the origin of SI entrepreneurs does not well reflect the transition model (agriculture-modern sector).

The other side of the model is the question where the SI entrepreneurs are destined to move in the future. Of course this is not directly measureable by data on existing SI units, but inferences can be drawn from the *past development of the enterprises* and the *future plans* of the entrepreneurs.

In terms of tools and workers, the *blacksmith* units do not show any steady growth pattern, but a stagnating pattern. Blacksmith units normally have two workers and may expand temporarily if there is a need. Only one blacksmith plans to expand his business to a metal workshop, the rest is happy to continue as before. Blacksmiths do not fit into the picture of a transitional phase. Of the *tinsmiths*, two show growth in terms of machinery, three in terms of employees, and one a decline in this regard. Only one considers to expand his business, eight plan to continue on the present level, and two would like to change to other, unrelated activities. Tinsmithing presents itself as a receiving point of agricultural people, to some degree (one unit) also for a reversed movement from the modern sector to the informal sector, but not as an avenue for further upward movement.

As mentioned above, most *metal workshops* expanded in terms of machinery (73%). Of the electric metal workshops, 16 (84%) expanded in terms of workers, of the non-electric a little more than half expanded, while three declined in this respect. Of the first group, 13 (59%) plan to continue on present scale, while 8 plan to expand and/or diversify their activities, and only one contemplates to change to another activity (trade). Thus the sector seems to present itself not as something transitional, but rather as a place to stay.

In *carpentry*, at the upper margin of the analysed SI branches, this picture is even more clear. 16 workshops (62%) expanded in terms of machinery, 14 (54%) in terms of employment, two declined in this respect. 17 (65%) plan to expand, while the rest plans to continue on the present scale - no one intends to leave the sector for another activity.

It can be concluded that neither capital nor education constitute an entry barrier to the analysed SI branches in Nyala.

5.10 Ability to innovate and flexibility

It is hypothesized that SI's ability to innovate and its flexibility are central distinct advantages, allowing them not only to survive, but also making them functional for structural adjustment processes. It is argued that these characteristics, rooted in their small size, close contact to clients, prevalence of family work, small fixed costs and a combination of diverse income sources, allow them to react quickly to market changes and market chances[165] - qualities which are often absent from LI[166]. There is, however, an argument that the need to remain flexible in a risky environment prevents enterprise growth and results in a spread of investments on small firms rather than the accumulation of capital in existing units[167]. For this reason, it is suggested that SI may be "unlikely to be the foundation of capitalist development"[168].

The above-mentioned argument runs counter to traditional beliefs that SI is ill-disposed for innovation because of "traditional social structures", risk avoidance[169] and that LI would be in a better position to innovate as with respect to the requirements of innovation in developing countries (learning about, choosing, importing, absorbing, and modifying foreign technology) LI would have considerable advantages[170].

Inferences about the ability to innovate can be drawn from an analysis of changes in product structure and range, technology, and inputs. Inferences on flexibility can be drawn from analyses of income sources, markets they operate on, character of products (are they varied and demand-adapted?), kind of technology (do they have

---
165 cf. Lipton (1980), Schmitz (1982b), Berry (1985), Elwert (1985), Cortes et al. (1987), Escher (1988), McCormick (1988), Schmitz (1989)
166 cf. King (1974: 28)
167 cf. Chapter 6.2.
168 McCormick (1988: 173)
169 cf. ILO (1972: 505)
170 cf. Little et al. (1987: 4)

a multi-purpose technology?), and worker qualifications (are they wide-spread or is there strict division of labour?).
The evidence is sketchy; no generalization is possible.

Ability to innovate and flexibility: Sudan

The "traditional" view on SI as being inimical to innovation and/or unable to innovate, is widely spread among government officials, development experts[171] and academics. Many of the micro-level studies, on the other hand, generally emphasize just these points as distinct advantages of SI. However, the empirical bases to decide about the extent of ability to innovate and flexibility[172] are less studied.

Ability to innovate and flexibility: Nyala

Innovation activities differ by industry branch. The *blacksmithing* products have been inherited since a long time and little change has taken place since. The only addition to the product range is the animal drawn plough, the use of which has spread from Egypt. The spreading of this innovation is limited by the low purchasing power of the agricultural population - most farmers are just too poor to afford the animals they would need. Most blacksmiths do produce ploughs, which shows that there is no antagonism against innovations. The reason why they don't produce more, is due to the demand conditions. The blacksmiths did not change their technology for a long time, which is probably due to the fact that the adapted technology is quite appropriate and sufficient for their purpose. In the past they made their own iron out of local ore, but this practice seems to have faded out completely - ore has been substituted by scrap metal. The stagnation of the blacksmith trade in terms of technological change and product differentiation is a result of the stagnation of agriculture. Local development projects (Western Savannah Development Corporation, Jebel Marra Rural Development Project) have experimented for some years with introduction of improved animal ploughs by delivering sufficient amounts of suitable raw materials and training blacksmiths in production. Blacksmiths have proven to be able and willing to produce improved goods. The experience[173] confirms the assessment above, i.e. that the

---

171 cf. Niazi (1987: 53) claiming that in Darfur cultivation is mostly done by hand because better implements are not available.
172 cf. Howard (1988), Streck (1982b) stressing the flexibility of SI entrepreneurs.
173 cf. WSDC (1988), JMRDP (1988)

constraints to technological improvement are the low demand from the side of the agricultural population, rather than the inability to produce new goods.

The *tinsmiths* did not change their product range and their technology during the last years, according to the statements of the interviewed entrepreneurs. However, they make a maximum use of different types of second-hand materials and most of their tools and other raw materials are also imported. This can be taken as an indicator of their openness for innovation.

The *metal workshops* have few changes in product structure as well. The only recorded change is the stop of production of decortication machines due to lack of demand - a negative product diversification. There are few examples of minor innovation, e.g. attempts to copy foreign furniture designs recognized in catalogues. The picture is also one of demand-led non-innovation. In the field of technological change, the diffusion of modern electric technology has been rapid and refutes the claim of disability to innovate.

In *carpentry*, the product structure is subject to rapid diffusion of western tastes through the Sudanese nationals working abroad, but also through media like the cinema - which is available in the city -, tv - which very few can afford - and catalogues of foreign carpentry styles. Also foreign advanced technologies are rapidly diffused, disproving any theory about "people inimical to innovation". For inputs, a far-reaching substitution of local raw materials by imported materials has taken place. The reasons behind this are the product changes due to import of foreign tastes and the ecological degradation which already led to the disappearance of many local tree species.

For SI in Nyala, in general, the evidence on ability to innovate can be summarized as follows: The existence of modern SI as carpentry and metal workshops can be taken as a proof of the ability and willingness of local entrepreneurs to innovate. With respect to the inputs, the rapid substitution of local raw materials by imports illustrates this. In the field of technology, a bimodal industrial structure came into being: on the one hand, the traditional industries (blacksmithing and tinsmithing) which operate on a very low technological level, and on the other hand, the modern industries (carpentry, metal workshops), which operate on a high level. There is a problem of a "missing middle", i.e. of intermediate or appropriate technologies.

The *flexibility* of SI can be measured by several indicators. One is the analysis of the *different income sources* of the SI entrepreneurs. This indicates their possibility to react to changes in external economic conditions by shifting their activity and in general to spread their risk. The most important other income source is, as expected, *agriculture*. However, the reliance on agriculture turned out to be much smaller than expected.

Among the *blacksmiths*, three (23%) of the interviewed entrepreneurs have no farm, the rest use their farm only for own consumption, i.e. they get no monetary income from them. All those who have a farm, nevertheless continue their blacksmithing work even during the rainy season. This is their primary source of income. Among the *tinsmiths*, almost half (45%) do not have a farm, as well as no other source of income at all. Of the rest, one half also produces farm goods for the market. Most continue work during the rainy season. One has income from trade and agriculture.

Of the *metal workshops*, more than half do not have a farm - 74% and 32% of the electric and non-electric workshops resp. Of those who do, almost all continue their industrial work throughout the year, their farms only provide for own consumption.

Of the electric carpentry workshops only one has a farm, among the non-electric 47% have. Out of these about one half also produces for the market. One of the carpenters is active in trade and agriculture, one works in the government service.

In summary, of all the interviewed entrepreneurs 53% do not have a farm, 39% have a subsistence farm (production exclusively for own consumption), i.e. the cash income from agriculture is negligible for the SI entrepreneurs. There is a tendency that the modern industry entrepreneurs rely least on agriculture, i.e. they rely more exclusively on their SI income, and so are less flexible in this respect. 93% of all continue work during the rainy season - contrary to all predictions -, for 96% the SI is their main income source.

Flexibility is gained if SI operates on *different markets*. In terms of the *place of sale*, most SI entrepreneurs (86%) sell exclusively in their workshop, in all trades. Only for two SI branches the percentages are lower than 80%: tinsmiths (64%), some of whom sell on the markets as well, and electric carpentry workshops, two of whom have show-rooms in the city centre.

Flexibility is also gained if SI sells to different *kinds of customers*: private clients, merchants, the government, other producing enterprises (see Table 5.10.1.).

Table 5.10.1. Customers of small industry in Nyala

industry	only private	private most important	merchant most important	also to government
blacksmiths	2	5	5	6
tinsmiths	6	-	5	-
metal workshops	13	18	1	20
electric	8	12	1	14
non-electric	5	6	-	6
carpentry	16	9	1	8
electric	2	5	-	5
non-electric	14	4	1	3
total	37	32	12	34

Source: own survey

Private clients are the main customers, virtually everybody sells to them. This category is almost identical with private consumption, because inter-industrial linkages are almost non-existent. The only instances of inter-industry linkages are one metal workshop having produced decortication and snuff mills and the blacksmiths producing wedges. About half of the blacksmiths also sell to the government (which resells ploughs to farmers), for 38% merchants are the most important customers. Merchants are most important for tinsmiths, for almost half of them they are the most important customers. In contrast, merchants are of no importance for the metal and the carpentry workshops. Of all the analyzed industrial units, 45% sell only to private customers, for another 39% they are the most important customers, and only for 14% merchants are most important. Those who depend on merchants are in danger of losing their independence and flexibility. This danger also exists for some of the tinsmiths and blacksmiths.

Another indicator of flexibility is the *geographical range* which SI enterprises supply. 12% of the SI enterprises are confined to Nyala, 61% to Darfur region. The modern industries (metal, carpentry) also reach beyond the region: 17% of them deliver also to Khartoum, 24% also export - this is mostly carpentry going to Central Africa.

An important feature of SI in Nyala is the predominance of *production on order*. Most of the production is not carried out in a continuous way for sale on the market, but on special demand by clients (see Table 5.10.2.).

Table 5.10.2. Production on order by small industries in Nyala (number of units producing on order)

industry	none at all	for the minor part	for the major part	exclusively
blacksmithing	1	10	2	-
tinsmithing	3	4	3	1
metal workshops	-	6	16	11
electric	-	6	14	2
non-electric	-	-	2	9
carpentry	-	6	12	8
electric	-	1	6	-
non-electric	-	5	6	8
total	4	26	33	20

Source: own survey

Production on order is an important feature of Nyala's SI. Only in blacksmithing and tinsmithing a few dispense with this kind of production. The majority of these trades produce "on order" only in limited amounts - 31% of the total of analyzed SI enterprises in Nyala. 40% produce on order for the major part of their production. These make up 48% of the metal workshops - 64% and 18% of the electric and non-electric resp. - and 63% of the carpentry workshops - 86% and 32% of the electric and non-electric resp. 24% produce exclusively on order. This category is of none or little importance in blacksmithing and tinsmithing, but it covers a great part of the enterprises in the other categories.

Production on order has different aspects from the development point of view. In most cases it is a result of cash shortage which forbids the entrepreneurs to buy big amounts of raw materials in advance and in many cases it results in frequent work stoppages. However, this mode of work also often reflects a varied production pattern and an adaptation to the wishes of the customer.

The kind of technologies utilized by SI in Nyala can broadly be described as *multi-purpose technologies* which are in the rule not specialized on the production of only one good, but are applied to all sorts of different production patterns. This helps to secure a high degree of flexibility.

The same is true for the *worker qualifications*. With very few exceptions every worker is capable to do most, if not all, of the different tasks, and the apprentices are trained in all these different fields. There is no strict division of labour.

5.11 Characteristics of small industries: a summary

The comparative analysis of the evidence with respect to SI on the macro- and micro-level from Sudan and Nyala resp. confirms some of the distinct advantages ascribed to SI. However, others are refuted. More importantly, the comparison of the data on SI on the national level and the Nyala field data show that the former do not represent more than a fraction of existing SI. This implies that many generally held judgments about SI are not any more tenable.

The data on employment generation are a case in point. While the official data on industry give a picture of LI predominance (though declining), the Nyala data indicate a reverse picture. Despite of the much more extensive character of industry, compared to other activities, industry remains small. With respect to labour intensity, the national statistics show much higher and rising figures (though not across the board) for SI. However, Nyala SI puts both of them into the shade.

The income data on the national level show a narrowing gap between LI and formal sector wages on the one hand and SI wages on the other hand. Profits are higher in SI (as well as traditional industry). In Nyala both wages and profits are high and variable.

The scarce data on capital saving and capital mobilization in Sudan tend to confirm the positive hypotheses. The Nyala experience shows a dichotomy between traditional and modern SI with respect to the kind of technology used: The former widely use self-produced and second-hand capital goods, while the latter rely almost completely on imported machinery. However, all of them save capital by self-training and rely almost exclusively on own finance.

The different character of SI and LI activities (with respect to products, technologies, input channels etc.) qualifies an efficiency comparison between the two. The Sudan data show not only higher capital efficiency, but also a trend towards higher labour productivity. Nyala data, as compared to both SI and LI, show lower labour productivity on the one hand and much higher capital productivity on the other hand.

The inter-economic linkages of SI and LI, as indicated by the statistics, are weak: both produce mainly consumer goods and appear to be weakly linked to either industry or agriculture. Nyala industry shows again a bimodal structure: While the traditional SI branches have strong backward and forward linkages, the modern SI branches tend to be strongly linked abroad (with respect to backward linkages) and consumer goods-oriented. As the latter category is much more important, this result refutes one of the alleged distinct advantages of SI.

Higher processing rates of SI point to a higher reliance on local resources. Nyala industry is characterized by a dichotomy: Traditional industries, on the one hand, use primarily machinery as well as raw materials of local origin; modern SI branches, on the other hand, rely mostly on imported (to a small degree other domestic) machinery and raw materials.

An analysis of the markets in which SI operates also destroys the picture of a uniform SI characterized by the above-mentioned distinct advantages: According to the statistics, SI concentrate on the production of urban wage goods, rather than general mass consumption goods - they do not belong to the consumption basket of most of the rural population. Nyala industries show a dichotomy between traditional SI oriented on the needs of the low-income population, while modern SI directs its production at the needs of the middle- and high-income population.

SI is indeed less geographically concentrated, especially if one considers the statistical bias towards the more visible large and urban industries.

SI qualifies itself as a training ground for entrepreneurs, if low entry barriers (capital, education) are taken as a criterion. However, the social background of SI entrepreneurs is too varied to regard the sector as a transitory stage in an upward movement from agriculture to the modern sector.

Modern SI is innovative. The low technological level and the limitation on the production of few products of the traditional industries was found to be due to a lack of demand rather than to any innate inability.

With respect to flexibility, the reliance on agriculture was found to be much smaller than expected, especially for the modern SI branches. For all entrepreneurs SI income is their main income, for most even the only income. While the dependence on traders for inputs is large, with respect to sale it is small.

6 Growth constraints of small industries

This chapter considers what the literature on SI has to say on the growth constraints of this sector, proceeding from the assumption that growth of SI can be considered desirable. Growth of SI has two dimensions: growth of enterprises and growth of the number of enterprises. Although both processes go together, their relation and its changes in the course of development is not well established. They depend on branch, technology, location. It is possible that growth occurs mainly through the second effect. Furthermore, on the micro-level, lack of growth of enterprises does not necessarily imply failure or lack of success. Small size may be an ideal size, and the enterprises may not wish to expand[1]. Thus, in contrast to most studies taking enterprise growth as a proxy for SI growth, in this study both dimensions are considered[2].

The term *growth* has to be defined further. In the literature, *evolutionary* and *involutionary* growth are distinguished. Evolutionary growth means an absorption of a larger labour force at higher income levels in contrast to an involutionary growth which implies that a larger labour force is absorbed at a stagnant or declining level of real income[3]. For a reform of SAP as outlined in chapter 1.3. the yardstick has to be evolutionary growth.

The structure of this chapter follows, to a large extent, the analysis of Schmitz (1982a). It classifies the constraints into "internal" and "external" constraints. While at a closer look this categorization becomes blurred, because of the interdependence of its elements, it was found to be useful to structure the topic.

Internal constraints are the constraints originating in the enterprises or the entrepreneurs. Broadly speaking, four kinds of internal constraints are focused on in the literature:
1. lack of entrepreneurship,
2. managerial deficiencies,
3. deficiencies in technical skills,
4. relation of business to family.

6.1 Lack of entrepreneurship

In the discussion on development of SI in developing countries an alleged "lack of entrepreneurship" plays a central role[4]. This is especially emphasized in the

---
1 cf. Stearns (1985: 38), Peattie (1984: 180)
2 e.g. Mars (1977), Schmitz (1982a)
3 cf. Weeks (1975); cf. also the concept of Geertz (1968), for whom an involutionary growth exists when the same amount of goods is produced with a higher number of people.
4 e.g. Gerschenkron (1952), Di Tullio (1974)

African context[5]. This perception was the reason (or justification) for politicians in many African countries to give a prominent role to public investments and foreign management[6].

Although lack of entrepreneurship began to be widely discussed in the context of the "modernization" theories in the 1960s and some believed that it had ceased to be a topic in the 1970s[7], it is still widely held as a presumption, at least for the African continent[8].

The concept of entrepreneurship is, unfortunately, very elusive. It is difficult to operationalize it, to translate it into measureable terms. Partly as a result of this, it has rather been assumed than proved. Many different definitions are in use and there are great differences in the importance attached to entrepreneurship and the judgement about its existence in developing countries. One of the reasons is that this concept is used by scholars of different disciplines (economy, sociology, psychology, political science).

The concept was first developed by economists in the discussion on the industrialization of the metropolitan countries. The first classical economist to define the entrepreneur as occupying a critical position in the economic development process was Jean Baptiste Say. However, the first major theoretical work emphasizing the role of the entrepreneur was Schumpeter (1935). This work, in turn, was greatly influenced by Weber (1934). Schumpeter's basic points were the inclusion of non-economic factors to explain economic behaviour and the importance of the individual's actions in the market.

Schumpeter defines development as the general enforcement of new combinations of the means of production[9]. He distinguishes five possibilities to achieve this:
1. production of new goods;
2. introduction of a new production method;
3. opening of a new market;
4. opening of a new source of raw materials;
5. implementation of a new organization.

For him entrepreneurs are those individuals whose function is to achieve the enforcement of these new combinations and who are the active elements in this process[10]. It is important to note that for Schumpeter the only characteristic of the entrepreneur is his innovating capacity. He explicitly excludes his functions of managing and risk-taking, by arguing that these can be bought on the market. In

---

5   cf. de Wilde (1971), Child and Kempe (1973), Dinwiddy (1974: 7), UNIDO (1988), World Bank (1989a: 135-147)
6   cf. Lawson and Kwei (1974: 9)
7   cf. Leff (1979)
8   e.g. de Wilde (1971), who regards it as the most critical constraint, and Little et al. (1987: 3), who claim that "an entrepreneurial class in Africa (is) virtually non-existent"
9   Schumpeter (1935: 100-101)
10   Schumpeter (1935:111)

his vision any society has only a small number of entrepreneurs, much smaller than the number of those, who have the material ability to innovate. Moreover, the entrepreneurs are often even those people who lack every material means to innovate[11]. For Schumpeter to be an entrepreneur is not a profession, but rather an activity. He defines the entrepreneur in the narrowest way. Most others include several other characteristics and functions.

After 1945 the concept of entrepreneurship began to be applied to the developing countries, which before had not at all been in the focus of attention of economists. Those who applied the entrepreneurship concept to developing countries generally saw them as "underdeveloped", "backward" societies, trying (and having to try) to catch up with the industrialized, Western countries. Thus they were not studied in their own right - it was believed that they were going to leave their present state rapidly[12]. The concept of entrepreneurship, as visualized by Schumpeter, was modified in one important aspect: potential entrepreneurs are not randomly distributed in societies, but their existence is dependent on special preconditions in the society. Now it was held that the developing countries are characterized by a lack of those conditions allowing entrepreneurship to emerge. Development was seen as primarily handicapped by cultural factors, which can only be changed in a slow, time-consuming process. Typical characteristics ascribed to the developing countries were *uneconomic behaviour, non-responsiveness to incentives, high propensities to consume, prestigious consumption, risk avoidance, lack of ideological imperatives, strong inertia*[13].

An insufficient supply of entrepreneurship, rather than a lack of capital or other production factors, was seen as the primary obstacle to development[14]. This claim has two dimensions: first, the number of existing entrepreneurs is low and second, the supply response to created economic opportunities will be weak, leading to a low absorption capacity for investment and development aid. Prominent studies with this orientation are Hirschman (1958), McClelland (1961), Hagen (1962), and Levine (1966)[15].

---

11 Schumpeter (1935: 119)
12 cf. Greenfield and Strickon (1981: 471)
13 Especially with regard to Africa there was a debate if conventional economic theory was appliable to this continent or not. Following the travel literature, an argument was made that economic behaviour in the "traditional" society of Africa contradicts conventional economic theory. The main argument was that rising incomes would lead to decreased, rather than increased labour - "backward-sloping curves of effort" (e.g. Boeke 1953, Moore 1965). The counter-argument holds that this behaviour can be explained by economic theory, i.e. that "man is economic in Africa" (e.g. Higgins 1955, Neumark 1958, Jones 1960, Berg 1961, Miracle and Fetter 1970). This discussion has not been very illuminating. While the first position was clearly ethnocentric and racist, the rationality assumption of the second position is purely theoretical (economistic) and bridges the fact that actually one does not know (Ellis 1981).
14 e.g. Stepanek (1960)
15 Hirschman regards the ability to make decisions as the scarce factor in development. He argues that in developing countries the individual ability to make entrepreneurial decisions is severely limited (cf. Papanek (1962). McClelland argues that entrepreneurship - and with it economic development - primarily depends on the strength of a particular psychological variable - the

As early as in the 1960s these views were criticized with regard to methodology, empirical evidence and transferability of a concept being developed for a society with very different characteristics[16]. McClelland's evidence supporting his theory does not stand up to a critical analysis[17]. The other theories are not measurable. None of them have achieved an acceptable level of empirical verification[18]. Many argue that the transfer of the Western idea as to what an entrepreneur has to be, is at the heart of the diagnosis "lack of entrepreneurship in developing countries"[19]. He is normally identified with a full-time businessman. However, this misses a large part of entrepreneurs because in developing countries many of them are engaged in informal and part-time business. In its original binary form (presence vs. absence of entrepreneurship) the argument is discredited.

The irrelevance of the Western concept of entrepreneurship does, however, not imply that entrepreneurship does not play a role. It can be argued that entrepreneurship is even more important in developing countries - because of prevalent market deficiencies (segmented markets, impeded factor mobility, lumpiness, pervasive administrative controls, input nonavailabilities)[20]. As a corollary it is argued that entrepreneurs in developing countries face many more difficulties than European entrepreneurs in the process of industrialization because of large discrepancies as compared to the existing up-to-date technology with its higher capital investment per worker, different labour skills and different organization of work as well as higher price and quality competition[21].

There is a need to re-define entrepreneurship for the present situation in developing countries. Firstly, the ability to innovate in the narrow sense is not a central requisition for entrepreneurs because of the availability of innovations in the industrial countries. The task is rather to adapt foreign innovations to local needs. Secondly, other abilities which are performed by the market in industrial countries have to be carried out by entrepreneurs in developing countries.

Different definitions of entrepreneurship in developing countries and in Africa have been put forward. Leibenstein (1968) sees as characteristics of the entrepreneur: gap-filling (to make up for market deficiencies), to connect different markets, to be an input-completer, to create or expand time-binding, input-transforming entities. Katzin (1964) defines the African entrepreneur as the

---

need for achievement. This in turn depends on child-rearing practices. Levine applies this concept to Nigeria. Hagen regards the supply of entrepreneurship as extremely inelastic and stagnating at a low level. Nurkse (1953) suggests that the social origin of entrepreneurship is largely the middle class, which is "virtually non-existent" in the developing countries (cf. also Papanek 1962: 48).

16 For a general critique of modernization theory in ideological, empirical and methodological respect cf. Tipps (1973).
17 cf. Kilby (1971: 17-18), Schatz (1971); for a general criticism see Redlich (1963)
18 cf. Kilby (1971: 17)
19 cf. Katzin (1964), Hart (1970), Kennedy (1980a), Elkan (1988)
20 cf. Leibenstein (1968), Kilby (1971), Leff (1979)
21 cf. Kilby (1971: 3)

"independent self-employed manager, who carries the risk and claims of an enterprise conducted with the object of obtaining money profits". She distinguishes between the innovating, the imitating (following the innovator) and the traditional entrepreneur (following traditional practices). For Hart (1970) the "small-scale entrepreneur" is anyone who controls the management of capital which he has invested in some enterprise in order to realize profit. Elkan (1988) sees three essential attributes of entrepreneurship in developing countries: the ability to perceive potentially profitable business opportunities, the willingness to act on what is perceived, and the necessary organizing ability[22].

Probably the most comprehensive definition of an entrepreneur in developing countries is given by Kilby, who conceptualizes entrepreneurship as the performance of services that are required but not available in the market[23]. He distinguishes 13 potential tasks for the entrepreneur:

1. perception of market opportunities (novel or imitative);
2. gaining control over scarce resources;
3. purchasing inputs;
4. marketing of the input and responding to competition;
5. dealing with the public bureaucracy;
6. management of human relations within the firm;
7. management of customer and supplier relations;
8. financial management;
9. production management;
10. acquiring and overseeing assembly of the factory;
11. industrial engineering (minimizing inputs with a given production process);
12. upgrading processes and product qaality;
13. introduction of new production techniques and products.

One can distinguish between those characteristics necessary to set up an enterprise and those necessary to run a business. This chapter will limit itself to the discussion of the first group, the second will be discussed in the next chapter.

There is a wide agreement that entrepreneurial abilities are vital for development, but not if there is any lack of these abilities in developing countries. Some argue that there is not any difference between industrial countries and developing countries concerning the supply of entrepreneurs, i.e. a sufficient number of entrepreneurs would come up if economic opportunities are available[24]. From this point of view, the supply of entrepreneurs is constrained by demand factors, e.g. by a preemption of entrepreneurs by state-owned corporations[25].

---

22 This is also the definition used in World Bank (1989a), which devotes a chapter on "Fostering African entrepreneurship".
23 cf. Kilby (1971: 27-28)
24 cf. Papanek (1962), Leibenstein (1968), Beveridge and Oberschall (1979), Leff (1979)
25 cf. Leff (1979)

A lot of evidence has been compiled over the years which shows that there is an abundance in people who react positively to economic opportunities to go into business and show a high degree of flexibility, in developing countries in general and in Africa in particular[26]. This refutes the early theories of intractable sociocultural obstacles to development[27]. Many argue that there is no shortage of entrepreneurs/entrepreneurship[28]. Leff (1979) argues that the studies provide evidence that the problem of entrepreneurship is "solved"[29].

However, it is argued by others that entrepreneurship cannot be ignored, because "the supply response among all groups is neither as full nor as efficient as it might be"[30]. This is stated to be due to technical and managerial inefficiencies in existing firms and to "factors that preclude many people from establishing firms at all"[31]. Kilby (1971) holds that there is no deficiency in entrepreneurship for the first 7 of his 13 entrepreneurial requirements. Elkan (1988) sees the first two of his three essential entrepreneurial attributes as available in Africa[32]. In literature reviews on SI Schmitz attributes "great initiative, inventiveness, responsiveness, readiness to jump at opportunities, hard work, preparedness to take risks" to SI producers[33].

As mentioned above, the concept of entrepreneurship is too broad to be operationalized. Efforts have been made to take educational level as a proxy for potential entrepreneurship and to measure correlations between education and entrepreneurial success (by some equated with profit)[34]. The results are mixed. Studies available do not give sufficient evidence to prove a relation between education/ training and success[35]. While House (1984) and Marris and Somerset (1971) arrive at a positive relationship between size of profit and school attendance, many studies arrive at no, weak or negative relationships between formal education and entrepreneurial success[36].

A related topic is the question to which degree craftsmen can develop into industrial entrepreneurs. According to the traditional view, their ability is severely limited by lack of entrepreneurship - industrial entrepreneurs will mostly originate from the merchant class. But others stress the ability of craftsmen to grow into industrial entrepreneurs and point to a significant share of former craftsmen in industrial entrepreneurs.

---

26 cf. Papanek (1962), Katzin (1964), Kilby (1965, 1971), Harris (1970), Hart (1970), Lawson and Kwei (1974), Leff (1979), Kennedy (1980a), Elkan (1988)
27 Few people still hold this view, e.g. Brown (1983).
28 cf. Katzin (1964)
29 This view seems now to be widely held (cf. Fasbender and Holthus 1990:8)
30 cf. Anderson (1982: 927)
31 op.cit.; on entry barriers see above chapter 5.9.
32 The same position is taken by Harris (1970: 317)
33 cf. Schmitz (1982a: 431), see also idem (1982b: 164)
34 cf. Chuta (1983). It is assumed that some education (literacy) is necessary to supervise the labour process, to keep accounts, to make contracts (cf. Hart 1970).
35 cf. Anderson (1982: 932)
36 cf. Harris (1970: 310), Nafziger (1970), Liedholm and Chuta (1976), Child (1977)

If there is any inefficiency in the supply of entrepreneurs, the interesting question is whether this can be enhanced by special policy and programme measures or whether it is a function of the general economic climate. Many studies point to the second alternative[37].

Entrepreneurship: Sudan

As in other developing countries, in Sudan many approaches to SI, be it as programmes or academic studies, emphasize a lack of entrepreneurship, explicitly[38] or implicitly by declaring the need for programmes which "encourage" entrepreneurs[39]. Although some claim that this assertion is based on empirical research, a closer look reveals that the basis is rather a contention, learned from textbooks, for instance "educated people operate better as entrepreneurs"[40], which justifies the adoption of the "McClelland" approach (see above). The contention that entrepreneurs are "potentially" present, but lack motivation[41], appears to contrast with the abundance of businessmen and women. The relevance of formal education for business success appears also to be missing[42].

To testify for the lack of entrepreneurs one could take reference to the fact that the first modern entrepreneurs in Sudan were mainly not of Sudanese, but of foreign origin: they were Levantine, Turkish, Egyptian, and other Arab businessmen[43]. However, the study of Mahmoud (1984) shows how far the process of indigenization has gone: Out of the 100 "leading businessmen" studied by her, only 24 were of non-Sudanese origin[44].

While the question of the role of entrepreneurs in Sudan's economic history is undoubtedly of importance[45], in the context of this study only one aspect of this problem is of interest: Does a lack of entrepreneurs hinder the development of SI? In his extensive study on industrial entrepreneurship in Sudan Hammeed (1974) explains why some enterprises grow and others do not by entrepreneurial characteristics. The approach of this study is different: Is there a constraint with respect to entrepreneurship?

The cited studies fail to operationalize the term "entrepreneurship" and to provide the link between the low level of development and the alleged lack of

---

37 cf. Harris (1972: 23), Elkan (1988: 181)
38 e.g. Güsten and Künkel (1963), Fadlalla (1973), Sen (1985), Ahmed (1988c, 1989a)
39 e.g. Bakhit Idris (1979), El Tahir (1988)
40 cf. Ahmed (1988c)
41 e.g. Sen (1985), Ahmed (1988c)
42 see above chapter 5.9. There are few studies on the possible correlation between education and earnings; Mulat (1986) finds a weak correlation with respect to self-employment.
43 cf. McLoughlin (1963: 83), Lageman (1989: 132)
44 cf. Mahmoud (1984: 73)
45 cf. the studies of Hammeed (1974), Mahmoud (1984), Lageman (1989: 123-140)

entrepreneurs. It is not clear which form the lack of entrepreneurship takes and how it prevents development. Accordingly, other analysts praise the abilities of indigenous businessmen, emphasize the difficult environment in which they operate[46], and dismiss the notion of lack of entrepreneurship[47].

Some light on this question can be thrown by analyzing the origin of industrial entrepreneurs: Do they develop from traditional industries, or do they tend to come from outside? The extensive study of Hammeed provides information on this (see Table 6.1.1.).

Table 6.1.1. Operational background of industrialists (in %)

previous activity	large industrialists	small industrialists
merchants	52.4	2.2
small traders	4.2	34.8
craftsmen, technicians, supervisors	17.3	43.8
business executives	12.5	5.6
professionals	11.3	3.4
farmers	1.2	6.7
other	1.2	3.4
total no.	168	89

Source: Hammeed (1974: 161)

The table shows significant differences between LI and SI. While more than half of the large industrialists had been merchants before and only 17.3% had been craftsmen, for SI the picture is quite different: the greatest group - almost half - had been craftsmen. This throws doubt on the allegation of the inability of traditional industrialists to develop to modern SI entrepreneurs.

Lack of entrepreneurship: Nyala

The concept of entrepreneurship does not fit in very well with the socio-economic milieu of Nyala. While in the more modern parts of the economy people conform to the picture of entrepreneurs, in the rather traditional parts dominated by the family economy, that concept of individual entrepreneurs is less suitable. In this survey those parts of the economy are represented by metal and carpentry workshops on the one hand and blacksmithing and tinsmithing on the other hand.

Basically entrepreneurship refers to the ability to establish and run a business. The second part of this will be tackled in the following chapters - this chapter considers the ability to establish businesses. Is there a lack of enterprises in Nyala?

---
46   cf. McLoughlin (1963)
47   e.g. Babiker (1982), Streck (1982b)

Looking at the four analyzed industries, this is clearly not the case - rather the contrary. The history of industry in Nyala cannot be exactly reconstructed, but it is clear that the number of people active in industrial activities has increased significantly, in the long-standing industries like blacksmithing, tannery, leather work etc. as well as in the modern industries which are of a very young age. In the last years the recession has led to a slump in demand, but to an increase in numbers of people active in industry instead of a parallel decrease. In most industries people complain about the lack of demand as one, if not the only, main problem (see below).

For the products which are produced locally there is no supply problem due to any "lack of entrepreneurship". The Nyala case confirms the picture of people reacting positively to market opportunities. The limited range of products does not indicate a lack of innovation[48]. In any case, in the face of wide-spread poverty a gaining of markets through innovation, i.e. the production of new products can have but a very limited effect, because it can enlarge only the limited markets of high-income earners. The production of SI in Nyala is demand-determined. The demand of the overwhelming majority of potential consumers is confined to the basic needs. The innovation of new products is not the issue for a basic-needs oriented development strategy.

A central requirement of entrepreneurs is to gain control over scarce resources. As was shown above[49], the SI entrepreneurs of Nyala, while not having access to any outside funds, manage to mobilize own resources to start up their businesses. Lack of entrepreneurship does not appear to be an issue in Nyala.

Formal education has been taken as a proxy for entrepreneurship in an attempt to render it measureable. Behind this is the assumption that those with a higher education are the more successful entrepreneurs. *Success* itself is of course a vague concept. Profits and labour productivity can be taken as proxies. The data on Nyala SI do not show any clear correlation between education and success, neither in terms of profit and productivity, nor in terms of an intuitive evaluation of entrepreneurs' success.

Blacksmiths show a uniform picture of low education[50]. No correlation was found between profits, productivities, or other signs of success and education. *Tinsmiths*, on the other hand, have wide differences in education, but in terms of business success no correlation can be found.

Higher levels of education are reached in the modern SI branches. Among the *electric metal workshops* those with a higher education, i.e. 9 years (secondary school degree or more) are situated on the lower-middle range of profits and the middle range of productivity. Those who attained highest profits have enjoyed only

---
48 see chapter 5.10.
49 see Chapter 5.3. on capital mobilization
50 see above Table 5.9.2.

a medium level of school education, most of them 4-7 years. The *non-electric metal workshops* have a lower educational level, and a somewhat lower profit level, but the variations in both are too large to arrive at any clear relation.

In *electric carpentry* the two entrepreneurs with a higher education attained a medium profitability and a low productivity. Of the *non-electric carpentry workshop* owners four have a higher education, which shows that there is no clear relation between education and electrifying workshops, i.e. lower education does not turn out as a barrier in this regard.

In summary, it can be stated that on the one hand there are distinct levels of education in the different SI branches, and those industries with the highest levels of education obtain the highest profits. On the other hand, within the industries there are high variations and there are many examples of uneducated and traditionally educated (*khalwa*) successful entrepreneurs. The data do not support any suggestion of an educational influence on entrepreneurial success - successful SI entrepreneurs may have any educational background. The data may, on the contrary, support the notion of a negative relation between the two. However, this remains speculation, the data are not unequivocal. The main lesson is, that although some education is probably beneficial for business success, other factors are much more important.

A related question concerns the *social origin of industrial entrepreneurs*: do craftsmen develop into industrial entrepreneurs, or are they superseded by capital owners from outside, i.e. mainly by merchants? An answer to this question can be indicated by a look at the job history and social origin of the SI entrepreneurs in the modern branches, which can be best taken to represent industries in the narrow sense.

Among the electric metal workshop owners (22 in total), only one was previously a merchant, three come from the formal sector, the others, i.e. the overwhelming majority, started with the same professions. Three are from merchant families, the same number out of craftsmen families. Among the electric carpentry entrepreneurs (seven), one was working in the formal sector before, all others started in the same profession. Of their fathers, none was a merchant, but one a carpenter. Among all carpenters in Nyala, there is one reported case of merchant investment. This shows that the involvement of merchant capital is marginal in Nyala SI. On the other hand, the ability of craftsmen to develop into industrial entrepreneurs seems to be proved.

6.2 Managerial deficiencies

The managerial and technical aspects of entrepreneurship have often been neglected arguing that these can be "bought on the market"[51]. However, these markets are poorly developed in the low-income developing countries. Page and Steel believe that SI units are "not managed as efficiently as they could be", but regard this shortcoming also as an asset, "in that small scale enterprises conserve on scarce managerial skills."[52] They provide a means for utilizing and generating basic managerial and technical skills that would not be sufficient for the LI and would otherwise go unused and undeveloped.

Different managerial deficiencies are claimed to exist in SI of developing countries:
- a lack of management control[53];
- solo management as a barrier to success[54];
- little skill in carrying out the organizational functions[55];
- lack of effective supervision and direction of labour[56];
- a misperception of problems and unawareness of management deficiencies[57]; it is claimed that often financial constraints are perceived as the main problem, which reflect, however, more basic problems[58];
- a lack of specialization[59];
- early diversification[60];
- inadequate accounting and costing[61];
- a lack of book keeping[62];
- a lack of stock control, overbuying of inventories[63];
- inadequate coordination of raw material purchases with product orders[64];

---

51 cf. Papanek (1962) Bauer and Yamey (1965), Hirschman (1958)
52 Page and Steel (1984: 24)
53 cf. Kilby (1965: 110)
54 cf. Kilby (1971: 31), Marris and Somerset (1971: 123-124); Beveridge and Oberschall (1979: 297), however, observed the same point but did not find that it led to difficulties
55 cf. Kilby (1965: 111), Page (1979: 30)
56 cf. Kilby (1965: 110-111), Kilby (1971: 51), de Wilde (1971)
57 cf. Kilby (1969: 338)
58 cf. Chuta (1983: 278), de Wilde (1971)
59 This can, however, be explained as a rational response to the "economy of uncertainty" (cf. Hart 1970: 108)
60 However, there is a possible rationale behind this: Motives may be to conceal money from relatives, there may be obstacles to firm expansion (cf. Kennedy 1980). For many the spreading of investments over a large number of small enterprises rather than accumulation in existing units is a strategy of small scale enterprises to cope with a risky environment (cf. McCormick 1988: 173; see also MacEwan Scott 1979, Hugon 1982, Moser 1984, Lewin 1985)
61 cf. de Wilde (1971), Nihan and Jourdain (1978)
62 cf. Kilby (1971: 51), Nihan et al. (1979: 635), Chuta (1983: 278); Hugon (1990: 73) believes that a lack of book-keeping implies a non-profit maximizing attitude.
63 cf. Child (1977), Chuta (1983), de Wilde (1971), Harper (1975, cited in: Page 1979: 30)
64 cf. Kilby (1971: 51)

- marketing deficiencies (competitive marketing because "the whole conception of marketing (is) outside their experience"[65]);
- little effective interest in improving the quality of their product[66];
- a tendency to confuse personal and business finance[67];
- an inability to calculate profits[68];
- a lack of knowledge of price trends over time[69];
- deficiencies in financial planning: a limited ability to anticipate the need to plan for service of debt, replenishment of stocks, replacement of equipment[70].

These observations have been criticized or qualified in two respects: First, whether the observed phenomena - assuming they are correct observations - are really problems depends on the size of the SI. For the lower end of SI - single craftsmen - many of the points are just irrelevant.

Second, it can be argued that what is considered a deficiency - from a view based on experience in Western industrialization - may actually be a strength of SI in developing countries. Instances are lack of separation between enterprise and family[71] and diversification. The observed lack of book keeping is a case in point. Not only the necessity has been doubted[72], but also it is claimed that the introduction of book keeping (e.g. in the context of a credit programme) may have negative results on the development of the enterprise, cutting across the integrated finance system which secures the need to be flexible[73].

Generally, it can be said that a large part of the observations of alleged managerial deficiencies are due to a narrow-minded transfer of Western management conceptions to very different realities. Instead, the managerial behaviour has to be understood in the context of the existing socio-economic structure and the managing practices have to be related to the general strategies, instead of simply advising Western management styles[74]. This does not imply that there are no deficiencies, but many of them are rational answers to external constraints[75].

---

65 cf. Marris (1968); however, Kilby (1965) claims the contrary
66 cf. Kilby (1965: 111)
67 cf. de Wilde (1971), Page (1979: 30)
68 cf Chuta (1983: 278), Child (1977, cited in: Page 1979: 30)
69 cf. Chuta (1983: 278)
70 cf. de Wilde (1971: 9)
71 see below chapter 6.4.
72 Marris and Somerset (1971: 221) report of profitable businesses whose only records are a jumble of invoices, and of others where neat books simply record accumulating losses. Elkan (1988: 179) argues that book-keeping becomes only important when ownership and control are separated and when an enterprise is subject to taxation.
73 cf. Lipton (1980)
74 cf. Richardson (1984)
75 Berry (1985: 153-154), discussing the managerial behaviour of Nigerian motor mechanics, convincingly demonstrates that what appears to be poor management is, in fact, rational behaviour to minimize the risk of serious loss. Also Scmitz (1990) in his study on Ghana finds that there is no general or intrinsic problem of managerial ability.

Managerial deficiencies: Sudan

Similarly to the lack of entrepreneurship, management deficiencies are mentioned as development constraints of SI, either for the existing enterprises[76] or for enterprise growth prospects[77]. However, rarely are these claims concretized. Furthermore, the apparent growth of the sector seems to contradict the contention. Here also the suspicion exists that ideology transfer is prevailing, rather than analysis of reality. Take, for instance, the study of Ahmed (1988c), which seems to be quite revealing in this respect. Three problems are emphasized : firstly, management training is necessary "to increase the efficiency and effectiveness of existing small businesses"; secondly, there is a lack of data concerning the training needs of small businesses; and the third major problem is "to convince small-scale industry managers that they need and can benefit from training"[78]. Three questions arise: How can one be so convinced of the need of SI entrepreneurs to be trained if the data which could support this are not available? And if even the entrepreneurs themselves are not aware of their need, is it really there? And lastly, even if the need for assistance were real, is it useful to assist entrepreneurs who are not aware of the need for assistance?

However, this point should not be stressed too far. Of course it is possible - in fact quite probable - that SI entrepreneurs are not perfectly aware of all aspects of their situation, and they could perhaps be helped by outside advice. However, a lot more insight and understanding is clearly needed to make such far-reaching statements concerning management deficiencies. By reading studies, which are taking alleged managerial deficiencies to substantiate the need for a proposed assistance scheme, the suspicion arises that they are a justification for the employment of experts rather than driven by a sincere concern about the fate of SI entrepreneurs.

Again, much seems to be a question of size. Practices as book-keeping, accounting, employment of trained managers, cash-flow analysis, budgetary control[79] are simply not needed by the vast majority of SI businesses.

Furthermore, the practices and standards of management in SI must be evaluated in the Sudanese context - and not be compared with an ideal textbook situation. A part of this context is the government and its operations. In comparison with its

---

76 e.g. Ahmed (1978), Bakhit Idris (1979), Sen (1985), BCHLI (1987), Niazi (1987), Shadeed Mohamed Zein (1988), Ahmed (1988c, 1989a), Ishaq and Adam Mohamed (n.d.)
77 e.g. Curtis (1980: 17), Hammeed (1974: 226)
78 cf. Ahmed (1988c: 28, 29). The last citation is from an "ILO authority", with which the author obviuosly agrees.
79 proposed by Ahmed (1978), Sen (1985), Niazi (1987), Ahmed (1988c)

planning and implementation capacity the SI may look much better, even in the eyes of Western "development experts"[80].

The state of knowledge on management practices and deficiencies on the one hand, and of the existing institutions of management training[81] on the other hand seems to point to severe limitations of any useful measure in the field of management training.

Managerial deficiencies: Nyala

There are many different claims concerning managerial deficiencies. These must be seen and analyzed, however, on the background of the actually necessary managerial needs of SI, i.e. it must be asked, if the abilities perceived as deficiencies, are actually needed by the SI establishments.

A case in point is *bookkeeping*. This practice is very rarely practiced among SI industrialists in Nyala. Blacksmiths don't use it at all, one tinsmith does use it, six metal workshop owners apply it. Among these five have electric workshops. One more of them abandoned this practice, because his business had declined, so he claims. Of the carpentry workshop owners, two practise it. This means that, in total, 11% of the analyzed SI units apply book-keeping. Furthermore, the kind of bookkeeping practised would not meet the requirements of any tax consultant or revenue authority.

Those who believe in the necessity of bookkeeping proceed from the assumption that a lack of it would result in *inadequate costing and accounting*, an *inability to calculate profits* and a *lack of stock control* leading to *overbuying of inventories*. In a similar argument, it is stated that they have a *lack of knowledge of price trends over a period of time*.

However, in Nyala these shortcomings could not be identified in any meaningful sense. Many enterprises are simply too small and operate in a too simple way to make any elaborated accounting system worthwhile, as for instance the two-man blacksmith units, most of the tinsmiths, and some of the non-electric carpentry and metal workshops. But also the slightly larger SI establishments manage well without bookkeeping. In many discussions about the situation on the input markets, the production process and the product markets, it became apparent that the entrepreneurs are well aware of their cost- and profit-structure. It is essential for them to be constantly aware of the prices of their inputs, as many fluctuate to a high degree[82]. They are well aware of these fluctuations, but very few are in a

---

80 For the weaknesses in the government management capacity on national planning, industrial policy, and industrial project level cf. Brüning (1986: 96-162), Moharir and Kagwe (1987)
81 cf. the evaluation of the MDC (El-Jack 1975)
82 see below chapter 6.7.

position to benefit from this knowledge to buy large amounts of raw materials at times of low prices. Their problem is not one of overbuying of inventories, but rather the contrary: very small inventories - if they have them at all (see below). Those who have inventories, know very well how large they are and why. They are the more successful in the face of the prevailing raw material market conditions.

It is also clear that the entrepreneurs know about their production costs and the prices they can obtain on the market. They have a clear idea about the different costs entailed in their production process and about the profits they obtain on the market.

In summary, the evidence of SI in Nyala does not support the notion of a necessity or even benefit of book-keeping. It simply appears not to be necessary to get a written picture of the SI operations, due to the small scale and the low degree of complexity of their operations.

Solo management is seen by many as a barrier to success. In fact, the huge majority of Nyala SI establishments are managed in this way. Only three blacksmiths, seven metal workshops, and three carpenters are jointly managed (which does not make a big difference in any case). But this form of management is perfectly adequate to the scale of enterprises, and it does not appear to be a constraint to a possible growth, because other constraints prevent this anyway.

The same arguments apply to a perceived *lack of management control, lack of effective supervision and direction of labour*, and *little skill in carrying out the organizational tasks*.

It is believed that there is a *misperception of problems* and an *unawareness of management deficiencies*. For instance, financial constraints are often perceived as the main problem, while in fact other points would be more important. In fact, in the interviews people regularly mentioned finance as the main problem if they were asked with an open-ended question. But this reflects, quite obviously, the expectations of the interviewees concerning the benefit they could get out of the interviewer, but it must not be confused with the actual conviction of the entrepreneurs about their main problems. It is very understandable that they do mention finance as the main problem, as naturally finance can relieve any kind of problem from the assisted individual's point of view. It does not appear that Nyala's SI entrepreneurs put an undue emphasis on financial constraints to the neglect of other factors.

Another perceived impediment to enterprise growth is an *early diversification*. Firstly, an early diversification is a rational strategy of risk spreading. Secondly, in the case of Nyala, the degree of diversification of activities was found to be astonishingly low (see above). For the huge majority the SI income is their only income - they rely to a very low degree on other incomes, especially on agricultural income.

A final deficiency is perceived in *marketing*. It is true that marketing is very competitive and very little effort is made in this regard by most of the small industrialists. The usual practice is just to display their products in front of their workplaces. The only exception to this are the few carpentry shop owners who have a show room in the market area.

It is a common practice that many competitors are situated in the same area. For example, almost all the shoe producers are at one area on the main market, all tanneries are at one place, and almost all blacksmiths are on one market. At the same time, small industrialists are well aware of the difference it makes where to situate their workplace. The new market *Suq ash Shabi*, for instance, is located at the edge of the town, not well connected to the city, and thus disliked by producers. The blacksmiths have been ordered to move out of the central market area by the authorities, and the tinsmiths much prefer the central market area. It is felt that the differences in marketing techniques are due to basic cultural differences. That means, what is perceived by Westerners as a deficiency and where possibilities of increased sales by improved marketing are seen, this may not be compatible with Sudanese cultural standards. Apart from this, an improved marketing could increase the sales of an individual producer, but in the face of the income situation, it is hardly conceivable that it would increase the total turnover of SI. If this is true, an improvement in marketing would simply drive out some of the existing enterprises, which would be a negative rather than a positive overall effect. The basic problem is the lack of effective demand (see below). In the context of a reform of SAP (see chapter 1.3.) a production directed at the basic needs is claiming priority, and in this context it doesn't seem that marketing would make the difference.

A related accusation against SI entrepreneurs is their *little interest in improving the quality of their product*. Indeed, there are wide differences in the quality in many product fields. This points to a large scope for improvement of product qualities. However, the impediment to actually achieve these improvements is not an internal inability or unwillingness, but the market conditions. The quality of the SI products is clearly determined by their markets: Products destined to high-income markets tend to be expensive high-quality products. The electric carpentry workshops are a case in point. Products destined to the low-income markets are inexpensive and of low quality. An example for this is the second-hand furniture.

A further determining factor for the quality of many SI products is their relative innovative character, bringing with it a lack of knowledge of quality standards on the part of the customers.

In summary, it appears that the prevailing management techniques are perfectly adequate for the level of operations of SI establishments in Nyala, but of course not, if the enterprises want to expand. However, other obstacles are in the way of expansion.

6.3 Lack of technical skills

Many studies regard a lack of technical skills as a major or the deciding growth constraint of SI[83]. The ILO study on Kenya (1972) blames the traditional training system as responsible for the following deficiencies: practice of copying the master craftsmen's techniques, and - as a result - lack of product differentiation and lack of versality in adjusting to new opportunities[84]. Another deficiency is a "failure to regularly maintain equipment"[85].
Others, however, hold that existing technical skills rarely constitute a problem, but they are "generally a sufficient basis to pick up the missing technical aspects through a process of learning-by-doing"[86]. There are positive assessments of traditional training systems on the grounds that they respect traditional values, they cost society nothing, and provide the best preparation for self-employment. It is maintained that the quality of the traditional training system is comparable to formal training systems[87]. A lot of literature claiming a lack of technical skills appears to confuse this issue with the level of technology considered as low. This is, however, a different issue[88]. The two issues would only be identical if a lack of technical skills would be not only one, but the only reason for the low level of technology. What will be discussed under the heading of technical skills, however, is the question if the technical skills are adequate at the presently employed technologies.

Lack of technical skills: Sudan

Several studies identify this as a major deficiency of SI production[89], which is claimed to result in products of low quality[90]. As in the first two chapters, a suspicion creeps up here as well, that "technical deficiencies" are a mere justification for engagement of development aid. As a rule, the technical practices are not evaluated in their socio-economic context, but simply attributed to a lack of skills.

---

[83] e.g. de Wilde (1971), Berg (1978b), Nimpuno (1978)
[84] cf. ILO (1972: 192)
[85] Kilby (1971: 31)
[86] cf. Schmitz (1982b: 165); see also King (1977) on the capability of the informal training system.
[87] cf. Nihan and Jourdain (1978), Nihan, Demol and Jondoh (1979)
[88] see below chapter 6.9.
[89] cf. Fadlalla (1973), Ahmed (1978), Anand and Nur (1984), Niazi (1987), Shadeed Mohamed Zein (1988)
[90] cf. Güsten and Künkel (1963: 225-226), Bakhit et al. (1987: 7), Howard (1988).

An exception is the study of de Coninck et al. (1984), which explains the low level of technology of the production of agricultural implements in Southern Sudan explicitly as not due to any lack of skills on the part of blacksmiths, but by external factors (the low technological level of agriculture[91]). Others attribute the "modest quality" of SI products to a high fluctuation, which results in a very limited interest in a profound training[92].

The informal training is prevalent in Sudan. According to a recent estimation of the SCSEU, the government provides only 16.25% of the training given. The remainder is provided by workshops[93]. As this estimation includes only the more modern fields in which the SCSEU is active, for the more traditional and informal SI units an even lower participation rate of the government is to be assumed.

Lack of technical skills: Nyala

The blacksmiths utilize inherited techniques, transferred by the apprenticeship system. It is well adapted to the prevailing technology. The experiences of development projects in introducing new products (animal drawn ploughs) and improved techniques with this, shows that the blacksmiths are skilled enough to be capable to improve their technologies. The lack of product differentiation is not due to a lack of versatility in adjusting to new opportunities - the low technological level is not due (at least primarily) to technical skills[94].

The electric SI branches show an impressing ability to keep their machines running despite the adverse conditions of a lack of spare parts. Also the entrepreneurs do not regard technical skills as any problem of their workforce - with only one exception (out of 29).

The prevalent opinion is that the formal technical training of the government institutions is not adequate for SI needs: First, it has a theoretical bias, and second, the technologies taught are often appropriate to a machinery which is not available to the workshops themselves.

The general impression, reinforced by expert opinions, is that technical training may only become an issue when new technologies are introduced. And even this is not unequivocal, because the existing SI establishments having introduced electric machinery prove that people with a minimum of formal technical training are capable to perform a technological leap. Furthermore, many of the presently

---

91   cf. chapter 6.12.
92   cf. Güsten and Künkel (1963: 225-226)
93   cf. SCSEU (1989: 9); see also Menck (1982) on the neglect of technical and vocational training by the government. El Jack and Ali Taha (1977) consider the formal vocational training system as a failure; see Rasheed and Sandell (1980) on the variety of forms of non-formal education.
94   On the encouraging experiences of agricultural development projects to train blacksmiths in the production of intermediate agricultural implements see JMRDP (1988) and WSDC (1988).

utilized modern technologies are rather too capital intensive, too modern, than the reverse. That means, it is doubtful that technical skills can be regarded as a major constraint.

6.4 Integration into family

It is widely held that SI establishments are to a large extent family businesses and that social obligations towards the family would mean a considerable drain on resources, impeding capital accumulation if not making it impossible[95].

The counter-thesis holds that the integration into the family is one, if not the central, distinct advantage of SI. The family may provide capital (especially initial capital)[96] and manpower[97] at more advantageous terms than the market - if the market is providing these resources at all. Families can be regarded as an insurance against failure[98]. Formulated more generally, the fungibility of resources (labour, capital) between production, preparation of consumables and reproduction of the family's capacity for both of these allows to maximize expected utility to the household[99].

From this point of view, development measures like supervised credit, introduction of book-keeping and any measures to separate family and enterprises will be harmful. It has to be noted that this argument takes the enterprise as a function of family's utility maximization. If it is accepted as valid, the family may nevertheless be a constraint for growth of SI enterprises. Another implication is that the family can be regarded as a decision unit. The subordination of the individual is widely regarded as a characteristic of African societies, but undoubtedly this structure is presently breaking down, and a process of individualization is taking place.

To analyze this complex it is also necessary to analyze the extent of the relation family-enterprise and its character in relation to business success and expansion. The extent can be measured in terms of family manpower and capital flows. For the second issue, it has to be measured if and how there is a correlation between family involvement and success/expansion of SI enterprises.

---

95   cf. Higgins (1955), Dinwiddy (1974: 7), ILO and JASPA (1985: 14) Schneider (1986: 86), Vorlaufer (1988: 78)
96   For de Wilde this may outweigh the "heavy burden" of the extended family system - he regards it doubtful that the family is a serious bar to development success; cf. also Hirschman (1965) and Kennedy (1980: 45)
97   This is emphasized by Scott (1979), Lipton (1984), McCormick (1988)
98   cf. Lawson and Kwei (1974)
99   cf. Lipton (1980)

Integration into family: Sudan

Most of the studies confirm the assumption of strong ties between SI and the entrepreneurs' families. Although less material is available on the impact of these ties, several studies emphasize the importance of entrepreneurs' families in financing[100]. Others, however, point to the social obligation of sharing in the family, which would constitute a development constraint ("comparable to communism")[101].

Integration into family: Nyala

To illuminate the drain on resources, the structure of the households of the entrepreneurs has to be taken into account. To get a hint on the number of people supported by the SI income, the number of supported people is divided by the people who work. The interviewees do not consider household and agricultural subsistence work as work. This means, that only work to earn money is included in this category (see Table 6.4.1.).

Table 6.4.1. Dependence rate of SI entrepreneurs in Nyala (no.of supported/no.of working people per household)

industry	average	range
blacksmiths	3.5	1-8
tinsmiths	5.0	2-10
metal workshops	5.4	1-13
electric	5.7	2-13
non-electric	4.7	1-10
carpentry	6.2	1-14
electric	6.7	5-10
non-electric	6.1	1-14
total	5.3	1-14

Source: own survey

This table shows that there are marked differences between the various branches - the highest dependence rate is almost double as high as the lowest. Increasing dependence appears to correspond to increasing modernity in terms of applied technology (measured by capital intensity) with blacksmiths on the lower extreme and branches working with electric machines on the upper extreme. However, it does not fit into this relation that the non-electric metal workshops have a lower rate than the tinsmiths and that both carpentry categories have higher rates than

---

100 cf. Hammeed (1974: 74-82), Mahmoud (1984: 122), Gumaa et al. (1987: 159), Ahmed (1989b: 15)
101 cf. Streck (1982: 63-64); see also Ahmed (1989b) for this argument.

all others, despite the fact that electric metal workshops have the highest capital intensity.

It is, at first sight, surprising that the modern SI branches have a higher dependence rate than the more traditional trades. This contradicts the assumption that especially the traditional industries are subject to the "family constraint". On the contrary it implies that during the course of development the drain on resources will increase.

The conclusion that in modern SI the families of the entrepreneurs constitute a higher drain on resources than in traditional industries is confirmed when the information on non-monetary incomes is added. The most important non-monetary source of income is, of course, agriculture. The traditional industries' entrepreneurs do tend more to have a subsistence farm than the modern SI. 77% of the blacksmiths and 55% of the tinsmiths have a farm, while only 26% and 5% of the electric metal and carpentry workshop owners resp. have one.

In terms of capital formation, the linkage to family is surprisingly small, as discussed above (see Table 5.3.1.): only 17% of the entrepreneurs relied on family credit as a source of initial capital. For 11% family savings were the most important source of finance. On both counts, blacksmiths are the most reliant on family finance.

For the ongoing finance, only one of all (83) reported family finance. Of course, these data are also confined to the monetary sphere, i.e. the important non-monetary finance through subsistence agriculture is disregarded. However, as discussed above, this does not alter the picture, but reinforces it: In the traditional industries families are less a drain and more a support to SI.

On the participation of family labour in SI see Table 6.4.2..

Table 6.4.2. Family manpower in small industries of Nyala (family workers as % of employed)

industry	% of family workers
blacksmiths	85.7
tinsmiths	10.0
metal workshops	12.5
electric	12.8
non-electric	11.4
carpentry	18.9
electric	17.0
non-electric	20.9
total	20.1

Source: own survey; in the dry season

Overall, the reliance on family labour is surprisingly small. The only exception to this rule is the blacksmith trade relying mostly on family labour. Among the others, no trend of an association with modernity is discernible.

6.5 Other internal constraints: contempt of industrial labour, segregation of traditional industries

There is a notion that in Sudan manual labour is widely regarded as the task of slaves and thus considered as onerous and degrading[102]. This pattern is conspicuous for the visitor to Sudan, and it is reported in several studies about SI[103]. In a similar context, reportedly several activities (blacksmithing, pottery, foundry) are exclusively carried out by selected ethnic groups. Also industries are strictly segregated by sex. This might limit the labour supply to industries as well as the earning capacities of ethnic groups, as well as women. However, it is not clear if this operates as a constraint to the development of SI, i.e. if it results in a lack of people ready to be active in this work.

This proposition can be tested by analysing the ethnic and social background of SI entrepreneurs and their workers and by qualitative interviews of them and of non-industrialists.

Contempt of manual labour: Nyala

A sort of contempt of work in the field of SI, as part of a general contempt of manual labour, is in fact strongly rooted in the minds of the "educated people". The image of the superiority of the white collar professions is widely spread, not only among those having the white collar jobs and high school students, but also among most other groups in society, including even people working in SI themselves. This idea is, of course, not confined to Nyala or even the developing countries, and it has its justification in the real superiority in terms of payment, working conditions etc. What is relevant in the context of growth constraints of SI, is the question if this idea prevents people from entering the world of SI and thereby might prevent growth of SI.

In this context one has to distinguish between the SI as such and some traditional trades which were contempted and restricted to special ethnic groups for centuries. In our context, a case in point is the blacksmith trade.

To start with, in Nyala the sufficient number of entrepreneurs itself is a strong argument against any constraint to exist. In the survey, in order to illuminate the importance of the contempt for industrial labour in general and for special trades as blacksmithing in particular, the ethnic identity of the entrepreneurs and their workers was asked for.

---
102 cf. McLoughlin (1962)
103 cf. Babiker (1982: 52), Streck (1982a, 1983), Oesterdiekhoff (1984: 61), Bakhit et al. (1987: 17)

During this exercise one becomes aware of the immense ethnic variety of Nyala and its function as a melting pot of peoples. For most trades, the number of ethnic groups named by the entrepreneurs and workers almost approaches the number of those interviewed. For instance, the 22 electric metal workshop owners belong to 17 different ethnic groups, their workers to 31 ethnic groups. The only significant concentration on one group is among the blacksmiths, where the *Tama* provide 62% of the entrepreneurs. However, even this shows that the strict segregation of traditional crafts by ethnic group is beginning to be something of the past. It seems to be reasonable to assume that Nyala is representative for a general change in urban society: the breakdown of the discrimination of manual work in general and some traditional trades in particular. The main force behind this change is the erosion of the incomes of white collar jobs.

6.6 Internal constraints: a summary

Although the allegation of a lack of entrepreneurship is also raised in Sudan, the evidence from Nyala belies this claim. Furthermore, no clear relationship between business success and educational level is found. In the same manner, major managerial deficiencies operating as a constraint could not be identified in Nyala - the prevailing management techniques were found to be perfectly adequate for the level of operations. The same is true for the technical skills.

The role of the family is ambivalent. In Nyala, surprisingly little family labour is involved in SI. The financial support of the family for SI establishments is even more marginal. On the other hand, the supporting role of SI for the family is important - more so for the modern SI.

Contempt of manual labour is wide-spread among the "educated people", but this does not constitute a barrier for SI.

Altogether, the conclusion of Schmitz in his evaluation of SI studies is confirmed: He concludes that external constraints seem to be more important than internal factors and assumes that the wide-spread emphasis on measures which apply to the internal factors (managerial training) serves partly an ideological function: It puts the blame for lack of development of these enterprises "on the people who run them rather than on the environment in which they operate". At the same time he warns that a "fascination with the external factors can easily lead to gloomy and deterministic predictions, to the denial of all accumulative prospects and to a general theory of marginalization"[104]. To this remark one must add that this view can also lead to an overly optimistic view, giving the impression that only some

---

[104] cf. Schmitz (1982a: 445)

external constraints, mainly relating to government policy, must be relieved to set loose a huge potential[105].

6.7 External constraints: Exploitation of small industries by LI and the economy at large

Among the external constraints, broadly three groups can be distinguished. The first group of arguments concerns the relationship of SI to LI or the economy at large, on a sectoral or firm level. The second group of arguments concerns the access to raw materials, product markets, technology and credit. The last group emphasizes the pervasive role of the government in both of those areas.

The first group of arguments hypothesizes that SI (as a part of the informal sector) holds a subordinate position and is exploited by LI, the formal sector, or, in general, the larger economy[106]. Three linkages are relevant for this argument:

1. SI produces consumption goods for those working in export production (in agriculture, industry) and/or the modern sector at very low prices, under very competitive conditions and in this way allow the incomes of export/ modern sector workers to be lower than they would otherwise be. This means high profits in these branches because the reproduction costs of labour are reduced[107]. Some formulate this as a subsidization of the formal sector or as a value transfer to this sector or generally from the peripheral states to the metropolitan states.
2. SI produces inputs for LI (in subcontracting arrangements or otherwise), at very low prices, under very competitive conditions and exploitative relations vis-à-vis LI. This is also stated to be a value transfer[108]. Subcontracting is regarded as disadvantageous because of a weak bargaining power (subordinate position) of SI establishments which would result in an exploitation through unfavourable prices and a shift of the cost of fluctuation in the production to SI[109].
3. SI buys raw materials from the formal sector on disadvantageous terms. This is also claimed to be a value transfer[110].

Another linkage is the provision of casual labour[111].

---

105 There is a tendency like this in ILO (1972); cf. Hansohm and Wohlmuth (1987: 175)
106 cf. Tokman (1978) for an overview of different approaches
107 cf. Bienefeld and Godfrey (1975), Portes (1978), Moser (1984: 1062)
108 cf. Portes (1983), Bienefeld and Godfrey (1975)
109 cf. Bromley and Gerry (1979), Abadie (1982), Schmitz (1982b), Lewin (1985)
110 This will be discussed under Chapter 6.8.
111 cf. Quijano (1974)

The first proposition is part of a wider argument emphasizing the role of the informal sector in general and the household economy in particular in securing the reproduction of labour[112]. It is argued that the household economy alleviates the cost of proletarianization, subsidizes the capitalist sector by cheapening the reproduction cost of its labour force. The relation of the informal sector and the formal sector is seen as symbiotic. Not only strong relations are assumed, but also a mutual dependence of the two sectors: not only the informal sector is dependent on the formal sector for markets (besides other factors), but also the formal sector is dependent on the informal sector providing the "cheap goods" necessary to achieve competitiveness on the export market[113]. This explains the persistence of informal activities. It is argued that SI and the traditional, non-capitalist economy are subject to two contradicting influences: 1. a dissolution through competition of superior LI and imports[114], 2. a conservation of their activities[115]. As a result, SI is marginalized[116], has no accumulation potential, is faced by severe competition, accelerating differentiation, progressive impoverishment, loss of accumulated skills, in general a bleak future, i.e. its growth is involutionary[117]. From this point of view, any traditional form of direct assistance to SI would only aggravate the tendency of differentiation. Nothing short of a "break with the transnational operating corporation economy" is adequate to develop the informal sector activities[118].

The relation informal sector-formal sector is formulated as a combination of different modes of production, or of different parts of one mode of production (forms of production)[119], in any case under the hegemony of the formal sector/modern sector/LI.

According to critics, this argument suffers from a one-sidedness, regarding LI, the formal sector and international capital as omnipotent and SI as powerless. It takes solely the perspective of the LI/ capitalism[120] and lacks supporting micro level studies. In this manner this school exposes itself as a variation of the classical modernization theory, and thus has to be criticized for its ethnocentric view, as well.

---

112 cf. Leys (1973), LeBrun and Gerry (1975), Meillassoux (1976), Quijano (1977), Portes (1978, 1983), Senghaas-Knobloch (1978), MacEwan Scott (1979), Elwert et al. (1983), Moser (1978, 1984)
113 This appears, however, to contradict the argument of bringing high profits.
114 see below chapter 6.9.
115 e.g. LeBrun and Gerry (1975), Gerry (1978), McGee (1979), Allen (1983), Wellings and Sutcliffe (1984)
116 For a critique of the concept of marginality cf. Peattie (1980).
117 cf. LeBrun and Gerry (1975: 30), Quijano (1977: 312), Gerry (1978: 1158)
118 cf. Senghaas-Knobloch (1978: 204; own translation)
119 cf. Bienefeld (1975a, b). In contrast, van Dijk (1986a, b) rejects the concept of separate modes of production.
120 Lipton (1980) argues strongly for the strength of the family mode of production. In his view its persistence is due not to the unwillingness but inability of capitalism to abolish it.

The argument implies that a large share of the labour force is satisfied by the household economy and by the informal sector. The services of the household economy include not only, and not even mainly, the products of household industry, but also child rearing, care for the old, social/emotional services etc. However, the role of the household is not analyzed here. The household industries have not been included in the data collection. Thus this argument is relevant for our context only insofar as it concerns non-household SI[121].

The counter-proposition regards the relation of SI to the wider economy as positive and consequently favours strengthening the linkages between the two sectors[122]. As favourable effects are seen:
1. development of new activities by SI;
2. diffusion of technologies from LI to SI;
3. diffusion of new raw materials and machines to SI (e.g. second-hand machines and materials from LI);
4. securing of flexibility (through subcontracting);
5. different forms of assistance for SI through subcontracting.

An examination of the propositions will have to answer the following questions:
1) Which linkages of SI to the LI/formal sector/modern sector do exist? How strong are they? Does SI produce cheap consumption goods for LI workers (wage goods)? Do SI products compete with LI products? Does SI produce inputs for LI as sub-contractors or independent producers?
2) Are these linkages benign or exploitative[123]?
3) Is there a relation between growth prospects of SI and intensity of linkages?

The evidence on the impact of linkages on growth prospects is not conclusive, which is due to a lack of data and to methodological difficulties. Most analysts agree that SI is strongly externally dependent, i.e. its growth pattern is not autonomous[124]. The "cheap wage goods" proposition is not supported by evidence.

---

121 For the arguments on the role of household economy in subsidizing the capitalist economy cf. Elwert (1985), Thomi (1988), Vorlaufer (1988).
122 cf. Staley and Morse (1965: 266-267), ILO (1972), King (1975), World Bank (1978: 25-26), Sethuraman (1981c: 188), ILO (1983: 85), House (1984: 218), Nanjundan (1986: 43), van Dijk (1986a, b), Vorlaufer (1988)
123 There are difficulties to measure exploitation of SI (cf. Schmitz 1982b: 169-170). First their efficiency must be established. Insofar as low prices for SI products reflect low efficiency, one cannot talk of an exploitative relationship. One could say that exploitation exists, if the return on labour in SI is less than the current wage rate multiplied by hours worked. However, there are difficulties to compare. First it is difficult to compare wages. Family workers used by SI may not be able to work outside, i.e. they may not be "free labour". Also, if work is done at home, it may be difficult to separate it from leisure time. Second it is difficult to compare returns to capital. The capital invested in SI may not have other chances to be invested (fragmented capital market). Also it may be difficult to discriminate between working capital and money needed for consumption.
124 Middleton (1981: 512) claims that the extent of linkages is widely overestimated.

On subcontracting, in his survey Schmitz concludes that "very little is known about the growth potential of small contractors", not even about their existence[125]. According to Page and Steel "It is believed that subcontracting is relatively rare in Africa - in contrast to South Asian countries - , one reason being the dominance in the modern sector of foreign owned import substituting firms, which are highly import dependent"[126].

Exploitation of SI by LI and the economy at large: Sudan

There is a lack of data illuminating the relation of SI to LI and the wider economy in Sudan. The diversity of experiences, the wide field of activities in which SI is active, the overall growth of the sector and the incomes in comparison with other sectors however disprove outright a general theory of marginalization or a subordinate position of the SI sector.
Subcontracting plays at most a marginal role in Sudan. No mention is made in existing studies about extent or quality of subcontracting. As the sector produces predominantly consumer goods and LI is highly import-dependent, any subsidization/exploitation of SI by LI/the wider economy plays no role. An exploitation of SI through the other link (provision of cheap consumer goods) can, however, not outrightly be rejected from available studies. Indeed, SI produces mainly urban wage goods, and it produces under very competitive conditions. These informations would fit into the picture of a subsidization of the formal sector or exports. However, no estimation of the importance of the goods produced by SI in the consumption budget is available.
The traditional SI (handicraft), however, appears to be subject to a tendency of marginalization[127]. Oesterdiekhoff (1984) claims that they are only surviving because of opportunity costs of zero or near zero in the face of superior competition. Increasing alternative income sources would imply a shift of labour force to other sources and a deterioration of handicrafts. These are at the same time less linked to the wider economy (reliance on local resources) - the picture of autonomous marginalization[128]. A contrast seem to be modern SI branches, which are more linked from the input as well as from the output side, and growing at the same time. A (very tentative) hypothesis can be formulated that those SI branches more linked to the wider economy have better accumulation prospects.

---
125 cf. Schmitz (1982a: 437)
126 Page and Steel (1984: 26)
127 cf. Oesterdiekhoff (1984). Streck (1982b, 1983) rejects strongly the hypothesis of marginalization and emphasizes emphatically the growth of handicrafts, which manage to benefit from the impacts of modern life in a process of "selective acculturation".
128 This is contradicted by others, e.g. Mohamed Nur (1988: 37), who claims that the informal sector is not autonomous, but well integrated with the rest of the economy through the demand-supply link.

Exploitation by LI and the economy at large: Nyala

How strong are the linkages of Nyala's SI? Forward linkages from Nyala's SI to LI are virtually non-existent (cf. Ch. 5.6.) - this is true not only for the analyzed four branches but for the SI in total; the local LI is totally import dependent. This means that the questions concerning negative or positive implications of subcontracting and other relations to LI are irrelevant.

SI produces overwhelmingly consumer goods. Only *blacksmiths* make predominantly capital goods - agricultural producer goods. The vast majority of farmers utilize only hand tools made locally by blacksmiths. Thus there is no competition for their agricultural tools. The only exception are the large farmers using tractors. In general, for the products of the blacksmiths there is very little competition.

The *tinsmiths'* products partly compete with other products available on the market. In any case, their products do not constitute a major part of the consumption goods of any income group. It is difficult to argue that they subsidize the formal sector/ export economy.

The *metal workshops* and *carpentry* products do not have any significant competition by other products available on the market. Their products can be regarded as "luxury products" in the sense that they do not satisfy basic needs. Thus the argument of a *subsidy* to those sectors in which the consumers work cannot be applied in a meaningful sense. For the high-income groups both product groups may be an important item in relative terms (to know about this one needs expenditure surveys). For lower income groups only the metal products may be of importance.

Altogether, one can assume that the SI products do not constitute a significant part of the consumption basket of either the low income or the high income groups.

The backward linkages of the Nyala SI to the formal sector or in general the wider economy are, on the other hand, on the whole very strong. This is because of their strong dependence on imported inputs which they receive through the trading system. This is even true for the blacksmiths who obtain most of their scrap and charcoal through traders (see below next chapter).

The link "provision of casual labour for LI" is non-existent.

In summary, one can say that SI has no links to LI, but strong linkages to the wider economy as a whole, because of a high dependence on imports and on consumers, who are themselves working in export oriented or generally foreign-economy-determined economic sectors. In contrast to widely held beliefs many SI branches in Nyala reveal themselves as having strong links to foreign economies.

Besides this, many of the SI activities are induced from outside. One group of examples are repair activities of imported products (the most important of this being car repair). Another group of examples are products imitated from foreign patterns. Actually most of the SI products fall in this category - all in carpentry. Thus, one can say that the development of SI should in no way be characterized as "autonomous", on the contrary SI is highly dependent on and determined by factors outside of it.

Are these links benign or exploitative? The *blacksmith* products are inexpensive, but they are also characterized by a very low productivity, and thus not comparable to the imported mechanized agricultural tools. This makes a conclusion that blacksmiths subsidize export agriculture by providing cheap products unviable. Incomes can be taken as an indirect indication of exploitative conditions in an industry. On this count also the blacksmiths do not appear as being exploited, because their incomes compare well with formal sector incomes. This is all the more correct, when the working conditions are taken into account. Blacksmiths work under a self-determined work system which is adapted to individual needs and thereby contrasts to the formal sector system which is imposed on the employees and in which their needs are secondary to the needs of the enterprise.

The *tinsmith* products which are inexpensive, are also of low quality and thus cannot be compared to formal sector products. In some cases they substitute for more expensive imported products, but in any case they do not constitute a significant part of consumption goods - of neither low nor high income earners. The incomes of many tinsmiths are low enough to speak of "exploitation", but in these cases the work is in no way intensive, so that in comparison to formal sector jobs they do not do badly.

Metal workshops do not produce any substitutes for other products, so that the "subsidization" hypothesis does not fit. Many of their products - e.g. doors, windows - are directed at a high income clientele (the poor have huts). For those high income clients SI products may constitute a significant part of their expenditure. The incomes of entrepreneurs and workers in this sector also figure comparatively high, so that there is no hint for an exploitative relationship.

The same is true for the *carpentry* subsector.

On the whole, one can say that SI mostly produces goods which are not in competition and do not act as a substitute for imported or LI products. Those SI products which do, are of lower quality and thus are also not comparable to imported or LI products. This means that the exploitation hypothesis cannot be confirmed in the case of Nyala. The incomes earned in SI also refute a theorem of general marginalization.

Looking at the correlation of growth prospects and the intensity of linkages to the formal sector/ wider economy, it appears that those SI branches which have the strongest linkages to the formal sector/ wider economy - the modern branches - also have the best growth prospects. On the other hand, those traditional industries which have stronger linkages to agriculture, but less to the formal sector because of less imports - and are thus more advantageous in terms of macro-economic development - have worst growth prospects. This constellation is to be explained by the impact of government policy (see below chapter 6.12.).

6.8 Difficulties in access to raw materials and machinery

Difficulties in access to raw materials is mentioned by several authors as one, if not the decisive, growth constraint[129]. The question of machinery is given less importance. As reasons for these difficulties are mentioned lack of capital (which would allow to buy large quantities), weak bargaining position, or in general a subordinate position, oligopolistic market structure[130], lack of infrastructure.

Trade liberalization ought to improve access by alleviating distortions. However, there is a danger that LI might benefit more from trade liberalization because SI establishments are too small to reap the benefits.

To analyze difficulties in access to raw materials and machinery the following issues have to be studied:
1. From where do SI enterprises acquire their raw materials and tools/machinery? How are these markets structured (numbers of buyers, sellers)?
2. From where do raw materials and tools/ machinery originate (local, domestic, imported)?
3. Are there scarcities?
4. What are the prices (retail, wholesale, import)?
5. How are the terms of payment?
6. What are the changes over time?

Evidence on these questions is scattered. As Schmitz shows in his analysis of Gerry's studies on Dakar[131], the data provided in studies emphasizing the raw materials constraint are not sufficient to allow to conclude dependence and inability to accumulate from the mere fact that SI enterprises purchase raw materials from large enterprises.

---

[129] cf. Gerry (1978, 1979), Allal and Chuta (1982: 18), Schmitz (1982b: 169-170)
[130] i.e. a market dominated by few suppliers
[131] cf. Gerry (1978, 1979), Schmitz (1982b: 431-440)

Difficulties in access to raw materials and machinery: Sudan

This is a major problem of industry in Sudan - LI as well as SI. Virtually every study on Sudanese industry emphasizes this point. According to the Industrial Survey 1981/82 shortage of raw materials was the major factor behind the close down of LI in the year of the survey (none of the recorded SI closed down during this period). It is well established that LI suffers of a lack of raw materials, due to foreign exchange shortages. In the 1980s import licenses were granted by the Ministry of Industry for only 50% of the required industrial inputs (in value terms)[132]. This is an unexpected result. In the presence of the relative market power of LI the access to raw materials was believed to be mostly a SI problem.

How does SI perform in this respect? We have to discriminate between those more traditional SI branches relying mostly on local raw materials and the more modern branches which rely more on imported raw materials. The second group faces two interrelated problems: shortages and interruptions of the supply of raw materials as well as high prices of these. Behind these problems are the import dependence, deficient transport structure, and the dependence on an oligopolistic marketing system. SI has a competitive disadvantage because it is not able to import directly, but has to rely on merchants.

Unexpectedly, as well those SI branches which rely predominantly on local materials appear to face supply problems: because of the ecological degradation on the one hand, and because of the oligopolistic market structure on the other hand[133].

No studies focusing especially on the trade with industrial inputs (or products) in Sudan are available. However, there are studies on the *marketing system* in general[134] and the agricultural marketing system in particular[135]. These bring out the following picture of the marketing system:
- marketing is restricted by low incomes and the importance of subsistence production;
- further difficulties are the dispersed population and a fragmented and unreliable transport system;
- the supply (and demand) - and accordingly the prices - of a large part of the agricultural population are not steady, but cyclical;
- the marketing system is complicated; several steps of intermediate trade are involved;
- this results in a high share of trading margins in the consumer's price of goods; they are often higher than the producer's share;

---
132   cf. World Bank (1987a: 13)
133   cf. Hansohm (1986a), Bakhit et al. (1987)
134   cf. Ahmed Hamza Khalifa (1976), Abdel Rahman A. Ibrahim (1984), Haaland (1984), Manger (1984b), and others in Manger (1984a)
135   cf. Oesterdiekhoff (1979c, 1988)

- often the trade with the producers (especially farmers) is part of a larger relation including financing, buying and selling (*sheil* system), which results in an oligopsonic/oligopolistic formation;
- thus, the trading system is generally regarded as exploitative, by both producers and consumers;
- accordingly the government has attempted time and again to control marketing by administrative measures (controlled prices); these attempts, however, largely failed.

Table 6.8.1. Differences between official and actual prices for small industry raw materials (selected items) in Khartoum, January 1989 (actual price as % of official price, LS)

industry	material	actual price/ official price
blacksmiths	scrap	170
	charcoal	113
tinsmiths	oil barrel, second hand	107
	edible oil container	167
	tin sheet, imported	143
	small nails, imported	200
	big zinc sheet	125
	tin flux	280
metal workshops	metal rod, imported	150-385
	metal pipe, imported	200
	hammer, imported	180-200
	soldering rod	133
carpentry workshops	white wood, imported	167-200
	Gimbil wood, domestic	167
	Sandal Radom wood, domestic	175
	marsonite, imported	133
	glue, imported	167
	glass, imported	150
	small lock, imported	170

Source: own survey

There is, however, no consensus, if this system is "exploitative". Some claim that the market structure tends to be olipopolistic and oligosonistic and point to the draining of resources out of productive sectors into the tertiary sector[136]. While this opinion is wide-spread and accordingly it is believed that the government has to play a vital role, others describe the system as efficient and competitive, and the high costs of marketing as adequate to the difficulties described above[137]. An evaluation of the existing marketing system has to take into account the alternatives: are they more efficient? In the past, the attempted alternative (government control) seems not to have been efficient, due to the limited

---
[136] cf. Oesterdiekhoff (1988), Seisi Mohamed and Fadlalla (1989)
[137] cf. Haaland (1984)

administrative capacity of the government, and a rigidity not adequate to the conditions defining the constraints on marketing in Sudan[138].
SI is almost totally dependent on merchants for the purchase of inputs, both local and imported. The available studies do not give detailed information on prices, availabilities, terms of payment for raw materials, but a 1989 comparison of the differences of official and actual prices brings out the very limited influence of government control (see Table 6.8.1.).

Difficulties in access to raw materials and machinery: Nyala

Different forms of markets for machinery and raw materials co-exist. They will be discussed separately by industry.

The *blacksmiths* produce their tools themselves - with very few exceptions. The import dependence with regard to machinery is negligible (see above Table 5.6.5.). All of the blacksmiths buy the *scrap* they need both for producing their tools and their products on the local market, either from traders or workshops in the Industrial Area, very seldom directly from lorry drivers. The most important source are traders. There are four traders specialized in scrap in Nyala, on *Suq ash Shabi* and in the Industrial Area. Sometimes traders come from Khartoum - the scrap they bring is more expensive. At times there are scarcities in scrap. This supply situation is reflected in high price fluctuations. Compared with Khartoum, the prices are 25% higher - twice the amount of the official price (see Table 6.8.2.).

Because of a lack of cash blacksmiths are generally not in the position to buy big amounts of scrap when the price is low. Instead they buy small amounts, several times a week. Because of this pattern they occasionally have to stop work when there is no scrap available on the market. Some get part of their scrap from one trader, but most compare prices between different traders before buying. The supply of scrap is more a problem now than in the past. One can imagine that the main reason is the higher demand, not being compensated by a supply, which has also risen due to more motor traffic. The absolute shortage of scrap is aggravated by the more or less oligopolistic market structure - few traders control a large part of the supply.

The other raw material used, *charcoal*, is bought from traders, in the nearby villages, but mostly in Nyala city. Traders buy it from producers in the vicinity of Nyala and transport and sell it in Nyala. With respect to charcoal there are also shortages sometimes, especially during the rainy season. Nevertheless, prices are

---

138 cf. Haaland (1984: 274-282)

Table 6.8.2. Price differences between Nyala and Khartoum (actual and official prices, LS) in January 1989

industry	material	Nyala as % of Khartoum (actual)	Nyala as % of Khartoum (official)
blacksmiths	scrap	125	208
	charcoal	57	88
tinsmiths	oil barrel, second hand	188	200
	edible oil container	140	233
	tin sheet, imported	300	429
	small nails, imported	300	429
	big zinc sheet	59	73
	tin flux	64	180
metal workshops	metal rod, imported	150-200	225-769
	metal pipe, imported	118	235
	hammer, imported	111	200
	soldering rod	175	233
carpentry workshops	white wood, imported	120-150	200-300
	Gimbil wood	100	167
	Sandal Radom wood	314	550
	marsonite, imported	150	200
	glue, imported	160	267
	glass, imported	133	200
	small lock, imported	147	250

Source: own survey

much lower than in Khartoum (see Table 6.8.2.); the price difference reflects the different degrees of urban congestion and ecological destruction. Different modes of payment are in use for the purchase of tools as well as raw materials (see Tables 6.8.3. and 6.8.4.)

Table 6.8.3. Modes of payment for tools and machinery of small industries in Nyala

industry	all at once paid from own sources	partly by credit from relatives	partly by credit from seller of machine
blacksmiths	13	-	-
tinsmiths	11	-	-
metal workshops	29	2	2
electric	20	1	1
non-electric	9	1	1
carpentry	24	-	2
electric	5	-	2
non-electric	19	-	-
total	77	2	4

Source: own survey; each enterprise counted once

Table 6.8.4. Modes of payment for raw materials of small industries in Nyala

industry	in cash immediately	with advance payment by clients	trader credit	provided by client
blacksmiths	13	2	5	7
tinsmiths	11	2	2	4
metal workshops	15	21	-	18
electric	12	18	-	10
non-electric	3	3	-	8
carpentry	15	23	4	21
electric	7	7	1	7
non-electric	8	16	3	14
total	54	48	11	50

Source: own survey; each enterprise may be counted more than once

As can be seen in Table 6.8.3., all of the blacksmiths pay the raw material for their tools at once from own sources. As far as the raw materials for their ongoing production are concerned, all pay at least part in cash immediately (see Table 6.8.4.). More than half of the customers bring their own material at times, about 40% take trader credit occasionally, and advance payments by clients are of no big importance.

All of the *tinsmiths* buy their tools from local traders or workshops. As shown in Table 5.6.5., more than one third is imported. No scarcities are reported by the tinsmiths. All but one state that the supply is better now as compared to the years before. As seen in Table 6.8.3., all pay their tools immediately. As far as their raw materials are concerned, all are bought locally from traders. Two tinsmiths buy partly from one trader, but otherwise there is a variety of many traders to choose from - the market is not oligopolistic. Nevertheless, the prices are much higher than in Khartoum (see Table 6.8.2.). From the modes of payment the immediate payment is also prevalent. All use it, at least for part of their purchases. Trader credit on the other hand is only used by two. In between, prepayment of raw materials by customers either in form of cash payment or provision of raw materials is used by 55% (see Table 6.8.4.). Despite the fact that the raw materials are partly second-hand materials, shortages do occur at times and may force tinsmiths to stop work. In the past the situation was better.

The situation is different in the more modern SI branches. The *electric metal workshops* use almost exclusively imported machinery (see Table 5.6.5.). While six (27%) buy their tools from different traders in Nyala, fifteen (68%) buy at different places in Sudan, i.e. mainly both in Nyala and Greater Khartoum, one only bought exclusively in Greater Khartoum. This reflects both the insufficient supply of electric machinery in Nyala - many machines are simply not available in Nyala - and the relative independence of SI entrepreneurs of local traders. Almost all of the entrepreneurs paid all their machinery at once (see Table 6.8.4.).

The raw material markets give a different picture. Also a high percentage is imported (see Table 5.6.6.). 86% buy only in Nyala, from different traders. Only one buys exclusively from one trader. One buys both from Khartoum and Nyala, while another one buys from one trader in Khartoum. There are severe scarcities in this market. Occasionally raw materials can be found neither in Nyala nor in Khartoum. These scarcities are exacerbated by the trading system. Although the number of traders dealing in this sphere is quite high, it is a speculative activity characterized by high price fluctuations. The practice to create artificial shortages is common. Prices may be more than twice the Khartoum prices - not to speak of the official prices (see Table 6.8.2.). Different modes of payments are combined by the workshop owners to cope with the situation. 54% pay in part at once, 82% demand advance payment from clients, and 45% use the practice of clients bringing the raw materials (see Table 6.8.4.). 27% only use the practice of advance payments. Trader credits are not used at all. Due to foreign exchange shortages and the general economic decline in Sudan the supply of raw materials has become much worse compared to the years before.

Half of the *non-electric metal workshop* owners also purchase their tools in Nyala from different traders, the same number also buys from Greater Khartoum, while one buys partly from abroad. The import intensity is almost as high as among electric metal workshops (see Table 5.6.5.). For the non-electric tools shortages do not constitute a severe problem. There is no unequivocal opinion if the supply situation became worse or not over the years. These tools are also for the most part paid immediately (see Table 6.8.3.).

The raw materials supply affects most SI producers in an indirect way, because they do not buy any raw materials themselves (64%). Those who do, buy from different traders in Nyala. As discussed above (see Table 5.6.5.), over 90% are imported. There are frequent raw material shortages, absolute or artificial, in Nyala, especially during the rainy season (for the price difference see Table 6.8.2.). Among the modes of payment, the provision of raw material by the clients is most common (see Table 6.8.4.). No one pays all of the raw material at once. The supply became worse compared to the years before.

From the *electric carpentry* workshop owners, surprisingly more than half bought their machines in Nyala (two also from abroad), despite the fact that they are almost totally imported (see Table 5.6.5.). This points to a highly developed trading structure in this sphere. However, there are frequent shortages in Nyala, sometimes even in Khartoum. Two received a seller credit for part of their expenditure on machinery, the rest paid at once (see Table 6.8.3.). According to the opinion of the concerned entrepreneurs the supply of machinery became better or did at least not deteriorate.

The raw materials were by all bought on the Nyala market, from different traders (oligopolistic market structure). About 3/4 are imported. Especially in the rainy season there are severe shortages at times - absolute and artificial (for the price difference see Table 6.8.2.). All of the workshop owners combine different modes of payment: in cash at once, customers' advance payment, and provision of raw materials by clients. Only one also uses trader credit. The supply situation clearly deteriorated during the last years, not the least because of the ecological destruction.

The *non-electric carpentry* workshops have the highest import dependence with regard to machinery (see above Table 5.6.5.). Nevertheless, almost 2/3 bought all their tools on the Nyala market. Scarcities do occur at times in Nyala - even in Khartoum. The tools are paid exclusively at once (see Table 6.8.3.). On this market, the supply is better now than in the years before.

The import dependence is much lower than for the electric carpentry (see above Table 5.6.5.). The raw materials are exclusively bought in the Nyala market from different traders. Especially during the rainy season there are shortages. For the imported items, prices are high (see Table 6.8.2.). Among the modes of payment, advance payments by clients are most common (see Table 6.8.2.). 42% also pay part in cash at the time of purchase, but only one practices this mode exclusively. The supply situation deteriorated over the years.

The supply of raw materials and machinery emerges as a major problem of Nyala's SI, mainly for the highly import-dependent modern branches. But also traditional SI is dependent on the oligopolistic trading system for its supplies.

6.9 Difficulties in access to product markets

It is argued in different quarters that lack of demand would be a decisive barrier to growth of SI. Hymer and Resnick argued that in the course of development with rising incomes the demand for industrial goods would shift away from local non-agricultural activities to superior LI products or imports - the SI products are considered as inferior[139].

In the face of a reality of *declining* - rather than rising - incomes in many developing countries it seems reasonable to hypothesize that there might be opposite substitution effects, i.e. - assuming that SI products are inferior - these do substitute for LI products or imports.

The *marginalization* theorists[140] have a different theoretical background but arrive at the same pessimistic conclusion as Hymer and Resnick: stagnating or declining

---
139 - called "Z"-goods; cf. Hymer and Resnick (1969); see also Resnick (1970) supporting this argument by three Asian country cases
140 cf. Quijano (1977)

demand for SI products. Others see a depression of demand due to deficiencies in government policy and especially in agricultural policy[141]. It is argued that a bimodal development strategy as pursued in many developing countries would lead to the co-existence of a high-income modern agricultural sector, dependent on imported inputs and a low-income traditional agricultural sector dependent on local inputs and consumption goods[142].

A related approach attributes a displacement of SI products by products of transnational corporations to "taste transfer" through advertising, copying of lifestyles of expatriates and other mechanisms in the course of cultural influences (cultural imperialism)[143].

SAPs are expected to have positive impacts on SI by increasing the income of those who demand SI products (e.g. the rural and the agricultural population)[144]. But no evidence is yet available on the truth of this assertion.

To test these various propositions the following issues have to be analyzed:
1. For whom do SI and LI produce (industry, exports, low-income, high-income consumers)? On which markets do LI and SI products compete? What is their relative importance in the household budgets of consumers?
2. What are the income elasticities of SI and LI products?

The limited evidence is not unequivocal. It shows that SI overwhelmingly produces consumer goods. SI products are not necessarily inferior. Although many hold that SI produces for low-income markets, this view is not undisputed[145].

Neither Hymer and Resnick nor the marginalists support their arguments with empirical evidence. The arguments seem to be based on two related arguments: first, improved infrastructure, giving an advantage to standardized products of LI or imports, and second, the economies of scale[146]. Both arguments have to be acknowledged, but must be qualified. Several authors mention regional and sectoral exceptions, in which informal, or family based enterprises maintain their position[147]. Economies of scale appear not to be significant in a number of production lines[148]. It is held that the impacts of modernization and colonialism is too differentiated to be subsumed as marginalization[149].

---

141 cf. Anderson (1982: 929), Binswanger (1983)
142 cf. ILO (1972), Johnston and Kilby (1975), Mellor (1976), Anderson and Leiserson (1980),
143 cf. Langdon (1975), Kaplinsky (1979)
144 cf. Haggblade et al. (1986)
145 Berg (1978b) holds that they produce luxury goods. Wohlmuth (1990b) claims that the informal and formal sectors compete on identical markets.
146 cf. Page and Steel (1984: 18). This view sees a choice between labour intensive small-scale production and capital-intensive large-scale production, when demand rises.
147 cf. King (1974), Lipton (1980) and Schmitz (1982a)
148 cf. Chuta and Liedholm (1979)
149 cf. Chuta and Liedholm (1984), O'Hear (1987)

Although several studies on Africa suggest that SI concentrates on the production of inferior goods[150], there seem to be hardly any studies on income elasticities of demand which are disaggregated by sector of origin. Liedholm and Chuta (1976), who distinguish product groups manufactured by small and large enterprises calculate high and positive expenditure elasticities for the first category in Sierra Leone. A 1985 study of Chuta and Liedholm also shows high and positive figures. King and Byerlee's study (1978), also in Sierra Leone, reveals that the rural expenditure elasticity for rurally produced non-farm consumption items is 1.4.
It is not quite clear how the agricultural demand is related to income levels. Most studies hold that the expenditures for rurally produced consumer goods as well as agricultural equipment are higher for small farms. For East Africa, however, Johnston (1984) maintains that there is a purchasing power constraint which prevents the spread of even simply improved technologies. Hazell and Röell (1983) suggest that richer households and larger farms may have more desirable expenditure patterns and that thus there may be a trade-off between growth and equity.
Exports are not a major market for SI. The share of exports in total production of SI tends to be less than 1%[151]. However, for particular product groups (crafts, "culturally-oriented" products) exports can be a significant market with high income elasticities of demand[152].

Difficulties in access to product markets: Sudan

The imports of manufactured products - combined with active disencouragements - led to a deterioration of traditional industries. The same effect resulted from modern import-substituting industries which did not develop from the existing industrial base, but depended on imported technologies. Some of the traditional industries seem actually to be extinguished (e.g. spinning and weaving), others had to compete with superior products (e.g. pottery, blacksmiths, tinsmiths, tannery, leather work). The new products were superior in terms of price, comfort, durability, odour, or were prefered because of the Western image they provided[153]. This would fit into the theory of inferior products. On the other hand, new SI branches were coming into existence.
But recently there seems to be another trend. Recent studies on existing SI (modern and traditional) argue that demand is no problem - there is excess

---

150 cf. Page and Steel (1984: 10)
151 cf. Liedholm and Mead (1987: 59)
152 cf. Ho and Huddle (1976)
153 cf. El-Bushra (1980: 270, 285), Kuhn (1970), Oesterdiekhoff (1984), Streck (1982b: 64-65)

demand for SI products[154], due to the supply constraints of LI as well as insufficient imports due to foreign exchange constraints.
Few studies analyse if SI products substitute for LI products or imports. There is disagreement if imports compete for LI and SI products. According to a World Bank report, smuggled imports are presently mostly goods not produced in Sudan[155]. Others, however, mention competition between the two[156]. Mohamed et al. argue that there is a change in pattern of final demand in favour of goods and services produced informally[157]. No information is available which income groups are changing their consumption structure.

Difficulties in access to product markets: Nyala

Overall markets are declining because of declining incomes. The differences in living standards between Nyala and Khartoum can be assessed from the price differences of consumption goods (see Table 6.9.1.).
While some locally produced food (most importantly the staple foods millet, sorghum, and edible oil) are cheaper in Nyala, other essentials as bread (nowadays the most important urban staple food, made from imported wheat), sugar (mostly from East and Central Sudan) and others are much more expensive. It is, however, noteworthy that the prices in Nyala are not consistently higher than in Khartoum.
The markets of SI in Nyala have been discussed in Chapters 5.5. and 5.7. The question is now the potential of these markets, the position of local SI on these markets and the future chances SI has from the demand point of view.
The *blacksmiths* produce mainly agricultural hand tools. In this respect there is neither competition by LI products or imports nor any danger of such competition. The production of animal drawn ploughs shows that the blacksmiths are able to keep pace with an introduction of intermediate technologies which are affordable to the mass of the small farmers. Blacksmiths can produce the necessary tools much cheaper than imported goods and in a sufficient quality. The problem is that the low incomes of farmers prevent most of them even to go beyond the use of hand tools. A tractorization would of course displace most blacksmiths by substituting imported tractors for hand tools. But such a development can neither be expected nor is it desirable (because of resulting land concentration and damaging ecological effects).
The situation is different with respect to the other goods blacksmiths produce (e.g. hammer, trowel, knife). These are competing with imported goods which are both

---
154 cf. Anand and Nur (1985), Bakhit Idris (1979: 4.5.2.), Niazi (1987)
155 cf. World Bank (1987a: 44)
156 cf. Babiker (1982)
157 cf. Mohamed et al. (1985: 38)

Table 6.9.1. Official and actual prices for domestic and imported consumption goods in Nyala and Khartoum, January 1989 (LS)

domestic products	Nyala as % of Khartoum (actual)	Khartoum actual as % of official	Nyala as % of Khartoum (official)
beef	77	125	96
mutton	57	117	67
eggs	89	117	104
sorghum	61	112	68
millet	74	120	89
sugar	150	400	600
salt	223	100	224
edible oil	53	136	18
local soft drink	57	233	133
Bringi cigarettes	63	150	94
toilet soap	100	125	125
batteries	210	111	233
damouria (cloth)	33	113	38
imported products			
wheat flour	86	117	100
rice	56	120	67
bread	400	167	667
tea	100	150	150
milkpowder	93	113	104
Pepsi cola	180	167	300
Benson cigarettes	83	150	125
petrol	120	250	300
diesel	125	500	625

Source: own survey

more expensive and of better quality (more durable). This implies that the danger of displacement with rising incomes is looming, these goods are inferior.

The statements of blacksmiths concerning their demand prospects are not unequivocal. Most regard them as good or medium, only 2 (15%) as insufficient. Most of them assess the demand as having increased compared to the past, while 38% say that it declined; most of the latter group attribute this to a rising number of workshops. On the other hand, more than half feel that there is a lot of competition from other blacksmiths. Almost half say that they have to sell with losses sometimes, which also points to a demand problem.

On the demand side, the *tinsmiths* also fall into two categories. Almost half regards the demand as good and having increased compared to the years before. On the other hand 36% regard the demand as insufficient and as having declined compared to the years before. Astonishingly only one regards competition as a problem. 36% also sell with losses. Those at the lower end are the same workshops

which produce inferior goods, and which are situated at unfavourable markets (Suq ash Shabi, Suq Congo).
Most goods of the tinsmiths are inferior consumption goods and directed at low income markets. When incomes rise, they will be substituted by imports. However, the reverse substitution effect, i.e. the substitution of expensive imports by cheap local tinsmith products is very small. Apparently the incomes of many are too low to afford even these substitutes.
The demand assessments of the *metal workshop* owners also vary. There are no significant differences between electric and non-electric units. In both categories the largest group considered demands as having declined. However, the two subgroups differ in another respect: While almost half of the electric units have to sell with losses at times, only one non-electric unit reports this.
All of the metal workshop goods can be regarded as luxury goods. Even the cheapest and most common goods - chairs - are substitutes for local material based and inexpensive stools. In terms of income elasticities the demand situation of this industry implies that with rising incomes the demand for their products will rise. However, at the same time it means that with declining incomes it will also fall.
Concerning the *carpentry workshops*, the electric units assess the demand more positively than the rest. 71% label it as "good", while only 42% of the non-electric units do so. About half of the electric workshop owners regard the demand as having increased, while only 37% of the non-electric units do so. These results are enforced by the information on sale with losses. Of the electric units 29% have to sell with losses at times, while more than half of the non-electric workshops report this practice. On the other hand, the electric units have a stronger feeling about competition - 71 vs. 58%.
Carpentry products are mostly luxury goods, the share of those making cheap furniture out of second-hand material is very small. In spite of this, the market of the first sub-group - but not the second - is growing. This implies that this SI copies and reinforces the unequal income structure, rather than overcoming it. In any case, for the carpentry workshops there is no difficulty to produce quality goods.

6.10 Difficulties in access to technology

Technology is here used in a broad sense, including everything concerning the transformation of inputs into outputs[158]. Formerly, technology was not in the centre of attention of economists concerned with development[159]. It was considered as a parameter of economic analysis. Furthermore, technical change

---
158 cf. Fransman (1984)
159 For Africa cf. Johnson (1978), Austen and Headrick (1983)

was considered as neutral[160]. In this framework, transfer of technology from the industrial countries was regarded as an unequivocal blessing. A main basis for this opinion was a belief in extremely weak technological capabilities of the developing countries. Later all of these assumptions have been challenged. It was acknowledged that there is a choice of technology, which is determined by economic policy and development - and that there is an opposite causation as well, i.e. the choice of technology influences the pattern of development, growth, income distribution etc. More than that, one became aware that technology is a major factor explaining the success - or failure - of development efforts[161]. It is recognized that it was misleading to regard technical change as such as something positive[162]. The focus of attention shifted from the import of technologies to the "indigenous technological capability", i.e. the abilities of developing countries to achieve technological progress as a central prerequisite of development[163]. Also it became clear that the conditions for achieving this cannot be properly analysed in the dichotomy of import-substituting industrialization vs. export-oriented industrialization as alternatives - an explanation of success stories is much more complicated[164]. Some elements of both strategies seem to be relevant (at different points of time) and a directed government policy plays a central role - technological development cannot be achieved by merely accumulating experience. For technologically backward countries, neither an undiscriminated take-over of technologies from industrial countries nor technological self-sufficiency are appropriate, but a proper combination of foreign and local technological elements[165]. There is a wide consensus on the importance of a domestic capital goods sector for facilitating indigenous technological change[166]. This seems all the more important in view of the apparently increasing technological gap to low-income developing countries, especially in Africa - of course with the exception of the NICs[167]. This gap increases technological dependence and foreign exchange costs, and, more importantly, results in the transfer of increasingly inappropriate technologies (in terms of factor endowments and of products)[168].

There are still a lot of open questions concerning the role of technology in development and how it is affected and affects other factors, but some points seem to have emerged from research: It has to be assessed in the wider context of the

---

160 cf. Stewart (1977)
161 e.g. Stewart (1977), Ranis (1984)
162 cf. Marsden (1970), Cooper (1972)
163 cf. Fransman and King (1984), Dahlman et al. (1987)
164 cf. Fransman (1984: 19)
165 cf. Dahlman et al. (1987)
166 cf. Marsden (1970: 490), Fransman (1984: 24)
167 cf. Bienefeld (1984), Kaplinsky (1984); concerning Africa cf. Goody (1973), Austen and Headrick (1983)
168 cf. Cooper (1972), Stewart (1972, 1977), James and Stewart (1981)

social organisation of production[169]. In contrast to former, static analyses, it has to be seen in a dynamic and historical perspective[170]. The traditional view of SI painted it as using technologies with a low productivity and over time failing to significantly improve its technologies. As a result a technological gap between SI technologies and up-to-date technologies used by LI and/or represented by imports would increase. This would make SI increasingly uncompetitive[171].

In view of the above-mentioned discussions the argument that SI faces a constraint concerning access to technologies has to be reformulated. To investigate this proposition it has to be analyzed:

1. Which technologies are employed by SI? How do they compare to the technologies employed by LI?
2. Are their technologies appropriate to their socio-economic environment, i.e. in terms of factor endowment and in terms of products?
3. Which technological change is taking place in LI and SI?
4. What determines the level of technology and its change (or lack of change)?

Although there is a general impression confirming the proposition that SI in developing countries - especially traditional SI - employ low-level technologies, Schmitz (1982a) shows that there is no conclusive evidence to support the notion of an increasing technological gap. Technological discontinuities appear to be not very severe. Little research has been done on the actual impact of the introduction of new technologies on SI. This is partly due to the fact that this must be seen in a historical perspective. The discussion of the technological aspect of SI development as a whole is of quite recent nature. Cortes et al. refute the view that SI - including the very small - fails to improve its technology over time. In their view SI enterprises do not take over superior technologies from LI - or fail to do so - (the traditional view), but they adapt their technology to their financial situation and the factor prices they face, i.e. technological changes reflect objective changes in a firm's economic circumstances[172].

Concerning Africa, there is evidence that the low level of SI is due to its economic environment, especially to the low technological level of agriculture[173] - as shown above, SI has a strong relation to agriculture. It is assumed that SI is inherently in a position to improve its technology if an appropriate environment is created. Müller in a study on blacksmiths in Tanzania argues that their simple technology is due and adequate to their situation, i.e. their production potential is fully exploited,

---

169 cf. Marsden (1970), Leys (1984); concerning Africa cf. Goody (1971), Austen and Headrick (1983)
170 cf. Marsden (1970), Kaplinsky (1984)
171 cf. Bienefeld (1975), LeBrun and Gerry (1975: 24)
172 cf. Cortes et al. (1987: 201-205)
173 cf. Goody (1973), Austen and Headrick (1983), Ahmed and Kinsey (1984), Vitta (1988)

given the policies towards LI and imports, the demand and the development of the industrial service infrastructure. A change in these issues would be not only necessary, but also sufficient, to induce the development of blacksmiths, including technological development[174].

Difficulties in access to technology: Sudan

Little research has been done about the technological aspect of industrialization in Sudan. The upper range of SI, which is included in the industrial statistics, does appear to use a different technology, but does not appear to become inefficient comparatively to LI - on the contrary. This indicates that SI selects the appropriate technology[175]. For the lower range of SI, the situation may be different[176]. Many informal traditional industries are stagnating in terms of technological development - they use still the same techniques as ages ago (e.g. blacksmithing, pottery). According to Kuhn (1971) the rapid injection of new technologies did not give craftsmen an opportunity to adapt their work to new machines and tools. Thus others who had never been craftsmen were recruited for modern industries, which establish their market partly at the expense of the traditional SI.

Difficulties in access to technology: Nyala

Technologically, Nyala's SI is split into traditional industries using primitive technologies on the one hand and modern industries using up-to-date technologies on the other hand: There is a technological dichotomy.
The *blacksmiths* use hand tools and were hardly affected by technological change since decades. What is the reason for this technological stagnation? As the introduction of intermediate technologies produced by blacksmiths (camel ploughs and donkey seeder-weeders) shows, blacksmiths are in a position to produce improved instruments[177]. This and the limited spread of an Egyptian model of an animal-drawn plough points to another reason: lack of demand due to low incomes and neglected agriculture.
The modern industries (*electric metal and carpentry workshops*), on the other hand, use up-to-date instruments, although the local availability of them is very limited. They are partly bought in Khartoum, but the main corridor of introduction is

---
174 cf. Müller (1980: 146-147), idem (1984)
175 Streck (1982) emphasizes the capability of traditional industry to select the appropriate technology from the wide range available.
176 Bakhit Idris (1979) claims a low technology used by SI due to non-availability of technical information.
177 cf. JMRDP (1988), WSDC (1988: 31-41)

working abroad - and buying the machines abroad. Shortcomings of these technologies are their very limited relation to the indigenous technological base: they are very highly dependent on imported spare parts (the local production of spare parts is rudimentary). This makes them subject to frequent supply interruptions. A related factor is the dependence on imported energy. Furthermore, these technologies have limited employment effects. What is missing is the middle: intermediate technologies.

6.11 Difficulties in access to credit

Lack of credit is widely regarded as a barrier to enter the SI sector[178] and as a main growth constraint of SI, by academics[179] as well as by SI entrepreneurs[180]. It is widely accepted that SI enterprises are largely self-financed, have little access to credit, and have to pay higher interest rates if they take credit ("capital segmentation")[181]. As a result, the provision of credit, by special programmes or directives to commercial banks to allocate credit to SI, often at subsidized rates, is a major part of SI promotion programmes.

However, this policy is controversial. The counter-proposition argues:
1. Higher credit costs for SI and difficulties to access are appropriate to their position, they reflect their risky and unstable environment, high transaction costs, high failure rates and other constraints they face[182].
2. Credits at subsidized, non-market rates would run the risks to encourage unviable investment projects and undue capitalization and to replace personal savings. They would undermine some of SI's main distinct advantages, namely its labour intensity and efficient use of capital. At the same time, supply-side assistance does not ensure a market for higher output[183]. Furthermore, interest ceilings make it unprofitable to lend to SI[184].

However, there is evidence that the principle of provision of credit at rates which reflect costs and risks alone will not solve the problem because of exceedingly high initial risks, a great increase of risk because of high interest rates, possible market failure, possible default of good borrowers because of failures of others. Furthermore, financial institutions are not adapted to deal

---

178 cf. Anderson (1982: 932)
179 cf. Hoselitz (1959: 617), Schatz (1965: 309), Steel (1977: 171), Page (1979: 22), Sethuraman (1981c: 29-30) idem (1981c: 196), Richardson (1984: 25), Stearns (1985: 9-13), Nanjundan (1986: 25-26)
180 cf. Liedholm and Mead (1986: 321)
181 cf. Page (1979: 22), Kilby et al. (1984: 277), Richardson (1984), Cortes et al. (1987: 216). On capital segmentation cf. chapter 6.12.
182 e.g. Little et al. (1987: 311). The critical views on the policies of cheap credit are summarized in von Pischke et al. (1983), Adams et al. (1984) and Adams and Vogel (1986)
183 e.g. Page (1979), Steel and Takagi (1983)
184 cf. Liedholm and Mead (1986: 318)

with SI and do not have the necessary information and experience, which results in very high initial administrative costs. This implies that SI programmes cannot pay for themselves[185]. These shortcomings in capital markets, mostly of an institutional nature, have to be addressed by interventions as lending by development banks (at non-concessionary rates) and publicly backed risk-sharing schemes. It is widely agreed that there is a need for financial innovations to reach the SI entrepreneur. In this context, the informal financial sector is highlighted and especially the moneylender has been rehabilitated to some degree. However, the scope to channel finance through the informal financial sector appears to be limited in Africa, as compared with other regions[186].
3. The idea of a capital scarcity is a myth or at least debatable[187]. First, SI establishments and the socio-economic environment from which they spring have a high capacity to save and to invest[188]. Second, only a small part of the apparent credit need of SI is an effective demand for credit. A considerable, if not the major part of the apparent demand conceals other problems[189].

This argument is supported by high failure rates of credit programmes and by some evidence that huge amounts of capital are not necessarily important for success of SI[190], and a lack or correlation between business success and the amount of initial capital[191].

It is difficult to assess the effective demand for credit of SI enterprises, let alone whole sectors. The perceived credit need has to be analyzed in the context of supply and demand factors as well as the economic position of the enterprise. Factors to be analyzed include the composition of capital and the sources of capital.

Difficulties in access to credit: Sudan

SI in Sudan is largely self-financed. Its access to credit is very limited. Three kinds of credit can be distinguished: commercial banks, development banks and informal credits. *Commercial banks* were an important source of working capital finance for industry (almost exclusively LI) up to the end of the 1970s, but in the course of the economic crisis bank activities shifted more and more to short-term lending for

---

185 cf. Anderson and Khambata (1982), van Dijk and Molenaar (1983)
186 cf. van Dijk (1983)
187 cf. Nihan and Jourdain (1978), Nihan et al. (1979), Schneider-Barthold (1984a: 71), Cortes et al. (1987: 216)
188 cf. Ewing (1968: 113-127), Katzin (1964: 194), Cortes et al. (1987: 216)
189 cf. Schatz (1965), Nihan and Jourdain (1978), Chuta and Liedholm (1984: 306-307), Kilby et al. (1984)
190 cf. Kennedy (1980: 45)
191 cf. Chuta and Liedholm (1985: 73)

commercial (mainly trade) activities, which they regard as easier, more secure, and more profitable[192]. Nowadys commercial banks play a very limited role in industrial financing. In 1987 79.2% of their total advances to the private sector were short-term credits; only 17.8% of these went to industrial enterprises[193]. Furthermore, their credits tend to be heavily concentrated on the *Three Towns* and the Central Region. This tendency is enforced by the heavily centred administrative structure of the commercial banks. Their branches outside Khartoum - which are quite limited anyhow - are not authorized to lend more than a small proportion of their resources to the private sector without referring to their headquarters in Khartoum[194]. SI did hardly benefit even from the small share of credit devoted to industry, because of the very traditional approach[195] of the banks: risk avoidance, very little information on SI enterprises, the lack of documentation and the often unconventional practice as well as a lack of collateral of SI. Furthermore, commercial banks fail to mobilize long-term domestic savings. The finance available for SI is also highly concentrated on the *Three Towns* and the Central Region. This is reflected by the astonishingly high rate of finance available for SI in these areas: A 1987 study found that 27% of the surveyed enterprises in these areas received bank credits[196].

A financial innovation is represented by the *Islamic banks* (there are six Islamic banks presently operating in the country). Because of their conception and their economic ethical principles one can assume that they are more inclined to promote investment which is development-oriented. In fact, the largest Islamic bank active in Sudan - the *Faisal Islamic Bank (Sudan)* - began to take interest in medium-term financing of industries in the small business and artisans sectors. A special branch for this activity was opened in Omdurman and is operating successfully. According to a recent study, this branch plays an important role: It provided 63% of all credits (1981-85) for the surveyed enterprises in Khartoum Industrial Area[197]. However, in the total context of the banks activities and of the SI financing needs, it plays a marginal role. 4.1% of the surveyed enterprises in the Khartoum Industrial Area received credits from the Craftsmen Branch, and the share of this branch in the bank's activities comes to about 5%[198]. On the whole, the Islamic banks did not perform better than other commercial banks in Sudan: Their financing is even of a shorter term, small and medium customers are even more discriminated against (exceptions are only the Craftsmen Branch of the Faisal Islamic Bank and the Sudanese Islamic Bank, a minor bank with only 8.7%

---
192 cf. Ali (1966), Abdel Aal Salih (1977), World Bank (1987b: 55-57)
193 cf. BoS (1988)
194 cf. Seisi Mohamed and Fadlalla (1989: 15)
195 cf. Ali (1966), Yassin (1987), Ahmed (1988a, 1988b), Staab (1989)
196 cf. Gumaa et al. (1987); however, the very small sample (81) from many different areas and branches cannot claim representativity.
197 cf. Miro et al. (1986: 62)
198 cf. Miro et al. (1986: 65), Staab (1989: 184)

of the capital of the Islamic banks in 1985), productive sectors (agriculture and industry) are neglected, the banks contribute to increased regional inequality by chanelling mobilized savings from rural to urban areas, and almost all of the banks are influenced by religious groups and accordingly distribute their credits[199].

The government set up several *development banks* to compensate for the financial shortcoming of the productive sectors in general and SI in particular: the Agricultural Bank of Sudan (ABS), the Industrial Bank of Sudan (IBS), the Sudan Rural Development Corporation, and the Sudanese Savings Bank (SSB). Their performance has been mixed[200], but their overall effect with respect to SI has been negligible[201].

In the face of this very limited access to the formal credit system, SI enterprises have only two choices: either to search on the *informal credit markets* or to rely on self-finance. Unlike agricultural producers[202], small industrialists apparently hardly take the first choice. Informal credits tend to imply high interest rates. Evidence on informal credit markets in Sudan is, however, limited. While there is a consensus that the interest rates are high, there is disagreement if this is appropriate to the prevailing conditions or exploitative. A study on credit in the Gezira Scheme finds an average interest rate of 726% for the "sheil" credit and concludes that this is far beyond a reasonable charge taking into account appropriate allowances for the special circumstances[203]. Others, however, evaluate the informal financial markets more positively. The structure of informal credit markets is competitive and suited to the high-risk and high-cost environment of lending, it is argued[204].

SI relies strongly on *self-finance*. The opinions are divided on the question whether this indicates a genuine problem, or whether it is reflecting other problems or a credit-avoidance on the part of the SI entrepreneurs. A large group of academics and government representatives tends to assume that finance is a serious, if not the major, problem of SI, resulting in inability to buy reasonable stocks of raw materials, leading to idleness and production on order, and low prices for SI products because of a need to sell products quickly[205]. However, there are also other opinions. It is argued that SI entrepreneurs need little capital and are inclined to avoid credit[206].

Evidence is not sufficient to evaluate the contrasting claims. However, some doubt is thrown on the "capital scarcity" argument. The evidence is often very shaky. For instance, claims of SI entrepreneurs that they face a capital shortage are often

---
199 cf. Staab (1989)
200 cf. the next chapter for an analysis of them.
201 cf. Gesim Marhoum (1980: 73)
202 see below chapter 6.12.
203 cf. Ahmed (1983)
204 cf. Wilmington (1955), Haaland (1984)
205 cf. Fadlalla (1973), Bakhit Idris (1979), Anand and Nur (1985), Bakhit et al. (1987), BCHLI (1987), Ishaq and Adam Mohamed (n.d.)
206 cf. Hammeed (1974), Nimeiri (1976b), Curtis (1979, 1980)

taken as a basis[207]. This is, however, not convincing. Even if these claims could be taken to represent the perceived credit need (which would be naive), this is not necessarily equal to the real credit need. The persistent over-liquidity of commercial banks[208] points rather to a lack of viable projects.

Difficulties in access to credit: Nyala

It was shown above that SI in Nyala rely to a high degree on self-finance. The traditional branches rely totally on own resources to finance their tools and machinery, modern branches to a high degree. Formal sources of credit play no role, family credit a marginal one. The main credit source are the suppliers of machinery (see Table 6.8.3.). The larger of the modern SI establishments, for which bank credit would be an option, avoid credits because of the loss of independence and the credit terms which they regard as too unfavourable. An interest in a credit service by government development banks on better terms (with respect to interest rate and duration) is expressed by many, but generally this does not represent a real interest.

With respect to current finance, the situation is different, as indicated by the multitude of different finance arrangements (see Table 6.8.4.). The practices of buying small amounts and of production on order and the frequent production interruptions also point in this direction. Their capital scarcity puts them at the mercy of the traders in the face of the transport difficulties and the oligopolistic market structure. Those larger establishments which have enough capital to buy larger amounts of raw materials in Khartoum are in a favourable position.

6.12 Government discrimination

Many studies give this constraint a prominent place[209], not least because of the pervasive role governments (try to) play in developing countries[210]. All of the above-mentioned external constraints are directly or indirectly influenced by

---
207 e.g. Miro et al. (1986), Ahmed (1988b)
208 cf. Staab (1989)
209 cf. ILO (1972), Di Tullio (1973), World Bank (1978), Page (1979), Schwarz (1980), Schneider-Barthold (1981, 1984a, 1984b), Allal and Chuta (1982: 27-37), Bruch (1983), House (1984), Stearns (1985), Engelberg et al (1988), Schamp (1988). Cortes et al. (1987: 220), however, report that in Colombia "on balance, public policy appears to have been neither a major support for small and medium industries nor a strong deterrent". Discrimination measures are not very strong and positive discrimination is taking place by minimum wage legislation, unionization, social benefits and taxation which are applied to LI but not to SI.
210 It is, however, a controversial issue how pervasive this role really is. Hyden (1983) claims the contrary as a central feature in Africa. On the range of different government attitudes with respect to regulation of SI and their determining factors cf. Eades (1985).

government policy. The headline of this chapter, "government discrimination", seems actually to be biased, because there are policies having a positive impact, as well as those which have a negative impact. It is important to become aware of how large the range of government policies, which have an impact on SI, really is. Research on SI has not yet done justice to this fact. However, on balance the overall negative policy impacts on SI appear to be clear enough to justify such a headline.

Government policies can be categorized in several dimensions. One of them is a temporal dimension. In the African context, historically one can distinguish between two phases: First, the phase of "classical" discrimination of SI in the course of industrialization efforts in Africa, emphasizing LI. Second, the phase of stabilization policies. These policies are believed to have a positive impact on SI, mostly because of redressing the distortions which discriminated against SI[211]. However, hardly any studies exist proving (or disproving) this hope. Critics argue that other negative side-effects of SAP might more than outweigh the positive impacts[212].

Another dimension is to divide between those measures having a direct impact on SI, i.e. affecting only them, and the much more numerous indirect impacts, which are also more difficult to assess.

A third dimension is to divide between project and policy impacts. Policies are affecting categories of enterprises, while projects operate directly through individualized relationships with selected beneficiaries. Formerly, promotion policies - and the attention of research - were concentrated on the second category. From a strict economic point of view, however, policies seem to be preferable to projects, which try to correct distortions against SI by introducing new distortions and thus arriving at an even more distorted environment. Distortions, however, by definition imply costs in terms of economic efficiency. More recently, attention has shifted to policy - there is a danger that presently too much blame or credit is attributed to these[213]. In short, some balance between both is necessary.

The emphasis in this chapter is on policies, rather than projects. The evidence on project impacts is scattered[214]; comparatively, the impact of projects on the SI sector is negligible - the vast majority of SI enterprises are not directly affected by projects - while all are influenced by policies.

The policies of a government, of course, cannot be fully understood in a pure economic analysis. They have a political dimension. Apparently "inappropriate"[215] policies make sense when they are seen in this context[216]. The political dimension

---

211 e.g. World Bank (1989a)
212 cf. Fitzgerald (1989), Hugon (1990)
213 cf. Haggblade et al. (1986: 2)
214 cf. chapter 1.4.
215 cf. Balassa (1981)
216 cf. chapter 1.3., footnote 16, for literature on this.

explains a good deal of the lack of success of SAP: why "inappropriate policies" are continued again and again, despite the sometimes economically good and well documented advice of institutions as the World Bank.

However, the political dimension of policies towards SI is beyond the scope of this study[217]. A pure economic analysis seems to be useful in order to find out the costs of different options in policies with regard to SI. If it can be shown that discrimination of SI implies high costs for a national economy, this may be useful for policy makers, despite their particular interests - or those of others -, which may divert actual policies from what is rational in terms of economic welfare. This seems all the more true in the context of present Africa - a context of scarce resources.

For such an economic analysis of policy impacts on industrial producers Haggblade et al. (1986) developed a comprehensive framework of policy distortions. By definition, policy distortions lead to allocative inefficiencies and thus to lower output than would prevail in a distortion-free world. However, not all price differences on factor and product markets are due to policy interventions. First, there are price differences due to quality differences (for labour or products) and differences in terms of risk and administrative costs. Second, there are price differences due to lack of information and to power of some participants to manipulate markets. These have to be separated analytically, but in practice this is very difficult and has not been done rigorously. Table 6.12.1. summarizes the points of policy intervention influencing production, employment, and the size distribution of enterprises.

On the factor markets, four types of distortions can be distinguished, refering to the labour market, the capital market, availability and price of other inputs, and those which operate through regulatory policies, affecting the relative profitability of different producers or different production technologies.

Concerning labour market distortions, the segmentation often parallels the distinction between SI and LI. Generally speaking, the prices for labour in SI are relatively undistorted and closely approximate opportunity cost of that labour, while LI is frequently subject to minimum wage laws. However, also the effects of minimum wage laws for LI appears often to be limited, and much evidence shows that the magnitude of wage differentials due to distortions is rather small. Data on the impact of policy distortions on the economy are scarce. Data on Colombia

---

217 The following reasons are put forward to explain the discrimination of SI by governments:
   1. lack of knowledge and ignorance on the part of bureaucrats
   2. economic and social weakness of SI, lack of political strength, lack of organization
   3. interests of state bureaucracy (comprador bourgeoisie, alliance with metropolitan countries, with LI).
Arriving at the conclusion that all three elements are involved - which few deny - policy documents find themselves in a dilemma: advising governments to revise policies which are in their own interest. This is Leys' (1973: 421-425) critique of the ILO (1972) Kenya report; cf. also Werlin (1974) for a critique of the "pluralistic" political model behind the report.

Table 6.12.1. Policy effects on industrial producers

factor and other input markets	output markets

1. policies affecting the price of labour
  a. minimum wage laws
  b. labour legislation
  c. public sector wages
  d. policies towards unions
  e. labour based taxes
2. policies affecting the price and availability of capital
  a. interest rates and credit availability
  b. import duties and quotas
  c. exchange rates and controls
  d. capital-based taxes (e.g. accelerated depreciation)
3. policies affecting the availability and price of other inputs
  a. import duties
  b. exchange rates and controls
  c. price controls
  d. access to and price of infrastructure
4. regulatory policies affecting the relative profitability of different producers and production techniques
  a. land allocation and tenure
  b. zoning
  c. licensing and registration
  d. monopoly privileges
  e. application of production standards
	1. policies affecting demand for domestic products through the price of competitive traded goods
	  a. effective rates of protection (import duties and quotas on inputs and outputs)
	  b. exchange rates and controls
	  c. export taxes and subsidies
	2. policies affecting demand through sectoral income distribution (agriculture vs. industry; rural vs. urban; SI vs.LI)
	  a. differential structure of protection
	  b. differential export taxation
	  c. differential foreign exchange rates and controls
	  d. differential expenditure on services and infrastructure
	  e. differential taxation
	  f. differential output pricing
	  g. direct investment in production
	3. policies affecting demand through vertical income distribution
	  a. fiscal policy, transfers and taxation
	  b. item 2 above
	4. price controls for finished products

adapted from: Haggblade et al. (1986: 10)

estimate 2.7-10.7% of loss of GDP due to labour market distortion[218]. It is generally believed that in the course of the economic crisis in low-income developing countries, especially in Africa, in general, and in the context of SAP, in particular, the income gaps have narrowed considerably because of declining real incomes in LI as well as in urban areas[219].

Concerning distortions on the capital market, three types can be distinguished: those arising from the operation of domestic capital markets, those arising from the operation of trade regimes (tariff structure, foreign exchange market), and those arising from direct taxes and related tax concessions and exemptions. SI

---
[218] de Melo (1977), cited by Haggblade et al. (1986: 45). For more evidence on labour market segmentation cf. Steel and Takagi (1983), Haggblade et al. (1986: 16).
[219] cf. Jamal and Weeks (1988) on declining differences of incomes on different labour markets in Africa.

almost entirely relies on traditional sources of finance, i.e. personal and family savings, and to a smaller degree on traders and money lenders. LI, on the other hand, has access to the formal credit system. These two markets are very different: it is estimated that the real interest rate small enterprises are facing is 3-over 10 times higher. This reflects partly higher risks and higher transaction costs, but these are estimated to amount to no more than 10% of total costs[220]. SAP is believed to eliminate cost advantages of LI with respect to capital and thus to be advantageous for SI.

The tariff structure discriminates against SI. Many of its capital and intermediate inputs are classified as consumer goods, while LI is granted investment incentives enabling it to import capital goods duty free for an extended period. Because of currency overvaluation in many developing countries quantitative restrictions on imports through quotas and licensing are necessary. The practices tend to discriminate against SI[221]. Bhagwati lists the following reasons for this: ease of administration in dealing with smaller numbers of successful applicants; a feeling that LI establishments were more reliable; an idea that LI would get better terms from foreign suppliers; the greater access (and contacts) of LI to the bureaucracy; a tendency to allocate according to past shares or other quantity-related variables[222]. SAP should redress these biases. However, there are dangers that without protective measures SI (being less powerful economically and politically) might lose out because of increased speculation and marketing margins as a result of shortages[223].

The foreign exchange rationing, which is often necessary because of overvaluation, also tends to imply a bias towards LI, which have a better access to foreign exchange at the official rate. Devaluations in the context of SAP are believed to decrease this disadvantage of SI. They are also advantageous for SI, assuming that they are less import-intensive.

SI does generally not qualify for tax exemptions and may be discriminated against by indirect taxes (if they apply to all stages of production) vis-à-vis integrated LI. However, SI is often not subject to taxes, which partly offsets, but does not eliminate, the overall capital cost advantage of LI. The summary of available studies arrives at capital market distortions in favour of LI of 30-65%[224].

The effects of the other two kinds of distortions are uncertain, as data is lacking. There are contrasting assessments of the relevance and impact of regulations for SI. While irrelevance of regulation is a defining characteristic of informal sector

---

[220] For evidence on capital market segmentation cf. Steel and Takagi (1983)
[221] cf. Di Tullio (1974: 80-81), ILO and JASPA (1985: 33)
[222] cf. Bhagwati (1978: 28)
[223] cf. Hugon (1990)
[224] cf. Haggblade et al. (1986: Table 7, p.31); the exception is Hong Kong (having no discrimination).

enterprises and has been emphasized as a distinct advantage[225], more recent evidence seems to allow the conclusion that they follow largely regulations and taxation[226].

Public expenditure on infrastructure (water, electricity) is generally geared towards LI and the formal sector in general[227]. Different regulatory policies[228] also tend to discriminate against SI.

A lot of evidence documents that factor substitution of labour and capital is possible (high elasticities of substitution)[229]. However, the factor market distortions operate in different directions for SI and LI and the net impact of an alleviation of policy distortions on production and employment in SI and LI is not clear[230].

The distortions on product markets are less well researched. One can distinguish between policies affecting demand for domestic products through the price of competitive traded goods, policies affecting demand through sectoral (agriculture/industry, rural/urban) and vertical income distribution. Concerning the first item, the literature on different trade strategies (import substitution vs. export promotion) paid little attention to their impacts on the size distribution of industries. While there is an argument that export promotion would provide a uniform bias to exporters[231], the limited evidence indicates that SI are often not eligible for export promotion. Furthermore, tariff protection against competing imports tends to discriminate against SI, because the sectors in which SI is concentrated tend to be discriminated against[232]. A shift from import-substitution to export-promotion - as advised by SAP - implies a chance for SI to participate in an export drive, but also the danger of displacement by imports in the course of trade liberalization[233].

Concerning the relation of agriculture and industry, there is abounding evidence about the anti-agricultural and urban biases in many developing countries on the one hand[234], and the strong linkages between agriculture, rural incomes and industry, especially SI, on the other hand[235]. Thus, an anti-agricultural and an urban bias is also an anti-SI bias[236].

---

225 e.g. Bromley (1985b: 328)
226 cf. Wohlmuth (1990b)
227 cf. ILO and JASPA (1985: 34)
228 cf. Table 6.12.1., left column, no.4
229 cf. Haggblade et al. (1986: 46-50) for literature on this
230 cf. Haggblade et al. (1986: 51-52)
231 cf. Krueger et al. (1981: 41)
232 cf. Haggblade et al. (1986: 38-40)
233 Ho (1980) gives evidence for worse performances of SI in South Korea and Taiwan under trade liberalization.
234 cf. Lipton (1977), Little et al. (1970)
235 cf. chapter 5.6.
236 e.g. Child and Kaneda (1975), Haggblade et al. (1987: 150)

Governments also have an influence on the size distribution of industries through their own investment in industry. In most countries, there is a bias towards LI. Nevertheless, shortcomings in this strategy may have had positive impacts on SI: both generation of demand which could not be met by LI and intra-industrial linkages which did not materialize may have created an impetus for SI[237]. Different assessments exist with respect to the potential of government demand for SI products[238].

A last link is the effect of income distribution on the size distribution of industries. There is a hypothesis that increased incomes for the poor will shift demand patterns in favour of more labour-intensive products and thus increase employment and promote SI (assuming they are more labour-intensive)[239]. While most studies support this hypothesis, the magnitude of even major income redistribution appears to be rather modest[240]. While SAP are expected to benefit - at least in the long term - the low-income groups, the actual impacts are - at least in the short term - negative. On the other hand, the income of higher-income groups is also affected negatively, which might result in a shift from imported and LI consumer goods to SI products.

SAP have opposite effects on the demand for SI products. On the one hand, income shifts to agriculture, rural areas, and to low-income groups should increase this demand. On the other hand, the overall contractionary effects reduce demand for SI consumer goods as well as for SI intermediate goods. Furthermore, because of structural rigidities (lack of access to technologies, finance) SI enterprises might not be in the position to respond to increased demand and to adopt appropriate technologies. The LI in its stronger political and economic position might be able to benefit much more from SAP measures and thus to shift the main adjustment burden to SI and consumers.

Government discrimination: Sudan

The role of the government with respect to SI and industry as such is characterized by paradoxes. As other sectors, industry is highly regulated by the government with plans, laws, ordinances, and institutions and the government plays an important role also as industrial producer. In fact, Sudan's modern industry is a product of government concessions rather than developing spontaneously[242]. At the same

---
237 Fuhr (1987) provides evidence from Latin America.
238 While Weeks (1975: 9) and ILO and JASPA (1985: 36) see a considerable potential, Wohlmuth (1989a: 15) regards it as rather limited.
239 e.g. Weeks (1975)
240 cf. Morawetz (1974)
241 cf. ILO and ARTEP (1987), Fitzgerald (1989), Hugon (1990); in their view the negative results of SAPs are likely to more than outweigh the positive effects.
242 cf. Umbadda (1985: 147)

time, the government never had an industrial strategy in the true sense of the expression: There were only a lot of intentions, more or less unrelated objectives expressed in many documents, plans and programmes.

Despite the heavy role of the government, the government policy towards SI is a clear case of neglect and negative bias. As shown above, all of the external constraints are more or less influenced by government policy. It is a continuation of the colonial policy, which started to drive out the traditional industries (which totally fell into the category of SI), mostly by import of manufactured goods, but also by direct measures as bans[243]. The national government continued in this line by promoting exclusively LI and capital-intensive technologies. Its policy has been combined with and based on ignorance and prejudices. This biased ideology turned out to be extremely persistent and stubborn and determines government policy until today[244].

This policy can be analysed on three levels: plans and programmes, legislation, and practice. The first plan to mention SI was the *Five-Year-Plan* (1970/71-1974/75). It emphasized the necessity to modernize and to promote the traditional industries and the handicrafts[245]. The *Six-Year-Plan* (1977/78-1982/83) included "development of small scale industries based on local materials" as one of 11 objectives in the field of industry[246]. These statements were, however, neither reflected in allocations, nor in concrete policies.

In the course of stabilization policies the donors advised several times to promote SI. In the most comprehensive industry report of the World Bank, for instance, the promotion of SI is one of 14 proposed fields of action[247]. Seemingly in the same spirit the *Four Year Salvation, Recovery and Development Programme* (1988/89-1991/92) declares:

"The strategy of industrial development also includes encouraging the development of small scale industrial undertaking as well as the traditional handicrafts, with particular emphasis on the need to develop rural areas. Policies towards this end shall include special concessions and attractive incentives for enterprises proposed to be located in the rural areas, particularly in the less developed districts of the Sudan."[248]

How these objectives could be reached was explained in more detail in the recommendations of the concerned committees. The workshop on the industry sector recommended in its report on handicraft and SI[249]:

---

243 cf. Abu Affan (1985: 10), Mahmoud (1984: 53), Nimeiri (1976b: 77), Oesterdiekhoff (1984), Wohlmuth (1989: 363)
244 see chapter 4.1.
245 cf. MNP (1977a)
246 cf. MNP (1977b: 54)
247 cf. World Bank (1987a: 67)
248 cf. MFEP(P) (1988: 28)
249 cf. BCHLI (1987)

- to collect information and to make a comprehensive plan;
- to register all establishments and to arrange a law to encourage this sector;
- to distribute land and build industrial areas;
- to make available machinery for nominal rent;
- to decrease taxes for imports of raw materials;
- to remove or decrease taxes and customs or allow payment in installments;
- to protect temporarily against imports;
- to control the quality of products;
- to give special incentives for rural industry;
- to oblige development and commercial banks to provide fixed rates of their credits for the sector;
- to fix minimum wages;
- to establish technical schools;
- to establish special centres for marketing.

The recommendations of the Committee of Rural and Crafts Industries[250] are similar:
- to encourage and organize investment in the sector;
- to create a special body to supervise the sector;
- to issue a law to legalize and define all aspects;
- to provide financial and non-financial incentives (land, tax and customs concessions);
- to establish a corporation within the Ministry of Industry to collect information, to supervise and control prices and quality, to provide administrative services, and to train workers;
- to increase the capital of the SRDC;
- to earmark 5% of commercial bank credit for the sector.

These recommendations are, up to now, of a mere academic interest, as they have not been implemented (by June 1990), except for the establishment of a Department for Small Industries in the Ministry of Industry with exclusively advisory competence[251]. The approach indicated by these measures is an extension of the industrial acts (see below) to the field of SI.

Later even this at least "formal interest" vanished, despite the more and more obvious failure of LI. The *National Conference for Economic Salvation* (November 1989) as well as a 1990 policy declaration of the government[252] put no emphasis on SI. Another indicator for the neglect of SI is the gross underestimation of its

---

250 cf. CRCI (1987)
251 This had been planned since the mid-seventies (cf. Bakhit 1979: 5.5.3.); the speed of implementation of measures for the promotion of SI indicates the strength of interest by the government in SI.
252 cf. GoS (1990: 22-27)

importance in the latter document: "There is, in addition (to the manufacturing sector with 8% of GDP), a traditional handicrafts/small-scale manufacturing sector which accounts for about 2 per cent of GDP."[253] This is the only comment the document wastes on SI.

This development gives the lie to optimistic statements which diagnose that due to increasing dissatisfaction with LI a more positive approach to SI became prevalent[254]. Actual developments during the late 1970s and the 1980s revealed this as wishful thinking.

Coming to the level of actual policies, one finds that there is not any great difference between the phases in which the importance of SI was recognized in the plans and those phases in which they were totally ignored, because there was a clear lack of implementation of the good intentions concerning the promotion of SI.

There have been five consecutive laws to regulate investments in the industrial sector, in 1956, 1967, 1972, 1974, and 1980[255]. There have been deliberations for a long time to replace the 1980 law, but this has only been implemented by the military government in 1990[256]. The last of these acts (1980) refers to all economic activities (the former acts refered exclusively to industry), but all the acts are modifications of the first law, without any major change. Only the 1974 Act underlined small-scale enterprises, but this was not translated into directive principles, and thus had no obligatory character. In reality, the industrial legislation heavily discriminated against SI. SI - projects with an investment of LS 25,000 or belonging to one of 29 "light industries"[257] - are refered to regional and local governments whose licenses entitle to much less concessions.

This will be discussed in detail below, where the impact of government policy is analysed in the framework of Table 6.12.1. Main features of the laws are[258]:

- A great number of far-reaching concessions are provided.
- The eligibility criteria are very vague and general. They are not able to reflect the stated objectives of industrial policy.
- The concessions are not provided automatically; there is a high degree of discretion, which opens the door for corruption.
- Existing and approved enterprises are as a rule entitled to new incentives, irrespective of whether they need them[259].

---

253 cf. GoS (1990: 5)
254 cf. Bakhit Idris (1979)
255 MCI (1956), MIM (1967), MCI (1973), MIM (1974), MFNE (1980)
256 This law is not considered in detail in this study. Basically, the same regulative approach of the former acts is retained. This act also refers to all economic fields (cf. Investment Public Corporation 1990).
257 see Appendix 6
258 for a comprehensive evaluation cf. Abu Affan (1985: 25-48), further see Awad (1970) and Nimeiri (1976b)
259 In the first act there was a clause to this effect; later it was dropped.

- Most of the concessions are not limited to a certain period (contrary to the underlying "infant industry" argument).
- There is no explicit discrimination between SI and LI, foreign and local, public and private enterprises.
- Most of the concessions became more generous over time.
- While in the first act licenses are only necessary for those enterprises seeking concessions, the 1968 act extended the direct controls to all enterprises, whether assisted or not.

As mentioned, the eligibility criteria are very vague and general, unsuitable to direct investment to specific areas. Furthermore, they were "guiding lines" rather than definite criteria for a committee, whose decision was in any case not binding for the minister of industry, who had the decision power.

A further dimension to discuss the government policy is the practice of implementation of the laws. The necessary procedures for approval and concessions involve many institutions and are very complicated and time-consuming. The approvals and concessions are not provided on the basis of socio-economic desirability, but on a first-come-first-serve basis. However, there is no security at any stage to receive all the possible advantages - everything is left to the discretion of government officials in different ministries and institutions. Although it is reported that the bulk of concessions is provided in a more or less automatic manner, the entrepreneur has always to reckon that possibly his project is interrupted for no good reason[260]. On the other hand, once the privileged status is attained, it is likely to last for a long time: Except for the business profit tax, the concessions tend in practice not to be limited; enterprises tend to enjoy their privileges even after the end of the specified periods. Furthermore, new superseding acts usually gave the same concessions again for the formerly approved enterprises[261].

Because of the great number and extent of concessions on the one hand and the relative high effort to obtain them on the other hand, the result is that the industrial entrepreneur has to concentrate his efforts on obtaining as high concessions as possible. Once this step is been done, success is almost secure in the face of the supply constraints[262]: "A successful applicant more often than not finds himself in a monopoly or quasi-monopoly situation"[263]. This practice of course opens the door widely for corruption. Although the wide existence of corruption is

---

[260] cf. Awad (1970: 185)
[261] cf. Nimeiri (1976b: 99)
[262] Hammeed (1974: 89) reports that among the firms he analysed 2/3 of the businesses which went out of businesses did so because they failed to get the concessions they applied for.
[263] cf. Umbadda (1985: 153)

widely known (it is nothing particular for Sudan of course), there are hardly any studies on this at hand[264].

This situation implies a clear bias against SI, because (besides not being eligible for most of the concessions in any case) they are not able to compete in terms of finance, time, social relations, education. To apply successfully for license and the different concessions means travelling to Khartoum and staying there for some time for follow-up.

The impacts of government policy on SI will now be discussed in detail according to the system shown in Table 6.12.1. classifying government policies by the entry points on the input and output markets.

Policies directed at the input markets:
Policies affecting the price of labour

The labour market can be divided into three segments: the public sector (controlled by the government), the formal private sector (regulated), and the informal private sector (unregulated). Up to the 1970s the Sudanese labour market fitted in the picture of "segmented labour markets" with a protected, high-wage and permanent employment sector (public and private formal sectors) on the one hand and a competitive, unregulated, low-income sector (informal, casual, manual, peasant, and other activities) on the other hand[265]. Entry barriers to the formal sector were requirements of literacy, training, prior work experience. The public sector was the wage leader with the highest incomes and guaranteed promotion according to criteria not related to performance. Public sector employment was guaranteed to all university graduates. In 1974 minimum wage laws were issued which brought minimum formal sector incomes in line with the minimum public incomes[266]. Labour legislation secured formal employment[267] and the formal sector was exclusively served by the labour administration. It is important to note that the division between high incomes and low incomes was not equal to that between SI and LI, but crossed it: Low-paid, temporary, unskilled labour was employed by LI and even casual workers could earn more than the government minimum wage[268].

Since the end of the 1970s the picture changed dramatically (see above chapter 5.2.1.). The segmentation of labour markets lost in significance[269] - income

---
[264] cf. Kameir and Kursany (1985), Kameir and El Bakri (1987)
[265] cf. Kannappan (1977), Oesterdiekhoff (1979: 102-136); on regulation of the formal sector cf. Ali Taha and El Jack (1973), Ali Taha (1976)
[266] see above chapter 5.2.1.
[267] cf. Ali Taha (1976), Fallon (1987)
[268] cf. Kannappan (1977: 251-252), Oesterdiekhoff (1979b: 119-120), Kameir (1980: 262), Shazali (1988: 240)
[269] On the breakdown of agricultural labour market segmentation cf. O'Brien (1983b).

differences are narrowing and inter-sectoral movements are increasing. The formal/ informal model is no longer adequate to describe the flexible, diverse, and highly mobile structure of the labour market. The comparatively low incomes in the public sector are to some degree compensated by the higher social security.
Trade unions had been weak and scattered before 1970[270]. During the 1970s several laws strengthened their position considerably. However, their influence is weakened by the government pay regulations and the low profitability of the formal private sector. The influence of trade unions is almost totally restricted to large enterprises. They have no relevance for the labour force in SI and other labour relations.
Taxes on labour incomes play no role in Sudan - they are less than 1% of the total tax income.

Policies affecting the availability and price of capital

As discussed above, the government has pursued a capital-intensive, LI oriented policy of industrialization. For this policy it is crucial to provide large amounts of capital. To facilitate this, the government took extensive measures to regulate the capital market in order to cheapen capital:
- persistent overvaluation;
- artificially low, actually negative interest rates;
- capital tax exemptions without a specified maximum period[271].

These features caused, however, evasion of credit suppliers and excess demand for credits, resulting in credit allocation[272]. Within the industrial sector, this credit is not distributed according to efficiency of the project, but to the size of the investments. This implies an encouragement of increases in capital intensity. As shown in the preceding chapter, SI has little access to the priviliges of subsidized credits. Furthermore, the access of industry in general is restricted, because banks reacted by evasion of the credit market regulation.
The government established several financial institutions to alleviate the financial constraints of industry: notable are the *Industrial Bank of Sudan (IBS)*, the *Sudan Rural Development Corporation (SRDC)*, and the *Sudanese Savings Bank (SSB)*.
The oldest of these institutions is the IBS, which started its operations in 1962 with a capital of LS 3 mill.[273]. From 1962-1987 the bank provided 382 loans amounting to LS 36.3 mill. The rather limited impact of the IBS activity is also shown by the

---
[270] On the trade unions cf. Ali Taha (1976), Fallon (1987: 33-35), Shazali (1988)
[271] cf. Mohamed Nur (1988: 24)
[272] On the financial sector cf. World Bank (1987b: 57-64)
[273] cf. IBS (1962-1988)

number of employees of the promoted enterprises: 6741 - in 27 years. Although most of the benefiting enterprises have been small, i.e. less than 25 employees, the branches promoted are not the most worthwhile from the point of view of SAP reform: All of them are "modern", higher-income branches, the traditional industries are ignored. Most belong to the upper range of SI, and, although some small credits are involved, the credits are highly concentrated on few borrowers. With its policy the IBS thus contributed to capital-intensity[274]. Furthermore, credits are regionally concentrated on Khartoum. This bias was, however, slightly alleviated: While in the first years about 90% of the credits were concentrated on Khartoum, this rate declined to 48.6% in 1987 - contrasting with 2.6% for Darfur & Kordofan and 1.1% for the Southern Region.

To contribute to alleviate this high concentration of investment on Khartoum is the central objective of the SRDC (operating in all areas except Khartoum), which was founded by the government in 1982[275]. Compared to the IBS, its activities are even tinier. Up to February 1988 22 projects were assisted (13 of them in industry, 8 in agriculture, and 1 in services) with a total contribution of more than LS 6 mill. The total investment in the projects varied between LS 21510 and LS 4.5 mill., with an average of LS 855,000; most of the projects involved investments higher than LS 300,000. Also the SRDC concentrates its activities on few borrowers, which belong also mostly to the upper range of SI[276]. The industrial projects concentrate on the production of consumer goods for the urban classes. Employment generated (1984-1987) amounts to 869, 469 of them in industry[277]. The difficulties to find access to SI is illustrated by the relation of the low number of implemented projects (22) - far lower than resources would allow - to the high number of lapsed projects (176)[278]. An analysis of the 18 operating projects in 1987 found that 7 operated with a capacity utilization between 33 and 66%, while 11 operated with less than 33%[279].

Another attempt to reach the small producers is the SSB founded in 1974. This bank has the explicit objective to promote regional development. It is also the only bank not having its headquarters in Khartoum. This is the only development banking institution reaching the lower levels of SI. Besides giving credits to industry (8.5% of total credits), the bank provided 110 small credits to craftsmen with an average of LS 9.300 in 1984. This activity came, however, not to more than 1.7% of total credits[280].

---

[274] cf. Awad (1974)
[275] cf. SRDC (1985-88)
[276] No information about employment per project is available.
[277] cf. El Nafar Ibrahim (1987)
[278] SRDC documents
[279] cf. El Nafar Ibrahim (1987)
[280] cf. SSB (1985)

Altogether, the development banks reach only a tiny fraction of the SI - and the upper range.

Other production inputs

Due to the government policy the market for industrial inputs is divided into two parts. On the one hand there is a highly regulated sector (mostly concerning imports) with restricted access and far-reaching advantages, which, however, is plagued by supply constraints. The firms participating in this sector are mostly highly import-dependent. One the other hand, there is a free market (called "black market" in Sudan), to which most producers have to refer.

The condition for participation in the regulated market is a license. This, however, is not sufficient. The regulated input market is characterized by a multitude of regulations as well as by a multitude of changes in the system[281]. Two kinds of import regulations are operating: tariffs and quantity regulations. The tariffs are 40% for most of machinery items and 40-60% for raw materials and intermediate goods[282]. The encouragement of investment laws provide, however, wide possibilites for reduction or outright abolition. The conditions for import tax reductions became more generous over the years. Time limits as well as conditionality (e.g. domestic non-availability) were dropped. According to the most recent act (1980), partial or total exemption from import duties on machinery, spare parts and raw materials is possible (by decision of the minister).

More important than the tariffs, however, are the quantity restrictions. The practice of foreign exchange allocation was characterized by a bias for capital goods and against spare parts and raw materials, in the intention to expand capacity, but with the result of declining capacity utilizations[283]. The system of foreign exchange allocations fails to encourage efficiency, because foreign exchange was not allocated according to efficiency, but on the basis of the installed capacity[284]. The obtaining of licenses is a procedure which is extremely complex, complicated and time-consuming. This system discriminates between five kinds of commodities. Each of the categories involves a large number of different institutions to be addressed, forms to be filled, and time to be invested[285]. Furthermore, success is not ensured, because the system is arbitrary - approval is left to the discretion of the officials (this is again a door for corruption). This structure excludes most of the SI units, which do not have the necessary resources

---

281 cf. Umbadda (1984b), World Bank (1987a: 15-20; 1987b: 4-8)
282 cf. World Bank (1987a: 16)
283 cf. Naseem (1977: 78), Abu Affan (1985: 115-116)
284 cf. Umbadda (1985: 152); on the foreign exchange losses due to the differences between official and market prices, e.g. through overinvoicing, cf. Shaaeldin and Umbadda (1984)
285 For a description of the system cf. World Bank (1987b: 4-8)

(money, time, "connections"). As in the permission of business licenses, the system of import licenses is characterized by high benefits for those who succeed (because of the high overvaluation of the LS) on the one side, and a high uncertainty if the effort will turn out to be worthwhile. Due to delays because of government inefficiencies, but mostly because of lack of foreign exchange, this has increasingly become a constraint. It is illustrated by the fact that in 1987 only half of the foreign exchange budget applied for by the Ministry of Industry was actually included in the budget, i.e. only half of the requirements of industrial enterprises entitled to the formal imports, could be satisfied by this market[286]. The remainder had to be satisfied on the "black market".

SI enterprises are theoretically entitled to be excepted from customs duties for plant and machinery. However, in practice full exception is hardly given. This discriminatory treatment is based on the argument that SI works with local raw materials[287]. Thus they have to buy imports from the oligopolistic domestic trade sector, resulting in scarcities (due to lack of foreign exchange and aritificial scarcities created by traders) and high prices.

These import regulations are a major contribution to capital-intensity, and discriminate against industries which use simple technologies, are labour-intensive and use local raw materials. Due to the economic crisis the advantages for LI through this system were, however, eroded and often swung to the contrary: lack of imported inputs is a major factor behind low capacity utilization. Before this policy had created the structures dependent on this. Presently it cannot be decided which of the two tendencies is more important.

The domestic industrial inputs are largely bought on a free market. However, also here the government plays a role as a main supplier, e.g. of agricultural inputs. In this field SI is reported to have difficulties of access due to the requirement to buy in bulk and pay immediately. This requirement has generally pushed entrepreneurs to activities where local inputs controlled by the government are not needed[288].

In the field of infrastructure there are also two conflicting tendencies. On the one hand, the government provided the protected enterprises with generous, below-price facilities. On the other hand, increasing inability of the government often turned this artificial advantage into its contrary. In the practice of rationing of electricity and transport services, the industrial enterprises are regularly the first to be cut off[289].

---

286 cf. World Bank (1987a: 16)
287 cf. Sen (1985: 39)
288 cf. Awad (1970: 196), Curtis (1980: 24)
289 cf. Abu Affan (1985: 109)

Licensing

As mentioned above, SI establishments (as defined by investment of less than LS 25,000 or belonging to one of 29 "light" industrial branches[290]) have to apply for licensing at regional or provincial authorities. These are only able to give concessions concerning the allocation of land at concessional prices. For all the other concessions, SI units are refered to the General Secretariat of Investment in Khartoum. In practice, however, SI units are only regarded as eligible for one concession: exception from customs duty for plant & machinery.

While the first act (1956) only covered those enterprises which applied for concessions, the later acts covered all industrial enterprises - assisted or not. However, this did not make a big difference, because, as argued above, the decisive step to business success in the formal sector is the obtaining of a license and of concessions. The acts formulated criteria for eligibility to receive a license, apparently with the aim to direct investment somewhere. Although it soon became obvious that the criteria totally failed to direct investments anywhere, they were not abandoned. However, in the course of time, they became - perhaps in realization of the futility to direct investment - more in number but also more vague and arbitrary. The first act provided five criteria which the enterprises had to fulfill: It had to be beneficial to the general interest[291], had to have "reasonable prospects of successful development", had to have a field of activity "not already sufficiently covered", initial assistance must be necessary, and lastly it must have "sufficient capital and managerial resources". The significance of these five conditions was qualified by the facts that the advisory committee deciding about the qualification of any firm was, as its name says, not more than advising the minister, whose decision was clearly above the judgement of anyone else. The law even stated clearly that the minister's decision was final and could "not be called into question before any court or any other authority"[292] - a pattern which remained until the present.

The following acts diluted the eligibility criteria more and more, enforcing the tendencies of arbitrariness, i.e. the high degree of decision power of the government bureaucracy, on the one hand, and the high subsidization on the other hand. The fourth criterion (necessity of assistance) was already dropped in 1968. Two aspects of this are important: First, it meant a clear, unveiled subsidy, not justified either by infancy or socio-economic desirability. Second, it necessarily

---

[290] see Appendix 6
[291] defined as to have some "defense or strategic importance", to utilize or encourage the production of raw materials, to employ, directly or indirectly, a large number of Sudanese employees and train them to replace foreign personnel serving in the enterprise, contribute to import substitution or assist in export to save foreign exchange, and to assist in the establishment of new industries and in increasing national income (Ministry of Commerce, Industry and Supply, cited by: Abu Affan <1985: 26-27>)
[292] cf. MCIS (1956)

created a dependence on exactly this assistance. Besides, from 1968 onwards any enterprise did not have to fulfill a number of criteria, but just one of them. While in the 1968 Act there were six criteria, in 1980 their number had increased to nine: to contribute to national income increase, to contribute to the removal of development obstacles, to provide necessary services, to depend on local resources, to help to attain self-sufficiency or to create export surpluses, to contribute to the balance of payments, to contribute to employment creation (directly or indirectly), to have defence or strategic importance, or to contribute to economic cooperation with African and Arab countries[293]. It is quite obvious that any industry is able to fulfill more than one of these criteria, and thus the criteria have lost any meaning.
It was shown above that it is very profitable to obtain licenses. An important question arising is: Is there any follow-up in order to prevent misuse? While the licenses are issued by the General Secretariat of Investment, which is under the Ministry of Finance, the follow-up is the "right" of the Ministry of Industry. This, however, made the last follow-up in the year 1979, and only in Khartoum. The General Secretariat of Investment made its own follow-up twice since 1980. During the last follow-up (1985) each licensed plant in the Central, Eastern and Northern Regions was visited. It was found that the implementation did not exceed 30%[294].

Zoning

From Khartoum instances of moving informal SI units (among other informal activities as well as squatter housing) out of central market places to special areas are reported. Under the "Khartoum Evacuation Policy" in an authoritarian and inhumane manner squatter areas, in which also SI activities had been practiced, were destroyed, and their inhabitants and users deported - sometimes back to their rural areas[295]. The ideology behind it was the idea of a "clean city", ignoring the informal activities' vital function, for the served population as well as for the activists.
This policy is only reported from Khartoum. In the other areas a policy of benign neglect seems to have been practised.

Other regulations

Other incentives provided to licensed industrial establishments are allocation of land at below-market rates, and deduction of costs of electricity and transport. For

---
293 cf. MFNE (1980)
294 General Secretariat of Investment
295 cf. ILO (1976: 388), Mohamed Nur (1988: 28)

the licensed SI establishments only the provision of land seems to be relevant - for the upper range of SI.

However, these privileges are also a double-edged sword, because of the inability of the government to provide electricity and transport on a reliable and constant basis.

There is some evidence from Sudan confirming high elasticities of substitution between labour and capital, which points to some potential of alleviation of the policy distortions[296].

Policies directed at the output markets:
Competing foreign products

Sudanese manufactured products play no role in exports - at least not in the officially registered exports. Sudan was incorporated into the world economy as an exporter of agricultural raw materials. That this did not change since independence, is largely attributable to government policies: All exports are subject to burdensome bureaucratic regulations (license system) and partly restricted by bans (in case a domestic supply gap is established)[297]. But more importantly, the system of industrial incentives is biased towards the domestic market, i.e. most of the incentives are given for the production which is directed to this market. The following table quantifies the bias against exports:

Table 6.12.2. Bias against exports: ratios of proceeds obtainable from domestic sales and from exports

ISIC	industry	bias
3115	vegetable oil	2.57
3116	grain milling	1.77
3118	sugar factories	2.25
3211	spinning & weaving	3.21
3231	tanneries	0.87
3523	soap & cleaners	1.98
3692	cement	3.08

Source: World Bank (1987a: 40). The bias against exports is measured by the rate of the actual domestic price (including observed scarcity rates) divided by the actual export price.

With the exception of tannery, for all of the analyzed industries domestic sales are much more profitable, because of the high overvaluation of the LS and because of the scarcity premia on domestic sales: This implies that Sudanese manufactures are hardly competitive in the world market.

---

296 cf. Ali (1977a), Mohamed Ahmed (1980)
297 cf. World Bank (1987b: 8-9)

But the products of Sudan's industry are competing with foreign products on the domestic market. Here the government has a tradition of intervention to protect the domestic industry. Starting from the first industrial investment law (1956), guaranteed protection for industrial goods was a major part of investment incentives. Like other measures, protection became more articulated over the years. Presently two kinds of measures are taken: quantitative restrictions and tariffs. Tariffs for final consumption goods are extremely high - in contrast to capital goods, raw materials and intermediate goods. For most consumption goods the tariffs range between 80 and 125%, while for high-income products the tariffs are in excess of 100%[298]. However, import tariffs have to be considered more as a measure of income generation than for industrial policy: They contribute about 2/3 of total tax income[299].

The main instruments for import regulation are *quantitative restrictions*. Here two measures have to be distinguished: import bans and import licenses. The list of banned imports has grown over the years (there is no established procedure of removing them) : in 1986 it consisted of 97 items[300]. Permitted imports are regulated by a license system. This system underwent many changes and is presently extremely comprehensive, complicated, and time-consuming. Objectives of the import bans are protection for selected LI units, reduction of luxury imports, and religious restrictions (e.g. alcohol).

This extensive system contrasts, however, with the low capacity of the government to enforce its laws. The combined effects of the highly restricted official imports, the high time effort and the uncertainty of import procedures, and the insufficient domestic industrial production result in a high incentive for smuggling. Thus it is no surprise that the amount of smuggled imports is estimated to be as high as the official imports[301]. Most of the unofficial imports can be regarded to be consumer goods. This reduces the protection considerably, but most of the smuggled imports are products not competing with the domestic production.

A survey by the World Bank of 15 LI establishments in the major industrial branches in 1984/85 provides estimates of the rate of protection of LI provided by the discussed measures (see Table 6.12.3.). As SI does not enjoy most of the measures, the estimates are also indicative of the degree of SI discrimination.

---

298 cf. World Bank (1987a: 83-86)
299 cf. World Bank (1987a: 28)
300 cf. World Bank (1987a: 17); for a list of banned imports cf. World Bank (1987a: 87-88)
301 cf. World Bank (1987a: 44); on the foreign exchange losses due to smuggling cf. Shaaeldin and Umbadda (1984); for a local study on smuggling cf. Doornbos (1983)

Table 6.12.3. Nominal and effective rates of protection (NRP and ERP resp.) for industry based on regulated and adjusted prices (1984/85)

ISIC	industry	based on regulated prices		based on adjusted prices	
		NRP	ERP	NRP	ERP
3115	vegetable oil	120	195	208	508
3116	grain milling	104	106	113	130
3118	sugar factory	35	57	170	290
3211	spinning & weaving	187	690	286	1003
3231	tanneries	4	123	4	123
3523	soap & cleaners	138	103	138	103
3692	cement	167	232	270	370
	weighted average	124	240	189	416

Source: WB (1987a: 39-40). The nominal rate of protection expresses the domestic price of an industry's output (PD) as a percentage of its price in the world market (PW; NRP = <PD/PW-1>x100) - a positive rate indicates a protection. The effective rate of protection takes into account both input and output prices; it expresses the domestic value added (DVA) of an industry as a percentage of its theoretical value added valuing all traded goods at world market prices (WVA; ERP = <DVA/WVA-1>x100). Regulated prices are the prices controlled by the Ministry of Industry. The adjusted prices include a premium of 50% in order to account for the scarcity rents which can be extracted due to severe shortages.

The table shows high degrees of protection for Sudan's modern industry, although there are wide differences (which are also an indication of the great impact of government intervention). The average nominal rate of protection is 124%, if regulated prices are assumed, and 189% if more realistic prices are assumed by adding a scarcity premium. The rates of effective protection, taking into account also the protection on the input side, are even much higher: 240% and 416% resp. Compared with 1971 data, the rates increased almost everywhere[302].

Policies affecting agricultural demand

Agriculture is by far the most important productive sector, and thus also of utmost importance as a source of demand for industrial products, directly (agricultural inputs) and indirectly (consumer goods for the agricultural population).
Nevertheless, in a typical fashion for developing countries, agricultural policies have been designed in a way to drain off resources to finance the development of other sectors - notably industry -, rather than to support agriculture itself to become a motor of development. In this respect no change from colonial policies took place. Agricultural policies have, thus, contrasted with industrial policies. While these protected industry (i.e. LI), the opposite is done with agriculture. If the indicators for protection cited above (nominal and effective rates of protection) are applied to agriculture, the rates are negative (producer prices

---
[302] cf. Nimeiri and Shaaeldin (1977: 46)

below their economic value), reflecting a strong discrimination against agriculture (implicit input subsidies reduce the discrimination, however, to some degree, so that effective protection rates are less negative than the nominal protection rates)[303]. Another indication of the discrimination of agriculture is the fact that while agriculture earns almost 100% of the export earnings and is highly squeezed by taxes[304], the imports flowing into agriculture are minimal (estimated to be 6-7% in 1979, and have no direct impact on agricultural productivity[305]). Although there is a long history of agricultural planning and administration (since long before independence), the state of data is weak, there is no integrated and implementable programme, in reality agricultural development was erratic, structurally and functionally imbalanced[306].

However, the development in agriculture is not uniform. As explained above, one important feature of agricultural underdevelopment is the heterogeneous character of the sector and its imbalanced development. It is useful to discriminate between three sub-sectors: the two modern sub-sectors of irrigation and mechanized farming, and the "traditional"[307] sector. The shares of the sub-sectors in crop areas are estimated to be 8.0%, 37.0%, and 55.0% for the irrigated, mechanized farming, and traditional sectors resp.[308].

In chapter 5.5.1. it was shown that these sub-sectors differ significantly with respect to their backward linkages to industry. While the traditional sector relies almost completely on the domestic industry for its inputs (the only exception being negligible amounts of imported fertilizers and insecticides), the modern sectors, especially mechanized farming, are heavily import dependent. This heterogeneous structure is an outcome of government policy. The two modern sub-sectors were imposed on the existing socio-economic systems, first by the colonial administration, later by the independent governments. They operate with foreign technology and are dependent on external resources, but encroaching on traditional agriculture, with little positive spill-over effects on their surrounding environment, but sucking dry its resources (land, labour). Parallel to the discrimination against and exploitation of agriculture by the other economic sectors, the same mechanism is taking place at the sub-sectoral level with respect to the traditional sector and the modern sectors: While the traditional sector, besides providing a living for the majority, is most important in production and

---

303 cf. World Bank (1987a: 38-39)
304 For instance, the combined effect of taxes on cotton is calculated at 43% (Abdel Salam 1986: 416); on taxation see also Shaaeldin (1986: 32)
305 cf. Bedri (1979: 141)
306 cf. Oesterdiekhoff (1979a), Wohlmuth and Hansohm (1984: 7-17), Eltom (1986), Sattar and Zaki (1986), Wohlmuth (1987); on the inadequacy of the planning framework and institutional shortcomings cf. Simpson (1980).
307 On the problematic nature of the terms "traditional" and "modern" with respect to Sudanese agriculture cf. O'Brien (n.d.). To take account of this, in strict terms the two terms should be used in quotation marks throughout the text. However, to simplify matters, this is not done.
308 Average for the years 1980/81-1985/86 (cf. El Hanan et al. 1987: 2)

foreign exchange earning, it is not only neglected in terms of allocation of government resources, but is also a victim of heavy policy discrimination and its resources are exploited by the other sub-sectors.
The traditional sector up to now has remained at the periphery of the government's attention. Although since the Six-Year Plan (1977/78-1982/83) its importance is regularly mentioned and it is featured as a priority, in fact all programmes (the Breadbasket Strategy of the 1970s as well as the ensuing stabilization policies) are characterized by an almost complete lack of implementing measures. Also the comprehensive and far-reaching Strategy for Development of Rainfed Agriculture (1986)[309], emphasizing the higher social rates of return in rainfed agriculture, up to now has not had any impact on actual agricultural policy, as seen in the expenditure structure. The funds going to traditional agriculture have not only remained negligible compared with the sizes and the funds going to the other sectors, but also the benefit of even those small amounts has been doubtful, as they are mostly not used for the improvement, i.e. upgrading of the existing farming systems, but rather for the expansion of "modern" cultivation practices into traditional rainfed agriculture - this is a strategy which does hardly reach the small traditional farmer[310].

In addition the credit allocation of government development banks as well as commercial banks practice a double-level discrimination against traditional agriculture: First, the small share dedicated to agriculture, second, the concentration of these funds on the modern sectors of irrigated and mechanized rainfed agriculture[311]. It is estimated that not more than one percent of commercial bank credits go to agriculture, a pattern which did not change over the years. This is due to the risky nature of its production systems, farmers' lack of liquid assets, and especially to government policy: commercial banks are not allowed to charge more than 12% interest on credits to the agricultural sector, and in case of crop failure or other delays they have to borrow from the Bank of Sudan at a rate of 14.5%. The main remaining formal source of finance is the government-run Agricultural Bank of Sudan (ABS). Its funds go primarily to the modern sectors: about 3/4 to mechanized farming, most of the rest to irrigated agriculture, and only about 6-7% to the traditional sector. Other institutional sources are the SSB and the SRDC. It is assumed that all formal credits cover only 3% of the traditional farmer's needs[312]. These have to turn to informal sources, the most important being the sheil system. This is characterized by very high interest rates. It is argued that these high rates are appropriate, reflecting the high risks involved[313], but empirical data seem to disprove this[314]. They seem rather to

---
309   cf. MFEP (1986)
310   cf. Wohlmuth and Hansohm (1984: 30)
311   On agricultural credit cf. Ahmed Ali (1986) and Hansohm (1990a)
312   cf. MFEP (1986b)
313   cf. Wilmington (1955)

be determined by the oligopolistic/monopolistic and oligopsonistic/monopsonistic position of the moneylenders, who as a rule are also the buyers of and sellers to the credit takers. Nevertheless, as long as no institutional alternative is in sight, the sheil system cannot be blamed as a central reason for the slow growth of Sudan's agriculture. It plays an important role in removing the financial constraints faced by small farmers. Without this credit system, large numbers of traditional farmers would have given up farming.

In the same way critiques of the marketing system have to be relativized. Several studies give evidence that the marketing system with respect to the traditional sector is characterized by combined oligopsons and oligopols, if not monopsons/ monopols and leads to a marginalized position of the producers and a drain of resources from traditional agriculture to the urban sectors[315]. But this reflects largely underlying problems as lack of infrastructure (storage facilities, roads, railway), the dispersed structure of agricultural population, cyclical demand and supply, etc. The concentration of government expenditures for agricultural infrastructure on the modern sectors contributed a lot to this state.

Another dimension of neglect of the traditional sector is the research. Up to now, the knowledge on traditional agriculture is patchy and contradictory, reflecting the dearth of studies, contrasting with the comparative wealth of information on other agricultural sub-sectors. This dearth is, at the same time, reason and result of a wide-spread ignorance and biased ideology about Sudanese traditional agriculture. Basic notions of this ideology are that of "vast, unutilized areas" on the one hand and, on the other hand, a "primitive, inefficient traditional agriculture", practiced by peasants who are at best ignorant, if not foolish and lazy. The logical way out of this situation is a radical intervention from outside, with massive amounts of capital, technology, and expertise. An approach of "appropriate technology" as adviced by some foreign advisers is, not surprisingly, regarded with suspicion, as an attempt to prevent development, rather than to implement it.

However, the reality of traditional agriculture is different. The technological level is, no doubt, very low. With few exceptions, hand tools are used. A recent study calculated the average value of machinery used on traditional farms in 1985/86 at only LS 22[316]. But this is not due to any innate ignorance or inability of the peasants, but to a complex environmental system in which the peasants operate: often the soils are of low fertility, rainfall is meagre and uncertain, the population is scattered, traffic connections are in a bad state, markets are difficult to reach, incomes are low, the availability of consumer goods is very limited, and the

---

314 There are little data on the sheil system, but an empirical study in the Gezira Scheme (Ahmed 1983) confirmed the hypothesis that charges for sheil credits are excessive. A "justified" interest rate of 122% p.a. is calculated (by adding the opportunity cost, administrative charges, premium for risk of default, and premium for inflation). This compares with an actual rate of 726%.
315 cf. Oesterdiekhoff 1979c, Manger 1984b, Steenwinkel 1986, Oesterdiekhoff (1988)
316 El Hanan et al. (1987: 19)

marketing system is oligopsonistic and oligopolistic. Considering all these constraints to agricultural development, the existing practices are not only rational, but also efficient (with respect to labour and to land)[317]. Actually no superior system has as yet been found. The potential for intermediate technologies is promising from the technical point of view, but limited by low incomes of farmers and limited ownerships of animals[318]. To increase the technological level of traditional agriculture is not an insoluble problem, but one which needs a much more comprehensive and sensitive approach as has been tried in the past. First of all, it needs to say good-bye to dreams of the possibility of rapid and dramatic increases of agricultural production just as a result of massive injections of capital, which characterized past approaches, as for instance the 1976 ILO approach of a parallel development of modern and traditional agriculture[319].

Many micro-level studies on mechanized farming schemes have accumulated[320] which allow to draw a picture on this sector. Salient features of the sector are:
- High initial investments make it inaccessible for traditional peasants. The investors come from outside, primarily from the trade sector.
- Yields are high after initial clearing but decline after a short time. In comparison with traditional agriculture, yields are at best slightly higher, but production costs are twice that much.
- The financial feasibility is due primarily to different forms of direct and indirect government subsidies (subsidized imports, currency overvaluation, export subsidies, subsidized credits with low repayment rates by ABS or Mechanized Farming Corporation, provision of land at nominal rates) and profits in the marketing sphere.
- The benefits are distributed very inequally. While investors' profits are normally high, the benefits for the local community are small. While the wages for temporary employment in the mechanized farming schemes are considered high (as compared with the traditional farmer's income) by some analysts, the disruption and displacement of traditional agriculture cannot be offset by employment, if it is considered that all land is used to a greater or lesser degree by traditional producers (farmers or nomads) and how high the degree of encroachment became (6 mill. feddan as compared to 8.9 mill. feddan of traditional farming[321]).
- The ecological effects are disastrous, especially in the western regions. In the present system the investor is not interested in long-term consolidation and

---
317 cf. Ali (1977b), Adams and Howell (1979), Huntington et al. (1981), De Coninck et al. (1984)
318 cf. JMRDP (1988: 1-5), WSDC (1988: 161)
319 cf. ILO (1976); for a critique cf. Adams and Howell (1979)
320 cf. Affan (1978), Simpson and Simpson (1978), Alkafi (1980), Saaed (1980), M. Simpson (1980), UNDP and World Bank (1982), Adam et al. (1983), O'Brien (1983a), Shepherd (1983), Affan (1984b), World Bank (1984b), Elhassan (1988); the results of most of these studies are summarized in Wohlmuth and Hansohm (1984: 36-41).
321 (average of crop areas in 1980/81-1985/86); cf. El Hanan et al. (1987: 2)

sustained yields, but in a quick return on the huge investments. It is more feasible for him to move to new areas. Land has practically a price of zero and the government gives even incentives to expand. The government-run Mechanized Farming Corporation is not in a position to enforce its regulations. Furthermore, a large part of mechanized farming is taking place in "uncontrolled areas".

It is clear that the system of mechanized farming, as it has been practiced, represents the opposite of "equitable development" as promised in the *Breadbasket Strategy*. It is also obvious that this system is largely a result of government intervention - it is, in fact, only sustainable with government intervention. With respect to industries, this tilts the demand structure: The demand for industrial goods of the agricultural population (agricultural inputs and consumer goods), largely covered by rural SI, is declining, while the created income, mostly accruing to urban traders, is spent on imported agricultural machinery and consumer goods, which are mostly also imported - or produced by urban industry.

The irrigated sub-sector is also an example of imposed enclave-kind development. Up to now it is at the centre of government attention. Despite plans emphasizing the rainfed sector, current thinking among planners is reinforcing the predominance of irrigated agriculture even more radically than before, in the technocratic belief that this would by-pass the drought problems - it would also by-pass the majority of the population. Its imposition was accompanied by a destruction of the existing socio-economic structures and the existing crafts as a part of it. The Gezira Scheme has been the model for many other government-directed irrigation schemes[322]. A classical example of government-induced development characterized by high cost, misplanning, extreme external dependence is the Kenana Scheme[323].

In summary, government policy has promoted capital-intensive, import-dependent agricultural sub-sectors, while neglecting the traditional agriculture, which has strong linkages to the domestic industry. Thus it turns out as a major impediment for SI development.

Policies affecting the urban-rural and regional relations

Although the urban-rural gap as measured in income terms narrowed from 2.5 to 1.9 between 1967/68 and 1978/80[324], it is still considerable. This is obvious, when

---
[322] cf. Al-Arifi (1975), Pollard (1981), Hassan et al. (1989)
[323] cf. Oesterdickhoff (1982), Wohlmuth (1983), Grawert (1984), Wohlmuth and Hansohm (1985); on an appropriate small-scale altenative cf. Seisi Mohamed (1976)
[324] cf. ILO (1987: 38)

one compares the standards of living in the rural and urban areas. The difference is of a qualitative nature and thus not quantifiable. The income gap is not a good indicator for the differences in living standards, because different goods and services can be bought with these incomes, and they have different prices. On the one hand, it has been estimated that the poverty line is double as high in urban than in rural areas[325], on the other hand, in qualitative terms the rural life is very poor as compared to the urban areas. Thus to compare rural and urban life in quantitative terms would need a lot of value judgements. But even then a comparison would be impossible - almost all available data are on urban areas. This holds despite the facts of considerable rural[326] as well as urban[327] differentiation. Comparisons of the incomes of the urban poor with those of traditional farmers and the availability and prices of goods and services give evidence for this.

The government has strong influence on this, mainly by the provision of services. Table 6.12.4. provides information of government services by region. The table shows a strong discrimination in favour of Khartoum as well as the Northern Region. Although different government programmes emphasized the development of rural areas and the attainment of regional equity, the actual government spending policy remained uninfluenced by it[328]. This is a logical result of the pressure population groups can exert in the respective areas. The political history

Table 6.12.4. Government health and education services by region (per population)

	doctors	hospital beds	primary school teachers	secondary school teachers
Khartoum	1351	501	329	1058
Central Region	10210	218	315	3986
Northern Region	6260	683	170	1682
Eastern Region	9828	960	603	6022
Kordofan Region	26438	1828	586	7715
Darfur Region	38671	1719	456	17946
Southern Region	69358	1728	678	8407
Sudan	8203	1223	431	4204

Source: El Sammani (1987: 378, 397)

---

325 cf. Abu Shaikha (n.d.: 91)
326 On rural differentiation cf. IFAD (1987) and the literature cited on the impacts of mechanized farming, for irrigated agriculture cf. Hassan et al.(1989), Shaaeldin (1983)
327 On the great differences in living conditions in the Three Towns cf. Herbert and Hijazi (1984), El-Agraa et al.(1985), ESRC (1988), World Bank (1988)
328 On the failure of regional policy cf. Roden (1974), Affan (1984a), Fadlalla (1986)

of Sudan gives evidence throughout that major policy changes were initiated by "the street" in Khartoum - not by any development in the regions[329].

Policies affecting income distribution

The development in Sudan has been characterized by increasing inequality[330] and eroding urban wage incomes. This implies *relative* improvements of rural incomes; however, due to the marketing structure and the unequal development of the agricultural sub-sectors, the majority of the rural population did not benefit from these relative improvements.

The effect of these developments on SI is not unequivocal. It was shown above that SI produces for different markets: While the traditional branches tend to produce for the low income population, the modern branches tend to produce for the higher income urban population. The dramatic income losses of urban wage earners depressed demand for those modern branches. While small urban markets are there for modern SI products, the mass market is stagnating.

Price controls for finished products

Since independence a system of price controls is existent in Sudan, its rational being to protect the consumers from the upward pressure on prices due to the insufficiency of domestic production and imports to satisfy domestic needs. Imports, domestic manufactures, agricultural products, and "strategic commodities" (sugar, wheat, petroleum) are controlled. Prices are fixed according to a cost-plus system[331]. For domestic manufactured products, allowable costs are labour costs, raw materials, water and fuel, electricity, depreciation, rent, and insurance costs. A profit margin of 7.5-15% is allowed. Price increases can be applied for, if evidence on cost increases is provided. Prices are controlled at the factory gate, rather than at the market. This system does not encourage efficiency, because most LI producers follow a cost-plus calculation system, rather than a cost-minimizing one[332]. The system is also disadvantageous for the industrial producers because there are delays of several months in the process of price revisions (implying heavy losses in the face of the high inflation rates), and because of the use of the commercial bank exchange rates in the price calculation, while most imports actually have to be financed at the black market exchange rate.

---

329 The lack of attention given to wide-spread hunger in regions as not only the South, but also Darfur, Kordofan and the East is a sad proof for this.
330 cf. ILO (1987b: 35-39)
331 cf. World Bank (1987: 20-25), UNIDO (1989: 42-43)
332 cf. Gameil (1982)

Furthermore, field studies have shown that the actual retail prices the consumers have to pay are usually much higher than the factory ones- or other controlled prices. A World Bank study comparing controlled and retail prices in 1986, for instance, found that the latter are often more than double as high, but higher in any case. They reflect the scarcity, rather than government control[333]. An own comparison of controlled and actual retail prices in Khartoum in January 1989 also found retail prices of consumer goods being 11-300% higher than the official ones. Outside of Khartoum there are usually no controls, so that the prices there reflect scarcities. But also in Khartoum a 1988 study found that the retail prices are differing according to the residential area. Besides from being much higher than the official price, it was found that retail prices are even higher in the areas of very poor people, i.e. those people whose welfare is the justification for the price controls. 9 basic goods were in an unscheduled area on an average 270% more expensive than the official prices and 167% more expensive than in a Third Class area. On an average the 32 domestically-produced goods were found to be 64% more expensive than their official prices. The 46 imported items were 127% more expensive[334].

This is an important finding, because the welfare of the consumers is the justification for price controls. From the national economy point of view, the system of price control is also highly undesirable, because it means that the scarcity rates go to the traders, rather than to the producers. In any case, trade profits are mostly higher than 7.5-15%, the profit rate allowed for industrial producers. This is a major deficiency of the price control system, because incentives which should go to the producer to alleviate the scarcities, go instead to the trader. The price controls are one of the few discriminations in favour of SI, because these are in the majority out of the control system.

Government discrimination: Nyala

SI producers are almost only indirectly influenced by government policy - the local environment in which they are operating conforms very much to the free market picture. Their labour market is completely unregulated: no minimum wages, no labour legislation, no services of the labour office, no trade union activities. As shown above, SI has no access to the regulated and subsidized capital market - neither to commercial nor to development banks. In the same manner, SI is excluded from the regulated input markets. The publicly provided infrastructure (electricity, water) is not available for the traditional SI, and its supply is irregular

---
333 cf. World Bank (1987a: 22)
334 cf. World Bank (1988: 7-24)

for those enterprises which have access to it. Those enterprises which utilize electric machines either own a generator or have to reckon with frequent production interruptions. Water supply is carried by donkeys.
The licenses which the analysed Nyala SI enterprises possess are all issued by the city council. Practically no advantage is provided by these licenses. Few of the larger enterprises obtained land (at concessional prices) at the New Industrial Area. This area is, however, a symbol of the government policy of neglect and discrimination: It is situated far outside the city (see map), which is very unfavourable with respect to market access (as well as the labour force), and is up to now (April 1990) not connected to the public supply of electricity, nor to the water supply. Consequently, no activity has started as yet. Other concessions would only be obtainable from the General Secretariat of Investment in Khartoum. No case of such concessions granted is known.
On the other hand, 56 entrepreneurs have been granted licenses from the regional government in El Fasher[335]. According to investigations in Nyala, only 3 of these planned enterprises actually worked at the time of the survey. Reported reasons for this significant discrepancy are: lack of finance, lack of foreign exchange, but most importantly, misuse of licenses to obtain land and invest in trade (many of the planned factories are reportedly used as warehouses).
The relocation of industries outside the city centre is a typical phenomenon of SI discrimination: The alleged reasons are sanitation and health, but the real reason appears to be a deep-seated resentment of bureaucrats against the world of industry. The result breaks the organic entity of the city centre and is to the disadvantage of not only the SI entrepreneurs and workers, but even more importantly, of the consumers. Another instance of this zoning policy is the relocation of blacksmiths and tinsmiths away from the main market (*Suq Um Dafaso*) to a new, drawing board-market at the margin of the city (*Suq ash Shabi*)[336].
Concerning the policies with respect to the output market, as outlined above, Nyala SI is hardly competing with imports. Exports play a marginal role for the modern metal workshops; these exports do not pass government control. The described bimodal agricultural policy has its negative impact on Nyala's SI. Although the city is the centre of one of Sudan's major agricultural areas, the industry-agricultural linkages are weak and fall far behind their potential: they are limited to seasonal agro-processing and the production of agricultural inputs by blacksmiths. The low incomes in traditional agriculture (which is dominating in Darfur Region) limit the purchasing power of the agricultural population, which works as a demand constraint for the overall SI. Government demand is very

---
335 Regional Ministry of Finance, El Fasher
336 see map on p. 50

limited despite a large potential (production of agricultural inputs, furniture, doors, windows for public buildings). One of the advantages of the free market climate of Nyala is the lack of price controls. On the output side, most Nyala's SI is neither dependent on traders nor subject to government control.

7 Summary and conclusion

This chapter summarizes the main results of the study, draws theoretical conclusions and closes with some policy conclusions.
Starting point of the analysis is the multi-dimensional crisis of African economies, with special regard to the industrial crisis. After more than a decade of largely failing efforts to overcome the crisis and fierce debates about the course of reform policies some degree of consensus about the contents of a necessary reform has been reached. One element of this reform package is the promotion of SI. This idea is based on the belief in several distinct advantages of SI, i.e. advantages of SI as compared to LI. The study examines these claims. The second issue the study addresses is the various constraints that exist for the development of SI.
The study evaluates existing theoretical approaches in the light of empirical evidence. The state Sudan is taken as an example for an African low-income country. The analysis is carried out at the national level (secondary data) and at the local level (primary data: case study of Nyala city). A detailed analysis on the local level is made of four industrial branches, two of them representing traditional, and two more modern SI branches: blacksmiths, tinsmiths, metal workshops and carpentry.
The results give interesting insights and allow to put existing theories into a new perspective. However, the limitations of the study do not allow final conclusions. The following limitations are noteworthy:
- no information is provided on rural areas;
- no comparison with other urban areas (based on primary data) is made;
- no temporal comparison is made;
- no detailed analysis of the consumption structure is provided.

Although it is plausible that Nyala can be regarded as typical for a Sudanese city and that the results have a lot of relevance for Sudan and for Africa, to arrive at firm conclusions, more research is necessary to put the results on a more generalizable basis.
The main results of the study can be summarized in 26 points:
1. The starting assumptions with respect to methodology have been proven as adequate by the results: the conventional methods (standardized questionnaires, one-shot (single) visits) are not suitable. Instead of quantitative methods, an open-minded and flexible approach and qualitative methods are necessary to arrive at meaningful information. The combination of macro- and micro-level analysis is suitable to highlight the different dimensions of SI development. Existing studies neglect the macro-economic environment in which SI operates.

2. The national statistics and assumptions on SI fall short of the size as well as the diversity of this sector: Recent government plans proceed from the assumption that SI contributes not more than 20-30% of industrial employment and production. However, according to the field survey SI in Nyala constitute almost 80% of industrial employment - and even this is an underestimate because of the neglect of "invisible" industries as home industries. Furthermore, rural industries are not considered. In fact, contradicting existing data, SI is an important sector of Sudan's economy, even under present biases against this sector (see below).

   As important as the severe underestimation of SI is the biased view the statistics give: Only the larger, urban SI establishments and only the more visible SI branches are recognized. The result is an incorrect picture of the sector's characteristics. Existing theories on SI concentrate only on a small part of the existing establishments.

   In spite of this, in relation to the size of Nyala city, industrial activities still remain rather small.

3. In the light of Sudanese evidence traditional concepts of the sector appear inadequate: the activities of the "informal sector" are not as a group unequivocally different from more formalized enterprises. The SI as defined in Sudan (enterprises with less than 25 employees) includes very heterogeneous activities, and the larger SI enterprises are not much different from LI enterprises. Although one can discriminate between "traditional" (with a long history and operating at a low technological level) and "modern" branches, the variety of different combinations of production factors also blurs this distinction. In fact there is a continuum of establishments in the dimensions of size, formality and tradition-modernity.

4. The statistics show that SI needs only half of the capital per employee, as compared with LI. What is more, the Nyala figures concerning those modern and traditional industries not included in the statistics, show that these work with a fraction of the capital either class needs. In the face of the scarcity of capital Sudan faces, this is an important finding. Theoretical assumptions are confirmed.

5. SI manages to save capital and to build "human capital" by training on the job. Traditional industries also save capital by self-production of machinery and utilization of second-hand material. However, these activities are rarely practised by the modern SI branches. As these branches are by far the more important (at least in the urban areas), the assumption that SI produces its machinery and utilizes second-hand material has to be questioned.

6. SI establishments rely almost exclusively on self-finance. In this way they mobilize additional resources - resources which would otherwise not be used

productively. This finding confirms existing assumptions and fits in the requirements of SAP.
7. Wage incomes in SI are highly variable, but they are not on a clearly lower level than those in LI and the modern sector, as generally assumed. Profit rates and profit incomes tend to be higher. This contradicts the wide-spread idea that SI is a low-income activity and contradicts pessimistic assumptions with respect to the future potential of SI development.
8. Also with respect to efficiency, there is no gap between SI and LI. Capital productivity is much higher in SI, especially in the very small establishments. Labour productivity is lower in the informal and traditional branches, but higher in the upper echelons of SI. Many LI branches are highly inefficient due to their insulation from competition. This defeats theories emphasising the low efficiency of SI.

However, a comparison of SI and LI is qualified by the different character of SI and LI activities (with respect to products, technologies, inputs) and their different environment (with respect to input channels, government discrimination etc.). This questions theoretical approaches concentrating on efficiency comparisons between SI and LI.
9. Linkages between the economic sectors are important, because they secure the mutual stimulation of economic activities. The traditional and informal industries have comparatively stronger backward linkages (reliance on local inputs) as well as forward linkages (production of agricultural implements and capital goods). The modern SI, on the other hand, rely mainly on imported inputs (machinery, raw materials) and produce almost exclusively consumer goods. This implies that their backward linkage effects leak out abroad and they have no forward linkages. As these modern SI branches constitute the majority in terms of employment and production, at least in the urban areas, the linkage argument is qualified. Under present conditions, only the traditional SI branches would clearly fit into a reformed industrialisation strategy based on the concept of agricultural-demand-led industrialisation.
10. Higher processing rates of SI point to a higher reliance on local resources. Nyala industry is characterised by a dichotomy: Traditional industries, on the one hand, use largely machinery as well as raw materials of local origin; modern SI branches, on the other hand, rely highly on imported - to a lower degree other domestic - machinery and raw materials. Thus only the traditional industries fit into the positive picture of highly locally linked SI.
11. SI do not generally produce for low-income markets, as often assumed. According to secondary data, SI concentrates on the production of urban wage goods, rather than general mass consumption goods - the goods they produce do not belong to the consumption basket of most of the rural

population. Nyala industries show a dichotomy between traditional SI oriented primarily at the needs of the low-income population, while modern SI directs its production to the needs of the middle- and high-income population.

12. SI is indeed less geographically concentrated than LI, all the more if one considers the statistical bias towards the more visible large and urban industries. Thus they help to redress the existing bias towards the capital city and contribute to the aim of regional development.

13. SI qualifies itself as a training ground for entrepreneurs: the entry barriers (capital, education) are generally low. However, the picture of the sector as a transitory stage in an upward movement from agriculture to the modern sector is not appropriate - the social background of the entrepreneurs is too varied. Instead, more entrepreneurs come from the formal sector, especially the public sector. Thus, SI does increasingly emerge as an outlet for the politics of privatization, which is a part of SAP.

14. The low technological level and the limitation on the production of few products of the traditional industries is due to a lack of demand rather than to any innate inability to innovate. The modern industries, on the other hand, are quite innovative. Theoretical assumptions that SI is ill-disposed for innovation are refuted.

15. Inferences on flexibility can be drawn from analyses of income sources, markets operated on, and other indicators. The reliance on agriculture as a second source of income was found to be much smaller than expected, especially for the modern SI branches. For all entrepreneurs analyzed SI income is their main income, for most the only income. While the dependence on traders for inputs is large, with respect to product sales it is small. Although SI does not conform to the expected picture of flexibility, because of their small size, demand-adapted products, multi-purpose technologies and their experience to operate in a market economy, SI enterprises are better equipped to respond to the impacts of SAP.

16. Although some of the assumed distinct advantages are confirmed, many of them are only true for the traditional SI branches, which are a minority, at least in the urban areas. Only these branches conform fully to the requirements of SAP and long-term development. Thus SI on its own cannot, as hoped for by many, be regarded as the panacea. Most SI enterprises adapt to the distorted economic structures - only a general economic restructuring, far beyond the SI sphere, will bring out the distinct advantages of SI.

17. The constraints to SI development can be divided into internal (those originating in the enterprises or the entrepreneurs) and external constraints. At the present stage of development, the primary constraints of SI are not

internal. The theories on SI growth emphasizing any innate constraints are refuted. Although "lack of entrepreneurship" is mentioned in several relevant studies, Sudan data do not provide any evidence to substantiate this allegation. Nyala data contradict this statement: There is overwhelming business activity and reaction to economic incentives. Furthermore, although the educational background of entrepreneurs varies highly, no meaningful relation between educational level and business success can be established.

18. No major managerial deficiencies could be identified either (examples for alleged deficiencies are lack of book keeping, inability to calculate profits, insufficient knowledge of prices, lack of stock-control, misperception of problems). The prevailing management techniques were found to be perfectly adequate to the level of operations. The same is true with respect to technical skills.

19. The role of the family is not as important as supposed by different theoretical approaches. In Nyala, very little family labour is involved in SI. Only in one of the analyzed traditional SI branches (blacksmiths) it constitutes the majority of the labour force. The financial support of the family for SI establishments is even more marginal. But the supporting role of SI for the family is quite important - surprisingly more so for the modern SI. This contradicts the assumption that especially in traditional SI the family is a drain on SI: In traditional SI families are less a drain and more a support to SI.

20. Although contempt of manual labour, an alleged major constraint to labour supply, is still wide-spread among the "educated people", this attitude no longer constitutes a supply problem for SI.

21. The hypothesis that SI holds a subordinate position and is exploited by LI, the formal sector or the larger economy in general, has to be rejected. Most of the goods produced by SI are not in competition and do not act as a substitute for imported products, or for goods produced by LI. Generally, they do not constitute an important share in the consumption basket of any group which would be necessary to make the argument meaningful. Furthermore, the incomes earned in SI do not fit into the picture of exploitation. Lastly, those branches in closest contact with the larger economy (the modern branches) have better, rather than worse, growth prospects.

22. The supply of machinery and raw materials is a main constraint to the development of SI in Sudan, especially for the extremely import dependent modern SI. These are a victim of Sudan's balance of payments crisis in the same manner as the LI. This problem is aggravated in Nyala by supply interruptions due to the deficient infrastructure and the oligopolistic market structure (artificial shortages created by traders to increase prices). But also the traditional industries, which rely mostly on local and other domestic

materials, face problems because of declining supply of raw materials (ecological crisis) and because they also depend on the oligopolistic market system.

23. A main constraint to the development of SI in Sudan are low and declining incomes. These limit consumption to a minimum and make even simple consumption goods appear as luxuries for wide parts of the population. The substitution effects of SI products for imports and LI products are very limited. Modern SI is mainly active on limited wage income urban markets - urban wage earners face continuous income erosion. The traditional and informal SI branches refer to low income markets - markets which are also stagnating.

24. With respect to technology SI shows a dichotomy. On the one hand, traditional industries operate at a very low technological level. This is primarily due to the neglect and discrimination of traditional agriculture, the main sector these industries refer to. The few attempts of development projects to increase the technological level of agriculture with the help of locally produced implements prove that indigenous entrepreneurs are in a position to raise their technological level if external constraints are removed.
On the other hand, modern SI branches partly use very up-to-date technologies (often acquired abroad), which are not always optimal in terms of capital/labour relation, availability of spare parts and energy supply.

25. Credit is often mentioned as a main constraint. However, with respect to initial investments, the system of self-finance seems appropriate: entrepreneurs are able to raise enough funds to start business. If successful, they manage to grow. But with respect to working capital, the system of self-finance results in a dependence on supplier and customer credits, higher cost and interrupted production.

26. Government policy turns out as a major factor behind the external constraints of SI. The government plays a strong role in the Sudanese economy in general and the industrial sector in particular. This sector is highly regulated with plans, laws, ordinances, and institutions, besides the role of the government as an industrial producer. With respect to SI, government policy is a clear case of neglect and negative bias. It is a continuation of the colonial policy, which started to drive out the traditional industries, mostly by import of manufactured goods, but also by direct measures as bans. The national government continued in this line by promoting exclusively LI and capital-intensive technologies, by-passing the existing industrial structure. Despite some hints for a more positive attitude in different plans, this policy remained basically unchanged. Results of the bias are:

- no access for small enterprises to a subsidised capital market, limited access to development banks;
- no access to the regulated and subsidised market for industrial inputs;
- subsidies for LI by tax and customs exceptions, electricity & water supply, transport and provision of land (at nominal prices); in sum, a high protection of this sub-sector against imports, i.e. a high discrimination of SI;
- removal of SI from city centres to unfavourable areas;
- policies discriminating against traditional agriculture, a main sector of demand for SI products; the favoured sub-sectors of mechanised farming and irrigated agriculture are dependent on imported inputs.

These results confirm those theoretical approaches to SI growth constraints emphasizing the government role. The present situation of SI is highly influenced by policy impacts, and thus SI could be a viable part of a reformed SAP.
SI branches as studied in Sudan and particularly in Nyala do not appear as a panacea, as hypothesised by some, nor do they conform to pessimistic assumptions of inevitable decline. A diversified picture emerges. SI as a whole is a major sector of economic activity. The traditional branches conform fully to the hypothesised distinct advantages, while the modern branches fail to conform to some hypotheses. External constraints hinder SI development and government policy is a major factor behind. Policy reform could promote the development of traditional SI branches and redirect modern SI branches in order to conform better to the assumed distinct advantages of SI.
The following policy conclusions for the case of Sudan emerge:
1. Most important is the resumption of economic growth and development. The preconditions for this are a peaceful solution of the political problems and a comprehensive national development programme. This would pave the way for large-scale investments of remittances in productive activities (especially in SI) and for a support of domestic efforts by resumed injections of foreign aid.
2. In the face of the complex biased environment in which SI establishments operate, isolated projects are not the best way to promote SI. These would add new biases to existing ones, reach only a minority and would probably increase the welfare loss to the economy. The first step to promote SI is the alleviation of the policy biases. This would also mean promoting those SI establishments which are conforming to the presumed developmental advantages and bring the other enterprises closer to these characteristics.
3. Administrative procedures should be simplified and controls be reduced to a minimum.

4. Existing LI establishments should be thoroughly evaluated with respect to their efficiency as well as in the macro-economic context. A rehabilitation at all costs is not feasible.
5. In order to promote the environment in which SI operates, especially a bundle of measures to promote the traditional agriculture as a major source of demand, is necessary. This is an important end in itself, because this neglected sector is the most important economic sector, but also with respect to SI, because there is a large potential of SI-agriculture linkages.
6. Additional research on SI has to be done (on the limitations of this research see the beginning of this chapter).
7. Based on and supplementary to the policy changes, direct measures are appropriate to speed up SI development. Important areas for intervention by projects are: technology advice, especially for traditional industries and schemes of credit-supported raw material supply.

Abbreviations

ACR	African Contemporary Record
AIDO	Arab Industrial Development Organisation
ARTEP	Asian Employment Programme
BfA	Bundesstelle für Außenhandelsinformation
BCHLI	Branch Committee of the Handicraft and Local Industries
CRCI	Committee of Rural and Crafts Industries
DoS	Department of Statistics (MFEP)
DSRC	Development Studies and Research Centre (UoK)
ECA	Economic Commisson for Africa
ESRC	Economic and Social Research Council
GDP	gross domestic product
GoS	Government of Sudan
IBS	Industrial Bank of Sudan
IDS	Institute of Development Studies, Brighton
IFAD	International Fund for Agricultural Development
ILO	International Labour Office
IMF	International Monetary Fund
ISIC	International Standard Industrial Classification
JASPA	Jobs and Skills Programme for Africa
JMRDP	Jebel Marra Rural Development Project
LI	large industry
LS	Sudanese Pound
MAFNR	Ministry of Agriculture, Forestry and Natural Resources
MANR	Ministry of Agriculture and Natural Resources
MCI	Ministry of Culture and Information
MDC	Management Development Centre
MFEP	Ministry of Finance and Economic Planning
MFEP-E	Ministry of Finance and Economic Planning (Economy)
MFEP-P	Ministry of Finance and Economic Planning (Planning)
MFNE	Ministry of National Economy
MIM	Ministry of Industry and Mining
mn	million
MVA	manufacturing value added
n.d.	no date
NIC	newly industrialized country
OAU	Organization for African Unity
ODA	official development assistance
OECD	Organisation for Economic Cooperation and Development
o/w	of which
PCP	petty commodity production
RGADP	Research Group on African Development Perspectives, Bremen
ROAPE	Review of African Political Economy
SAP	structural adjustment policies
SBA	Statistisches Bundesamt
SCSEU	Sudanese Craftsmen and Small Enterprises Union
SERG	Sudan Economy Research Group at the University of Bremen
SI	small industry
SIA	Sudanese Industry Association
SRDC	Sudan Rural Development Company Ltd.
SSA	sub-Saharan Africa
SSB	Sudanese Savings Bank
SSE	small-scale enterprise
UNDP	United Nations Development Programme

UNIDO	United Nations Industrial Development Organization
UoG	University of Gezira (Wad Medani)
UoK	University of Khartoum
USAID	United States Agency for International Development
WSDC	Western Savannah Development Corporation

References

Abadie, Nhu Le, 1982, La Sou-Traitance: Complementarité ou Subordination du Secteur Informel, in: Deblé and Hugon (Eds), pp. 193-201

Abdel Aal Salih, Mohamed, 1977, An Assessment of Commercial Banks Lending Role, in: Sudan Journal of Development Research, Vol. 1, pp. 18-32

Abdel Gadir Mohammed, Mohammed, 1989, The Negative Impact of Emergency-Food-Aid on the Traditional Agricultural Production Systems in the Sudan, Khartoum: Institute of Environmental Studies, UoK, Environmental Monograph Series, No. 7

Abdel Salam, M.M., 1986, Agricultural Policy Formation and Administration, in: Zahlan and Magar (Eds), pp. 409-423

Abdel Wahab, Abdel Rahman, 1976, Development Planning in the Sudan: Policy and Organization, in: El-Hassan (Ed.), pp. 216-234

Abu Affan, Bodour Osman, 1985, Industrial Policies and Industrialization in the Sudan, Khartoum: University of Khartoum, Graduate College Publications No. 16

Abu Shaikha, Ahmad, n.d., Towards the Alleviation of Rural Poverty in the Sudan, Roma: Food and Agriculture Organization

Abu Sin, Mohamed El Hadi, 1980: Nyala: a Study in Rapid Urban Growth, in: Valdo Pons (Ed.), Urbanization and Urban Life in the Sudan, Khartoum/Hull, pp. 352-380

Adam, Farah Hassan, El Tayeb Amin Mohamed and Kamil Ibrahim Hassan, 1983, Mechanized Agriculture in the Central Rainlands of the Sudan, in: Oesterdiekhoff and Wohlmuth (Eds), pp. 54-80

Adams, Dale W. et al. (Eds), 1984, Undermining Rural Development with Cheap Credit, Boulder: Westview Press

Adams, Dale W. and Robert C. Vogel, 1986, Rural Financial Markets in Low-Income Countries: Recent Controversies and Lessons, in: World Development, Vol. 14, No. 4, pp. 477-487

Adams, Martin E., 1982, The Baggara Problem. Attempts at Modern Change in Southern Darfur and Southern Kordofan (Sudan), in: Development & Change, Vol. 13, pp. 259-289

Adams, Martin E. and John Howell, 1979, Developing the Traditional Sector in the Sudan, in: Economic Development and Cultural Change, Vol. 27, No. 3, pp. 505-518

Adelman, Irma, 1984, Beyond Export-Led Growth, in: World Development, Vol. 12, No. 9, pp. 937-949

Adelman, Irma, 1986, A Poverty-Focused Approach to Development Policy, in: John P. Lewis and Valeriana Kallab (Eds), pp. 49-65

Adelman, Irma, Jean-Marc Bourniaux and Jean Waelbroeck, 1989, Agricultural Development-led Industrialization in a Global Perspective, in: Jeffrey G. Williamson and Vadiraj R. Panchamukhi (Eds), The Balance between Industry and Agriculture in Economic Development, Vol. 2, Houndmills et al.: Macmillan, pp. 320-339

Affan, Khalid, 1978, Output, Employment and Income Distribution in Mechanized Farming, in: Willem Keddeman and Ali Abdel Gadir Ali (Eds), Employment, Productivity and Incomes in Rural Sudan, Khartoum, pp. 27-50

Affan, Khalid, 1984, Towards an Appraisal of Tractorisation Experience in Rainlands of Sudan, Khartoum: DSRC, UoK, Monograph Series No. 19

Africa Watch Committee, 1990a, Denying "The Honor of Living". Sudan - A Human Rights Disaster, London: Africa Watch Report, March

Africa Watch Committee, 1990b, Sudan. Nationwide Famine. Culpable Negligence in the Management of Food Security, War, and the Use of Food as a Political Weapon, London: News from Africa Watch, Nov. 7

African Contemporary Record, 1977-78

Ahmad, Minhaj Uddin, 1978, A Survey of Small-Scale Industry Potential in the Gezira, UNIDO, unpubl. Report for the SSB

Ahmed, Abdel Ghaffar M. and Gunnar M. Sorbo (Eds), 1989, Management of the Crisis in the Sudan. Proceedings of the Bergen Forum, Feb. 23-24 1989, Bergen: Centre for Development Studies, University of Bergen

Ahmed, Iftikhar and B. H. Kinsey, 1984, Farm Equipment Innovations in Eastern and Central Southern Africa, Aldershot: Gower

Ahmed, Saad El Medani, 1983, Interest Rates in the Informal Credit Markets of Underdeveloped Rural Areas. The Case of the "Sheil" Credit in the Sudan Gezira Scheme, Khartoum: Dept. of Rural Economy, UoK, Rural Development Series, No. 1

Ahmed, Sayed Abbas, 1988a, Financial Institutions' Behaviour Towards Small Business Financing in the Sudan, Wad Medani: UoG

Ahmed, Sayed Abbas, 1988b, The Small Business Financing Gap in the Sudan. An Empirical Examination, Wad Medani: UoG and Friedrich Ebert Stiftung

Ahmed, Sayed Abbas, 1988c, Small Enterprise Development Policy in a Developing Economy - Sudan, Wad Medani: UoG
Ahmed, Sayed Abbas, 1989a, Towards an Integrative Framework to Recruit Un-Employed School Leavers and University Graduates in the Informal Sector. Sudan Case, Khartoum: Employment Opportunities for Graduates and School Leavers Workshop
Ahmed, Sayed Abbas, 1989b, Towards an Analytical Framework for the Definition of Small Business in Sudan. An Exploration, Wad Medani: UoG
Ahmed Abdel Ali, Hassan, 1988, The Process of Famine: Causes and Consequences in Sudan, in: Development and Change, Vol. 19, pp. 267-300
Ahmed Ali, Ahmed Humeida, 1986, Finance and Credit, in: Zahlan and Magar (Eds), pp. 332-357
Ahmed Suliman, Ali, 1975, Issues in the Economic Development of the Sudan, Khartoum
Al-Arifi, Salih Abdalla, 1975, Landlordism among Small Farmers: The Case of the Gezira Farmers in the Sudan, in: Sudan Journal of Economic and Social Studies, Vol. 1, No. 2, pp. 10-14
Ali, Ali Abdel Gadir, 1977a, A Note on the Substitution Possibilities in the Industrial Sector in the Sudan, in: Sudan Journal of Development Research, Vol. 1, No. 1, pp. 125-135
Ali, Ali Abdel Gadir, 1977b, Some Aspects of Productivity in Sudanese Traditional Agriculture: The Case of the Northern Province, Khartoum
Ali, Ali Abdel Gadir Ali (Ed.), 1985, The Sudan Economy in Disarray. Essays on the IMF Model, Khartoum
Ali, Ali Abdel Gadir, 1988, How Long is Long Enough: The World Bank and Economic Policy Making in the Sudan, Khartoum: DSRC, UoK, Seminar Series No. 77
Ali, Mohamed Said, 1973, The Role of Commercial Banks in the Industrial Development of the Sudan, in: Bashir Imam (Ed.), pp. 176-189
Ali El Dawi, Taj Al-Anbia, 1972, Social Characteristics of Big Merchants and Businessmen in El Obeid, in: Ian Cunnison (Ed.), Essays in Sudan Ethnography, London: C. Hurst & Co., pp. 201-216
Ali El Dawi, Taj Al-Anbia, 1975, Migration in Western Sudan, in: Sudan Notes and Records, Vol. 56, pp. 160-175
Ali Taha, Abdel-Rahman E., 1976, The Industrial Relations System in the Sudan, in: Ali Mohamed El-Hassan (Ed.), pp. 183-200
Ali Taha, Abdel-Rahman E. and Ahmed H. El Jack, 1973, The Regulation of Termination of Employment in the Sudanese Private Sector, Khartoum: Khartoum University Press
Alkafi, Mohammed Al Azim, 1980, Traditional and Mechanized Farming under Rainfed Agriculture in Sudan, Khartoum
Allal, M. and E. Chuta, 1982, Cottage Industries and Handicrafts. Some Guidelines for Employment Promotion, Geneva: ILO
Allen, Rob, 1983, The myth of a redundant craft: potters in Northern Nigeria, in: Journal of Modern African Studies, Vol. 21, No. 1, pp. 159-166
Allison, Caroline and Reginald Green, 1983, Stagnation and Decay in Sub-Saharan Africa: Dialogues, Dialects and Doubts, in: IDS Bulletin, Vol. 14, No. 1, pp. 1-10
Allison, Caroline and Reginald Green, 1985, Editorial: Toward Getting Some Facts Less Snarled?, in: IDS Bulletin, Vol. 16, No. 3, pp. 1-8
Al-Shazali, Salah Al-Din, 1988, The Structure and Operation of Urban Wage-Labour Markets and the Trade Unions, in: O'Neill and O'Brien (Eds), pp. 239-276
Amara, Mohamed, 1987, Assistance for the Examination of Ways & Means to Support Small Scale Industries in the Sudan, contribution to Industrial Development Programme, June 8-July 17
Amedon, Etsé Honmapo, 1982, La Petite Production Marchande: Base d'un développement Endogène?, in: Deblé and Hugon (Eds), pp. 202-207
Amin, Samir, 1977, Zur Theorie von Akkumulation und Entwicklung in der gegenwärtigen Weltgesellschaft, in: Dieter Senghaas (Ed.), Peripherer Kapitalismus. Analysen über Abhängigkeit und Unterentwicklung, Frankfurt am Main: Suhrkamp, pp. 71-97
Amin, Samir, 1982, A Critique of the World Bank Report Entitled "Accelerated Development in Sub-Saharan Africa", in: Africa Development, Vol. 7, No. 1/2, pp. 23-29
Amnesty International, 1989, Sudan. Human Rights Violations in the Context of Civil War, London, Dec. 12
Anand, Vinod K. and El Tahir Mohamed Nur, 1984, A Report on the Results of a Census Survey of the Small Scale Enterprises in Wad Medani, Wad Medani: UoG
Anand, Vinod and Tahir Mohammad Nur, 1985, The Role of Small Scale Enterprises in Developing Countries - A Case Study of Wad Medani in Sudan, in: Asian Economic Review, Vol. 27, No. 1/2, pp. 137-159
Anderson, Dennis, 1982, Small Industry in Developing Countries: a Discussion of Issues, in: World Development, Vol. 10, No. 11, pp. 913-948

Anderson, Dennis and Farida Khambata, 1982, Financing Small-Scale Industry and Agriculture in Developing Countries. The Merits and Limitations of "Commercial" Policies, Washington: World Bank, Staff Working Papers No. 519
Anderson, Dennis and Mark Leiserson, 1980, Rural Nonfarm Employment in Developing Countries, in: Economic Development and Cultural Change, Vol. 28, No. 2, pp. 227-248
Andersson, Tommy D., 1987, Profit in Small Firms. A Model Based on Case-studies from the Informal Sector in a Developing Country, Aldershot et al.: Avebury
Anheier, Helmut, 1987, Indigenous Voluntary Associations, Nonprofits, and Development in Africa, in: W. Powell (Ed.), The Non-Profit Sector, New Haven: Yale University Press, pp. 416-433
Arab Fund for Economic and Social Development, 1976, Basic Programme for Agricultural Development in the Democratic Republic of the Sudan 1976-1985, Kuwait
Arrighi, Giovanni, 1973, International Corporations, Labour Aristocracies, and Economic Development in Tropical Africa, in: Arrighi, Giovanni and John S. Saul (Eds), Essays on the Political Economy of Africa, New York: Monthly Press Review, pp. 105-151
Aryee, George, 1981, The Informal Manufacturing Sector in Kumasi, in: Sethuraman (Ed.), pp. 90-100
Auciello, K. E. et al., 1975, Employment Generation Through Stimulation of Small Industries: An International Compilation of Small-Scale Industry Definitions, Atlanta: Georgia Institute of Technology
Austen, Ralph A. and Daniel Headrick, 1983, The Role of Technology in the African Past, in: African Studies Review, Vol. 26, No. 3/4
Awad, Mohamed Hashim, 1970, Government Policy Towards Private Industry in the Sudan, in: L'Egypte Contemporaine, Vol. 61, No. 340, pp. 181-200
Awad, Mohamed Hashim, 1973, Sudan's Five Year Plan (1970-1975). Soviet Planing for a Developing Country, in: Orient, No. 3, pp. 115-118
Awad, Mohamed Hashim, 1983, Why is the Breadbasket Empty?, Khartoum: DSRC, UoK, Seminar Series No. 40
Babiker, Abdelbagi A., 1982, The Role of Rural Industries in the Arid and Semi-Arid Areas of the Sudan, in: GeoJournal, Vol. 6, No. 1, pp. 49-55
Bacha, Edmar L., 1987, IMF Conditionality: Conceptual Problems and Policy Alternatives, in: World Development, Vol. 15, No. 12, pp. 1457-1467
Bakhit, Abdel Hamid, Fouad Ibrahim and Frauke Rheingans, 1987, Small-Scale Industries in Darfur, Sudan, Hannover and Khartoum, published for State of Lower Saxony, Federal Republic of Germany
Bakhit Idris, Yousif, 1979, The Small Scale Enterprise in Sudan, Dublin: Trinity College, unpublished report
Balassa, Bela, 1981, Structural Adjustmment Policies in Developing Countries, World Bank Staff Working Papers, No. 464, Washington
Balassa, Bela, 1983, Outward versus Inward Orientation Once Again, in: The World Economy, Vol. 6, No. 2, pp. 215-218
Balassa, Bela, 1984, Adjustment Policies in Developing Countries: A Reassessment, in: World Development, Vol. 12, No. 9, pp. 955-972
Banerji, Ranadev, 1978, Small-Scale Production Units in Manufacturing: An International Cross-Section Overview, in: Weltwirtschaftliches Archiv, Vol. 114, No. 1, pp. 62-83
Bank of Sudan, various years, Annual Reports
Barker, Jonathan, 1984, Politics and Production, in: idem (Ed.), The Politics of Agriculture in Tropical Africa, Beverly Hills: Sage, pp. 11-31
Barnett, Tony and Abbas Abdelkarim (Eds), 1988, Sudan. State, Capital and Transformation, London et al.: Croom Helm
Barth, Frederik, 1967, Economic Spheres in Darfur, in: Raymond Firth (Ed.), Themes in Economic Anthropology, London, pp. 149-174
Bashir Imam, Faisal (Ed.), 1973, Industry in the Sudan. Papers Presented to the First Erkowit Conference, Erkowit: School of Extra-Mural Studies, UoK
Bauer, P. T. and B. S. Yamey, 1965, The Economics of Underdeveloped Countries, Digswell Place Nesbit: Cambridge Economic Handbooks
Bautista, Romeo M., 1989, Agricultural Growth as a Development Strategy, in: Economic Impact, No. 66, pp. 24-28
Bedri, M.A., 1979, Agricultural Machinery Industry and Rural Industrialization in the Sudan, in: UNIDO (Ed.), Appropriate Industrial Technology for Agricultural Machinery and Implements, New York, pp. 141-148
Berg, Bruce L., 1989, Qualitative Research Methods for the Social Sciences, Boston et al.: Allyn and Bacon

Berg, Elliott J., 1961, Backward-Sloping Labor Supply Functions in Dual Economies - The Africa Case, in: Quarterly Journal of Economics, Vol. 75, pp. 468-492
Berg, Elliott, 1984, The Africa Report: An Overview, in: Rural Africana, No. 19-20, pp. 41-48
Berg, Liv, Krisno Nimpuno, Roger van Zwanenberg et al., 1978, Towards Village Industry. A Strategy for Development, London: Intermediate Technology Development Group
Berg, Liv, 1978b, Small-Scale Production, in: Berg/ Nimpuno/ van Zwanenberg et al., pp. 37-50
Berry, Sara S., 1984, The Food Crisis and Agrarian Change in Africa: A Review Essay, in: African Studies Review, Vol. 27, No. 2, pp. 59-112
Berry, Sara, 1985, Fathers Work for Their Sons. Accumulation, Mobility, and Class Formation in an Extended Yoruba Community, Berkeley: University of California Press
Beveridge, Andrew A. and Anthony R. Oberschall, 1979, African Businessmen and Development in Zambia, Princeton: Princeton University Press
Bhagwati, Jagdish, 1978, Anatomy and Consequences of Exchange Rate Control Regimes, Cambridge (Massachusetts): Ballinger
Bickersteth, J.S., 1990, Donor Dilemmas in Food Aid. The Case of Wheat in Sudan, in: Food Policy, June, pp. 218-226
Bienefeld, 1975a, The Informal Sector and Peripheral Capitalism: the Case of Tanzania, in: IDS Bulletin, Vol. 6, No. 3, pp. 53-73
Bienefeld, 1975b, The Self-Employed of Tanzania, Dar es Salaam: Economic Research Bureau, Economic Research Bureau Paper 75.11
Bienefeld, Manfred, 1983, Efficiency, Expertise, NICs and the Accelerated Development Report, in: IDS Bulletin, Vol. 14, No. 1, pp. 18-23
Bienefeld, Manfred, 1984, International Constraints and Opportunities, in: Fransman and King (Eds), pp. 161-174
Bienefeld, Manfred, 1985, The Lessons of Africa's Industrial "Failure", in: IDS Bulletin, Vol. 16, No. 3, pp. 69-77
Bienefeld, Manfred and Martin Godfrey, 1975, Measuring Unemployment and the Informal Sector. Some Conceptual and Statistical Problems, in: IDS Bulletin, Vol. 7, No. 3, pp. 4-10
Biguma Napoleon, Constantin, 1990, Les Politiques d'Appui au Secteur Informel: Un Exemple Paradoxal de Réussite: Le Rwanda, in: Revue Tiers Monde, Vol. 31, No. 122, pp. 393-404
Bilal, Gassoum K., 1985, On the Role of the Informal Sector in Development: A Case Study of Medani Town, Khartoum: DSRC, Bulletin No.128
Binswanger, Hans P., 1983, Landwirtschaftliches Wachstum und außeragrarische Aktivitäten, in: Finanzierung & Entwicklung, Vol. 20, No. 2, pp. 38-40
Bishop, Robert A., 1962, The Spearhead as a Factor in Economic Development Illustrated by Reference to Iran and the Sudan, in: Rivista di Politica Economica, Vol. 52, pp. 321-345
Bliss, Frank, 1989, Sudan: Recycling-Handwerker und Recycling-Märkte in der Provinz Darfur, in: Werobèl-La Rochelle and Bliss (Eds), pp. 83-100
Boehm, Ullrich and Robert Kappel (Eds), 1990, Kleinbetriebe des informellen Sektors und Aushildung im sub-saharischen Afrika, Hamburg: Institut für Afrika-Kunde
Boeke, J. H., 1953, Economics and Economic Policy of Dual Societies as Exemplified by Indonesia, New York Institute of Pacific Relations
Bond, Marian E., 1983, Agricultural Responses to Prices in Sub-Saharan African Countries, in: IMF Staff Papers, Vol. 30, No. 4, pp. 703-726
Bottomley, Anthony, 1965, The Fate of the Artisan in Developing Economies, in: Social and Economic Studies, Vol. 14, No. 2, pp. 194-203
Bowen, Eleonore Smith, 1964, Return to Laughter. An Anthropological Novel, New York: Doubleday
Brandt, Helmut, 1982, Die Weltbankvorschläge zur Neuorientierung der Entwicklungspolitik in Schwarzafrika, in: Deutsche Institut für Entwicklungspolitik (Ed.), Arme Länder Afrikas. Strukturprobleme und krisenhafte Entwicklung, Berlin, pp. 163-177
Bragina, Elena A., The Role of Small-Scale Industrial Production in the Struggle for Economic Independence of the African Countries, in: Bulgarina Academy of Sciences (Ed.), Developing Countries on the Non-Capitalist Road, Sofia, pp. 127-129
Branch Committee of the Handicraft and Local Industries (BCHLI), 1987, Tagrir ... Al Sina'at Al Harafiya wa Al Rifiya (Report on Small and Local Industries)
Bratton, Michael, 1987, The Politics of Government-NGO Relations in Africa, draft
Braun, Hans-Gert, 1981, Concepts and Problems of Decentralized Industrialization in Developing Countries, in: Economics, Vol. 24, pp. 68-86
Breman, Jan, 1976, A Dualistic Labour System? A Critique of the "Informal Sector" Concept, in: Economic and Political Weekly, Vol. 11, No. 48-50, pp. 1870-1876, 1905-1908, 1939-1944

Bromley, Ray, 1978, Introduction - The Urban Informal Sector: Why is it Worth Discussing?, in: World Development, Vol. 6, No. 9/10, pp. 1033-1039

Bromley, Ray (Ed.), 1985a, Planning for Small Enterprises in Third World Cities, Oxford et al.: Pergamon

Bromley, Ray, 1985b, Small May Be Beautiful, But It Takes More Than Beauty to Ensure Success, in: idem (1985a), pp. 321-341

Bromley, Ray and Chris Gerry (Eds), 1979, Casual Work and Poverty in Third World Cities, Chichester: Wiley

Brown, Raymond L., 1983, Indigenous entrepreneurship in Less Developed Countries: The Importance of Entrepreneurs to the Developing Process, Claremont: Claremont Graduate School

Bruch, Mathias, 1983, Kleinbetriebe und Industrialisierungspolitik in Entwicklungsländern. Eine vergleichende Analyse der ASEAN-Länder, Tübingen: Mohr

Brüning, Dietrich-Karsten, 1986, Management Problems in Africa: Under Special Consideration of the Formation of Management Training Projects in Public Enterprises. Empirical Study in Six African States, Berlin: Quorum Verlag

Buchanan-Smith, Margaret, 1990, Food Security Planning in the Wake of an Emergancy Relief Operation: The Case of Darfur, Western Sudan, Brighton: IDS Discussion Paper 278

Bulmer, Martin and Donald P. Warwick (Eds), 1983, Social Research in Developing Countries. Surveys and Censuses in the Third World, Chichester et al.: John Wiley & Sons

Bundesstelle für Außenhandelsinformation (BfA), 1989, Sudan. Wirtschaftsentwicklung 1988/89, Oktober

Bush, Ray, 1988, Hunger in Sudan: The Case of Darfur, in: African Affairs, Vol. 87, pp. 5-23

Byerlee, Derek, Carl K. Eicher, Carl Liedholm, Dunstan S. C. Spencer, 1983, Employment-Output Conflicts, Factor-Price Distortions, and Choice of Technique: Empirical Results from Sierra Leone, in: Economic Development and Cultural Change

Centre of African Studies (Ed.), 1980, Post-Independence Sudan, Edinburgh: University of Edinburgh

Chandavarkar, Anand, 1988, The Informal Sector: Empty Box or Portemanteau Concept? (A Comment), in: World Development, Vol. 16, No. 10

Chaudhuri, Tamal Datta, 1989, A theoretical analysis of the informal sector, in: World Development, Vol. 17, No. 3, pp. 351-355

Chenery, Hollis et al., 1974, Redistribution with Growth, Cambridge: Oxford University Press

Chenery, H. and M. Syrquin, 1975, Patterns of Development, 1950-1970, New York: Oxford University Press

Chenery, H., S. Robinson and M. Syrquin, 1986, Industrialization and Growth: A Comparative Study, New York: Oxford University Press

Child, Frank, 1977, Small-scale Rural Industry in Kenya, Los Angeles: University of California, African Studies Center Occasional Paper 17

Child, Frank C. and Hiromitsu Kaneda, 1975, Links to the Green Revolution: A Study of Small-Scale, Agriculturally Related Industry in the Pakistan Punjab, in: Economic Development and Cultural Change, Vol. 23, No. 2, pp. 249-275

Child, Frank C. and Mary E. Kempe (Eds), 1973, Small Scale Enterprise. Proceedings of a Conference Organized by the Institute for Development Studies, University of Nairobi, and held at Masai Lodge, Nairobi, 26 and 27 February, 157 pp.

Choucri, Nazli, 1985, A Study of Sudanese Nationals Working Abroad, Vol. 1, Final report, Cambridge: Massachusetts Institute of Technology

Chuta, Enyinna, 1983, Upgrading the Managerial Process of Small Entrepreneurs in West Africa, in: Public Administration and Development, Vol. 3, pp. 275-283

Chuta, Enyinna and Carl Liedholm, 1979, Rural Non-Farm Employment: a Review of the State of the Art, Michigan State University, Rural Development Paper No. 4

Chuta, Enyinna and Carl Liedholm, 1984, Rural Small-Scale Industry: Empirical Evidence and Policy Issues, in: Carl K. Eicher and John M. Staatz (Eds), Agricultural Development in the Third World, Baltimore, pp. 296-312

Chuta, Enyinna and Carl Liedholm, 1985, Employment and Growth in Small-scale Industry. Empirical Evidence and Policy Assessment from Sierra Leone, London, Basingstoke: Macmillan

Cline, William, 1982, Can the East Asian Model of Development be Generalized?, in: World Development, Vol. 10, No. 2, pp. 81-90

Cohen, Ronald, 1973, Warring Epistomologies: Quality and Quantity in African Research, in: O'Barr et al. (Eds), pp. 36-47

Coing, Henri, Hélène Lamicq, Carlos Maldonado and Christine Meunier, 1982, in: Déble and Hugon (Eds), pp. 50-62

Colclough, Christopher, 1983, Are African Governments as Unproductive as the Accelerated Development Report Implies?, in: IDS Bulletin, Vol. 14, No. 1, pp. 24-29
Commissioner for Refugees, Ministry of Interior, and Ministry of Labour and Social Security (Eds), 1988, Seminar on Employment Potential and Income Generating Opportunities of Small Scale Ventures, Khartoum, Dec. 12-14, Conference papers
Committee for Peace and Reconstruction in Sudan, 1989-1990, Sudan Update, London, Vol.1, Vol.2, various issues
Committee of Rural and Crafts Industries (CRCI), 1987, Discussison Report about Rural and Craft Industries for the Four Year Programme 1988-1992, Khartoum, unpublished
Connolly, Priscilla, 1985, The Politics of the Informal Sector: A Critique, in: Nanneke Redclift and Enzo Mingione (Eds), Beyond Employment. Household, Gender and Subsistence, Oxford: Basil Blackwell, pp. 55-91
Cooper, Charles, 1972, Science, Technology and Production in the Underdeveloped Countries: An Introduction, in: Journal of Development Studies, Vol. 9, No. 1, pp. 1-18
Cordova, A., 1973, Strukturelle Heterogenität und wirtschaftliches Wachstum, Frankfurt
Cornia, Giovanni Andrea, 1987, Adjustment at the Household Level: Potentials and Limitations of Survival Strategies, in: Cornia et al. (Eds), pp. 90-104
Cornia, Giovanni Andrea et al. (Eds), 1987, Adjustment with a Human Face, Vol. 1, Oxford: Clarendon Press
Cortes, Mariluz, Albert Berry and Ashfaq Ishaq, 1987, Success in Small and Medium-scale Enterprises. The Evidence from Colombia, New York: Oxford University Press
Craig, Gillian M. (Ed.), 1991, The Agriculture of the Sudan, Oxford: Oxford University Press
Crockett, Andrew D., 1981, Stabilization Policies in Developing Countries: Some Policy Considerations, in: IMF Staff Papers, Vol. 28, No. 1, pp. 54-79
Curtis, Donald, 1979, Training and Administrative Development: a Khartoum Experiment, in: IDS Bulletin, Vol. 10, No. 4, pp. 66-70
Curtis, Donald, 1980, Small Scale Industry Promotion, Report on a Field Project, Birmingham: Development Administration Group, University of Birmingham
Dahlman, Carl J., Bruce Ross-Larson and Larry E. Westphal, 1987, Managing Technological Development: Lessons from the Newly Industrializing Countries, in: World Development, Vol. 15, No. 6, pp. 759-775
Daniel, Philip, 1983, Accelerated Development in Sub-Saharan Africa: An Agenda for Structural Adjustment Lending?, in: IDS Bulletin, Vol. 14, No. 1, pp. 11-17
Dar Fur Region and UNDP, 1985, Rehabilitation & Development Strategy to Combat the Effects of Droughts & Desertification in Dar Fur, April
Davidson, Basil and Barry Munslow, 1990, The Crisis of the Nation-State in Africa, in: ROAPE (Ed.), pp. 9-21
Deblé, Isabelle and Philippe Hugon (Eds), 1982, Vivre et Survivre dans les Villes Africaines, Paris: Presses Universitaires de France
de Coninck, J. D., A. Duncan and P. E. Winter, 1984, Agricultural Equipment and Innovation in Southern Sudan, in: Ahmed and Kinsey (Eds), pp. 253-271
de Janvry, Alain, 1983, Growth and Equity: A Strategy for Reconciliation, in: Kenneth C. Nobe and Rajan K. Sampath (Eds.), Issues in Third World Development, Boulder: Westview, pp. 19-33
de Janvry, Alain and Elisabeth Sadoulet, 1983, Social Articulation as a Condition for Equitable Growth, in: Journal of Development Economics, Vol. 13, pp. 275-303
Dell, Sidney, 1982, Stabilization: The Political Economy of Overkill, in: World Development, Vol. 10, No. 8, pp. 597-612
de Melo, Jaime A. P., 1977, Distortions in the Factor Market: Some General Equilibrium Estimates, in: Review of Economics and Statistics, Vol. 59, No. 4, pp. 398-405
Demery, Lionel and Tony Addison, 1987, The Alleviation of Poverty under Structural Adjustment, Washington: World Bank
Deng, Francis Mading, 1986, Seed of Redemption. A Political Novel, New York: Lilian Barber Press
Deng, Francis Mading and Prosser Gifford (Eds), 1987, The Search for Peace and Unity in the Sudan, Washington (DC): Wilson Center Press
Department of Statistics (DoS), 1974, Al-Hiraf Al-Jadawiya (The handicrafts) 1970/71, Khartoum
DoS, 1976, Selected Tables from the 1970-71 Industrial Survey for the Establishments Employing Less than 25 Workers, Khartoum
DoS, 1977, National Income Accounts and Supporting Tables 1972/73-1974/75, Khartoum
DoS, 1979, National Income Accounts and Supporting Tables 1975/76, Khartoum
DoS, 1987, National Income at Current and Constant Prices 1979/80-1983/84, Khartoum
DoS, 1988, Population and Housing Census 1983, Khartoum

Deutscher Bundestag, 1989, Öffentliche Anhörung zum Thema: "Der Sudan und die Menschenrechte", Stenographisches Protokoll der 24. Sitzung des Unterausschusses für Menschenrechte und Humanitäre Hilfe des Auswärtigen Ausschusses
de Wilde, John C., 1971, The Development of African Private Enterprise, Washington: World Bank
Diab, Mohamed Hag, 1984, Devaluation of Sudanese Pound. The IMF Panacea that Failes to Cure the Patient, Khartoum: ESRC, Bulletin No. 101
Diaz-Alejandro, Carlos F., 1980, Discussion (of Krueger 1980), in: Amerian Economic Review, Papers & Proceedings, Vol. 70, No. 2, pp. 299-300
Dick, H.W. and P.J.Rimmer, 1980, Beyond the Formal/ Informal Sector Dichotomy: Towards an Integrated Alternative, in: Pacific Viewpoint, Vol. 21, No. 1, pp. 26-41
Dinwiddy, Bruce, 1974, Promoting African Enterprise, London: Croom Helm
Di Tullio, Kathleen, 1974, Small enterprises in manufacturing: The Emerging Issues, in: OECD (Ed.), pp. 78-100
Doornbos, Paul, 1983, Some aspects of Smuggling Between Chad and Sudan, Khartoum: UoK, DSRC, Seminar Series No. 33
Drake, H. Max, 1973, Research Method or Culture-Bound Technique? Pitfalls of Survey Research in Africa, in: O'Barr et al. (Eds), pp. 58-69
Dritte Welt Haus Bielefeld, 1986, Hunger durch Agrarexporte? Afrikas Landwirtschaft zwischen Selbstversorgung und Exportproduktion, Bielefeld
D'Silva, Brian, 1983, Sudan's Agricultural Production "Potential". Prospects and Policy Choices. Paper delivered at Annual African Studies Association Meeting, Boston, Dec. 7-10
Dumont, René, 1988, False Start in Africa, London: Earthscan
Eades, J. S., 1985, If You Can't Beat 'Em, Join 'Em: State Regulation of Small Enterprises, in: Bromley (Ed.), pp. 203-218
Economic and Social Research Council (ESRC), 1988, Social Dimension of Adjustment. Khartoum Province: Case Study, Research Report No. 26, for: MFEP-P
Economic Commission for Africa (ECA), 1969, Small-Scale Industries in Africa, Addis Ababa
ECA (Ed.), 1982, Accelerated Development in Sub-Saharan Africa: An Assessment by the OAU, ECA and ADB Secretariats, in: Africa Development, Vol. 7, No. 3, pp. 109-137
ECA, 1988, The Khartoum Declaration. Towards a Human-Focussed Approach to Socio-economic Recovery and Development in Africa, Khartoum
ECA, 1989, African Alternative Framework to Structural Adjustment Programmes for Socio-Economic Recovery and Transformation, New York: United Nations
El Agraa, Omer M. A., Adil M. Ahmad, Ian Haywood and Osman M. El Kheir, 1985, Popular Settlements in Greater Khartoum, Khartoum: Sudanese Group for Assessment of Human Settlements
El Bagir, Ibrahim and Hussein Gibreal, 1984, Some Aspects of Employment in Sudan, Khartoum, Paper presented to the National Conference on Training & Manpower Planning
El Bashir Mohamed, Abdel Rasig, 1986, The Supply and Demand of Agricultural Labour, in: Zahlan and Magar (Eds), pp. 94-113
El-Bushra, El-Sayed, 1980, The Development of Industry in Greater Khartoum, in: Valdo Pons (Ed.), pp. 269-296
El Hanan, Mohamed M., Abdel Latif Ijaimi and Surjit S. Sidhu, 1987, Crop Production, Costs and Returns to Family Labor in the Traditional Rainfed Areas of Sudan. Results of 1985/86 Farm Survey, Khartoum: Dept. of Agricultural Economics and Statistics, MANR
Elhassan, Abdalla Mohammed, 1988, The Encroachment of Large Scale Mechanized Agriculture: Elements of Differentiation among the Peasantry, in: Barnett and Abdelkarim (Eds), pp. 161-180
El-Hassan, Ali Mohamed (Ed.), 1976a, An Introduction to the Sudan Economy, Khartoum: Khartoum University Press
El-Hassan, Ali Mohamed, 1976b, Structure of the Sudan Economy, in: El-Hassan (Ed.), pp. 1-23
El-Hassan, Ali Mohamed (Ed.), 1977, Growth, Employment and Equity. A Selection of Papers Presented to the ILO Comprehensive Employment Strategy Mission to the Sudan, 1974-75, Khartoum: Khartoum University Press
El Jack, Ahmed H. and Abdel Rahman E. Ali Taha, 1977, Vocational Training and Economic Development in the Sudan, Khartoum: DSRC, UoK, Monograph Series No. 2
Elkan, Walter, 1988, Entrepreneurs and Entrepreneurship in Africa, in: The World Bank Research Observer, Vol. 3, No. 2, pp. 171-188
Ellen, R. F., 1984, Ethnographic Research. A Guide to General Conduct, London et al.: Academic Press

Ellis, Gene, 1981, The Backward-Bending Supply Curve of Labor in Africa: Models, Evidence, and Interpretation - and Why It Makes a Difference, in: Journal of Developing Areas, Vol. 15, pp. 251-274
El Nafar Ibrahim, Sit, 1987, The Role of the Sudan Rural Development Corporation in Rural Development, Khartoum: DSRC, UoK, Diploma Diss.
Elnur Ahmed, Mohamed, 1977, Pattern of Industrial Development in the Democratic Republic of the Sudan, Kuwait: Arab Planning Institute, unpublished report
El Sammani, M. O. (Ed.), 1987, Baseline Survey for Darfur Region, Khartoum: MFEP-P and UNDP
El Sammani, Mohamed O. et al., 1977, Non-Agricultural Employment in Rural Areas, in: El-Hassan (Ed.), pp. 161-192
Elsenhans, Hartmut (Ed.), 1978, Migration und Wirtschaftsentwicklung, Frankfurt/Main: Campus
Elsheikh M. Ahmed, Ahmed and Beshir Omer M. Fadlalla, 1985, A Modelling Approach to Forecasting. A Critique of Some Essential Aspects of the Sudanese Six-Year Plan, Khartoum: DSRC, Monograph Series No. 23
El-Shibly, M. and A. P. Thirlwall, 1981, Dual-Gap Analysis for the Sudan, in: World Development, Vol. 9, pp. 193-200
El Tahir, El Tahir Mohamed, 1988, Employment Potential of Small Scale Income Generating Ventures and Training Needs, in: Commissioner for Refugees et al. (Eds), pp. 52-64
El Tayeb, Mohamed and Elblel Alla El Tayeb, 1984, On the Extent & Costs of Delays in Public Industrial Projects Implementation, Khartoum: ESRC, Bulletin No. 110
Eltom, Ali, 1986, Towards a Long-Term Agricultural Development Strategy and Related Policies, Khartoum: First National Economic Conference, Agricultural Sector Conference
Elwert, Georg, 1985, Überlebensökonomien und Verflechtungsanalyse, in: Zeitschrift für Wirtschaftsgeographie, Vol. 29, No. 2, pp. 73-84
Elwert, Georg, H.-D. Evers and W. Wilkens, 1983, Die Suche nach Sicherheit, in: Zeitschrift für Soziologie, Vol. 12, No. 4
Engelberg, Walter, Theo Rauch and Uwe Schmitter, 1988, Die Entwicklung des produzierenden Kleingewerbes in Sambia in ihrer Abhängigkeit von der gesamtwirtschaftlichen Entwicklung, in: Zeitschrift für Wirtschaftsgeographie, Vol. 32, No. 2, pp. 101-112
Escher, Anton, 1988, Modernisierung und Formalisierung traditioneller Handwerksbranchen in Marokko, in: Zeitschrift für Wirtschaftsgeographie, Vol. 32, No. 2, pp. 120-130
Ewing, A.F., 1968, Industry in Africa, London: Oxford University Press
Ezzat, Farag Abdel-Aziz, 1980, Measurement of Resource Requirements and Assessment of Future Growth Limits in the Sudan, in: L'Egypte Contemporaine, Vol. 70, No. 380, pp. 101-131
Fadlalla, Beshir Omer M., 1986, Financing Regionalisation in the Sudan: Centre-Region Fiscal and Financial Relations, in: Van der Wel and Mohamed Ahmed (Eds), pp. 187-238
Fadlalla, Sayed Abdalla, 1973, Government Policy Towards Industrialization, in: Bashir Imam (Ed.), pp.13-20
Fallon, Peter R., 1987, Labor Markets in Sudan: Their Structure and Implications for Macroeconomic Adjustment, Washington: World Bank, DRD Discussion Paper
Farag, Mahmoud M.I., n.d., Urban Population Growth in Northern Sudan: Patterns and Determinants, Cairo University, Institute of African Research and Studies, Occasional Papers, No. 9
Farrell, M.J., 1957, The Measurement of Productive Efficiency, in: Journal of the Royal Statistical Society, Series A, Vol. 120, Part III, pp. 253-281
Farzin, Y. Hossein, 1988, The Relationship of External Debt and Growth. Sudan's Experience, 1975-1984, Washington: World Bank, Discussion Papers, No. 24
Fashender, Karl und Manfred Holthus, 1990, Zur Übertragbarkeit der Sozialen Marktwirtschaft auf Entwicklungsländer, in: Aus Politik und Zeitgeschichte, B 30-31, pp. 3-10
Fitzgerald, E.V.K., 1989, The Impact of Macroeconomic Policies on Small Scale Industry: Some Analytical Considerations, Working Paper
Frank, Charles, 1968, Urban Unemployment and Economic Growth in Africa, in: Oxford Economic Papers, Vol. 20, No. 2, pp. 250-274
Fransman, Martin (Ed.), 1982, Industry and Accumulation in Africa, London: Heinemann Educational Books
Fransman, Martin, 1984, Technological Capability in the Third World: An Overview and Introduction to some of the Issues Raised in this Book, in: Fransman and King (Eds), pp. 3-30
Fransman, Martin and Kenneth King (Eds), 1984, Technological Capability in the Third World, London and Basingstoke: Macmillan
Friedmann, John and Flora Sullivan, 1974, The Absorption of Labor in the Urban Economy, in: Economic Development and Cultural Change, Vol. 22, No. 3, pp. 385-413
Fuhr, Harald, 1987, Economic Restructuring in Latin America: Towards the Promotion of Small-Scale Industry, in: IDS Bulletin, Vol. 18, No. 3, pp. 49-53

Galaleldin, Mohamed El Awad, 1985, Some Aspects of Sudanese Migration to the Oil-Producing Arab Countries During the 1970s, Khartoum: DSRC, UoK, Monograph Series No. 24
Galenson, Walter and Harvey Leibenstein, 1955, Investment Criteria, Productivity, and Economic Development, in: Quarterly Journal of Economics, Vol. 69, pp. 343-370
Gameil, Mohamed Y., 1982, The Determination of Selling Prices: An Empirical Investigation, in: Sudan Journal of Economic and Social Studies, Vol. 4, No. 2, pp. 40-63
Geertz, Clifford, 1963, Peddlars and Princes: Social Change and Economic Modernization in Two Indonesian Towns, Chicago: University of Chicago Press
Geertz, Clifford, 1968, Agricultural Involution: The Process of Ecological Change in Indonesia, Berkeley: University of California Press
Gerry, Chris, 1978, Petty Production and Capitalist Production in Dakar: The Crisis of the Self-Employed, in: World Development, Vol. 6, No. 9/10, pp. 1147-1160
Gerry, Chris, 1979, Small-Scale Manufacturing and Repairs in Dakar: A Survey of Market Relations within the Urban Economy, in: Bromley and Gerry (Eds), pp. 229-250
Gerschenkron, Alexander, 1952, Economic Backwardness in Historical Perspective, in: Bert F.Hoselitz (Ed.), The Progress of Underdeveloped Areas, Chicago: University of Chicago Press, pp. 3-29
Gesim Marhoum, Abdel Aziz, 1980, Planned Industrial Investment and its Sources of Financing in the Sudan During 1960/61-1982/83, Kuwait: The Arab Planning Institute
Girvan, Norman, 1973, The Development of Dependency Economics in the Caribbean and Latin America: Review and Comparison, in: Social and Economic Studies, Vol. 22, No. 1, pp. 1-33
Girvan, Norman, 1985, Adjustment via Austerity: Is There an Alternative?, in: IFDA Dossier, No. 45, pp. 45-54
Glewwe, Paul and Jacques van der Gaag, 1987, Confronting Poverty in Developing Countries: Definitions, Information and Policies, Draft
Godfrey, Martin, 1983, Export Orientation and Structural Adjustment in Sub-Saharan Africa, in: IDS Bulletin, Vol. 14, No. 1, pp. 39-44
Godfrey, Martin, 1985, Trade and Exchange Rate Policy in Sub-Saharan Africa, in: IDS Bulletin, Vol. 16, No. 3, pp. 31-38
Goody, Jack, 1971, Technology, Tradition, and the State in Africa, London et al.: Oxford University Press
Gordon, David F. and Joan C.Parker, 1984, The World Bank and Its Critics: The Case of Sub-Saharan Africa, in: Rural Africana, No. 19-20, pp. 3-33
Goulet, Dennis, 1989, Participation in Development: New Avenues, in: World Development, Vol. 17, No. 2, pp. 165-178
Government of Sudan (GoS), 1990, Country Presentation, Paper delivered to the United Nations Conference on the Least Developed Countries, Paris, September 3-14
Grawert, Elke, 1984, Die Steine im kapitalistischen Entwicklungsweg des Sudan: Auswirkungen der kleinbäuerlichen Produktionsweise auf die neuen Zuckerprojekte Kenana und Assalaya, Hamburg: Universität Hamburg, unpublished M.A. thesis
Green, Reginald, 1983, Incentives, Policies, Participation and Response: Reflections on World Bank "Policies and Priorities in Agriculture", in: IDS Bulletin, Vol. 14, No. 1, pp. 30-38
Green, Reginald, 1985a, From Deepening Economic Malaise Towards Renewed Development: An Overview, in: Journal of Development Planning, No. 15, pp. 9-44
Green, Reginald, 1985b, IMF Stabilisation and Structural Adjustment in Sub-Saharan Africa: Are They Technically Compatible?, in: IDS Bulletin, Vol. 16, No. 3, pp. 61-68
Greenfield, Sidney M. and Arnold Strickon, 1981, A New Paradigm for the Study of Entrepreneurship and Social Change, in: Economic Development and Cultural Change, Vol. 29, No. 3, pp. 467-499
Griffith-Jones, Stephany, 1983, A Chilean Perspective, in: IDS Bulletin, Vol. 14, No. 1, pp. 50-54
Gulhati, Ravi and Raj Nallari, 1988, Reform of Foreign Aid Policies: The Issue of Inter-Country Allocation in Africa, in: World Development, Vol. 16, No. 10, pp. 1167-1184
Gumaa, Yousif Taha, Abdelgadir Mohamed Ahmed and Abdelmageed Elamin Abdelmageed, 1987, Al-Sina'at Al-Saghira fi Al-Sudan (Small Scale Industries in Sudan), Khartoum: Faisal Islamic Bank Sudan
Gusten, Rolf, 1984, African Agriculture: Which Way Out of the Crisis?, in: Rural Africana, No. 19/20, pp. 55-61
Güsten, Rolf and Klaus Künkel, 1963, Probleme der Industrialisierung, in: Rudolf Stucken (Ed.), Entwicklungsbedingungen und Entwicklungschancen der Republik Sudan, Berlin: Duncker & Humblot, pp. 218-234
Guyer, Jane I., 1984, Women's Work and Production Systems: A Review of Two Reports on the Agricultural Crisis, in: Review of African Political Economy, No. 27/28, pp. 186-191
Haaland, Gunnar, 1984, The Jellaba Trading System, in: Manger (Ed.), pp. 269-284

Hagen, Everett E., 1962, On the Theory of Social Change. How Economic Growth Begins, Homewood: Dorsey Press
Haggblade, Steve, Carl Liedholm and Donald C.Mead, 1986, The Effect of Policy and Policy Reforms on Non-Agricultural Enterprises and Employment in Developing Countries: a Review of Past Experiences, USAID
Haggblade, Steve, Peter Hazell and James Brown, 1987, Farm/ Non-Farm Linkages in Rural Sub-Saharan Africa: Empirical Evidence and Policy Implications
Hammeed, K. A., 1974, Enterprises. Industrial Entrepreneurship in Development. Based on Case Studies from the Sudan, London: Sage
Hamza Khalifa, Ahmed, 1976, Marketing in the Sudan, in: El-Hassan (Ed.), pp. 201-215
Hansohm, Dirk, 1986a, Promotion of Rural Handicrafts, in: Republic of the Sudan. MFEP, Reassessment Rehabilitation Programme Kordofan and Darfur. Final Report, Euroconsult,pp. 241-259
Hansohm, Dirk, 1986b, The "Success" of IMF/World Bank Policies in Sudan, in: Lawrence (Ed.), pp. 148-156
Hansohm, Dirk, 1987, Explanations of the African Crisis: The World Bank Approach and its Critics, unpublished conference contribution, Dubrovnik: Inter-University Centre, March 2-14
Hansohm, Dirk, 1988a, Research Project: The Potential of Small Industries in Sudan. Preliminary Report, Nyala: Labour Office
Hansohm, Dirk, 1988b, Al-Sina'at Al-Saghirat fi Al-Sudan: Mawdua' Derasa Nyala (Small Industry in Sudan: Case Study Nyala), Khartoum: Ministry of Labour and Social Security
Hansohm, Dirk, 1989a, IMF/World Bank Policies in Sudan and Its Critics, in: Karl Wohlmuth (Ed.), Structural Adjustment in the World Economy and East-West-South Economic Cooperation, Bremen: University of Bremen, pp. 259-280
Hansohm, Dirk, 1989b, The Potential of Small Industries in Sudan. Case Study of Nyala, Bremen: SERG, Discussion Paper No.14
Hansohm, Dirk, 1990, The Role of African Non-Governmental Organizations in Development: An Introduction, in: RGADP (Ed.), pp. 563-574
Hansohm, Dirk, 1991a, Agricultural Credit, in: Craig (Ed.), pp. 117-123
Hansohm, Dirk, 1991b, Rural Small Industries and Crafts, in: Craig (Ed.), pp. 162-176
Hansohm, Dirk and Karl Wohlmuth, 1987, Promotion of Rural Handicrafts as a Means of Structural Adjustment in Sudan, in: Scandinavian Journal of Development Alternatives, Vol. 6, No. 2&3, pp. 170-190
Hansohm, Dirk and Karl Wohlmuth, 1988, East-South and South-South Cooperation: The Case of the Sudan, in: Istvan Dobozi (Ed.), Politics and Economics of East-South Relations, Tilburg: EADI, pp. 271-299
Hansohm, Dirk and Karl Wohlmuth, 1989, Sudan's Small Industry Development. Structures, Failures and Development, Bremen: Universität Bremen, Berichte aus dem Weltwirtschaftlichen Colloquium, Nr. 16
Hansohm, Dirk and Karl Wohlmuth, 1990, Sudan's Small Industry Development: Structures, Failures and Perspectives, in: Meine Pieter van Dijk amd Henrik Secher Marcussen (Eds), Industrialization in the Third World. The Need for Alternative Strategies, London: Frank Cass, pp.146-165
Hansohm, Dirk and Hanns-Eduard Woltersdorff, 1983, "Die wollen ja nicht arbeiten" - Sozioökonomische Bestimmungsfaktoren des Arbeitsverhaltens am Beispiel des Sudan und der BRD, Bremen: Universität Bremen, unpublished Dipl. Thesis
Harper, Malcolm, 1975, The Employment of Finance in Small Business, in: Journal of Development Studies, Vol. 11, No. 4, pp. 366-375
Harper, Malcolm and Tan Thiam Soon, 1979, Small Enterprises in Developing Countries. Case Studies and Conclusions, London: Intermediate Technology Group
Harris, John R. and Michael P.Todaro, 1970, Migration, Unemployment and Development: A Two-Sector Analysis, in: American Economic Review, Vol. 60, pp. 126-142
Harris, John R., 1972, On the Concept of Entrepreneurship, with an Application to Nigeria, in: Sayre P. Schatz (Ed.), South of the Sahara: Development of the African Economies, London: Macmillan, pp. 5-27
Harris, Peter, 1970, Nigerian Entrepreneurship in Industry, in: Carl Eicher/ Carl Liedholm (Eds), Growth and Development of the Nigerian Economy, Michigan State University Press, pp. 299-324
Harrison, Paul, 1987, The Greening of Africa, London: Paladin Books
Hart, Keith, 1970, Small-Scale Entrepreneurs in Ghana and Development Planning, in: Journal of Development Studies, Vol. 6, No. 4, pp. 104-120
Hart, Keith, 1973, Informal Income Opportunities and Urban Employment in Ghana, in: Journal of Modern African Studies, Vol. 11, No. 1, pp. 61-89

Harvey, Charles, 1982, The Economy of Sub-Saharan Africa. A Critique of the World Bank's Report, in: African Contemporary Record, pp. A 114-A 119
Harvey, Charles, 1983, The Case of Malawi, in: IDS Bulletin, Vol. 14, No. 1, pp. 45-49
Harvie, C.H. and J.G. Kleve, 1959, The National Income of Sudan 1955/56, Khartoum: DoS
Hassan, Rashid M., Lehman B. Fletcher and S. Ahmed, 1989, Unequal Wealth Accumulation and Income Inequality in a Unimodal Agriculture: Sudan's Rahad Irrigation Scheme, in: Journal of Development Studies, Vol. 26, No. 1, pp. 120-130
Hassan Ahmed, Rafia, 1986, Central Personnel Growth in Sudan, Khartoum: Khartoum University Press
Hazell, Peter, 1984, Rural Growth Linkages and Rural Development Strategy, in: Agricultural Markets and Prices, IVth European Congress of Agricultural Economists, Kiel, pp. 78-93
Hazell, Peter B.R. and Ailsa Röell, 1983, Rural Growth Linkages: Household Expenditure Patterns in Malaysia and Nigeria, International Food Policy Research Institute, Research Report 41
Helleiner, Gerald K., 1985, Aid and Liquidity: The Neglect of Sub-Saharan Africa and Others of the Poorest in the Emerging International Monetary System, in: Journal of Development Planning, No. 15, pp. 67-84
Helleiner, Gerald K., 1987, Stabilization, Adjustment, and the Poor, in: World Development, Vol. 15, No. 12, pp. 1499-1513
Henderson, P.D., 1982, Trade Policies and "Strategies" - Case for a Liberal Approach, in: The World Economy, Vol. 5, No. 3, pp. 291-302
Herbert, D. T. and Naila B. Hijazi, 1984, Urban Deprivation in the Developing World. The Case of Khartoum/ Omdurman, in: Third World Planning Review, Vol. 6, No. 3, pp. 263-281
Herskovits, Melville J. and Mitchell Harwitz (Eds), 1964, Economic Transition in Africa, Northwestern University Press
Higgins, Benjamin, 1955, The "Dualistic Theory" of Underdeveloped Areas, in: Ekonomi Dan Keuangan Indonesia, Vol. 8, No. 2, pp. 58-78
Hippel, Gerlinde, 1980, Untersuchungsmethoden zur Projektvorbereitung in ländlichen Gebieten Afrikas, in: Die Dritte Welt, Vol. 8, No. 2
Hirschman, Albert O., 1958, The Strategy of Economic Development, New Haven: Yale University Press
Hirschman, Albert O., 1965, Obstacles to Development: A Classification and a Quasi-Vanishing Act, in: Economic Development and Cultural Change, Vol. 13, No. 4, pp. 385-393
Hirschman, Albert O., 1981, A Generalized Linkage Approach to Development with Special Reference to Staples, in: Albert O.Hirschman (Ed.), Essays in Trespassing, Cambridge: Cambridge Univiversity Press, pp. 59-97
Ho, Samuel P. S., 1980, Small Scale Enterprises in Korea and Taiwan, Washington: World Bank, Staff Paper No. 384
Ho, Yhi-Min and Donald L. Huddle, 1976, Traditional and Small-Scale Culture Goods in International Trade and Employment, in: Journal of Development Studies, Vol. 12, pp. 232-251
Homoudi, Anna Beshir, 1976, Manufacturing Industry in the Sudan: Development, Structure and Distribution, Khartoum: UoK, M. A. Thesis
Hoselitz, Bert, 1959, Small Industry in Underdeveloped Countries, in: Journal of Economic History, Vol. 19, No. 4, pp. 600-618
House, William, 1984, Nairobi's Informal Sector: Dynamic Entrepreneurs or Surplus Labor?, in: Economic Development and Cultural Change, Vol. 32, No. 2, pp. 277-302
House, William J., 1987, Labor Market Differentiation in a Developing Economy: An Example from Juba, Southern Sudan, in: World Development, Vol. 15, No. 7, pp. 877-898
Howard, Stephen, 1988, Paper on Employment and Strategies in the Small-scale Industries in Urban Sudan, in: Commissioner for Refugees et al. (Eds), pp. 73-86
Huang, Yukon and Peter Nicholas, 1987, The Social Costs of Adjustment, CPD Discussion Paper No. 1987-6, Washington: World Bank
Hugon, Philippe, 1982, Secteur Souterrain ou Reseaux Apparents, in: Hugon and Deblé (Eds), pp. 26-49
Hugon, Philippe, 1990, The Informal Sector Revisited (in Africa), in: Turnham et al. (Eds), pp. 70-87
Hugon, Philippe and Isabelle Deblé (Eds), 1982, Vivre et Survivre dans les Villes Africaines, Paris: Presse Universitaires
Huntington, Richard, James Ackroyd and Luka Deng, 1981, The Challenge for Rainfed Agriculture in Western and Southern Sudan: Lessons from Abyei, in: Africa Today, Vol. 28, No. 2, pp. 43-53
Hyden, Goran, 1980, Beyond Ujamaa in Tanzania: Underdevelopment and an Uncaptured Peasantry, London: Heinemann

Hyden, Goran, 1983, No shortcuts to Progress. African Development Management in Perspective, Berkeley/ Los Angeles: University of California Press
Hyden, Goran, n.d., The Changing Context of Institutional Development in Sub-Saharan Africa, unpublished article
Hymer, Stephen and Stephen Resnick, 1969, A Model of an Agrarian Economy with Nonagricultural Activities, in: American Economic Review, Vol. 59, No. 3, pp. 493-506
Ibrahim, Abdel Rahman A., 1984, Trade and Regional Underdevelopment in Sudan, in: Manger (Ed.), pp. 109-138
Ibrahim, Badr Eldin A., 1989, An Evaluation of the Empirical Studies on Handicrafts and Small Scale Industrial Activities in Sudan, Bremen: SERG, Discussion Paper No. 17
Ibrahim, Fouad, 1984, Ecological Imbalances in the Republic of the Sudan - With Reference to Desertification in Darfur, Bayreuth: Druckhaus Bayreuth
Ijomah, B.I. Chukwumah, 1973, Some Problems of Quantitative Research in Africa, in: O'Barr et al. (Eds), pp. 48-57
Industrial Bank of Sudan (IBS), 1962-1988, Annual Reports 1962-1987
Industrial Sector Workshop, 1987, Waraga hawl Tahdeed ihtiya gaat Al-Hirafiyia min Mudachalaat al Intag (Paper about Exact Needs of Craftsmen for Production Inputs), Khartoum: Paper for Four-Year-Programme
International Fund for Agricultural Development (IFAD), 1987, IFAD Target Groups for Poverty Alleviation Measures in Sudan, unpublished report
International Labour Office (ILO), 1970, Towards Full Employment: A Programme for Colombia, Geneva
ILO, 1972, Employment, Incomes and Equity. A Strategy of Increasing Productive Employment in Kenya, Geneva
ILO, 1976, Growth, Employment and Equity. A Comprehensive Strategy for the Sudan, Geneva
ILO, 1983, Sixth African Regional Conference, Tunis, Report II, Application of the Declaration of Principles and Programme of Action of the World Employment Conference, Geneva
ILO, 1987a, Coping with Technological Dualism in the Farm Equipment Sector of the Sudan, Geneva: ILO and MANR, Papers and proceedings of a national workshop on farm tools and equipment technology, basic needs and employment, Khartoum, Nov. 12-14, 1985
ILO, 1987b, Employment and Economic Reform: Towards a Strategy for the Sudan, Geneva
ILO and Asian Employment Programme (ARTEP), 1987, The Role of Small Industrioes in Adjustment, in: idem, Structural Adjustment: By Whom, For Whom, New Delhi, pp. 25-34
ILO and Jobs and Skills Programme for Africa (JASPA), 1985, Informal Sector in Africa, Addis Ababa
Investment Public Corporation, 1990, The Encouragement of Investment Act, Khartoum
Ishag, Ibrahim Ali and Ibrahim Adam Mohamed, n.d., Mushakil Al-Sina'at Al-Saghirah (Problems of Small-Scale Industries), Khartoum: MDC
Jamal, Vali and John Weeks, 1988, The Vanishing Rural-Urban Gap in Sub-Saharan Africa, in: International Labour Review, Vol. 127, No. 3
James, Jeffrey and Frances Stewart, 1981, New Products: A Discussion of the Welfare Effects of the Introduction of New Products in Developing Countries, in: Oxford Economic Papers, March, pp. 81-107
Jebel Marra Rural Development Project (JMRDP), 1988, Fifth Annual Review - March, Adaptive Research Department. Animal Traction
Jenkins, S. J., 1981, Aspects of the Informal Economic Sector of Juba, Southern Sudan, Juba: University of Juba, Population and Manpower Unit, Research Paper No. 1
Johnson, Marion, 1978, Technology, Competition and African Crafts, in: Clive Dewey and A. G. Hopkins (Eds), The Imperial Impact. Studies in the Economic History of Africa and India, London, pp. 259-269
Johnston, Bruce, 1984, Farm Equipment Innovations in Eastern Africa: Policy Considerations, in: Iftikhar Ahmed and B.H.Kinsey (Eds), pp.19-88
Johnston, Bruce and Peter Kilby, 1975, Agriculture and Structural Transformation. Economic Strategies in Late-Developing Countries, New York: Oxford University Press
Jones, Emily L., 1963, The Courtesy Bias in South-East Asian Surveys, in: International Social Science Journal, Vol. 15, No. 1, pp. 70-76
Jones, William O., 1960, Economic Man in Africa, in: Food Research Institute Studies, Vol. 1, No. 2, pp. 107-134
Kaballo, Sidgi Awad, 1979, Surplus Value in the Sudanese Manufacturing Industry, Khartoum: ESRC, Bulletin No. 72
Kaballo, Sidgi Awad, 1984, The Supply Response of Traditional Oil Seeds Producers in Kordofan, Khartoum: ESRC, Bulletin No. 117
Kamarck, A. M., 1965, Economics and Economic Development

Kameir, El Wathig, 1980, Migrant Workers in an Urban Situation: A Comprative Study of Factory Workers and Building Site Labourers in Khartoum (Sudan), Hull: University of Hull, Ph. D.
Kameir, El-Wathig and Ibrahim Kursany, 1985, Corruption as the "Fifth" Factor of Production in the Sudan, Uppsala: Scandinavian Institute of African Studies, Resarch report No. 72
Kameir, El Wathig and Zeinab El Bakri, 1987, Corruption and Capital Accumulation: The Case of Urban Land in Khartoum, DSRC, Monograph No. 29
Kannappan, Subbiah, 1977, Urban Labour Market Structure and Employment Issues in the Sudan, in: idem (Ed.), Studies of Urban Labour Market Behaviour in Developing Areas, Geneva: International Institute for Labour Studies, pp. 86-106
Kannappan, Subbiah, 1989, Urban Labour Markets in Developing Countries, in: Finance & Development, Vol. 26, No. 2, pp. 46-48
Kaplinsky, Raphael, 1979, Inappropriate Products and Techniques: Breakfast Food in Kenya, in: Review of African Political Economy, No. 14
Kaplinsky, Raphael, 1984, Trade in Technology - Who, What, Where and When?, in: Fransman and King (Eds), pp. 139-160
Kappel, Robert, 1990, Zusammenfassung: Der informelle Sektor als Überlebensstrategie?, in: Boehm and Kappel (Eds), pp. 215-130
Kasfir, Nelson, 1986, Are African Peasants Self-Sufficient? A Review of Goran Hyden, in: Development and Change, Vol. 17, No. 1, pp. 335-357
Katzin, Margaret,1964, The Role of the Small Entrepreneur, in: Herskovits and Harwitz (Eds.), pp. 179-198
Kennedy, Paul, 1980, Ghanaian Businessmen. From Artisan to Capitalist Entrepreneur in a Dependent Economy, München, London: Weltforum Verlag
Khan, Mohsin S., 1987, Macroeconomic Adjustment in Developing Countries: A Policy Perspective, in: The World Bank Research Observer, Vol. 2, No. 1, pp. 23-42
Khan, Mohsin S. and Malcolm D. Knight, 1982, Some Theoretical and Empirical Issues Relating to Economic Stabilization in Developing Countries, in: World Development, Vol. 10, No. 9, pp. 709-730
Khogali, M.M., 1964, The Significance of the Railway in the Economic Development of the Sudan, with Special Reference to its Western Provinces, unpublished M.A. Thesis, University of Wales
Khundker, Nasreen, 1988, The Fuzziness of the Informal Sector: Can We Afford to Throw Out the Baby with the Bath Water? (A Comment), in: World Development, Vol. 16, No. 10, pp. 1263-65
Kilby, Peter, 1965, African Enterprise: the Nigerian Bread Industry, Stanford: Stanford University, Hoover Institution Studies
Kilby, Peter, 1969, Industrialization in an Open Economy: Nigeria 1945-1966, Cambridge: Cambridge University Press
Kilby, Peter (Ed.), 1971, Entrepreneurship and Economic Development, New York, London: Free Press, Collier-Macmillan
Kilby, Peter, Carl E. Liedholm, and Richard L. Meyer, 1984, Working Capital and Nonfarm Rural Enterprises, in: Dale W. Adams et al. (Eds), Undermining Rural Development with Cheap Credit, Boulder: Westview Press, pp. 266-283
Killick, Tony, 1981, Policy Economics, London: Heinemann
Killick, Tony et al, 1984, Towards a Real Economy Approach, in: Tony Killick (Ed.), The Quest for Economic Stabilisation. The IMF and the Third World, Aldershot: Gower, pp. 270-320
King, Kenneth J., 1974, Kenya's Informal Machine Makers: a Study of Small-Scale Industry in Kenya's Emergent Artisan Society, in: World Development, Vol. 2, No. 4/5, pp. 9-28
King, Kenneth J., 1975, Skill Acquisition in the Informal Sector of an African Economy: the Kenya Case, in: Journal of Development Studies, Vol. 11, No. 2, pp. 108-122
King, Kenneth J., 1977, The African Artisan. Education and the Informal Sector in Kenya, London: Heinemann
King, Kenneth, 1990, Research, Policy and the Informal Sector: African Experience, in: Turnham et al (Eds), pp. 131-149
King, Robert P. and Derek Byerlee, 1978, Factor Intensities and Locational Linkages of Rural Consumption Patterns in Sierra Leone, in: American Journal of Agricultural Economics, Vol. 60, No. 2, pp. 197-206
Korten, D.C., 1980, Community Organization and Rural Development: A Learning Approach, in: Public Administration Review, Vol. 40, No. 5, pp. 480-511
Krueger, Anne O., 1980, Trade Policy as an Input to Development, in: American Economic Review, Vol. 70, No. 2, pp. 288-292
Krueger, Anne O. et al. (Eds), 1981, Trade and Employment in Developing Countries: Individual Studies, Chicago: University of Chicago Press

Kuhn, Michael William, 1971, Markets and Trade in Omdurman, Sudan, Los Angeles: University of California, Ph.D.
Kuku, Ali El-Hassan, 1980, The Impact of Socioeconomic Plans on the Sudan, in: Centre of African Studies (Ed.), pp. 163-186
Kuznets, Simon, 1955, Economic Growth and Income Inequality, in: American Economic Review, Vol. 45, pp. 1-28
Kuznets, Simon, 1959, Economic Growth, New York: Free Press
Kuznets, Simon, 1966, Modern Economic Growth, New Haven: Yale University Press
Lachaud, J.P., 1990, The Urban Informal Sector and the Labour Market in Sub-Saharan Africa, in: Turnham et al. (Eds), pp. 111-130
Lageman, Bernhard, 1989, Wirtschaftswandel im Sudan. Ursprünge wirtschaftlicher Dynamik und Stagnation in einem arabisch-afrikanischen Entwicklungsland 1898-1985, Frankfurt a.M. et al.: Peter Lang
Langdon, Steven, 1975, Multinational Corporations, Taste Transfer and Underdevelopment: a Case Study from Kenya, in: Review of African Political Economy, No. 2
Lawrence, Peter (Ed.), 1986, World Recession and the Food Crisis in Africa, London: James Currey
Lawson, Rowena M. and Eric A.Kwei, 1974, African Entrepreneurship and Economic Growth: a Case Study of the Fishing Industry of Ghana, Accra: Ghana University Press
Lebon, J.H.G., 1965, Land Use in Sudan, The World Land Use Survey, Monograph No. 4, London
LeBrun, Olivier and Chris Gerry, 1975, Petty Producers and Capitalism, in: Review of African Political Economy, No. 3, pp. 20-32
Leff, Nathaniel, 1979, Entrepreneurship and Economic Development: the Problem Revisited, in: Journal of Economic Literature, Vol. 17, pp. 46-64
Leibenstein, Harvey, 1966, Allocative Efficiency vs. X-Efficiency, in: American Economic Review, Vol. 56, pp. 392-415
Leibenstein, Harvey, 1968, Entrepreneurship and Development, in: American Economic Review, Papers & Proceedings, Vol. 58, No. 2, pp. 72-83
Lele, Uma, 1986, Comparative Advantage and Structural Transformation: A Review of Africa's Economic Development Experience, Paper presented to 26th Anniversary Symposium on the State of Development Economics: Progress and Perspectives, Yale University
Lenin, V. I., 1936, The Development of Capitalism in Russia, in: idem, Selected Works, Vol. 1, London: Lawrence and Wishart, pp. 219-385
Leonard, David, 1984, What is Rational When Rationality Isn't? Comments on the Administrative Proposals of the Berg Report, in: Rural Africana, No.19/20, pp.99-113
Leonard, David, 1987, The Political Realities of African Management, in: World Development, Vol. 15, No. 7, pp. 899-910
LeVine, Robert Alan, 1966, Dreams and Deeds: Achievement Motivation in Nigeria, Chicago: University of Chicago Press
Lewin, A.C., 1985, The Dialectic of Dominance: Petty Production and Peripheral Capitalism, in: Bromley (Ed.), pp. 107-135
Lewis, Arthur, 1970, Economic Development With Unlimited Supplies of Labour, in: A. N. Agarwala and S. P. Singh (Eds), The Economics of Underdevelopment, Oxford (reprinted from: The Manchester School, May 1954), pp. 400-449
Lewis, John and Valeriana Kallab (Eds), 1986, Development Strategies Reconsidered, Washington: Overseas Development Council
Leys, Colin, 1973, Interpreting African Underdevelopment: Reflections on the ILO Report on Employment, Incomes and Equality in Kenya, in: African Affairs, Vol. 72, No. 289, pp. 419-429
Leys, Colin, 1984, Relations of Production and Technology, in: Fransman and King (Eds), pp. 175-184
Liedholm, Carl, 1973, Research on Employment in the Rural Nonfarm Sector in Africa, East Lansing: Michigan State University, Dept. of Agroicultural Economics, African Rural Employment Paper No. 5
Liedholm, Carl and Enyinna Chuta, 1976, The Economics of Rural and Urban Small-Scale Industries in Sierra Leone, East Lansing: Michigan State University, African Rural Economy Paper No. 14
Liedholm, Carl and Peter Kilby, 1989, The Role of Nonfarm Activities in the Rural Economy, in: Jeffrey G.Williamson and Vadiray R.Panchamukhi (Eds), The Balance between Industry and Agriculture in Economic Development, Vol. 2, Houndmills: Macmillan, pp. 340-366
Liedholm, Carl and Donald C. Mead, 1986, Small-Scale Industry, in: Robert J. Berg and Jennifer Seymour Whitaker (Eds), Strategies for African Development, Berkeley/Los Angeles/London: University of California Press, pp. 308-330

Liedholm, Carl and Donald Mead, 1987, Small Scale Industries in Developing Countries: Empirical Evidence and Policy Implications, East Lansing: Michigan State University, Dept. of Agriculturalö Economics, MSU Intzernational Development Paper No. 9
Lipton, Michael, 1977, Why Poor People Stay Poor, Cambridge: Harvard University Press
Lipton, Michael, 1980, Family, Fungibility and Formality: Rural Advantages of Informal Non-Farm Enterprise versus the Urban-Formal State, in: Samir Amin (Ed.), Human Resources, Employment and Development, . Proceedings of the 6th World Congress of the International Economic Association, held in Mexico City, Vol. 5, Developing Countries , pp. 189-242
Little, I.M.D., Dipak Mazumdar and John M.Page, 1987, Small Manufacturing Enterprises. A Comparative Analysis of India and other Economies, New York: Oxford University Press
Little, Ian, Tibor Scitovsky and Maurice Scott, 1970, Industry and Trade in some Developing Countries, London: Oxford University Press
Loxley, John, 1984a, The World Bank and the Model of Accumulation, in: Jonathan Barker (Ed.), The Politics of Agriculture in Tropical Africa, Beverly Hills: Sage, pp. 65-76
Loxley, John, 1984b, The Berg Report and the Model of Accumulation in Sub-Saharan Africa, in: Review of African Political Economy, No. 27/28, pp. 197-204
Loxley, 1986, IMF and World Bank Conditionality and Sub-Saharan Africa, in: Lawrence (Ed.), pp. 96-103
Lystad, Robert A., 1965a, The African World. A Survey of Social Research, London/ Dunmow: Pall Mall Press
Lystad, Robert A., 1965b, Introduction: The Integration of Social Research, in: idem 1965a, pp. 1-7
Macaulay, Sandy and Ahmed Karadawi, 1984, Income Generating Projects in Refugee Affected Areas of Sudan. Past Experience and Future Prospects, Khartoum: Office of the Commissioner for Refugees
MacBean, Alasdair I., n.d., Structural Adjustment in Commodity Based Economies, unpubl.
MacEwan Scott, A.M., 1979 Who are the Self-Employed?, in: Bromley and Gerry (Eds)
Madani, Yusuf Hasan, 1981, Development and Traditional Crafts in the Sudan, in: Ahmad Abd-Al-Rahim Nasr (Ed.), Folklore and Development in the Sudan, Khartoum: Institute of African and Asian Studies, UoK, pp. 181-212
Madavo, Callisto E., 1984, The World Bank Perspective: Goals and Potential of the Sub-Saharan Africa Report, in: Rural Africana, No.19-20, pp. 35-40
Märke, Erika, 1986, Ein Weg aus der Abhängigkeit? Die ungewisse Zukunft des informellen Sektors in Entwicklungsländern, Heidelberg: Forschungsstelle der Evangelischen Studiengemeinschaft
Mahmoud, Fatima Babiker, 1984, The Sudanese Bourgeoisie: Vanguard of Development?, Khartoum and London: Khartoum University Press and Zed Books
Malima, Kighoma, 1986, The IMF and World Bank Conditionality: The Tanzanian Case, in: Lawrence (Ed.), pp. 129-139
Management Development Centre (MDC), 1987, Al-Tawsayat Al-Chitamiyah li Seminar Tanmiyat Al-Sina'at wa Al-Amal Al-Saghira (Recommendations for the Seminar of the Development of Small Scale Industries and Handicrafts), unpublished seminar report
MDC, 1988, Al-Tawsayat wa Al-Mudawalat Al-Chitamiya li Seminar Tanmiyat As-Sina'at wa Al-Amal As-Saghirah Al-Muna'aghid Bidar Al-Sina'at As-Sudani (Recommendations of the Seminar on the Development of Small-Scale Industries in the SIA), unpubl.
Manger, Leif Ole, 1978, Some Remarks on the Use of Labour in Kheiran, The Sudan, in: Erik Erikson (Ed.), Aspects of Agro-Pastoral Adaptation in East Africa, Bergen, pp. 70-83
Manger, Leif Ole (Ed.), 1984a, Trade and Traders in the Sudan, Bergen: Dept. of Social Anthropology, University of Bergen
Manger, Leif Ole, 1984b, Introduction, in: idem (Ed.), pp. 1-24
Manger, Leif Ole (Ed.), 1987, Communal Labour in the Sudan, Bergen: Dept. of Social Anthropology, University of Bergen
Marris, Peter, 1968, The Social Barriers to African Entrepreneurship, in: Journal of Development Studies, Vol. 5, No. 1, pp. 29-38
Marris, Peter and Anthony Somerset, 1971, African Businessmen. A Study of entrepreneurship and development in Kenya, London: Routledge, Kegan Paul
Mars, Zoe, 1977, Small Scale Industry in Kerala, Brighton: IDS Discussion Paper
Marsden, Keith, 1970, Progressive Technologies for Developing Countries, in: International Labour Review, Vol. 101, No. 5, pp. 475-502
Marx, Karl, 1962, Das Kapital, Erster Band, Berlin: Dietz Verlag
Marx, Karl, 1963, Das Kapital, Zweiter Band, Berlin: Dietz Verlag
Mather, D.B., 1956, Migration in the Sudan, in: R.W. Steel and C.A. Fisher (Eds), Geographical Essays on British Tropical Lands, London, pp. 115-143

Mawut, Lazarus Leek, 1986, The Southern Sudan: Why Back to Arms, Khartoum: St George Printing Press
Mazumdar, Dipak, 1976, The Urban Informal Sector, in: World Development, Vol. 4, No. 8, pp. 655-679
McClelland, David, 1961, The Achieving Society, Princeton, London: Van Nostrand
McCormick, Dorothy, 1988, Small Enterprises in Nairobi: Golden Opportunity or Dead End? Baltimore: Johns Hopkins University, Diss.
McGee, Terence, 1973, Peasants in the Cities: A Paradox, a Paradox, a Most Ingenious Paradox, in: Human Organisation, Vol. 32, No. 2, pp. 135-142
McGee, Terence, 1979, Conservation and Dissolution in the Third World City. The 'Shanty Town' as an Element of Conservation, in: Development and Change, Vol. 10, pp. 1-22
McLoughlin, Peter F. M., 1962, Economic Development and the Heritage of Slavery in the Sudan Republic, in: Africa, Vol. 32, No. 1, pp. 355-391
McLoughlin, Peter F. M., 1963, Business and its Managers in the Sudan, in: California Management Review, Fall, pp. 81-88
Meier, Gerald M. and William F. Steel (Eds), 1989, Industrial Adjustment in Sub-Saharan Africa, New York: Oxford University Press
Meillassoux, Claude, 1976, Die wilden Früchte der Frau, Frankfurt/Main: Syndikat
Mellor, John, 1976, The New Economics of Growth, Ithaca: Cornell University Press
Mellor, John, 1986, Agriculture on the Road to Industrialization, in: John P.Lewis and Valeriana Kallab (Eds), Development Strategies Reconsidered, Washington: Overseas Development Council, pp. 67-89
Mellor, John, 1989, Rural Employment Linkages through Agricultural Growth: Concepts, Issues, and Questions, in: The Balance between Industry and Agriculture, Houndmills et al.: Macmillan, pp. 305-319
Mendels, Franklin F., 1972, Proto-industrialization: The First Phase of the Industrialization Process, in: Journal of Economic History, Vol. 32, No. 1, pp. 241-261
Mezzera, J., 1988, On the Usefulness of the Concept of the Urban Informal Sector, in: WEP Newsletter, No. 30, pp. 4-5
Middleton, Alan, 1981, Petty Manufacturing, Capitalist Enterprises and the Process of Accumulation in Ecuador, in: Development and Change, Vol. 12, pp. 505-524
Ministry of Agriculture, Food and Natural Resources (MAFNR), 1977, Food Investment Strategy 1977-1985, Khartoum
Ministry of Culture and Information (MCI), 1956, The Approved Enterprises (Concessions) Act, 1956, Khartoum
MCI, 1973, The Development and Promotion of Industrial Investment Act, 1972, Khartoum
Ministry of Finance and Economic Planning (MFEP), 1984, Household Income and Expenditure Survey 1978-1980, Khartoum
MFEP, 1986a, Strategy for Development of Rainfed Agriculture, Khartoum
MFEP, 1986b, Strategy for Development of Rainfed Agriculture, Annex 3, Institutions and Finance Task Force, Main Report, Khartoum
Ministry of Finance and Economic Planning (Economy)<MFEP-E>, 1990, Al Ard Al Iqtisadi (Economic Survey) 1989-1990, Khartoum
Ministry of Finance and Economic Planning (Planning)<MFEP-P>, 1982, Prospects, Programmes and Policies for Economic Development 1982/83-1984/85, Khartoum
MFEP-P, 1983, Prospects, Programmes and Policies for Economic Development - II, 1983/84-1985/86, Khartoum
MFEP-P, 1984, Prospects, Programmes and Policies for Economic Development - III, 1984/85-1986/87, Khartoum
MFEP-P, 1988a, The Four Year Salvation, Recovery and Development Programme 1988/89-1991/92, Vol. 1, Khartoum
MFEP-P, 1988b, Al-Barnamig Al-Rubai Lilingath wa Al-Islah wa Al-Tanmiah (Four Year Salvation, Recovery and Development Programme) 1988/89-1991-92, Vol. 2, Khartoum
Ministry of Finance and National Economy, (MFNE), 1980, The Encouragement of Investment Act, 1980, Khartoum
MFNE, n.d., Economic Survey 1976/77
Ministry of Industry and Mining (MIM), 1967, The Organization and Promotion of Industrial Investment Act, 1967, Khartoum
MIM, 1974, The Development and Encouragement of Industrial Investment Act, Khartoum
Ministry of National Planning (MNP), 1977a, The Six Year Plan of Economic and Social Development 1977/78-1982/83, Vol. 1, Khartoum
MNP, 1977b, The Six Year Plan of Economic and Social Development 1977/78-1982/83, Vol. 2, Khartoum

MNP, 1981, Second Three Year Investment Programme 1980/81-1982/83, Khartoum
Miracle, Marvin P. and Bruce Fetter, 1970, Backward-Sloping Labor-Supply Functions and African Economic Behaviour, in: Economic Development and Cultural Change, Vol. 18, No. 2, pp. 240-251
Mirghani, Hussein Mohamed, 1980, Government Policies and Income Distribution in the Sudan, in: J. F. Rweyemamu (Ed.), Industrialization and Income Distribution in Africa, Dakar, pp. 214-225
Miro, Abdelradi Ashrua, Arbab Ismail Babiker and Abdelbagi Mohamed Abbas, 1986, Al-Harafiyun Iqtisadiyatahum wa Tagiribit fra'Al-Harafiyin Bibank Faisal Al-Islami Al-Sudani (Craftsmen, Their Economic Activities and the Experience of Faisal Islamic Bank, Craftsmen Branch), Khartoum: Faisal Islamic Bank
Mitchell, Robert Edward, 1965, Survey Materials Collected in the Developing Countries: Sampling, Measurement, and Interviewing Obstacles to Intra- and Inter-national Comparisons, in: International Social Science Journal, Vol. 17, No. 4, pp. 665-685
Mkandawire, Thandika, 1982, The Lagos Plan of Action and the World Bank on Food and Agriculture in Africa: A Comparison, in: Africa Developmwent, Vol. 7, No. 1/2, pp. 166-177
Mohamed Abdelrahman, Hassan and Mohamed Baedaey Mohamed, 1984, Migration of Sudanese for Employment Abroad, Paper presented to the National Conference on Training & Manpower Planning, Khartoum
Mohamed Ahmed, Medani Mohamed, 1980, Capital-Labour Substitution Possibilities in the Sudanese Manufacturing Sector, Khartoum: MDC, Management Development Series, No. 10
Mohamed Ali, Galal El-Din El-Tayeb, 1980, Industry and Peripheral Capitalism in the Sudan: A Geographical Analysis, Los Angeles: University of California, Ph.D.
Mohamed Nur, El Tahir, 1988, Paper on Informal Sector Employment in the Sudan. Size, Strructure, and Constraints, in: Commissioner for Refugees et al. (Eds), pp. 18-44
Mohamed Osman, Mustafa et al., 1985, Development of Urban Informal Sector. Case Study of Sagana, DSRC, UoK, unpublished report
Moharir, V. V. and S. Kagwe, 1987, Administrative Reforms and Development Planning in the Sudan (1956-1975), Khartoum: DSRC, UoK, Development Studies Book Series No. 5
Molenaar, N., 1983, The Small Entrepreneur Really Does Know, in: idem et al. (Eds), pp. 70-89
Molenaar, N., M.S.S. El-Namaki and M.P.van Dijk (Eds), 1983, Small Scale Industry Promotion in Developing Countries, Delft: Research Institute for Management Science
Moore, Wilbert, 1965, Industrialization and Labour. Social Aspects of Economic Development, New York: Russell, Russell
Morawetz, David, 1974, Employment Implications of Industrialisation in Developing Countries: a Survey, in: Economic Journal, Sept., pp. 491-542
Morss, E.R., 1984, Institutional Destruction Resulting from Donor and Project Proliferation in Sub-Saharan African Countries, in: World Development, Vol. 12, No. 4, pp. 465-470
Moser, Caroline O.N., 1978, Informal Sector or Petty Commodity Production. Dualism or Dependence in Urban Development?, in: World Development, Vol. 6, No. 9/10, pp. 1041-1064
Moser, Caroline O.N., 1984, The Informal Sector Reworked: Viability and Vulnerability in Urban Development, in: Regional Development Dialogue, Vol. 5, No. 2, pp. 135-178
Mosley, P., J. Harrigan and J. Toye, 1991, Aid and Power: The World Bank and Policy Based Lending, Routledge
Müller, Jens, 1980, Liquidation or Consolidation of Indigenous Technology: A Study of the Changing Conditions of Production of Village Blacksmiths in Tanzania, Aalborg: Aalborg University Press
Müller, Jens, 1984, Facilitating an Indigenous Social Organisation of Production in Tanzania, in: Fransman and King (Eds), pp. 375-390
Mukhayer, Siddik Ibrahim, 1976, The Sociology of a Sudanese Factory. An Analysis of a Micro-Societal Setting as a Basis for Wider Domestic Viewpoint on Industrialization, Khartoum: ESRC, Bulletin No. 25
Mulat, Teshome, 1986, Education and Earnings in the Non-Government Sector: The Sudanese Case, in: Eastern Africa Economic Review, Vol. 2, No. 1, pp. 51-60
Munslow, Barry and A.B. Zack-Williams, 1990, Editorial: Democracy and Development, in: ROAPE (Ed.), pp. 3-8
Murtada Mustafa, Mohamed, 1988, Dimensions of Employment Generation and Productivity Enhancement in the Sudan, Khartoum: Ministry of Labour and Social Security
Mustafa Salih, Abdel Muhsin, 1977, The Structural Malformation of the Sudanese Economy. Part II. Some Suggestions for Restructuring the Economy: Khartoum: UoK
Mwene-Milao, Jalibu M. J., 1985, Industrial Development in Tanzania: The Case of Crafts and Small-scale Industries, Kiel: Institut für Weltwirtschaft

Myrdal, Gunnar, 1968, The Beam in Our Eyes, in: idem, Asain Drama: An Inquiry into the Poverty of Nations, New York: The Twentieth Century Fund, pp.16-26
Myrdal, Gunnar, 1969, Objectivity in Social Research, London: Gerald Duckworth
Nafziger, E.Wayne, 1970, The Relationship between Education and Entrepreneurship in Nigeria, in: Journal of Developing Areas, Vol. 4, pp. 341-360
Nanjundan, S., 1986, Small and Medium Enterprises. Some Basic Development Issues, UNIDO
Naseem, S. M., 1977, The Impact of Trade Policies on the Growth of Employment and Output in Manufacturing Industries in the Sudan, in: El-Hassan (Ed.), pp. 69-85
Nashashibi, Karim, 1980, A Supply Framework for Exchange Reform in Developing Countries: The Experience of Sudan, in: IMF Staff Papers, Vol. 27, pp. 24-79
Nashasbibi, Karim and Patrick Clawson, 1986, A Response, in: Oxford Bulletin of Economics and Statistics, Vol. 48, No. 1, pp. 73-82
Neumark, S.Daniel, 1958, Economic Development and Economic Incentives, in: South African Journal of Economics, Vol. 26, No. 1, pp. 55-63
Niazi, F.R., 1987, Survey of Small Scale Modern Iron Industry and Repair Workshops in Dar Fur Region, Consultant Report for UNIDO
Nihan, Georges, Erik Demol and Comlavi Jondoh, 1979, The Modern Informal Sector in Lomé, in: International Labour Review, Vol. 118, No. 5, pp. 631-644
Nihan, Georges and Robert Jourdain, 1978, The Modern Informal Sector in Nouakchott, in: International Labour Review, Vol. 117, No. 6, pp. 709-719
Nimeiri, Sayed, 1976a, The Five Year Plan (1970-75). Some Aspects of the Plan and Its Performance, Khartoum: DSRC
Nimeiri, Sayed, 1976b, Industry in the Sudan, in: Ali Mohamed El-Hassan (Ed.), An Introduction to the Sudan Economy, Khartoum: Khartoum University Press, pp.76-101
Nimeiri, Sayed and El Fatih Shaaeldin, 1977, Effective Rates of Protection for Industry in the Sudan, in: Sudan Journal of Economic and Social Studies, Vol. 2, No. 1,pp. 40-47
Nimpuno, Krisno, 1978, Community Development and Small Industry, in: Berg et al., pp. 7-12
Nureldin Hussain, M. and A.P. Thirlwall, 1984, The IMF Supply-Side Approach to Devaluation: An Assessment with Reference to the Sudan, in: Oxford Bulletin for Economics and Statistics, Vol. 46, No. 2, pp. 145-167
Nureldin Hussain, M. and A.P. Thirlwall, 1986, A Reply, in: Oxford Bulletin for Economics and Statistics, Vol. 48, No. 1, pp. 83-86
Nurkse, Ragnar, 1953, Problems of Capital Formation in Underdeveloped Countries, Oxford: Blackwell
O'Barr, William M., David H. Spain and Mark A. Tessler (Eds), 1973, Survey Research in Africa. Its Applications and Limits, Evanston: Northwestern University Press
O'Brien, Jay, 1983a, The Political Economy of Capitalist Agriculture in the Central Rainlands of Sudan, in: Labour Capital and Society, Vol. 16, No. 1, pp. 8-32
O'Brien, Jay, 1983b, Formation of the Agricultural Labour Force, in: Review of African Political Economy, No. 26, pp. 15-34
O'Brien, Jay, n.d., How Traditional is "Traditional" Agriculture?, in: Hussein M. Mirghani and Hassan A. Gadkarim (Eds), Essays on the Economy and Society of the Sudan, Khartoum: ESRC, pp. 80-93
Oehler, Reinhardt, 1989, Erfahrungen mit der Handwerkskammerpartnerschaft im Sudan, in: Wolfgang König et al. (Eds), Handwerk und Außenwirtschaft, Berlin: Duncker & Humblot, pp. 217-222
Oesterdiekhoff, Peter, 1979a, Agrarpolitische Orientierungen: Phasen, Tendenzen und Alternativen, Bremen: Universität Bremen, Forschungsbericht des Projektes Handlungsspielräume im unterentwickelten Agrarland Sudan
Oesterdiekhoff, Peter, 1979b, Industrieentwicklung und - struktur im Sudan, Bremen: Universität Bremen, unpubl., Forschungsberichte des Projektes Handlungsspielräume im unterentwickelten Agrarland Sudan, No. 2
Oesterdiekhoff, Peter, 1979c, Interne Vermarktungsbedingungen und Verteilung der Außenhandelseinkommen, Bremen: Universität Bremen, Forschungsberichte, No. 4
Oesterdiekhoff, Peter, 1982, Problems with Large-Scale Agro-Industrial Projects in the Sudan. The Example of the Kenana Sugar Corporation, in: Günter Heinritz (Ed.), Problems of Agricultural Development in the Sudan, pp. 51-68
Oesterdiekhoff, Peter, 1984, Handwerk im Sudan - Technische und sozioökonomische Aspekte, Bremen: SERG, Discussion Paper No. 2
Oesterdiekhoff, Peter, 1988, Landwirtschaftliche Vermarktung und Marktpolitik, Bremen: SERG, Discussion Paper No. 12

Oesterdiekhoff, Peter and Karl Wohlmuth, 1983a, The "Breadbasket" is Empty: The Options of Sudanese Development Policy, in: Canadian Journal of African Studies, Vol. 17, No. 1, pp. 35-67
Oesterdiekhoff, Peter and Karl Wohlmuth (Eds), 1983b, The Development Perspectives of the Democratic Republic of Sudan. The Limits of the Breadbasket Strategy, München et al.: Weltforum Verlag
Oestereich, Jürgen, 1980, Niches for Survival. Autochthonous Economic Systems in Cities of the Third World, in: Economics, Vol. 21, pp. 91-99
O'Hear, Ann, 1987, Craft Industries in Ilorin: Dependency of Independence?, in: African Affairs, Vol. 86, No. 345, pp. 505-521
Omer Beshir, Mohamed, 1968, The Southern Sudan. Background to Conflict, London: C. Hurst and Co.
Omer Beshir, Mohamed, 1975, The Southern Sudan. From Conflict to Peace, Khartoum: The Khartoum Bookshop
O'Neill, Norman and Jay O'Brien (Eds), 1988, Economy and Class in Sudan, Aldershot et al.: Avebury
Organization for Economic Cooperation and Development (OECD) (Ed.), 1974, Transfer of Technology for Small Industries, Paris: OECD
Organization of African Unity (OAU), 1981, Plan of Action for the Implementation of the Monrovia Strategy for the Economic Development of Africa, Geneva: International Institute of Labour Studies
Oshima, Harry T., 1971, Labor-Force "Explosion" and the Labor-intensive Sector in Asian Growth, in: Economic Development and Cultural Change, Vol. 19, No. 2, pp. 161-183
Osman, Mohamed, 1990, Verwüstung: Die Zerstörung von Kulturland am Beispiel des Sudan, Bremen: Edition Con
Osman Abdel Nur, Babiker, 1987, Marketing and Distribution of Farm Equipment in the Sudan, in: ILO (1987a), pp. 19-28
Osman Zein El Abdin, Omer, 1987, Demand and Supply of Farm Equipment, in: ILO (1987a), pp. 69-80
Ouattara, Alassane D., 1985, Reflections on the Crisis, in: Journal of Development Planning, No. 15, pp. 45-66
Page, John, 1979, Small Enterprises in African Development: a Survey, Washington: World Bank, Working Paper No. 363
Page, John and William F.Steel, 1984, Small Enterprise Development. Economic Issues from African Experience, Washington: World Bank
Papanek, Gustav F., 1962, The Development of Entrepreneurship, in: American Economic Review, Papers & Proceedings, Vol. 52, No. 2, pp. 46-69
Paul, James C.N., 1984, The World Bank's Agenda for the Crises in Agriculture and Rural Development in Africa: An Introduction to a Debate, in: African Studies Review, Vol. 27, No. 4, pp. 1-8
Peattie, Lisa. 1980, Anthropological Perspectives on the Concepts of Dualism, the Informal Sector, and Marginality in Developing Urban Economies, in: International Regional Science Review, Vol. 5, No. 1, pp. 1-31
Peattie, Lisa, 1984, Comment (to: Moser 1984), in: Regional Development Dialogue, Vol. 5, No. 2, pp. 179-180
Peattie, Lisa, 1987, An Idea in Good Currency and How It Grew. The Informal Sector, in: World Development, Vol. 15, No. 7, pp. 851-860
Pickett, James, 1989, Reflections on the Market and the State in Sub-Saharan Africa, in: African Development Review, Vol. 1, No. 1, pp. 59-86
Please, Stanley and K.Y.Amoako, 1984, The World Bank's Report on Accelerated Development in Sub-Saharan Africa: A Critique of Some of the Criticism, in: African Studies Review, Vol. 27, No. 4, pp. 47-58
Polak, J.J., 1957, Monetary Analysis of Income Formation and Payments Problems, in: IMF Staff Papers, Vol. 6, No. 1, pp. 1-50
Pollard, Nigel, 1981, The Gezira Scheme - A Study in Failure, in: The Ecologist, No. 1, pp. 21-31
Portes, Alejandro, 1978, The Informal Sector and the World Economy: Notes on the Structure of Subsidized Labour, in: IDS Bulletin, Vol. 9, No. 4, pp. 35-40
Portes, Alejandro, 1983, The Informal Sector: Definition, Controversy, and Relation to National Development, in: Review, Vol. 7, No. 1, pp. 151-174
Quijano, Anibal, 1977, Marginaler Pol der Wirtschaft und marginalisierte Arbeitskraft, in: Dieter Senghaas (Ed.), Peripherer Kapitalismus. Analysen über Abhängigkeit und Unterentwicklung, Frankfurt/Main: Suhrkamp, pp.298-341

Rafipoor, Faramarz, 1988, Die Grenzen und Möglichkeiten der Methoden empirischer Sozialforschung in den Ländern der Dritten Welt: Versuche einer allgemeinen Orientierung und ihre Konkretisierung auf der Basis der Erfahrungen im Iran, Social Strategies Forschungsberichte, Vol. 2, No. 3

Ranis, Gustav, 1984, Determinants and Consequences of Indigenous Technological Activity, in: Fransman and King (Eds), pp. 95-112

Rasheed, Sadig and Terry Sandell (Eds), 1980, Non-Formal Education and Development in the Sudan, Khartoum: DSRC, Development Studies Book Series, No. 3

Redlich, Fritz, 1963, Economic Development, Entrepreneurship, and Psychologism: A Social Scientist's Critique of McClelland's Achieving Society, in: Explorations in Entrepreneurial History, Second Series, Vol. 1, No. 1, pp. 10-35

Republic of Sudan, 1990, Al-Barnamig Al-Thalathi Al-Ingath Al-Iqtisadi (Three Year Economic Salvation Programme) 1990-1993, Khartoum

Research Group on African Development Perspectives Bremen (RGADP; Ed.), 1990, African Development Perspectives Yearbook, Vol. 1, 1989, Berlin: Schelzky & Jeep

Resnick, Stephen, 1970, The Decline of Rural Industry under Export Expansion: A Comparison among Burma, Philippines, and Thailand, 1870-1938, in: Journal of Economic History, Vol. 30, pp. 51-73

Review of African Political Economy (ROAPE; Ed.), 1990, Democracy and Development, No.49

Richardson, Harry W., 1984, The Role of the Urban Informal Sector: an Overview, in: Regional Development Dialogue, Vol. 5, No. 2, pp. 3-40

Riddell, Roger C., 1990, A Forgotten Dimension? The Manufacturing Sector in African Development, in: Development Policy Review, Vol.8, pp. 5-27

Riddell, Roger C. et al., 1990, Manufacturing Africa: Performance and Prospects of Seven Countries in Sub-Saharan Africa, London/ Portsmouth (New Hampshire): James Currey and Heinemann

Rivkin, Arnold, 1960, Incentives in African Life, in: Journal of African Administration, Vol. 12, No. 4, pp. 224-227

Roden, David, 1974, Regional Inequality and Rebellion in the Sudan, in: The Geographical Review, Vol. 64, pp. 498-516

Rodney, Walter, 1972, How Europe Underdeveloped Africa, Dar es Salaam and London: Tanzania Publishing House and Bogle-l'Ouverture Publications

Rweyemamu, J.F. (Ed.), 1980a, Industrialization and Income Distribution in Africa, Dakar: Codesria

Rweyemamu, J.F., 1980b, Introduction: An Agenda for Research, in: idem (Ed.), pp. 1-13

Saeed, Mohamed H., 1980, Economic Effects of Agricultural Mechanization in Rural Sudan: The Case of Habila, Southern Kordofan, in: Gunnar Haaland (Ed.), Problems of Savannah Development: The Sudan Case, Bergen, pp. 167-184

Santos, 1975, L'Espace Partagé: les Deux Circuit de l'Economie Urbaine des Pays Sous-Développés, Paris: Génin

Sattar, Abdus and E.A.A. Zaki, 1986, Structure of Sudanese Agriculture as Basis for Estimation and Projection of Agricultural Production, Khartoum: MFEP-P

Sau, Ranjit, 1983, Africa's Options in Development Strategy, in: Economic and Political Weekly, Vol. 18, No. 44, pp. 1897-1903

Schamp, Elke W., 1988, Zur Neuentdeckung des Kleinunternehmers in der Entwicklungsstrategie: Wachstumsbedingungen und Gewerbepolitik in Kamerun, in: Zeitschrift für Wirtschaftsgeographie, Vol. 32, No. 2, pp. 88-95

Schatz, Sayre P., 1965, The Capital Shortage Illusion: Government Lending in Nigeria, in: Oxford Economic Papers, Vol. 17, No. 2, pp. 309-316

Schatz, Sayre P., 1971, N Achievement and Economic Growth: a Critical Appraisal, in: Kilby (Ed.), pp. 183-190

Schmitz, Hubert, 1982a, Growth Constraints on Small-scale Manufacturing in Developing Countries: a Critical Review, in: World Development, Vol. 10, No. 6, pp. 429-450

Schmitz, Hubert, 1982b, Manufacturing in the Backyard. Case Studies on Accumulation and Employment in Small-scale Brazilian Industry, London: Pinter

Schmitz, Hubert, 1989, Flexible Specialization - A New Paradigm of Small-scale Industrialization?, IDS Discusssion Paper 261

Schmitz, Hubert, 1990, Growth Potential of Small-Scale Industry: Case Study from Ghana, in: Boehm and Kappel (Eds), pp. 115-124

Schneider, Helmut, 1986, Kleinindustrie in einem philippinischen Regionalzentrum: Das Beispiel der Municipality of San Fernando - Ilocosregion/ Nord-Luzon. Ein Beitrag zur Rolle der Kleinindustrie im Entwicklungsprozeß, Frankfurt (Main): Institut für Wirtschafts- und Sozialgeographie

Schneider-Barthold, Wolfgang, 1981, From Earthenware Pot to Plastic Bowl. The Role of Industry in African Agrarian States, in: Afrika, Vol. 22, No. 11, pp. 20-21
Schneider-Barthold, Wolfgang, 1984a, Entwicklung und Förderung des Kleingewerbes in der Dritten Welt, München/Köln/London: Weltforum
Schneider-Barthold, Wolfgang, 1984b, Industrie und Grundbedürfnisbefriedigung in Afrika, Frankfurt (Main): Campus
Schönherr, Siegfried and Badal Sen Gupta, 1975, Probleme und Erfahrungen empirischer Forschung in Entwicklungsländern unter besonderer Berücksichtigung standardisierter Erhebungstechniken, in: Gerhard Wurzbacher (Ed), Störfaktoren der Entwicklungspolitik, Stuttgart
Schultheis, Michael J., 1984, The World Bank and Accelerated Development: The Internationalization of Supply-Side Economics, in: African Studies Review, Vol. 27,. No. 4, pp. 9-16
Schulz, Michael and Judith Schulz, 1983, Port Sudan Small Enterprises Programme. Final Report of the Programme Design Phase 1982-1983
Schumacher, E.F., 1974, Small is Beautiful. A Study of Economics as if People Mattered, London: Abacus
Schumpeter, Joseph, 1935, Theorie der wirtschaftlichen Entwicklung, München: Duncker, Humblot
Schwarz, Gerhard, 1980, Mikroindustrialisierung: Handwerk und angepaßte Technologie als Elemente einer alternativen Entwicklung. Kolumbien als empirischer Bezug, Diessenhofen: Rüegger
Scott, A. MacEwan, 1979, Who Are the Self-Employed? in: Bromley and Gerry (Eds), pp. 105-129
Seers, Dudley, 1974, The Meaning of Development, in: International Development Review, Vol. 11, No. 4, pp. 2-6
Seibel, Hans-Dieter and Detlev Holloh, 1988, Handwerk in Nigeria: Unternehmensorganisation, Verbandsstruktur und Förderungsansätze, Saarbrücken: Breitenbach
Seisi Mohamed, Eltigani, 1976, Appropriate Technology for Sugar Manufacturing in the Developing Countries: A Further Evidence from Sudan, Khartoum: DSRC, UoK, Seminar Series No. 73
Seisi Mohamed, Eltigani and Bashir O.M. Fadlalla, 1989, Problems Arresting Private Sector Development in Western Sudan, Bremen: SERG, Discusssion Paper No. 13
Sen, A.R., 1985, The Development of Small Industries in the Sudan: Policies, Strategies and Programme, Vienna: UNIDO, unpublished report
Sender, John and Sheila Smith, 1984, What's Right with the Berg Report and What's Left of its Critics?, with a Response by C.Colclough, P.Daniel, M.Godfrey, Brighton: IDS, Discussion Paper, No. 192
Senghaas-Knobloch, Eva, 1978, 'Informeller Sektor' und peripherer Kapitalismus. Zur Kritik einer entwicklungspolitischen Konzeption, in: Elsenhans (Ed.), pp. 187-207
Sethuraman, S.V., 1976, The Urban Informal Sector: Concept, Measurement and Policy, in: International Labour Review, Vol. 114, No. 1, pp. 69-81
Sethuraman, S.V., 1977, The Urban Informal Sector in Africa, in: International Labour Review, Vol. 116, No. 3, pp. 343-352
Sethuraman, S.V. (Ed.), 1981a, The Urban Informal Sector in Developing Countries. Employment, Poverty and Environment, Geneva: ILO
Sethuraman, S.V., 1981b, Concepts, Methodology and Scope, in: idem, (1981a)
Sethuraman, S.V., 1981c, The Urban Informal Sector and Development Policy, in: idem (1981a), pp. 28-47
Sethuraman, S.V., 1981d, The Informal Sector and the Urban Environment, in: idem (1981a), pp. 171-187
Sethuraman, S.V., 1981e, Summary and Conclusions: Implications for Policy and Action, in: idem (1981a), pp. 188-208
Sethuraman, S.V., 1988, Informal Sector: Myth or Reality?, in: WEP Newsletter, No. 30, pp. 3-4
Shaaeldin, Elfatih, 1983, Tenants-Nontenants Relationships in the Gezira Scheme, in: Sudan Journal of Economic and Social Studies, Vol. 5, No. 1, pp. 3-15
Shaaeldin, Elfatih, 1986, The Role of the Agricultural Sector in the Economy, in: Zahlan and Magar (Eds), pp. 17-43
Shaaeldin, Elfatih and Richard Brown, 1988, Towards an Understanding of Islamic Banking in Sudan: The Case of the Faisal Islamic Bank, in: Barnett and Abdelkarim (Eds), pp. 121-140
Shaaeldin, Elfatih and Siddig Umbadda, 1984, Foreign Exchange Leakages in Sudan, Khartoum: ESRC, Bulletin No. 106
Shadeed Mohamed Zein, Amal, 1988, Problems and Constraints Facing Small-Scale Industry in the Sudan, DSRC, unpubl. report
Shapiro, Kenneth H., 1984, The Limits of Policy Reform in African Agricultural Development: A Comment on the World Bank's Agenda, in: Rural Africana, No. 19/20, pp. 63-68

Sharpley, Jennifer, 1984, The Potential of Domestic Stabilisation Measures, in: Tony Killick (Ed.), The Quest for Stabilisation. The IMF and the Third World, London: Gower
Shaw, Timothy M., 1983, Debates about Africa's Future. The Brandt, World Bank and Lagos Plan Blueprints, in: Third World Quarterly, Vol. 5, No. 2, pp. 330-344
Sheira, A. Z., 1968, Inter-Industry Relations in North Africa, in: Agricultural Economics Bulletin for Africa, No. 10, pp. 27-48
Shepherd, Andrew, 1983, Capitalist Agriculture in the Sudan's Dura Prairies, in: Development & Change, Vol. 14, No. 2, pp. 297-321
Simpson, I.C., 1980, Institutional Constraints to Agricultural Development in the Sudan, in: Centre of African Studies (Ed.), pp. 151-162
Simpson, Morag C., 1980, Large-scale Mechanised Rain-fed Farming Developments in the Sudan, in: Centre of African Studies (Ed.), pp. 197-212
Simpson, I.G. and M.C. Simpson, 1978, Alternative Strategies for Agricultural Development in the Central Rainlands of the Sudan, Leeds
Sinclair, Stuart W., 1976, The "intermediate" Sector in the Economy, in: Manpower and Unemployment Research, Vol. 9, No. 2, pp. 55-59
Singer, Hans, 1979, Policy Implications of the Lima Target, in: Industry and Development, No. 3, pp. 17-32
Singer, Hans and Patricia Gray, 1988, Trade Policy and Growth of Developing Countries. Some New Data, in: World Development, Vol. 16, No. 3, pp. 395-403
Singh, Ajit, 1986, The IMF-World Bank Policy Programme in Africa: A Commentary, in: Peter Lawrence (Ed.), pp. 104-113
Spiro, Benjamin B., 1972, Le Role de la Petite Industrie dans le Cadre d'une Stratégie pour le Développement des Pays les Plus Arriérés, in: Revue Economique et Sociale, Vol. 30, No. 2, pp. 99-118
Spradley, James P., 1979, The Ethnographic Interview, New York et al.: Holt, Rinehart and Winston
Staab, Christian, 1989, Die Bedeutung islamischer Banken für die wirtschaftliche Entwicklung im Sudan, Offenbach: Dieter Falk
Staley, Eugene and Richard Morse, 1965, Modern Small Industry for Developing Countries, New York: McGraw-Hill
Statistisches Bundesamt (SBA), 1990, Länderbericht Sudan 1990, Stuttgart: Metzler-Poeschel
Stearns, Katherine E., 1985, Assisting Informal-sector Microenterprises in Developing Countries, Ithaca, Cornell University, Dept. of Agricultural Economics
Steel, William F., 1977, Small-scale Employment and Production in Developing Countries: Evidence from Ghana, New York: Praeger
Steel, William F. and J.W.Evans, 1984, Industrialization in Sub-Saharan Africa, Technical Paper No. 25, Washington: World Bank
Steel, William F. and Yasouki Takagi, 1983, Small Enterprise Development and the Employment-Output Trade-Off, in: Oxford Economic Papers, Vol. 35, pp. 423-446
Steenwinkel, John, 1986, Control of Traders over Agriculture, in: van der Wel and Ahmed Mohamed (Eds), pp. 309-338
Stepanek, Joseph E., 1960, Managers for Small Industry. An International Study, Glencoe: The Free Press
Stewart, Frances, 1972, Choice of Technique in Developing Countries, in: Journal of Development Studies, Vol. 9, No. 1, pp. 99-121
Stewart, Frances, 1977, Technology and Underdevelopment, London and Basingstoke: Macmillan
Stewart, Frances, 1984, Alternative Conditionality, in: Development: Seeds of Change, No. 1, pp. 64-75
Stewart, Frances and Paul Streeten, 1971, Conflicts between Output and Employment Objectives in Developing Countries, in: Oxford Economic Papers, N.S., Vol. 23, No. 2, pp. 145-168
Streck, Bernhard, 1982a, Sudan. Steinerne Gräber und lebendige Kulturen am Nil, Köln: DuMont
Streck, Bernhard, 1982b, Was wird aus "unserer Entwicklungshilfe" gemacht? Kulturhistorische Gedanken zum Kulturtransfer, in: Freibeuter, No. 13, pp. 59-67
Streck, Bernhard, 1983, "Recycling" als Stammesgewerbe - Die Blechtonnenverarbeitung der Halab in Omdurman, in: Fritz Kramer and Bernhard Streck (Eds), Zwischenberichte des Sudanprojektes, Berlin: Institut für Ethnologie der Freien Universität Berlin, pp. 48-63
Streeten, Paul, 1974, Social Science Research on Development: Some Problems in the Use and Transfer of an Intellectual Technology, in: Journal of Economic Literature, Vol. 12, No. 4, pp. 1290-1300
Streeten, Paul, 1982a, A Cool Look at "Outward-Looking" Strategies for Development, in: The World Economy, Vol. 5, No. 2, pp. 159-169
Streeten, Paul, 1982b, Trade as the Engine, Handmaiden, Brake or Offspring of Growth?, in: The World Economy, Vol. 5, No. 4, pp. 415-417

Streeten, Paul, 1987, Structural Adjustment: A Survey of the Issues and Options, in: World Development, Vol. 15, No. 12, pp. 1469-1987
Sudan Rural Development Company Limited (SRDC), 1985-88, Annual Reports and Accounts 1984-87
Sudanese Craftsmen and Small Enterprises Union (SCSEU), 1986, Survey on Felt Needs Concerning Machinery and Equipment Expressed by 445 Craftsmen and Small Entrepreneurs in the Greater Khartoum Area During February and March 1986, unpublished report
SCSEU, 1989, Lime-Lights, Khartoum
Sudanese Savings Bank (SSB), 1985, Annual Report 1984
Thomas, Henk, 1988, Small-Scale Industrialization: A New Perspective on Urban Employment Policies, in: Development & South-South Cooperation, Vol. 3, No. 6, pp. 41-58
Thomi, W., 1988, Thesen zum Reproduktionszusammenhang des produzierenden Kleingewerbes im kleinstädtischen Milieu Afrikas, in: Zeitschrift für Wirtschaftsgeographie, Vol. 32, No. 2, pp. 113-119
Tignor, Robert L., 1987, The Sudanese Private Sector: An Historial Overview, in: Journal of Modern African Studies, Vol. 25, No. 2, pp. 179-212
Timberlake, Lloyd, 1985, African Crisis, London: Earthscan
Tipps, Dean C., 1973, Modernization Theory and the Comparative Study of Societies: A Critical Perspective, in: Comparative Studies in Society and History, Vol. 15, No. 2, pp. 199-226
Todaro, Michael P., 1969, A Model of Labor Migration and Urban Unemployment in Less Developed Countries, in: American Economic Review, Vol. 59, pp. 138-148
Tokman, Victor E., 1978, An Exploration into the Nature of Informal-Formal Sector Relationships, in: World Development, Vol. 6, No. 9/10, pp. 1065-1075
Tubiana, Marie-José and Joseph, 1977, The Zaghawa from an Ecological Perspective, Rotterdam: A.A. Balkema
Turnham, David, Bernhard Salomé and Antoine Schwarz (Eds), 1990, The Informal Sector Revisited, Paris: OECD
Twose, Nigel and Benjamin Pogrund (Eds), 1988, War Wounds - Development Costs of Conflict in Southern Sudan. Sudanese People Report on Their War, London et al.: Panos Institute
Umbadda, Siddig, 1984a, Border Trade in Darfur Region (in arabic), Khartoum: DSRC, Seminar No. 43
Umbadda, Siddig, 1984b, Import Policy in Sudan 1966-1976, Khartoum: UoK, DSRC, Monograph Series No.17
Umbadda, Siddig, 1985, Domestic Resource Costs for Sudanese Manufacturing Industry: A Preliminary Analysis, in: Development and Change, Vol.16, pp.147-158
Umbadda, Siddig and Elfatih Shaaeldin, 1983, IMF Stabilization Policies: The Experience of Sudan, 1978-1982, Hamburg
United Nations Development Programme (UNDP) and World Bank, 1982, Study of Cost of Production and Comparative Advantage of Crops in Sudan, Khartoum
UNIDO, 1985, The Democratic Republic of the Sudan, Industrial Development Review Series, Distr. limited
UNIDO, 1986, Technical Report: Industrial Survey of the Sudan, Prepared for the Government of the Sudan, Vienna
UNIDO, 1988, Accelerated Development of Indigenous Entrepreneurial Capabilities for Small- and Medium-scale Industries in Africa, Paper Delivered to International Conference on "The Human Dimension of Africa's Economic Recovery and Development", Khartoum, Sudan, March 5-8
UNIDO, 1989, The Sudan. Towards Industrial Revitalization, Industrial Development Review Series, Distr. limited
Van der Wel, Paul and Abdel Ghaffar Mohamed Ahmed (Eds), 1986, Perspectives on Development in the Sudan. Selected Papers from a Research Workshop in The Hague, July 1984
Van Dijk, Meine Pieter, 1983, Informal Finance Structures for Small Enterprises. West African and Indian Experiences, in: Molenaar et al. (Eds), pp. 151-165
Van Dijk, Meine Pieter, 1986a, Burkina-Faso. Le Secteur Informel de Ouagadougou, Paris: L'Harmattan
Van Dijk, Meine Pieter, 1986b, Senegal. Le Secteur Informel de Dakar, Paris: L'Harmattan
Van Dijk, Meine Pieter and N. Molenaar, 1983, Small Scale Industry Promotion in Developing Countries: Some Trends, in: Molenaar et al. (Eds), pp. 196-207
Vepa, Ram K., 1971, Small Industries in Africa, in: Small Industry in the Seventies, Delhi, pp. 124-156
Vitta, Paul B., 1988, Technical Change and Rural Development in Africa: Gaps between Knowledge and Practice, in: Rural Progress, Vol. 7, No. 1, pp. 6-17
von Pischke, J. D. et al. (Eds), 1983, Rural Financial Markets in Developing Countries: Their Use and Abuse, Baltimore: John Hopkins University Press

Vorlaufer, Karl, 1988, Produzierendes Kleingewerbe. Entwicklung und Raumorganisation in der Dritten Welt, in: Zeitschrift für Wirtschaftsgeographie, Vol. 32, No. 2, pp. 75-82

Wani Gore, Paul, 1986, Seasonal Labour Migration to the Renk Mechanized Scheme and Its Effect on the Subsistence Economy, in: van der Wel and Mohamed Ahmed (Eds), pp. 401-435

Warren, Bill, 1980, Imperialism. Pioneer of Capitalism, London: Verso

Warwick, Donald P. and Samuel Osherson (Eds), 1973, Comparative Research Methods, Englewood Cliffs: Prentice-Hall

Waterbury, John, 1985, A Review of the Contemporary Private Sector in the Sudan, Khartoum: USAID, unpublished report

Weber, Max, 1934, Die protestantische Ethik und der Geist des Kapitalismus, Tübingen: Mohr

Weeks, John, 1973a, An Exploration into the Nature of the Problem of Urban Imbalance in Africa, in: Manpower and Employment Research in Africa, Vol. 6, No. 2, pp. 9-36

Weeks, John, 1973b, Does Employment Matter?, in: R. Jolly et al. (Eds), Third World Employment, pp. 61-65

Weeks, John, 1975, Policies for Expanding Employment in the Informal Urban Sector of Developing Economies, in: International Labour Review, Vol. 111, No. 1, pp. 1-13

Wellings, Paul and Michael Sutcliffe, 1984, "Developing" the Urban Informal Sector in South Africa: the Reformist Paradigm and Its Fallacies, in: Development and Change, Vol. 15, pp. 517-550

Werlin, Herbert H., 1974, The Informal Sector: The Implications of the ILO's Study of Kenya, in: African Studies Review, Vol. 17, No. 1, pp. 205-121

Werobèl-La Rochelle, Jürgen M. and Frank Bliss (Eds), 1989, Einfälle statt Abfälle. Recycling-Handwerk in Afrika und Asien, Bonn: Arbeitskreis für entwicklungspolitische Bildung and Politischer Arbeitskreis Schulen

Western Savannah Development Corporation (WSDC), 1988, Western Savannah Project Phase II, Annual Report, July 1987-June 1988, Vol. 2, Nyala

Wheeler, David, 1984, Sources of Stagnation in Sub-Saharan Africa, in: World Development, Vol. 12, No. 1, pp. 1-23

White, Lawrence J., 1978, The Evidence on Appropriate Factor Proportions for Manufacturing in Less Developed Countries: A Survey, in: Economic Development and Cultural Change, Vol. 27, No. 1, pp. 27-59

White, Louise G., 1990, Implementing Economic Policy Reforms: Policies and Opportunities for Donors, in: World Development, Vol. 18, No. 2, pp. 49-60

Whittington, Dale and Craig Calhoun, 1988, Who Really Wants Donor Coordination?, in: Development Policy Review, Vol. 6, pp.295-309

Wilmington, Martin W., 1955, Aspects of Moneylending in Northern Sudan, in: The Middle East Journal, Vol. 9, pp. 139-146

Wohlmuth, Karl, 1983, The Kenana Sugar Project: A Model of Successful Trilateral Cooperation?, in: Oesterdiekhoff and Wohlmuth (Eds), pp. 195-236

Wohlmuth, Karl, 1987, Sudan's National Policies on Agriculture, Bremen: SERG, Discussion Paper No. 10

Wohlmuth, Karl, 1989, Sudan's Industrialisation after Independence: A Case of Africa's Crisis of Industrialization, in: N.Islam (Ed.), The Balance between Industry and Agriculture in Economic Development, Vol.5, Houndmills et al.: Macmillan, pp. 357-379

Wohlmuth, Karl, 1990a, Following-Up the Khartoum Conference and the Khartoum Declaration: An Introduction, in: RGADP (Ed.), pp. 3-40

Wohlmuth, Karl, 1990b, Strukturkrise und Entwicklung des informellen Sektors in Afrika - Alternativen der Förderungspolitik und der Strukturanpassung, in: Boehm and Kappel (Eds), pp. 11-38

Wohlmuth, Karl and Dirk Hansohm, 1984, Economic Policy Changes in the Democratic Republic of the Sudan, Bremen: University of Bremen, unpublished report

Wohlmuth, Karl and Dirk Hansohm, 1985, The Kenana Project. Macroeconomic Consequences of a Giant Development Project, unpublished training material for Seminar Project Management Training, Düsseldorf/ Rotterdam, April 27-May 26

Wohlmuth, Karl and Dirk Hansohm, 1987, Sudan: A Case for Structural Adjustment Policies, in: Development and Peace, Vol. 8, pp. 206-225

Wolde-Semait, Teferra, 1984, Stabilization and Adjustment Issues in Sub-Saharan Africa: Towards an Alternative Approach, in: Development: Seeds of Change, 1, pp. 37-45

World Bank, 1978, Employment and Development of Small Enterprises. Sector Policy Paper, Washington

World Bank, 1981, Accelerated Development in Sub-Saharan Africa. An Agenda for Action, Washington

World Bank, 1983a, Consultative Group for the Sudan, Chairman's Report on Proceedings, April 18

World Bank, 1983b, Sub-Saharan Africa: Progress Report on Development. Prospects and Programs, Washington
World Bank, 1984a, Consultative Group for the Sudan, Chairman's Report on Proceedings, April 27
World Bank, 1984b, Review of Mechanized Rainfed Farming (draft)
World Bank, 1984c, Toward Sustained Development in Sub-Saharan Africa. A Joint Program of Action, Washington
World Bank, 1985, Sudan. Prospects for Rehabilitation of the Sudanese Economy, Report No.5496-SU, Vol. 1: Main Report, Washington
World Bank, 1986, Financing Adjustment with Growth in Sub-Saharan Africa, 1986-1990, Washington
World Bank, 1987a, The Manufacturing Sector: Setting the Stage for Restructuring, Report No.6475-SU, Vol.1
World Bank, 1987b, The Manufacturing Sector: Setting the Stage for Restructuring, Report No.6475-SU, Vol.2
World Bank, 1987c, Sudan. Problems of Economic Adjustment, Report No.6491-SU, Vol.2. Main Report
World Bank, 1987d, World Development Report 1987, Washington
World Bank, 1988, Analysis of the Social Impact of Adjustment, in: Sudan: Programme to Alleviate Social Costs of Adjustment and Poverty, unpubl. report, pp. 1-44
World Bank, 1989a, Sub-Saharan Africa: From Crisis to Sustainable Growth, Washington
World Bank, 1989b, World Development Report 1989, Washington
World Bank, 1990, World Development Report 1990, Washington
Wynn, R.F., 1971, The Sudan's 10-Year Plan of Economic Development, 1961/62-1970/71: An Analysis of Achievement to 1867/68, in: Journal of Developing Areas, Vol. 5, pp. 555-576
Yeats, Alexander J., 1989, Do African Countries Pay More for Imports? Yes, Washington: World Bank, International Economics Dept., Working Paper
Yassin, Ibrahim H., 1982, "When Is Trade More Valuable than Aid?": Revisited, in: World Development, Vol. 10, No. 2, pp. 161-166
Yassin, Magmoud Mohamed, n.d., Ba'ad Gadaya Tamwil Al-Sina'at Al-Saghira wa Al-Hirafiya fi Al-Sudan (Aspects of Financing of Small Industries and Crafts in Sudan, Khartoum: IBS
Yongo-Bure, Benaiah, 1984, The Foreign Sector and Development Planning in Sudan, Dalhousie University, unpubl. Ph.D. thesis
idem, 1989, Economic Development of the Southern Sudan: An Overview and a Strategy, Bremen: SERG, Discussion Paper No. 16
Zahlan, A.B. and W.Y. Magar (Eds), 1986, The Agricultural Sector of Sudan. Policy & Systems Studies, London: Ithaca Press

Appendix 1

Important economic and social indicators of African countries

	calorie supply per capita/ day		life expectancy at birth	inhabitant per hospital bed	alphabets/ popul. (15 and older)	pupils/ age group
	no.	% of needs	years	no.	%	%
Algeria	2799	117	62	383(88)	50	94
Angola	1926	82	44(85)	563(83)	41	93(84)
Benin	2248	98	50	1016(81)	26	65
Botswana	2159	93	59	383(80)	71	104
Burkina Faso	2003	85	46	1359(84)	13	32
Burundi	2233	96	48	1564(83)	34(82)	58(86)
Cameroon	2080	90	56	373(85)	56	107(84)
Cape Verde	2614	111	65	512(80)	47	108
Central African Republic	2059	91	50	672(84)	40	73
Chad	1733	73	45	1278(78)	15(80)	38(84)
Congo	2511	113	58	225(81)	63	156(82)
Cote d'Ivoire	2308	100	52	891(80)	43	78(84)
Egypt	3275	130	61	788(86)	44(80)	96(87)
Ethiopia	1704	73	46	2787(80)	62(83)	36
Gabun	2448	105	52	228(85)	62	123(83)
Gambia	2229	94	43	928(80)	25	75
Ghana	1785	78	54	590(81)	53	66
Guinea	1731	75	42	585(76)	28	30
Kenya	2214	95	58	730(87)	59	94
Liberia	2373	103	54	654(81)	35	76(80)
Libya	3585	152	62	204(82)	67	127
Madagascar	2452	108	53	449(82)	67	121(84)
Malawi	2415	104	45	592(85)	41	62(84)
Mali	1810	77	47	1836(83)	17	23(83)
Morocco	2729	113	60	854(85)	33	81
Mauretania	2071	90	47	1572(84)	17(80)	37(82)
Mauritius	2717	120	66	357(83)	83	106
Mozambique	1617	69	48	1184(86)	38	84
Niger	2276	97	44	1389(84)	10(80)	29(86)
Nigeria	2139	91	51	1370(84)	42	92(83)
Ruanda	1935	83	48	633(82)	47	64
Senegal	2418	102	47	1342(85)	28	55
Sierra Leone	1784	78	41	892(84)	29	58(82)
Somalia	2074	90	47	691(79)	12	25(83)
Sudan	2168	92	50(87)	1202(83)	22(80)	49(84)
South Africa	2926	119	61	179(80)	-	105(72)
Tanzania	2316	100	53(87)	584(85)	85(87)	72
Togo	2221	97	53	749(84)	41	95
Tunisia	2796	117	63	462(86)	54	118
Uganda	2483	107	48	702(81)	57	58(82)
Zaire	2151	97	52	355(79)	61	98(83)
Zambia	2126	92	53	303(84)	76	103(84)
Zimbabwe	2144	90	58	771(84)	74	129(86)

Important economic and social indicators of African countries

	agri-culture/ GDP %	agri-cultural labour force %	processed goods/ total export %	cars/ 1000 inhabi-tants %	telephones/ 1000 inhabi-tants no.	GDP per capita US-$
Algeria	12	1034	1(85)	31(85)	36	2590
Angola	48(80)	202 12(81)	8(84)	5	-	
Benin	49	46	46(82)	3(79)	3	270
Botswana	4	430	-	15(86)	10	840
Burkina Faso	45	18	10(83)	3(83)	1	150
Burundi	58	21	5(85)	2(84)	1	240
Cameroon	22	142	4(83)	8(86)	3	910
Cape Verde	-	117(84)	3(84)	9(84)	8	460
Central African Republic	41	67	30	26(80)	17(84)	290
Chad	64(81)	78	8(75)	2(81)	0	-
Congo	8	61	7(80)	19(82)	6	990
Cote d'Ivoire	36	60	9(85)	19(84)	13(84)	730
Egypt	20	577	10(85)	16(85)	22	760
Ethiopia	48	77	1(85)	1(87)	2	120
Gabun	10	71	6(83)	14(85)	11	3080
Gambia	33(84)	82	0(77)	8(85)	4	230
Ghana	45	52(87)	1(81)	3(85)	3	390
Guinea	40	76(87)	-	2(81)	2	320(85)
Kenya	30	78(87)	11(83)	9(87)	6(87)	300
Liberia	37	72	0(84)	6(84)	3	460
Libya	2(84)	14	1(82)	154(81)	98	7170(85)
Madagascar	43	78	10(85)	2(85)	2	230
Malawi	37	79	4(83)	2(85)	3	160
Mali	50	83	23(79)	3(82)	1	180
Morocco	21	40	44(86)	26(86)	11	590
Mauretania	34	67	1(74)	8(85)	2	420
Mauritius	15	25	30(83)	35(86)	42	200
Mozambique	35	83(87)	1(84)	2(83)	3	210
Niger	46	89	2(81)	6(83)	1	260
Nigeria	41	66	0(81)	3(81)	2	640
Ruanda	40	92	0(76)	1(87)	1	290
Senegal	22	79	20(81)	12(85)	4	420
Sierra Leone	45	65	29(83)	5(84)	4	310
Somalia	58	72	0(81)	1(80)	1	280
Sudan	35	64(87)	1(81)	6(85)	3(87)	320
South Africa	6	15	14(82)	107(87)	76	1850
Tanzania	59	82(87)	11(81)	3(87)	2(87)	250
Togo	32	71	15(81)	1(87)	3	250
Tunisia	16	28	59(86)	38(86)	44(87)	1140
Uganda	76	83	0(76)	1(86)	2	230
Zaire	29	68	5(78)	1(84)	1	160
Zambia	11	71	3(82)	11(83)	7	300
Zimbabwe	11	70	16(84)	28(85)	13	620

Source: SBA (1990:12-15); year: 1986 (calorie supply 1985 or average 1983/85, alphabets and pupils 1985), if not indicated otherwise (year figures in brackets); pupil shares exceeding 100% result from recording method; few countries relate alphabet figures to the population older than 6 or 10 years

Appendix 2

International Standard Industrial Classification (ISIC)

31	food, beverages, tobacco
32	textile, wearing apparel & leather products
33	wood & wood products incl. furniture
34	paper & paper products
35	chemicals & chemical products
36	other non-metal miner. excl. petrol & coal
37	basic metal industries
38	fabricated metal prod. & machinery
39	other industries
3111	slaughtering and prep. of meat
3112	dairy prod. incl. ice cream
3113	canning & pres.of fruits & veg.
3114	canning & pres.of fish & fish prod.
3115	vegetable & animal oils & fats
3116	grain & mill products
3117	bakery,macaroni & noodle prod.
3118	sugar industry & refinery
3119	sugar confect., cocoa & choc.prod.
3121	food industries not elsewhere class.
3122	prepared animal food
3131	distilled alcoholic drinks
3134	soft & carbon drinks
3140	tobacco, cigar & cigarette industries
3211	weaving, spinning, dyeing & preparation
3212	blankets, bed sheets & towels
3213	knitting, needleworks, socks & stockings
3215	cordage, rope & twine
3219	weaving & spinning not elsewhere class.
3220	readymade apparel excl. footwear
3231	tanning & preparing of leather
3233	leather & substitute prod. excl. footwear
3240	footwear except plastic & rubber
3311	preparing wood & saw mills, planning mills
3320	wood products incl. furniture
3411	pulp, paper & papercard
3420	printing & publishing units
3511	basic chemicals excl. fertilizers
3521	paints, varnishes & others
3522	drugs & medicines
3523	soap, cleaners & toilet prod.(cosmetics)
3529	chemical products not elsewhere class.
3530	petroleum refineries
3551	tyre & tube industries
3560	plastic products not elsewhere class.
3620	glass and glass products
3692	cement, quicklime & plaste
3699	non-metallic minerals not elsewhere class.
3710	basic metal industries
3720	non-ferrous metal industries
3811	cutlery, handtools & metallic outfittings

3812	metallic furniture & fixtures
3813	structural metal products
3819	fabricated metal prod. not elsewhere cl.
3822	agricultural machines
3833	household appliances
3839	electrical apparatus not elsewhere cl.
3843	motorvehicles
3901	other industries not elsewhere cl.

Source: UNIDO (1986)

Appendix 3

Price Indices
(January 1970 = 100)

Year	Index
1970	106.7
1971	108.2
1972	120.9
1973	141.6
1974	178.7
1975	221.4
1976	225.1
1977	262.9
1978	314.9
1979	412.1
1980	516.6
1981	643.6
1982	808.2
1983	1055.9
1984	1417.2
1985	2060.3
1986	2673.0
1987	3365.6
1988	4762.8
1989	8094.4

Sources: BoS Annual Reports, MFEP-E (1990); 19´0-1979: indices for lower income population (less than LS 500 p. a.); 1980-1989: average income

Appendix 4:

Questionnaires for workshop owners and workers (English versions)

Questionnaire for owner of workshop

1. name of owner of enterprise

2. location

3. kind of activity
do you produce?
do you repair/provide maintenance?
do you trade?

4. activities in detail
what do you produce?
what do you repair or maintain?
what do you sell?
what do you produce most?
what is the price of the produced goods?

5. type of ownership/management
do you own the enterprise alone?
do you mange the enterprise alone?
do you share the ownership with someone else?
if yes: does he work there?
does someone not working here own the means of production or part of it?

6. book keeping
do you record your expenditures and profits?
if yes: in which form?

7. age of the enterprise
since when does the enterprise exist?

8. did you establish the enterprise?
if not: who established it?

9. what did you work before (directly)?

10. did you work in another line before this?

11. school education (kind, years)
did you attend a koran school or a school?
if school: how many years?

12. vocational training (kind)
where did you get your vocational training?

13. occupation of father
what does/did your father work?

14. place of birth
where are you born?

15. ethnic origin
what is your tribe?

16. age
how old are you?

17. marital status
are you married?
if yes: how many wives do you have?

18. occupation of wives
if yes: does your wive/do your wives work (outside)?

19. no. of children
do you have children?
if yes: how many?

20. no. of people supported
do you live with your family?
how many of your family members work?
how many people do you support?

21. does your family have a farm and/or animals?
if farm: does the farm produce for the market?

22. place of residence
do you live (permanently) in Nyala?
if yes: since when?

23. sources of income
do you have other sources of income?
if yes: which?
if yes: which is the main source?
do you work here the whole year?

24. duration of work
how many hours do you work here per day?
how many days do you work here per week?
do you work irregular hours?

25. excess capacity
do you work continuously during the working time?
if not: how many hours are you idle per week for lack of raw materials, electricity, demand, or other reasons?
do you work overtime sometimes?
would you work longer, if there was more demand?
how long did you work during Ramadan? did you work at night?

Workers

26. no.of workers
how many people are working with you?

27. no.of skilled workers
how many of them are skilled?

28. no.of permanent workers
how many of your workers are working permanently (all the year) with you?

29. initial no.of workers
how many workers were working with you, when you started your business?

30. highest no.of workers
has the no.of workers at some time been higher than now?
if yes:how many?

31. no.of male/female workers
how many of your workers are male/female?

32. no.of family workers
how many of the workers belong to your family?

33. weekly wage sum
how much do you pay per week for wages?

34. weekly payment for food
how much do you pay per week for the food of workers?

35. other expenditures for workers
do you have other expenditures for your workers?
if yes: how much weekly?

36. supply of workers
how is the supply of skilled and unskilled workers?

37. place of recruitment of workers
how do you recruit workers?

38. absenteism
do you have problems with absenteeism?

Tools/Machinery

39. employed tools and machines
which tools and machines do you use?

40. initial tools and machines
which tools and machines did you use, when you started your work?
are more tools and machines used now than at the beginning?

for each of the tools and machines:

41. place of purchase
from where do you get them?

42. place of production
where were the tools/machines produced?

43. state
did you buy the tools/machines new or second-hand?

44. price when bought
what was their price when you bought them?

45. date of purchase
when did you buy them

46. present price
if you had to buy this tool/machine now, what would it cost?

47. terms of payment
how did you pay the tools/machines (or the raw material for them)?

48. yearly expenditures for tools and machinery
how much do you spend for tools and machinery per year?

49. supply of tools and machinery (in Nyala and at other places)
is the supply of tools and machinery always sufficient in Nyala?
if not:is it sufficient in Khartoum?

50. supply in the past
how is the supply compared to the years before?

Workplace

51. kind of workplace

52. kind of ownership
do you rent the workplace?
do you own the workplace?
does your family own the workplace?
do you use it free of charge?

53. size of workplace (inside, outside)

54. value of workplace
if rented: how much is the rent?
if owned: since when do you own the workplace?
      how much did you pay?
      how much is the price now?

55. value of store and/or show-room
do you have an additional store and/or show-room at another place?
if yes: do you rent or own it?
if rented: how much is the rent?
if owned: since when do you own it?
    how much did you pay?
    how much is the price now?

56. value of raw materials
do you have any stock of raw materials?
if yes: what is their value?

57. value of products
do you have any stock of products?
if yes: what is their value?

58. value of other inventory
what is the value of the other inventory of your workshop?

59. electricity
do you work with electricity?
if yes: network and/or generator?
    is the supply always sufficient?
    how much do you pay monthly?

60. water
do you have water from the pipe?
is the supply always sufficient?
how much do you pay weekly?

Raw Materials

61. employed raw materials
which raw materials do you use?

for each of them:

62. place of purchase
from where do you get them?

63. place of origin
from which area do they originate?

64. price
what is their price?

65. price fluctuations
do the prices fluctuate?
if yes: between which prices (this year)?

66. price development
what was the price one year ago?
what was the price two years ago?

67. terms of payment
how do you pay?

68. frequency of purchase
how often do you buy?

69. quantities of purchase
how much do you buy?

70. supply
is the supply always sufficient?

71. supply development
how is the supply compared to the years before?

72. quality
are you satisfied with the quality of the raw materials?

73. storage
where do you store your raw materials?

74. transport
how do you transport them to your workshop/store?
what are the weekly costs of transport?

Production

75. production cooperation
do you cooperate in your production with other firms?

76. change of product composition
did you change your product composition since you began your work?

77. production development
compared to the last years, did your production increase?

78. production on order
do you produce on order?

79. weekly production
how much do you produce on an average per week, in a good week, in a
bad week, last week?

Marketing/Demand

80. weekly income
how much is your income in an average week, in a good week, in a bad week, last week?

81. place of sale
where do you sell?

82. clients
to whom do you sell?

83. place of consumption
where is your product/service used?

84. demand
how is the demand for your products?

85. demand development
since the last years, did the demand for your products increase?

86. price fluctuation
do the prices for your products fluctuate?
if yes: between which prices?

87. price development
since the last years, did the prices for your products rise compared
to other prices?

88. sale with losses
do you have to sell sometimes with losses?
if yes: what is the reason?

89. competition
do you think there is a lot of competition for small enterprises like you from other small enterprises,
from large enterprises or from imported products?

Sources of Finance

90. initial sources of finance
which were your sources of finance when you started your business?

91. present sources of finance
which are your present sources of finance?

92. credit
did you ever try to get a credit from a bank or government service?

93. credit need
if a bank or the government would offer credits on reasonable terms,
would you be interested?
if yes: for what would you use the credit?

Legal Status, Taxes, Institutions

94. license
do you have a license issued by the Town Council, Regional Government or Central Government?

95. taxes
do you pay taxes?
if yes, how much did you pay last year?

96. support from government
do or did you get any support from the government?
if yes: in which form?

97. support from other agencies
do or did you get any support from other agencies?
if yes: in which form?

98. membership in SCSEU
are you a member of the SCSEU?

99. membership in other organisation
are you a member in any other organisation concerning your trade?

Main Problems/Future Perspectives

100. main problems
what are your main problems (rank in importance)?

101. solutions to main problems
how could the mentioned problems be solved?

102. evaluation of business future
how do you evaluate the future of small industries/crafts in Nyala
and of your branch especially?

103. evaluation of income
how do you evaluate your income?

104. plans for future
what are your plans for the future?

105. plans for children
what would you like your children to do?

Questionnaire for Workers

1. occupation
what do you work as?

2. status
are you worker, assistant or student?

3. period of work
since when do you work here?
do you work only in holiday?

4. previous work
what did you work before (directly)?

5. other occupations
did you work in another line before this?

6. school education (kind, years)
what is your school education?

7. vocational training (kind)
what is your vocational training?

8. work of father
what does/did your father work?

9. place of birth
where are you born?

10. ethnic origin
what is your tribe?

11. place of residence
do you live permanently in Nyala?
if yes: since when?

12. kind of payment
how are you paid?

13. other sources of income
do you have other sources of income?
if yes: which?
    which is the main source?
do you work here the whole year?

14. duration of work
how many hours do you work here per day?
how many days do you work here per week?
do you work irregular hours?

15. excess capacity
do you work continuously during the working time?
if not: how many hours are you idle per week for lack of raw materials, electricity, demand or other reasons?
do you work sometimes overtime?
would you work longer, if there would be more demand?

16. age
how old are you?

17. marital status
are you married?
if yes: how many wives do you have?

18. occupation of wive(s)
does your wife/do your wives work (outside)?
if yes:what?

19. no.of children
do you have children?
if yes: how many?

20. no.of supported people
do you live with your family?
how many members of your family work?
how many people do you support?

21. agricultural activity
does your family have a farm and/or animals?
if yes: does the farm produce for the market?

Appendix 5

Employment in Sudanese industry (1981/82): a micro-perspective
(absolute employment <EMP>, capital intensity <K/EMP> in LS '000, for large and small industry)

ISIC	branch	all	SI	LI	all	SI	LI
3111	slaughtering and prep. of meat	299	-	299	12.55	-	12.55
3112	dairy prod. incl. ice cream	817	756	61	2.89	2.74	4.89
3113	canning & pres.of fruits & veg.	2312	152	2160	1.50	6.13	1.591
3114	canning & pres.of fish & fish prod.	110	-	110	-	-	-
3115	vegetable & animal oils & fats	7690	759	6931	18.54	8.73	19.64
3116	grain & mill products	12453	9747	2706	4.64	3.53	8.64
3117	bakery,macaroni & noodle prod.	14375	13195	1180	3.63	3.70	2.88
3118	sugar industry & refinery	43166	-	43166	8.26	-	8.26
3119	sugar confect., cocoa & choc.prod.	2217	639	1578	3.68	6.06	2.72
3121	food industries not elsewhere class.	1105	571	534	13.04	13.15	12.93
3122	prepared animal food	116	84	32	42.61	55.75	8.13
3131	distilled alcoholic drinks	271	-	271	2.26	-	2.26
3134	soft & carbon drinks	1816	399	1417	6.83	9.50	6.08
3140	tobacco, cigar & cigarette industries	992	-	992	3.28	-	3.28
31	food, beverages, tobacco	87739	26302	61437	7.54	4.25	8.95
3211	weaving, spinning, dyeing & preparation	23140	472	22668	7.41	4.68	7.48
3212	blankets, bed sheets & towels	312	-	312	1.71	-	1.71
3213	knitting, needleworks, socks & stockings	463	-	463	1.90	-	1.90
3215	cordage, rope & twine	145	-	145	1.73	-	1.73
3219	weaving & spinning not elsewhere class.	96	96	-	-	-	-
3220	readymade apparel excl. footwear	847	138	709	2.58	-	2.38
3231	tanning & preparing of leather	1558	-	1558	3.50	-	3.50
3233	leather & substitute prod. excl. footwear	182	182	-	20.92	20.92	-
3240	footwear except plastic & rubber	1666	96	1570	2.36	8.85	1.96
32	textile,wearing apparel & leather products	28409	984	27425	6.64	7.44	5.61
3311	preparing wood & saw mills, planning mills	626	207	419	1.95	2.52	1.67
3320	wood products incl. furniture	1462	1260	205	9.30	10.32	3.53
33	wood & wood products incl. furniture	2091	1467	624	7.15	9.22	2.28
3411	pulp, paper & papercard	569	-	569	6.70	-	6.70
3420	printing & publishing units	3656	796	2860	2.96	6.07	2.09
34	paper & paper products	4225	796	3429	3.46	6.07	2.86
3511	basic chemicals excl. fertilizers	214	44	170	8.57	18.64	5.97
3521	paints, varnishes & others	413	-	413	3.31	-	3.31
3522	drugs & medicines	412	-	412	5.58	-	5.58
3523	soap, cleaners & toilet prod.(cosmetics)	2299	763	1536	6.96	5.05	7.91
3529	chemical products not elsewhere class.	443	94	349	4.14	9.05	3.09
3530	petroleum refineries	206	-	206	112.89	-	112.89
3551	tyre & tube industries	425	-	425	139.66	-	139.66
3560	plastic products not elsewhere class.	924	331	593	7.50	10.08	6.06
35	chemicals & chemical products	5336	1232	4104	21.39	7.11	25.67
3620	glass and glass products	500	-	500	5.33	-	5.33
3692	cement, quicklime & plaste	3736	1999	1737	3.52	3.01	4.10
3699	non-metallic minerals not elsewhere class.	505	60	445	29.85	3.33	32.06
36	other non-metal miner. excl. petrol & coal	4741	2059	2682	6.51	3.31	8.97
3710	basic metal industries	332	30	302	2.10	2.70	2.04
3720	non-ferrous metal industries	445	34	411	4.61	7.85	4.34
37	basic metal industries	777	64	713	3.54	5.42	3.37
3811	cutlery, handtools & metallic outfittings	1451	1183	268	2.01	0.70	7.79

3812	metallic furniture & fixtures	2577	1936	641	2.81	2.24	4.52
3813	structural metal products	340	207	133	7.58	0.77	2.61
3819	fabricated metal prod. not elsewhere cl.	2676	1165	1511	1.85	1.86	1.85
3822	agricultural machines	94	-	94	3.26	-	3.26
3833	household appliances	755	171	584	3.97	0.04	5.12
3839	electrical apparatus not elsewhere cl.	945	220	725	16.34	0.65	21.11
3843	motorvehicles	1965	1549	416	4.79	4.40	6.24
38	fabricated metal prod. & machinery	10803	6431	4372	4.24	2.57	6.71
3901	other industries not elsewhere cl.	382	-	382	5.67	-	5.67

Source: UNIDO (1986)

Appendix 6

Light industries (industries under regional and provincial licensing)

1. Bakeries and bread baking
2. Wooden furniture
3. Brick making
4. Lime making
5. Maintenance workshops
6. Spice grinding
7. Confectionary (traditional)
8. Macaroni
9. Noodles
10. Biscuit making
11. Cold storage
12. Small printing presses
13. Leather pickling
14. Tiles incl. mosaic
15. Ice and soft drinks
16. Salt grinding
17. Auto servicing
18. Mechanized laundries
19. Other light industries
20. Coffee and coffee grinding
21. Bee-keeping
22. Picture houses and cinemas
23. Grain cleaning and sieving
24. De-shelling of groundnuts
25. Metal furniture
26. Dyeing of textiles, cloth etc.
27. Canning and packing of food, fruits etc.
28. Hotels (2nd class and lower)
29. Small foundries

Source: Ministry of Industry

Afrika - Hefte

AH 2 Sara Berry: Afrikanische Entwicklungsperspektiven- Ein kritischer Essay. (Übersetzung aus dem Amerikanischen). Bremen 1991. ISBN 3-927429-01-5. 43 Seiten. DM 10.00.

Obwohl bereits 1981 von der Boston University veröffentlicht, hat die Studie von Sara Berry nichts von ihrer Aktualität verloren. Sie skizziert in knappen Strichen Positionen und Schwächen der neoklassischen, orthodox-marxistischen, neokeynesianischen und dependenztheoretischen Richtungen in der Afrikaforschung und weist ihnen Defizite nach, die sie z.T. gemeinsam kennzeichnen. Sara Berry plädiert für eine stärkere Beachtung der Analysen "spezifischer Fälle", die auch für die Theorie mehr hervorbringen können als eine Anwendung generalisierender Konzepte, die leicht in die Irre führen, wie sie an etlichen Beispielen zeigt.

AH 3 Beate Martin: Von oben nach unten wächst gar nichts. Ländliche Entwicklung durch Selbsthilfe und Selbsthilfeförderung dargestellt am Beispiel einer senegalesischen Bauernorganisation. Bremen 1992. ISBN 3-927429-02-3. Ca. 100 Seiten.

AH 4 Barbro-Isabel Bruhns: Zur Situation Behinderter in Zimbabwe. Zwischen Institutionen und Integration. Bremen 1989. ISBN 3-927429-03-1. 71 Seiten. DM 10.00.

Nur 2 % der als behindert geltenden Bevölkerung Zimbabwes profitieren von institutionellen Rehabilitationsmaßnahmen, die eines von vielen Erbstücken der Kolonialzeit sind. Wie sieht diese institutionalisierte Arbeit mit Behinderten aus und was geschieht mit den restlichen 98 %, die zum größten Teil auf dem Lande in noch mehr oder weniger traditionellen Gesellschaftsformen leben? Mit diesen Fragen beschäftigt sich die vorliegende Studie vor dem Hintergrund der tradtionellen afrikanischen Gesellschaftsformen und der Kolonialgeschichte des relativ jungen Staates.

AH 5 Moema Parente Augel: Transatlantik - Begegnung zwischen Afrika und Brasilien. Bremen 1991. ISBN 3-927429-04-X. 80 Seiten. DM 8.00.

Das Buch beschreibt die Geschichte des transatlantischen Dreieckshandels und geht der Frage nach, wie es möglich war, daß die von Afrika nach Brasilien verschleppten Sklaven trotz ihrer unmenschlichen Lebensbedingungen und der Trennung von ihrer Heimat viele Elemente ihrer Ursprungskultur aufrechterhalten konnten. Es thematisiert Massendiskriminierung und die wirtschaftliche und soziale Situation von Menschen unterschiedlicher Herkunft und Hauffarbe und verdeutlicht anschaulich deren sozio-kulturelle Gemeinsamkeiten. Das reich bebilderte Heft wurde als Begleitbroschüre zur gleichnamigen Bielefelder Ausstellung konzipiert, ist aber auch unabhängig davon gut lesbar.

AH 6 Karl Peltzer: Traditionelle Heilkunde bei Ashanti und Shona. Bremen 1992. ISBN 3-927429-05-8. Ca. 120 Seiten.

Bremer Afrika-Studien

Band 1 Bruhns/Kappel (Hrsg.): "Ökologische Zerstörung in Afrika und alternative Strategien"Zur gleichlautenden Tagung des IZA vom 07. bis 09. März 1991.

Band 2 Dirk Hansohm: Small Industries Development in Africa. Lessons from Sudan. Bremen 1992. VI + 263 Seiten.

Außerdem erhältlich: Liberia Working Group. Leben wo der Pfeffer wächst. Bremen 1989. ISBN 3-926771-09-7. 151 Seiten. DM 15.00

Zu beziehen über: Informationszentrum Afrika (IZA)
Postfach 10 45 41 28 Bremen 1Tel.: 0421 / 74917

Hamburger Beiträge zur Überseegeschichte

herausgegeben von Leonhard Harding, Helmut Mejcher und Horst Pietschmann,
Universität Hamburg

Jörn Helmuth Arfs
Die Beziehungen der Hansestadt Hamburg zu den La Plata-Staaten 1815–1868
Der Aufstieg des Hamburger Außenhandels nach der Emanzipation Lateinamerikas Anfang des 19. Jahrhunderts stand ganz im Zeichen des Ausgreifens europäischer Mächte nach Übersee. Die vorliegende Studie untersucht die Entstehung, Rolle und Bedeutung hamburgischer Handelskolonien im politischen, ökonomischen und gesellschaftlichen Leben der La Plata-Staaten. Wie sicherte die kleine Stadtrepublik ihre kommerziellen Interessen in den instabilen Partnerländern und gegenüber den Großmächten ab? Und wie konnten sich hanseatische Konsuln und kaufleute in einem fremden geistig-kulturellen Milieu behaupten?
Bd. 1, 1991, ca. 432 S., ca. 48.80 DM, br., ISBN 3-89473-112-5

Dagmar Bechtloff
Bruderschaften im Kolonialen Michocán
Religion zwischen Politik und Wirtschaft in einer interkulturellen Gesellschaft
Der Aufstieg des Hamburger Außenhandels nach der Emanzipation Lateinamerikas Anfang des 19. Jahrhunderts stand ganz im Zeichen des Ausgreifens europäischer Mächte nach Übersee. Die vorliegende Studie untersucht die Entscheidung, Rolle und Bedeutung Hamburgischer Handelskolonien im politischen, ökonomischen und gesellschaftlichen Leben der La Plata-Staaten. Wie sicherte die kleine Stadtrepublik ihre kommerziellen Interessen in den instabilen Partnerländern und gegenüber den Großmächten ab? Und wie konnten sich hanseatische Konsulen und Kaufleute in einem fremden geistig-kulturellen Milieu behaupten?
Bd. 2, Winter 1991/92, ca. 360 Seiten, ca. 48.80 DM, br., ISBN 3-89473-231-8

Hamburger Studien zur Afrikanischen Geschichte

herausgegeben von Prof. Dr. L. Harding,
Historisches Seminar, Universität Hamburg

Eckart Rohde
Chefferie Bamiléké – Traditionelle Herrschaft und Kolonialsystem
Eine Studie zu den Veränderungsprozessen im Herrschafts- und Gesellschaftssystem der Bamiléké-Völker in West-Kamerun
Der europäische Kolonialismus hat unübersehbare Spuren in den traditionellen Herrschafts- und Gesellschaftssystemen Afrikas hinterlassen. In West-Kamerun bewirkte die koloniale Fremdbestimmung langfristig die Veränderung der Institution der Chefferie, die noch in vorkolonialer Zeit fest verankert schien, und auf einer klug ausgewogenen "Balance of Power" beruhte.
Der Autor beschreibt am Beispiel der Bamiléké-Chefferien die verschiedenen Phasen dieses Auflösungsprozesses. Er arbeitet dabei den Niedergang der traditionellen Rolle des Chefs heraus, der von einem "Primus inter Pares" zu einem exponierten Handlanger der Kolonialadministration mutiert.
Trotz dieser Veränderungen besitzt die Chefferie für die Bamiléké noch viel ihrer symbolischen Strahlkraft von einst, ist ihre Bedeutung weiterhin facettenreich. So bleibt der gesellschaftliche Aufstieg eines Mitglieds der modernen Elite ohne entsprechende Ehrung von Seiten des Chefs unvollständig.
Bd. 1, 1990, ca. 200 S., 38.80 DM, ISBN 3-88660-660-0

Andreas Eckert
Die Duala und die Kolonialmächte
Eine Untersuchung zu Widerstand, Protest und Prokonationalismus in Kamerun vor dem Zweiten Weltkrieg.
Nur wenige Aspekte der afrikanischen Geschichte haben in den vergangenen 25 Jahren ein so großes Interesse und so zahlreiche kontroverse Diskussionen erfahren, wie das Verhalten afrikanischer Gesellschaften gegenüber den Kolonialherren in den verschiedenen Phasen der europäischen Fremdherrschaft. Ziel dieser Arbeit ist es, Widerstand, Protest und die ersten Artikulationen eines nationalistischen Bewußtseins bei den Duala in Kamerun vor dem Hintergrund der durch den informellen und formellen Imperialismus initiierten ökonomischen, politischen und gesellschaftlichen Veränderungen zu untersuchen.
Der Autor macht deutlich, daß es eine undifferenzierte Sichtweise wäre, afrikanische Völker als jeweils homogene Blöcke zu betrachten, welche entweder ausschließlich als Widerstandskämpfer oder als Kollaborateure klassifiziert werden können. Er arbeitet die besonders große Ambivalenz der Duala-Politik gegenüber den Kolonialmächten heraus, die ständig zwischen Opposition und Kooperation lavierte.
Bd. 2, 1991, ca. 320 S., ca. 44.80 DM, br., ISBN 3-89473-095-1

Verena Westermann
Women's disturbances
Der Anlu-Aufstand bei den Kom (Kamerun) von 1958 bis 1960
Ende der fünfziger Jahre, am Vorabend der "Unabhängigkeit"Kameruns, führten nationalistische und modernistische Tendenzen zu einer krisenhaften Destabilisierung traditioneller Machtgefüge. Im Königtum Kom provozierten administrative Eingriffe einheimischer und europäischer Machtträger in die weibliche Produktions- und Reproduktionssphäre eine Revolte der Frauen. Im Verlauf dieses zwei Jahre währenden militanten Aufstandes aktualisierten die Kom-Frauen ihren traditionellen Ächtungs- und Bestrafungsritus Anlu zu einem modernen Instrument kollektiver politischer Herrschaft.
Die vorliegende Untersuchung basiert auf Interviews mit an der Revolte beteiligten Frauen und bislang unentdeckten schriftlichen Quellen. Der Anlu-Aufstand widerlegt sowohl das Vorurteil einer genuinen Passivität der afrikanischen Frauen, als auch die romantisierende Idee einer eigenständigen afrikanischen Geschichte weiblicher Militanz.
Bd. 3, 200 S., 34.80 DM, br., ISBN 3-89473--108-7

Leonhard Harding
Einführung in das Studium der Afrikanischen Geschichte
Dieses Buch will versuchen, die Beschäftigung mit dem afrikanischen Kontinent zu erleichtern, den Zugang zum Verständnis afrikanischer Gesellschaften und Zivilisationen zu ebnen.
Im Mittelpunkt stehen deshalb nicht geographische Strukturen, archäologische Probleme, ethnologische Zusammenhänge oder historische Fachfragen, sondern die Entwicklung des menschlichen Lebens; genauer: die Entfaltung menschlicher Gesellschaften in ihrer spezifischen Umwelt und ihren Außenbeziehungen.
Dabei soll versucht werden, an die besonderen Probleme heranzuführen, die sich diesen Gesellschaften durch ihre äußeren Existenzbedingen in ihrer jeweiligen, von europäischen Erfahrungen so stark verschiedenen ökologischen Situation gestellt haben; vor allem soll deutlich gemacht werden, daß die zahlreichen afrikanischen Gesellschaften sehr unterschiedliche und sehr vielfältige Lösungen für die Grundfragen ihres Überlebens gefunden haben, die in einer Vielfalt von politischen, sozialen, ökonomischen und kulturellen Organisationsformen ihren Ausdruck gefunden haben, die ihrerseits einem ständigen Anpassungsdruck ausgesetzt waren bzw. sind und sich entsprechend kontinuierlich verändert haben.
Bd. 4, 1991, 160 S. br., 19.80 DM ISBN 3-89473-233-4

Kulturanthropologische Studien

herausgegeben von
Prof. Dr. Rüdiger Schott, Seminar für Völkerkunde
der Westfälischen Wilhelms-Universität, Münster

Franz Kröger
Übergangsriten im Wandel
Kindheit, Reife und Heirat bei den Bulsa in Nord-Ghana
Bd. 1, 1978, 399 S., 54 Abb., 40.00 DM, ISBN 3-88660-688-0

Ingrid Heermann
Subsistenz- und Marktwirtschaft im Wandel
Wirtschaftsethnologische Forschungen bei den Bulsa in Nord-Ghana
Bd. 2, 1981, 277 S., 36.00 DM, ISBN 3-88660-689-9

Max Matter
Wertsystem und Innovationsverhalten
Studien zur Evaluation innovationstheoretischer Ansätze,
durchgeführt im Lötschental/Schweiz
Bd. 3, 1978, 305 S., 28.00 DM, ISBN 3-88660-690-2

Sabine Dinslage
Mädchenbeschneidung in Westafrika
Bd. 5, 1981, 185 S., 26.00 DM, ISBN 3-88660-691-0

Sabine Steinbrich
Gazelle und Büffelkuh
Frauen in Erzählungen der Fulbe und Haussa
Bd. 6, 1982, 249 S., 28.00 DM, ISBN 3-88660-692-9

Marianne Guckelsberger
Soul Food
Die Ernährung der Schwarzen in den USA als Ausdruck ihrer Kultur
Bd. 7, 1982, 142 S., 28.00 DM, ISBN 3-88660-693-7

Jürgen Grothues
Fischer in Südmarokko
Die Küstenfischerei an der südmarokkanischen Küste zwischen Agadir und Sidi Ifni
Bd. 8, 1982, 157 S., 28.00 DM, ISBN 3-88660-694-5

Franz Kröger
Ancestor Worship among the Bulsa of Northern Ghana
Bd. 9, 1982, 85 S., 28.00 DM, ISBN 3-88660-695-3

Peter Ositadinma Akogu
Leben und Tod im Glauben und Kult der Igbo
Eine empirische Untersuchung über die Glaubens- und Wertvorstellungen in der traditionellen Gesellschaft der Igbo
Bd. 10, 1984, 301 S., 10 Abb., 48.00 DM, ISBN 3-88660-696-1

Elisabeth Tietmeyer
Frauen heiraten Frauen
Eine vergleichende Studie zur Gynaegamie in Afrika
Bd. 11, 1985, 159 S., 32.00 DM, ISBN 3-88660-697-x

Sabine Dinslage
Kinder der Lyela
Kindheit und Jugend im kulturellen Wandel bei den Lyela in Burkina Faso
Bd. 12, 1986, 355 S., 36.00 DM, ISBN 3-88660-698-8

Anne Brüggemann
Amagdala und Akawuruk
Das Zwillingsmotiv in westafrikanischen Erzählungen der Bulsa, Mossi und Bambara
Bd. 13, 1986, 265 S., 36.00 DM, ISBN 3-88660-699-6

Ulrike Wanitzek
Kindschaftsrecht in Tansania unter besonderer Berücksichtigung des Rechts der Sukuma
Bd. 14, 1986, 439 S., 48.00 DM, ISBN 3-88660-700-3

Sabine Steinbrich
Frauen der Lyela
Die wirtschaftliche und soziale Lage der Frauen von Sanje (Burkina Faso)
Bd. 15, 1987, 487 S., 48.00 DM, ISBN 3-88660-701-1

Adelheid Weiser
Die Völker Nordsibiriens unter sowjetischer Herrschaft von 1917 bis 1936
Bd. 16, 1987, 325 S., 36.00 DM, ISBN 3-88660-702-x

Elisabeth Tietmeyer
Gynaegamie im Wandel
Die Agíkúyú zwischen Tradition und Anpassung
"Gynaegamie" ist eine in Afrika vorkommende soziale Institution und bedeutet "Heirat zwischen Frauen". Gegenstand des Buches ist die Beschreibung dieser Eheform, praktiziert von den Agíkúyú (Kikuyu) in Kenia in prä- und postkolonialer Zeit. Dabei werden die Fragen nach der Fähigkeit der Agíkúyú, eine traditionelle Eheform veränderten kulturellen Verhältnissen anzupassen, und nach der zukünftigen Praktizierung der Gynaegamie thematisiert. Anschließend folgt, basierend auf den zuvor dargestellten ethnographischen Daten, eine Diskussion ethnosoziologischer Heirats- und Familienbegriffe.
Bd. 17, 1991, 330 S., 29.80 DM, br., 58.80 DM, gb., ISBN 3-88660-653-8

Edvilla Talaroc
Tagbanua:
Ein philipinisches Fischervolk
Bd. 18, 1991, ca. 300 S., 58.80 DM, gb., ISBN 3-88660-654-6

Tobias Wendl
Mami Wata oder Ein Kult zwischen den Kulturen
Die mythische Gestalt der *Mami Wata* ist heute in mindestens 18 Ländern Afrikas zwischen Senegal und Tansania bekannt. Sie vereint Aspekte alter Wasser- und Schlangengeister mit den Zügen einer Europäerin: gefährlich und glückverheißend zugleich, grauenerregend und dennoch von großer erotischer Anziehungskraft.
Im Ritual lernen die von *Mami Wata* Auserwählten, den Geist der weißen Frau als Teil der eigenen Person zu achten und die fremdartigen Wünsche dieses Geistes zu erfüllen. Auf Altären halten sie bereit, was der exotischen Welt der Weißen entstammt: Puderdosen, Parfums, Plastikspielzeug und europäische Speisen. Im Besessenheitsritual stellen sich die Kultmitglieder bisweilen selbst als Europäer dar. Dann verkörpern sie im Tanz den Geist der weißen Frau und entwerfen – gleichsam einer getanzten Ethnographie – Bilder von uns Europäern und unserer Kultur.
Die vorliegende Arbeit steht in der Tradition einer hermeneutischen Ethnologie. Neben Literaturstudien stützt sie sich vor allem auf die Auswertung einer zwölfmonatigen Feldforschung bei den Ewe und Mina in Togo und Ghana. Abgehandelt werden: Entstehungsgeschichte, Kulturpraxis und die Lebensgeschichten von 60 Priesterinnen und Priestern. Im Mittelpunkt stehen dabei die symbolischen und rituellen Formen der Aneignung und Darstellung fremder Lebenswelten. Es wird gezeigt, daß die Abgrenzung gegenüber der eigenen Kultur Teil eines kontinuierlichen Inividuationsprosses ist, der von den Betroffenen selbst in einem Idiom der Bindungen an fremde Geister und deren Referenzkulturen artikuliert wird. Dabei erweist sich die kultische Praxis als

ritueller Gegenentwurf zur eigenen Kultur.
Bd. 19, 1991, 240 S., 38.80 DM, br., ISBN 3-89473-120-6

Forschungen zu Sprachen und Kulturen Afrikas/ Researches on African Languages and Cultures/ Recherches sur les langues et les Cultures Africaine

herausgegeben von Prof. Dr. Rüdiger Schott, Seminar für Völkerkunde
der Westfälischen Wilhelms-Universität, Münster

In dieser Reihe sollen Kulturen afrikanischer Völker durch Zeugnisse ihrer Sprachen wissenschaftlich dargestellt werden. Vereint und nicht getrennt werden daher die Linguistik und Ethnographie der Völker Afrikas in den "Forschungen zu Sprachen und Kulturen Afrikas"zu Wort kommen. Die Reihe soll vor allem der Veröffentlichung von mündlichen Überlieferungen afrikanischer Völker dienen - ihrer "oral history" ebenso wie ihren Erzählungen, Märchen, Sagen, Sprichwörtern und anderen Texten in afrikanischen Sprachen mit kommentierten Übersetzungen. Grundlage hierfür sind Wörterbücher, sofern sie über den lexikalischen Bestand der afrikanischen Sprachen hinaus auch die Kulturen der betreffenden Völker dokumentieren. Etwas vom Reichtum der Geisteswelt Afrikas soll mit den "Forschungen zu Sprachen und Kulturen Afrikas" sichtbar gemacht und festgehalten werden.

Franz Kröger
Buli – English Dictionary
With an Introductory Grammar and an Index English - Buli.
Bd. 1, Frühjahr 1992, 584 S., 78.80 DM, br., 148.80 DM, Ln., ISBN 3-88660-820-4

Schriften der Vereinigung von Afrikanisten in Deutschland (VAD e. V.)

Klaus von Freyhold/Rainer Tetzlaff (Hrsg.)
unter Mitarbeit von Regina Wegemund
Die "afrikanische Krise" und die Krise der Entwicklungspolitik
Referate der Jahrestagung der VAD 1986.
Aus dem Inhalt: *Franz Ansprenger*: Politische Systeme Afrikas; *Rainer Tetzlaff*: Überlegungen zur "Entstaatlichung" afrikanischer Gesellschaften: ein Ausweg aus der Krise?; *Volkmar Köhler*: Die Krise in Afrika und ihre Rückwirkung auf die Entwicklungszusammenarbeit. Weitere Beiträge beschäftigen sich mit "Bildung und Erziehung" (Sektion II), "Sprache und Kommunikation" (Sektion III) sowie "Umwelt, Sozialstruktur und sozialer Differenzierung" (Sektion IV).
Bd. 11, Herbst 1991, ca. 320 S., 34.80 DM, br., ISBN 3-89473-080-3

Rolf Hofmeier/Rainer Tetzlaff (Hrsg.)
Afrika – Überleben in einer ökologisch gefährdeten Umwelt
Ergebnisse der Jahrestagung der VAD 1991
Aus dem Inhalt: *Joe Lugalla*: Die ökonomische Krise, Strukturanpassung und Überlebensstrategien in Tanzania; *Andreas Mehler*: Klientelismus in Kamerun; *Rainer Tetzlaff*: Die Transition zur Demokratie: Ein Ausweg aus der Legitimationskrise?; *Gudrun Lachenmann*: Von der "Unsichtbarkeit" zur "Verletzbarkeit". Frauenpolitik in der Entwicklunspolitik; *Jürgen Heinrichs*: Umwelt und Bevölkerungsentwicklung; *Christa Wichterich*: Bevölkerungspolitik in Kenia; *Cord Jakobeit*: Die Zukunft der Rohstoffe in Afrika; *Jürgen Riedel*: Industrialisierungsperspektiven Afrikas; *Wolfgang Schöller*: Die Marginalisierung Afrikas auf dem Weltmarkt; *Karl Wohlmuth*: Die Erfüllung von Strukturanpassungsprogrammen in Afrika.
Bd. 13, Herbst 1991, ca. 350 S., 38.80 DM, br., ISBN 3-89473-074-9

LIT Verlag   Münster – Hamburg
Rothenburg 41   4400 Münster   Tel. 02 51 / 4 00 22
Hallerplatz 5   2000 Hamburg 13   Tel. 0 40 / 446 446